Demanding Justice and Security

Demanding Justice and Security

Indigenous Women and Legal Pluralities in Latin America

EDITED BY

RACHEL SIEDER

RUTGERS UNIVERSITY PRESS

NEW BRUNSWICK, CAMDEN, AND NEWARK, NEW JERSEY, AND LONDON

978-0-8135-8793-6
978-0-8135-8792-9
978-0-8135-8795-0
978-0-8135-8794-3
978-0-8135-9069-1

Cataloging-in-Publication data is available from the Library of Congress.

A British Cataloging-in-Publication record for this book is available from the British Library.

The paper used in this publication meets the requirements of the American National Standard for Information Sciences—Permanence of Paper for Printed Library Materials, ANSI Z39.48-1992.

www.rutgersuniversitypress.org

Manufactured in the United States of America

CONTENTS

PART THREE

Women's Alternatives in the Face of
Racism and Dispossession

PART FOUR

Methodological Perspectives

PREFACE

This book started life when a group of activist scholars, colleagues, students, and comadres decided we wanted to work together and learn from the different experiences and places where we conduct our research in Mexico, Guatemala, Colombia, Ecuador, and Bolivia. Our concern was to listen to how indigenous women are framing their demands for justice and security within their different organizational contexts and to understand their engagements with different forms of legality. Our hope was to witness and accompany, and to validate and amplify those claims through our scholarship and the different connections we could make. Building on our shared theoretical and methodological concerns, we devised a joint project, Women and Law in Latin America: Justice, Security and Legal Pluralism, as part of a collaboration between the Centro de Investigaciones y Estudios Superiores en Antropología Social (CIESAS) in Mexico City, where many of us are fortunate to be researchers, teachers, and students, and the Chr. Michelsen Institute in Bergen, Norway, where I am an affiliated senior researcher and part of an inspiring research network on law and gender. Great thanks are due to CIESAS and particularly its past and present directors, Virginia García Acosta and Agustín Escobar Latapí, for their unflagging support for the project and commitment to collaborative international research. In Bergen Siri Gloppen, director of Bergen's Centre for Law and Social Transformation, and Liv Tønnessen provided input and steadfast encouragement.

Central to our exchanges was the funding the project received from the Norwegian Research Council (project 199745), which enabled us to finance fieldwork, together with a series of workshops and meetings of the research team and representatives from organizations and communities. We are immensely grateful to the Council for their support. In 2011 we met in Cuetzalan, Puebla, at the Hotel Taselotzin, the first eco-tourist venture run by Nahua women from the organization Maseualsiuamej Mosenyolchicuani in the Sierra Norte. The space and care that Doña Rufi and her compañeras provided for us formed the perfect environment to listen, share, and strengthen our work together. In Mexico City, a workshop with Colombian psychologist Clemencia Correa helped us reflect on the challenges of working with histories of violence, and on the ethics of engagement, accompaniment, and mutual care. Earlier versions of the chapters contained here were presented in 2012 at panels at the Latin American Studies Association congress in San Francisco and at a meeting at CIESAS Pacífico Sur in Oaxaca. We are hugely indebted to Pamela Calla, Deborah Poole, and Lynn Stephen, all of whom read work in progress and made invaluable contributions at these different meetings, forcing us to think the extra mile. In Mexico Yacotzin Bravo provided research assistance and steered all of us through the inevitable paperwork with her keen eye and good grace, at the same time as developing her own research. In Guatemala, Lidia Osorio worked tirelessly to make the project a success and to facilitate visas and logística for visits to Mexico. On a personal level, I am lucky to count on Carlos Y. Flores for accompaniment and support, and grateful to him for initiating the very right decision to move our family to Mexico all those years ago.

Our special thanks are due to Kimberly Guinta, our editor at Rutgers University Press, who enthusiastically supported the book project from the very beginning. Thanks also to Alejandro Reyes Arias for his careful translation of the manuscript from Spanish into English. The volume benefited greatly from the careful and detailed suggestions made by two anonymous readers for Rutgers University Press.

Academic research can be a lonely pursuit, but the opportunity to work in a wonderful team of scholars, activists, teachers, and friends has been one of the greatest gifts of the past few years. I am constantly inspired by the passion and generosity of my compañeras and our students at CIESAS, their commitment to social justice, and their intellectual acumen and curiosity. Most of all our thanks to the women and men whose stories we tell in these pages, whose truths and struggles we are all privileged to know and accompany.

Rachel Sieder

August 2016

Demanding Justice and Security

INTRODUCTION

Demanding Justice and Security

Indigenous Women and
Legal Pluralities in Latin America

RACHEL SIEDER

Across Latin America, women have been at the forefront of indigenous people's struggles, challenging state violence and racial discrimination and demanding respect for their collective rights to group autonomy, including the right to exercise their own forms of law. At the same time, through different forms of organizing, they have also developed important critiques of gendered violence and discrimination within their communities, in particular of certain aspects of "tradition" or "culture" reflecting gender ideologies prejudicial to their life chances. Framing their claims within contexts of legal pluralism, indigenous women and their allies have deployed different discourses and strategies within a range of legal mechanisms, including community justice systems (*derecho propio*), national laws, constitutions and international human rights instruments, and domestic and international courts. This resort to law has involved examples of both judicialization (taking demands to legal tribunals) and juridification, when forms of social and political organization come to mirror or appropriate dominant legal discourses and forms.[1] Through their collective framings of grievances and what they consider to be appropriate forms of redress, indigenous women combine strategic recourse to discourses of human rights and international, national, and community legal forums with alternative constructions of "(in)justice" and "(in)security," theorizing on the basis of their lived experiences and in turn demanding we rethink accepted understandings of these terms.

This introductory essay frames a collection of ethnographic studies, products of a three-year project based at the Center for Anthropological Research and Graduate Study (CIESAS) in Mexico, involving eleven researchers engaged with different processes of indigenous women's organizing to secure greater gender justice within their communities, organizations, and societies. Five of the ten studies are from Mexico, where most of the team

1

members live and work; the remaining five analyze experiences from Guatemala, Ecuador, Bolivia, and Colombia, countries where the researchers either live or have long-standing activist research connections. All the case studies built on collaborations both between individual researchers and different organizations and between the researchers themselves, forged in a range of joint research endeavors prior to this project. Taken together, the chapters presented here examine how indigenous women collectively engage with different forms of legality in order to pursue their justice and security claims. In the following sections of this introduction and throughout the book, we highlight the ways in which our collaborative approaches to legal anthropology and ethnography can contribute new insights about indigenous women's engagements with legal pluralities. In particular, we explore the ways in which the intersectionalities of violence against indigenous women are expressed, reinforced, and resisted through resort to multiple justice forums and discourses, deploying different framings that, as we argue below, are both situated and relational. In the next section I briefly present the different cases analyzed in the following chapters. I then outline some of the key theoretical, conceptual, and methodological issues for analyzing indigenous women's mobilization for justice and security in Latin America.

The experiences described in the following chapters vary greatly. In Bolivia and Ecuador, processes of constitutional and legislative reform in the second half of the 2000s provided new opportunities for women to mobilize and lobby nationally for guarantees of gender equality and protection from violence to be included as part of the recognition of indigenous autonomy rights within the new constitutions and secondary laws (Rousseau 2011). In their coauthored contribution, anthropologist Emma Cervone and Kichwa rights activist Cristina Cucurí explore the nature and effects of the mobilization by Kichwa women in the province of Chimborazo, Ecuador, to secure the inclusion of women's rights to protection from violence within the provisions for indigenous autonomy set out in the 2008 Constitution. Their analysis documents the ways in which women's mobilization for gender justice in the constitutional reform in turn affected perceptions of justice and practices on the ground. Within their communities, women in Ecuador and Bolivia have also organized to ensure that local autonomy statutes reflect their specific concerns: in her contribution, Ana Cecilia Arteaga Böhrt considers the relationship between the 2009 Bolivian Constitution and the 2010 law of coordination between state law and indigenous law (*ley de deslinde*), and the elaboration of a local autonomy statute in the Marka of San Pedro de Totora, Oruro, documenting the discourses, practices, and strategies pursued by Aymara women to further culturally rooted forms of gender justice.

In Mexico, Guatemala, and Colombia, the other countries examined in this volume, women within indigenous social movements and organizations have engaged with issues of gender inequality as part of their struggles for culturally appropriate forms of justice and security within increasingly complex contexts of violence marked by militarization, paramilitarism, the spread of extractive industries, and new forms of territorial control exercised by organized crime. In her chapter, Rosalva Aída Hernández Castillo analyzes the legal and political struggles of the Organización del Pueblo Indígena Me'phaa (OPIM), in Guerrero, Mexico, focusing particularly on her own role as special anthropological witness in a case heard before the Inter-American Court of Human Rights in 2010. The court found the Mexican government guilty of violating the individual rights of Inés Fernández, a Me'phaa woman and OPIM activist raped by army soldiers in the context of the growing militarization of the region. In addition the court's landmark judgment condemned the rape as a violation of the collective rights of the Me'phaa people, revealing the possibilities that international judicialization offered for redefining harm and forms of restitution. Mariana Mora's ethnography focuses on her work with Mocipol, an initiative of human rights defenders working in Guerrero to monitor human rights violations by the police and armed forces. Mora analyzes the ways in which human rights NGOs produce legal knowledge in cases where the rights of indigenous people have been violated by government security policies, and considers the gendered effects of such processes. Also in Mexico, in the state of Oaxaca, Natalia De Marinis recounts her accompaniment of indigenous Triqui women from San Juan Copala in their struggle to achieve a measure of security following their forced displacement in 2010, when a short-lived experiment in municipal autonomy was terminated by sustained paramilitary violence. De Marinis's chapter documents the gendered dimensions of violence and political control in the Triqui region, and grassroots responses. And in Guatemala, Morna Macleod's analysis of the work of Maya-Mam women activists in San Miguel Ixtahuacán, San Marcos, to resist one of the largest open-pit gold mines in Latin America, reveals their situated perceptions of (in)security and (in)justice in the context of large-scale extractive industry projects, and the gendered environmental and social impacts of such forms of structural violence.

The languages and concepts that indigenous women use to analyze their situations, frame their claims, and present their demands vary depending on their own cultural specificities and broader hegemonic discourses; as María Teresa Sierra reminds us in her chapter, "cultural constructions of violence and gender affect the definition of grievances and understandings of security and justice for women." In addition, as we demonstrate in this volume, local organizational processes are also a central element in shaping women's claims. Sierra's work with Me'phaa and Na savi women who are part of the supracommunal autonomous regional coordination of community authorities (Coordinadora Regional de Autoridades Comunitarias, CRAC), or *policía comunitaria*, in the Costa-Montaña region of Guerrero, documents women's organizing as "justice promoters" trying to encourage forms of supracommunal justice more attentive to women's situations and needs. Through her mapping of the justice practices of the *comunitaria*, Sierra analyzes the changing gender ideologies that they reveal. Adriana Terven Salinas's work in Cuetzalan, in the Mexican state of Puebla, with Nahua women of the Centro de la Mujer Indígena (CAMI), an organization that has played a key role in promoting indigenous women's rights, analyzes the different constructions of justice and security at play within the CAMI and the dense network of organizations working to promote indigenous women's rights in Cuetzalan. Terven reveals how the CAMI's focus on "violence against women" has tended to mirror dominant policy definitions of gendered harm, privileging interfamilial violence over and above more structural forms of discrimination. In Guatemala, Rachel Sieder's ethnography focuses on organizational processes in Chichicastenango, Quiché, where grassroots organizers and civil society organizations developed an innovative "gender agenda" for municipal governance. Sieder analyzes the efforts by community leaders of the municipal women's council to strengthen Maya-K'iche' women's access to justice and protection from violence; her chapter points to the ways in which neoliberal agendas for decentralized governance shape the prospects for women's organizational autonomy and definitions of gender discrimination and harm. And in Colombia, Leonor Lozano Suárez's long-standing activist-research collaboration with the Indigenous Intercultural University, UAIIN, and the Regional Indigenous Council in Cauca, CRIC, forms part of one of the most established experiences of indigenous autonomy in Latin America—even within a context of ongoing armed conflict. Lozano's contribution to this volume analyzes the new forms of knowledge generated by processes of systematization and reflection about gender relations, indigenous identity, and justice within the UAIIN's diploma on family, participation, and gender equity.

The different contributions show that languages of claiming deployed by indigenous women vary across time and space, pointing in turn to the situated ways in which they experience different forms of injustice and violence, reflect on and theorize their multiple realities, and elaborate different visions for the future. As a number of the chapters suggest, reflection on specific histories of indigenous women's agency provides a vital resource for contemporary organizing for greater gender justice, pointing to women's roles in the historic struggles of their communities and peoples. For example, in her chapter Lozano highlights the extraordinary document drawn up in 1927 by women members of the Quintin Lamé movement on the "Rights of Indigenous Women," which bears witness to women's militancy alongside men in the struggle for land. Other examples of indigenous women's historical agency invoked by contemporary indigenous women's movements include Dolores Caguango in Ecuador and Mama Maquín in Guatemala. In Bolivia and Ecuador, contested debates around Andean notions of complementarity have provided a means for some women to develop intracultural critiques and press their claims for greater equity. In different specific contexts, Kichwa and Aymara women have used these to question gendered forms of oppression and representations of indigenous community law that emphasize its inherently harmonious characteristics. Debates about the "complementarity" between men and women that is often defended as an inherent characteristic of indigenous cultures have provided opportunities for some women to highlight the distances between such ideals and everyday practices. Importantly, they constitute alternative political idioms to the hegemonic language of "gender equality," which tends to dominate national and international development discourses. In her chapter, Ana Cecilia Arteaga Böhrt shows how Aymara women in Oruro have developed critical stances and theorized on the basis of their own culture, experiences, and practice, strategically mobilizing notions of complementarity in debates on regional autonomy in order to press for a less patriarchal local politics. This has involved a localized resignification of Aymara concepts of complementarity–*chachawarmi*–to develop reformulations (*warmichacha*) that include women's demands. Similarly, in Guatemala Mayan women intellectuals have resignified Mayan concepts of complementarity and duality to question gendered exclusions within indigenous communities and organizations (Chirix and Kaqla 2003; Macleod 2011). Framing their claims for justice in terms of appropriate ways of "good living together," or *lo debido y lo indebido*, indigenous women have challenged different forms of inequality and male violence against women when such ideas are debated at the national level, within their political movements, or in their communities. While maintaining their demands for guarantees of indigenous people's collective rights, they have consistently pointed to the obstacles they face as women. These include lack of access to land, lack of experience, training, or education, feelings of shame or fear, being subjected to gossip and slander, economic dependence on men, physical and sexual violence, abandonment, and systematic denial of women's participation and voice. Debates are simultaneously transnational and intensely local: for example, ideas of gender justice developed in Chiapas, Mexico, in the shape of the Zapatista women's revolutionary law, proved an important inspiration for Kichwa women organizing against domestic violence and racism in Cotacachi, Ecuador, indicating how gender-specific ideas of justice in indigenous communities have traveled across time and space (Barrera 2016). The continental indigenous women's movement—in particular through the Enlace Continental de Mujeres Indígenas (ECMIA) and the Foro Internacional de Mujeres Indígenas (FIMI)—has mobilized these alternative understandings of women's justice claims, invoking indigenous cosmovision as a site of resistance across multiple scales (Blackwell 2006). Although the resignification of indigenous epistemologies and concepts is a marked feature of contemporary indigenous women's organizing, rights also continue to be a powerful idea for naming gender injustices and seeking change; in the cases we examine from Mexico and Colombia, the idioms of claiming tend to be those of individual and collective rights, together with forms of development, justice, and security framed as being specifically indigenous. For example, in her chapter on women's organizing in the Cauca, Colombia, Lozano explores women's efforts to situate their claims within the indigenous development plans (*planes de vida*) and intercultural university curricula developed by the Consejo Regional Indígena del Cauca (CRIC). And in her analysis of the work of grassroots women justice promoters (*promotoras de justicia*) in the *policía comunitaria* in the Mexican state of Guerrero, Sierra identifies gendered claims within indigenous and mestizo people's alternative framings of justice and security. The following sections turns to some of the key conceptual and methodological issues underpinning this collective volume.

Gender Violence and Intersectionality

Violence against indigenous women is a complex and multidimensional phenomenon that cannot be reduced merely to physical or interpersonal violence; it is also structural, symbolic, and political (Bourgois 2001). Indeed, as Cecilia Menjívar has persuasively argued, rather than being some kind of episodic incident or measurable event, "violence constitutes a *process*, one that is embedded in the everyday lives of those who experience it" (Menjívar 2011: 29).[2] It is well established that women from different indigenous groups face multiple forms of physical, psychological, and structural violence because of their race/ethnicity, poverty, and gender. This includes violence either directly exercised by agents of the state or permitted because of governments' failures to protect citizens and uphold their rights. It also occurs within families and communities. Like their male kin, indigenous women are discriminated against and oppressed as part of racial and class hierarchies and suffer some of the highest levels of illiteracy and poor health, including extremely high levels of maternal mortality (CEPAL 2013; FIMI 2006; Sieder and Sierra 2010). Either their collective rights as indigenous peoples are not legally recognized, or where they are enshrined in state law they are seldom respected and defended in practice.

In many parts of Latin America the policies of limited multicultural recognition of the 1990s and 2000s have given way to the hardening of positions by governments and the private sector, and the increasing militarization of indigenous regions by state and nonstate armed actors, often in covert support of extractive industries, both "legal" and illegal (Sierra, Hernández, and Sieder 2013). Even in the supposedly "post-neoliberal" states of Ecuador and Bolivia where constitutional and legislative recognitions of indigenous autonomies have been significantly expanded (Goodale and Postero 2013), indigenous territories and the natural resources they hold continue to be the focus of extractive industries and other large-scale infrastructural projects (Erazo 2013; Sawyer 2004). Protests by indigenous peoples against such incursions are demonized by governments as an impediment to "development" or a threat to national security, and the use of physical and legal violence to repress manifestations of dissent has become commonplace. The death of thirty-three people in June 2009 in confrontations at the town of Bagua between Peruvian security forces and Amazonian indigenous peoples protesting concessions granted to transnational energy and mining companies on their historical lands was a significant watershed, but by no means an isolated case. The criminalization of protests against megaprojects involving the indictment and imprisonment of movement and community leaders is being documented in countries across the region (Bastos and de Leon 2014). In conflicts over territories and natural resources, indigenous women are often targeted in particularly insidious, gendered ways, especially if they are at the forefront of resistance (Belausteguigoitia Rius and Saldaña-Portillo 2015). The use of sexual violence by military and paramilitary forces to displace indigenous people from their land or halt their mobilization, for example, has been particularly common in Guatemala, Colombia, and Mexico (see, e.g., ECAP-UNAMG 2009; Hernández Castillo, 2010; Jaramillo 2014; Stephen 2011). Supposedly "nonstate" repression carried out by private actors is in fact intrinsic to new state forms and political economies linked to intensified exploitation of oil, mineral, forest, and water resources.

At the same time, women can face systematic discrimination and violence within their own communities and families, reflecting historical gender biases in society. "Custom" is often mobilized as a justification for localized, intimate, and patriarchal forms of exclusion and control. Such norms and practices reflect specific gender ideologies and are reproduced by men and women in order to enforce particular forms of female conduct, or to deny women equal access to land, education, or participation in community affairs. Yet despite these complex intersections between interpersonal, intracommunal, structural, and historical forms of violence, criminal law and courts tend to conceptualize "violence against women" as isolated, interpersonal incidents of aggression carried out by individual perpetrators against individual victims. Resort to dominant legal framings and mechanisms can risk decontextualizing and oversimplifying, focusing on direct manifestations of physical violence rather than addressing complex multiple causality and giving due weight to the perceptions and experiences of women themselves. The paradigm of intersectionality was elaborated through the contributions of black feminism, feminism of women of color, and decolonizing feminisms in Latin America and the Caribbean (hooks 2004; Crenshaw 1991; Collins 1990, 1998; Davis 2004; Lugones 2008). As an analytical perspective, it questions the utility of essentialist social categories, such as "indigenous," "Afro-Latin American," or "women," as a guide for understanding people's concrete life circumstances. Instead intersectionality focuses attention

on the specific ways in which these abstract social categories intersect in particular historical contexts to produce different hierarchies or what Patricia Hill
Collins calls a "matrix of domination" (Hill Collins 1998). In other words, it points
to the ways in which different forms of power and oppression intertwine to naturalize hierarchies and forms of violence including race, class, gender, and sexuality, and how these interact to shape the lives of men and women whose locations
within these multiply-constructed categories affect their ascribed social roles,
experiences, and life prospects. Intersectionality theory thus provides a key
starting point for exploring the connections between structural violence and
interpersonal forms of violence and oppression as experienced by indigenous
women, forms of violence which—as Sally Merry and others have observed—are
always intimately connected (Merry 2006; Lugones 2008). Indigenous activists
and theorists in Latin America have made important contributions to intersectionality theory, underlining the centrality of colonial categories and legacies
for understanding intersectional forms of exclusion and domination across
the continent.[3] For example, studies by Marisol de la Cadena and others point
to the ways in which social dynamics in the Andes are imbued not only with
colonial binaries and hierarchies of "Indians" and "mestizos" (despite actors'
fluid, ambiguous, and contextual performances of these identities), but also
with internalized gender hierarchies within indigenous families and communities that can often place indigenous women at the very bottom of racialized
systems of subordination (de la Cadena 1991; Seligmann 1993; Weismantel 1989;
Radcliffe 2015). Analyzing the intersecting axes of inequalities faced by Bolivian
highland women who migrate from rural areas to (semi)urban neighborhoods
to secure their subsistence through commerce or domestic service, Silvia Rivera
Cusicanqui observed that "to be a woman, indigenous (or *chola*, or *birlocha*) and
on top of that poor . . . constitutes a triple stigma which prevents a growing
number of people from enjoying the dignified status of human being" (1996:
22). Much more than is the case for men, "Indian-ness" is inscribed and reproduced through the bodies, language, clothing, and daily practices of women. The
International Federation of Indigenous Women (FIMI) has argued for a focus on
different interrelated forms of violence against indigenous women, "shaped not
only by gender discrimination within Indigenous and non-Indigenous arenas,
but by a context of ongoing colonization and militarism; racism and social exclusion; and poverty-inducing economic and 'development' policies" (FIMI 2006: 6;
see also ECMIA/Chirapaq 2012). The different situations and contexts described
in the following chapters are ones where "everyday" practices of gendered violence intersect with racial and ethnic discrimination, social exclusion, particular
forms of economic development, criminal exactions, and state security policies
imposed in the fight against so-called organized crime.

Although our research focuses on different cases from Latin America, it
contributes to debates about how to ground the concept of intersectionality

methodologically in order to explore gendered forms of violence, (in)security, and (in)justice. We also underline the ways in which indigenous women are theorizing intersectionality by reflecting on their lived experiences and proposing alternatives, even though they do not specifically use the term itself. We ask the following questions: How are different forms of gender violence perceived, experienced, and understood by women within specific contexts of socioeconomic, political, and racial violence? What actions do they take to try to confront these forms of oppression? And what effects do these actions generate? In order to answer these questions, we propose three starting points for research.

First, it is vital to historicize understandings of gender violence, particularly locating different forms of gender oppression within specific national and local histories of racialization and colonialism. Distinct colonial legacies place indigenous people, and specifically women, within certain economic, racial, and gender hierarchies in the present, shaping their possibilities for enunciation, organization, and resistance. For example, in her work on domestic servitude in Guatemala, Aura Cumes has argued that the debt slavery endured by Mayan populations on coffee plantations throughout the nineteenth and early twentieth centuries has contributed to a contemporary "culture of servitude" that makes all indigenous women synonymous with domestic servants, thereby fixing their place within colonial, racialized hierarchies (Cumes 2014).[4] In this volume, Emma Cervone and Cristina Cucurí also look to the histories of *pongeaje* or debt servitude on the haciendas in Chimborazo in order to explain the gendered, racialized orders of the present, which are characterized by extremely high levels of intrafamilial violence. They argue that the legacies of verbal and physical racialized violence against indigenous men within the hacienda system, with all the humiliation and shame that this implied, have in turn generated dynamics where violence is subsequently exercised by men within many families over the bodies of women and children. As all the contributors to this volume underline, we need to analyze the connections between interpersonal and intrafamilial violence in the present alongside the historical constitution of different forms of structural, racialized violence that makes these both possible and normal. And as Cervone and Cucurí explain in their analysis of the workshops that formed a central part of their research in Chimborazo, critical reflection by men on the colonial legacies and power dynamics that shape their behavior can provide a vital element in working toward greater gender justice.

Second, research should analyze how women in different contexts understand the distinct forms of structural and interpersonal violence that affect their lives: the categories and terms they use to describe them, the linkages they make between them, and the actions they take in response. In this respect the approach advocated in this volume adheres to a fundamental principle of anthropological research, namely to try to understand the emic perspectives and framings of the subjects themselves, the ways in which they make sense of their worlds, and how such understandings shape their actions. The method-ological challenge is to understand the complexity of relations between differ-ent elements that are always intertwined in practice, such as racial and gender discrimination, or economic exclusion and poverty, without assuming a priori that one form of violence is more salient for subjects than another, as many top-down policy interventions on "violence against women" often do.

Third, we propose that analyses of gender inequalities and violence—and of the responses to these—should be relational and situational: in other words, they should pay due attention to women's everyday relationships with other people—their families, partners, employers, and so forth, and also to their spe-cific political, economic, social, and cultural contexts. Dominant classifications of indigenous women in gendered and racial hierarchies vary significantly across time and space, and women's individual circumstances also differ. In her study of women from the Asian diaspora in postwar Britain, Avtar Brah argues that her interviewees' discourses and narratives about such issues as patriarchy and women's rights to participate in the workplace did not necessarily correspond with their own individual life circumstances. Rather these were shaped by such factors as the nature of their obligations of care toward others, the economic circumstances of their households, the opportunity structure of labor markets, the attitudes of those around them, racism in society, and race discrimination at work (2011: 180). In other words, women's understandings of their life worlds are situated, something Brah terms "contingent positionality" (2011: 179). As she argues, their narratives perform different modes of subjectivity from a space of positionality that simultaneously reflects social constructions of women's roles and more personal or individual perceptions of themselves (2011: 180). In short, our collective approach aims to historicize violence and discrimination against indigenous women, revealing connections between interpersonal and more structural, collective forms of race, class, and gender violence. It pays careful attention to the ways in which women talk about grievances, redress, and the collective solutions they propose, understanding these as culturally specific constructions rooted in time and place. Last, it considers different women's contingent positionalities and life circumstances as part of these dynamics. Such a perspective, we argue, can lead to more nuanced and grounded appre-ciations of indigenous women's multiple struggles for justice and security.

Organizing for Justice: Subaltern Cosmopolitan Legalities

The research presented in this volume locates the struggle for individual women's rights within the broader struggle for indigenous people's collective rights. The chapters show how women's contingent positionalities interact with their experiences of collective organization and understandings of their own histories as women and as indigenous peoples, generating new subjectivities.

By challenging the internalized codes and systems of domination that per-petuate women's subordination and normalize gender violence, and by making explicit the linkages between different forms of interpersonal and structural violence, indigenous women's collective organizing across Latin America has generated new forms of agency, resilience, and resistance (Figueroa Romero 2011; Hernández Castillo 2009, 2016; Millán 2014; Speed, Hernández Castillo, and Stephen 2006; Sieder and Sierra 2010; Belausteguigoitia Rius and Saldaña-Portillo 2015). Together these represent a struggle for social relations and forms of governance that are not based on the normalization of racial and gender inequality and violence, mirroring the broader justice claims made by indig-enous people's movements as a whole. Such processes invite us to question hegemonic understandings of what "access to justice" and "security" might mean for indigenous women. In a recent volume Martin Holbraad and Morten Axel Pedersen suggest that anthropologists should explore security as a matter of the plural forms of reproduction and survival of distinct social collectivi-ties over time. This involves understanding not just threats to the abilities of those collectivities to reproduce themselves and survive, but also their visions of change and hope for the future, the comprehension of which necessarily demands we go beyond what they refer to as "liberal political cosmologies" (Holbraad and Axel Pedersen 2013: 12–13).[5] Privileging organized, collective responses, we underline the importance of focusing on ontological security, livelihoods, and people's responses to the multiple forms of violence they face.[6] We see this as a necessary corrective to academic framings that often serve to reproduce and reinforce dominant discourses about "security/insecurity," or lack of "access to justice," such as the human security paradigm, which, while focused on the security of people's lives, remains grounded within universalist categories of rights (Fukuda-Parr and Messineo 2012).[7]

Boaventura de Sousa Santos and César Rodríguez-Garavito similarly point to the important role non-hegemonic or non-Western constructions of rights and human dignity have played in the ways in which marginalized communi-ties and social movements across the world have mobilized to transform and democratize national and transnational legal frameworks. They emphasize the importance of law and legal ideas in counterhegemonic globalization, focusing attention on the "growing grassroots contestation of the spread of neoliberal institutions and the formulation of alternative legal frameworks by [trans-national action networks] and the populations most harmed by hegemonic globalization" (Rodríguez-Garavito and Santos 2005: 2–3). What Rodríguez-Garavito and Santos term "subaltern cosmopolitan legalities" essentially refer to locally grounded forms of resistance and legal innovation by those most excluded and marginalized within the new global order. They argue that sub-altern cosmopolitan legality "seeks to expand the legal canon beyond indi-vidual rights and focuses on the importance of political mobilization for the

success of rights-centered strategies" (Rodríguez-Garavito and Santos 2005: 15).
Indigenous social movements in the Americas have been at the forefront of
counterhegemonic uses of law and legal discourses in processes of resistance
and mobilization against the effects of contemporary global capitalism. Indeed
Rodríguez-Garavito and Santos ground their critiques of universalist conceptions of law and rights in an analysis of colonialism, racism, and historical
violence against indigenous peoples, emphasizing the extent to which racism
structures the forms of poverty and exclusion that exist today. As indigenous
women's organizations have repeatedly emphasized, their justice claims cannot
be realized independently of guarantees for the rights of indigenous peoples.
Abstract philosophical debates often tend to assume that group autonomy
rights are bad for women and will deepen gender discrimination (Okin 1999),
and, conversely, that universal human rights are always beneficial for gender
equality. Yet by ignoring or underplaying the concrete circumstances of indigenous women's struggles, they risk portraying complex issues in absolute or
ahistorical terms. By contrast, ethnographic research reveals the "contingent
positionalities," possibilities, and compromises involved in everyday lived
experience and the pursuit of a better life through collective organization. It
also underlines how history and context shape individual perceptions, epistemological frames, and possibilities.

Building on the trajectories of each researcher, our project prioritized
engaged, collaborative forms of research and focused on the understandings of
law, justice, and security of ordinary women (and in some cases men) and the
translocal processes of which they are a part. Our concern was not only with
statutory law, but also with the alternative legal orders generated by subaltern actors, particularly the constructions and practices of what is generically
referred to in Latin America as "indigenous law," or *derecho propio*. Indigenous
people in many parts of the continent have organized to demand higher degrees
of legal and territorial autonomy as a means to defend their territories and specific ways of life. This involves ongoing efforts to strengthen their own forms of
law and security and communal and supracommunal forms of governance. In
recent decades the rights of indigenous peoples to exercise their *derecho propio*
have been recognized in international law and—at least partially—in national
constitutions. Yet the hierarchies and legacies of colonialism are invariably
reflected in indigenous legal practices; this may mean that some groups, such
as women or young people, are systematically discriminated against within
subaltern constructions of law, as they are within hegemonic legal orders
(Cumes 2009; Sieder and Sierra 2010; Barrera 2016). The contributors to this
volume analyze the shifting gender relations and ideologies reflected within
these alternative legal norms and practices, seeking to identify motors and
processes of change. Subaltern legal orders are shaped by transnational human
rights but also by other normative orders (such as religion and spiritual belief

systems) and reflect the moral and legal imaginations of different groups and individuals within communities, organizations, and networks as well as the power dynamics that structure them. Our ethnographic engagements explore subaltern cosmopolitan legalities with a particular emphasis on gender dynamics. How do culturally and historically situated understandings of violence, (in)security, and (in)justice change over time? What role do material factors play in these changing perceptions? How are they affected by different discourses, understandings, and imaginaries of "rights" and the mobilizations that demand their guarantee? What social, political, and legal strategies do women pursue to try to secure their visions of justice and security? And how are women's and men's social relationships, identities, and political subjectivities affected by their engagement with different justice systems? By emphasizing constructivist, intersubjective, and historically situated understandings of rights, justice, and security, we follow anthropological theorizing about human rights, which began in the 1990s and sought to explore how certain global discourses are understood, taken up, appropriated, rejected, and refashioned in local contexts, and mobilized for specific ends (Wilson 1997; Merry 2006; Cowan, Dembour, and Wilson 2001; Goodale and Merry 2007), together with recent anthropological studies that emphasize how understandings of justice and security are constituted through contextually specific social processes (Arias 2006; Goldstein 2004, 2012; Penglase 2014; Holbraad and Axel Pedersen 2013). We aim to contribute to these debates in legal and political anthropology, underlining how intersectional analyses of social movements and organizational processes can increase our understanding of struggles for gender justice in contexts of complex legal pluralities.

(Il)legal Pluralities, (In)justice, and (In)security: Shifting Terrains

Latin America's legal landscape at the start of the twenty-first century is one of overlapping and hybrid jurisdictions, including indigenous autonomies and *derecho propio*, national law, and international human rights, trade, and commercial law, all of which coexist in practice with other informal and often highly coercive regulatory orders. For example, in her chapter in this volume, Rosalva Aída Hernández Castillo shows how Me'phaa activist Inés Fernández appealed for redress for her rape at the hands of government soldiers to a range of forums and jurisdictions, including her community's justice authorities, state courts, and ultimately the Inter-American Commission and Inter-American Court of Human Rights. At the same time Inés, her family, and her organization (the Organización del Pueblo Indígena Me'phaa, OPIM) were constantly subjected to the fear and insecurity produced by the militarized forms of governance and control in Guerrero state that are part of the transnational "war on drugs." As Boaventura de Sousa Santos has observed, the articulation between different scales of law has become more complex, with increasingly porous boundaries between local, national, and global law giving rise to "legal hybrids" and new forms of legal meaning and action. The different scales of law are not bounded and can be understood only as part of complex, transglobal constellations that are also characterized in practice by constantly shifting and blurred lines between the legal and the illegal (Santos 2002; 2006; Comaroff and Comaroff 2009). This opaqueness and ambiguity of law in practice is particularly acute in the racialized regions and populations that have historically constituted what Das and Poole famously referred to as "the margins of the state," making any analysis of contemporary legal pluralities and their gendered effects complex and challenging (Das and Poole 2004).

While there has been a wealth of new research on legal pluralities in Latin America—and particularly on the challenges of coordination between state law and nonstate legal orders[8]—surprisingly little has focused on the gendered dimensions of law and women's access to justice and security.[9] During the 1990s and 2000s multicultural agendas prioritized reform of the state justice sector, combining with broader neoliberal, neo-institutionalist policy agendas to "strengthen the rule of law" by pluralizing and decentralizing parts of the judicial system. Indigenous women were the target of numerous initiatives (some of which are described in this volume) aimed at improving their "access to justice" and specifically at providing redress for interpersonal, intrafamilial violence. Measures included the creation of specialized state institutions, the promotion of alternative dispute resolution mechanisms and so-called "indigenous courts," specialized municipal and national programs to increase women's participation, and a host of public-private partnerships with domestic and international NGOs. At the same time the growing official recognition of indigenous people's rights to exercise their *derecho propio* meant that efforts to increase indigenous women's voice and participation also extended to non-state, community-based justice systems (Barrera 2016; Faundez 2011). Emerging evidence suggests that these new channels and institutions expanded possibilities for women to make claims and state their grievances, and in specific cases opened spaces for them to organize and advance their own proposals for justice (Terven 2009; Barrera 2016). However, as Adriana Terven indicates in her analysis of the work of the Casa de la Mujer Indígena in Cuetzalan, Puebla, engaging in such legal or quasi-legal spaces generates ambiguous effects. This is because hegemonic analytical and policy framings of indigenous women's lack of access to justice and security have tended to focus on intrafamilial or domestic violence to the exclusion of other structural forms of violence that underpin and enable it. In addition and connected to this, policy-oriented prescriptions to tackle "violence against women" frequently fail to take into account the experiences of women themselves, their perceptions of their lifeworlds, and their understandings of the nature and causes of the insecurities, suffering, and injustices they face on a daily basis. As Cecilia Menjívar has argued, "close attention to the words of women, to their stories, and to how they talk about their lives can lead to a rethinking of how we theorize and study violence" (2011: 238). Indigenous women's collective organizing has contributed "concepts such as structural violence, spiritual violence, violence against mother earth and processes of healing (*sanación*) . . . [all of which] should be a constitutive part of diagnoses and the definition of effective strategies" (CEPAL 2013: 132). In this volume, our theorizing about justice and security derives from our fieldwork observations and collaborations, rather than responding to preconceived categories. Indeed our original research questions focused on situated constructions of "justice," building on our earlier work on gender and legal pluralism, and indigenous women's rights organization (Sierra 2004; Hernández Castillo 2009; Sieder and McNeish 2012; Terven 2009; Cervone 2012; Arteaga Böhrt 2013; Macleod 2011). Yet as we analyzed and interpreted our field data we came to incorporate a greater emphasis on "security" and to understand the two concepts as intimately linked. Together the chapters in this book offer a gendered, emic perspective on what "security" and "justice" mean for indigenous women in different places and processes in Latin America. This is particularly urgent, given the top-down, state-centric, and institutionally focused nature of much academic research and policy debate on these issues. State security policies that emphasize the use of military force and deploy ideological justifications to criminalize "others" have a long history in the region. As Rosanna Reguillo has observed, a state-produced rhetoric of security "aim(s) to produce emotive responses through tropes . . . anchored in a principle of generalized insecurity" (Reguillo Cruz 2013: 203). Today hegemonic security discourses focus on institutional responses to so-called "organized crime" or "terrorism." Feldman, Menon, and Geisler have attempted to theorize the relationship between the global fixation on security and the militarization of civilian life that this increasingly entails, and the dramatic rise in day-to-day insecurity associated particularly with the effects of contemporary global capital's forms of accumulation through dispossession (Feldman, Menon, and Geisler 2011). Some researchers working on violence in Latin America have argued that such accumulation through dispossession affects not only territories but also bodies, and particularly those of poor and racialized women and men (Belausteguigoitia Rius and Saldaña-Portillo 2012). Others have noted growing tendencies in Europe and the global South toward "securitized" forms of governance, where development is increasingly tied to assessments of risk and targeted forms of intervention aimed at ameliorating poverty and providing security (Amar 2013; Maguire, Frois, and Zurawski 2014; McNeish and Sande Lie 2010).[10] The growing hegemony of such security/securitized frameworks has facilitated new forms of transnational accumulation at the expense of indigenous people's livelihoods. As dissent is increasingly rendered illegal by the state, indigenous people become a problem of security rather than, as in previous decades, a problem of "(under)development" (Mella 2014; Bastos and de Leon 2014). Such security framings invisibilize other structural, racial, and gendered forms of violence, yet at the same time they are in fact inextricably shaped by them—for example, criminalizing the poor or ethnic and racial minorities. By contrast, different forms of indigenous people's organizing constitute important counternarratives to dominant conceptualizations of security/insecurity, pointing instead to the structural forms of racism, discrimination, and dispossession that these serve to facilitate. Within these counternarratives, indigenous women's understandings of security often differ significantly from those of indigenous men. It is these gendered constructions, and their implications, that we seek to explore.

Methodological Routes

The contributors to this volume self-identify as activist scholars based in Latin America who are engaged in solidarity and collaborative dialogue with indigenous women's struggles for greater justice and security for themselves, their communities, and their organizations. Such a position, variously defined as public or activist scholarship (Hale 2008; Stephen 2007; Sanford and Angel-Ajani 2006; Hale and Stephen 2013), aims to provide insights into the ways in which the workings of power, history, and transnational forces affect indigenous people's lives and shape different processes of resistance and adaptation. It also privileges support of their collective aims and objectives, dialogue, and the coproduction of knowledge (FIMI 2013; Hernández Castillo 2016).[11] As now generally accepted at least within the discipline of anthropology, there is no objective or neutral position that is somehow "outside": all knowledge production is politically and ethically situated (Haraway 1988; Hale 2008), as well as being an intersubjective construction between different individuals and collectives. We understand indigenous women and men to be "simultaneously knowledge producers and political actors" and their organizational processes as sites where "theory-in-action" is produced (Perry and Rappaport 2013: 30–31). In recent years indigenous organizations and communities have increasingly demanded that researchers clearly position themselves and work in particular ways to defend their rights and advance their political struggles and agendas. The authors of this volume endorse the proposition enunciated by Charles Hale, that "research that is predicated on alignment with a group of people organized in struggle, and on collaborative relations of knowledge production with members of that group, has the potential to yield privileged insight, analysis, and theoretical innovation that otherwise would be impossible to achieve" (Hale 2008: 20). We believe that socially engaged knowledge production can generate new theoretical contributions as well as directly contributing to challenging situations of injustice and oppression in different ways. As Charles Hale and Lynn Stephen observe, "Theoretical innovation emerges from collaborative research methods because of the special proximity between political struggle and data gathering, or more broadly the production of knowledge" (2013: 22).

Such positionality implied a variety of research strategies in order to accompany and document the diverse processes described in this volume. First, the issue or problem to be analyzed was determined primarily by the actors and organizations themselves in dialogue with the researchers. This meant a degree of open-endedness about our research questions and implied considerable differences across the cases. As academics working together in a common intellectual and political project, we shared methodological and theoretical concerns and perspectives, but did not set out to ask exactly the same questions of each context. Second, we privileged ethnographic methods, with an emphasis on engagement. This implied combining participant observation with other, more self-evidently collaborative research methods and outputs such as workshops, focus groups, and the production of videos and popular education materials. Such spaces for collective reflection and co-labor were particularly important; as Keisha-Khan Perry and Joanne Rappaport observe (referring to workshops), "[these] are not only of academic interest, but are also arenas for political discussion and training, serving as spaces for self-discovery, as scenarios for 'concept mobilization,' and as stages on which organizational decisions are made" (2013: 36). In addition, and more practically, producing a range of different research outputs meant that the results of our collaborations were more accessible, useful, and timely for the people we work with than academic publications such as this book. By accompanying and supporting different organizational processes while at the same time paying close attention to the subtleties of discourse and practice, engaged ethnography can uncover situated and relational senses of grievance. In the field of legal activism, such research can contribute new perspectives on social justice struggles and on law itself, for example, using the applied field of special anthropological witness reports to communicate particular understandings and social realities to legal professionals who might otherwise view disputes through hegemonic lenses that tend to privilege abstract notions of individual rights over the situated histories of individuals who are part of specific collectivities. The kinds of legal and political anthropology proposed here therefore form part of legal and political advocacy in contexts of complex legal pluralities at the same time as they question hegemonic framings of law by highlighting alternative constructions of what "justice" might mean. As Craig Calhoun has observed, "[activist engagement] is not just about universal truths—though these do matter—but about producing truth in particular contexts and making knowledge useful in particular projects" (2008: xxi).

The different contributors to this volume underline the importance of putting the practices and narratives of indigenous women at the heart of analysis, meaning that testimony was of central importance to our project. As Adriana Terven Salinas observes in her chapter, women's narrations of mistreatment and grievances became integral to creating intersubjective research processes capable of generating new categories and perspectives on violence. Lynn Stephen proposes that testimony—which she defines as oral telling of a person's perception of an event that also implies witnessing—"allows silenced groups to speak and to be heard, to enact alternative visions for political and cultural representation, and to formulate new, hybrid forms of identity" (2013: 2). In her work on the APPO in Oaxaca, Stephen observes that personal testimonies serve as a fundamental means of political participation in indigenous community assemblies. Yet in many of our research contexts, women felt themselves to be marginalized within such communal spaces, finding it difficult to raise their concerns. Sharing their testimony in different, more intimate settings, such as the healing workshops described in Rachel Sieder's chapter on Chichicastenango, or the *plantón* (sit-in) of displaced Triqui villagers in the main square in Oaxaca that provided the setting for much of Natalia De Marinis's research, women elaborated new understandings of violence, rights, justice, and security, transforming their individual and collective senses of self in the process. In other, more public settings the performance of testimony permitted women to challenge dominant narratives of victimhood: in April 2012 a group of us traveled to Ayutla de los Libres in Guerrero to witness representatives of the Mexican state accept responsibility for the rape of Inés Fernández in a public ceremony, part of the implementation of the historic Inter-American Court judgment. Speaking in Me'phaa, Inés's trenchant testimony located her rape within a broader social context of violence against her organization and community. Rather than accept the status of "vindicated victim," she instead angrily questioned the good faith of the government officials on the podium beside her and denounced the presence of members of the local cartels in the audience. The forms of knowledge production implicit in testimony allowed us to share and document situated constructions of (in)justice and (in)security with a particular emphasis on women's understandings, exploring the ways in which intersectionalities of violence are experienced across time and space by different actors. As Mariana Mora illustrates in her chapter, the narratives of Nahua women in Guerrero about the insecurities they face in their everyday lives differed significantly from those of men. While men tended to identify specific acts of violence (such as those perpetrated by security forces or actors linked to organized crime), women also referred to different aspects that limit and fragment their capacities to sustain their families and their communities. Similarly, Morna Macleod's chapter on Maya-Mam women resisting the Goldcorp mine in San Marcos, Guatemala, points to women's concerns about the natural environment and the fate of future generations. The insecurities generated by thirty years of neoliberal economic policies with their associated "indianization of poverty" (Cervone 2012) and the struggles of daily existence are often at the heart of women's narratives of what Mora calls an "accumulation of insecurities." Physical and structural violence are intimately related in women's accounts: for example, in their chapters both Mora and Aída Hernández Castillo signal the perceptions of Nahua, Na'savi, and Me'phaa women in Guerrero, who argued that the distances they had to walk to access government schools or health clinics made them more vulnerable to sexual assault. The research presented in this volume points to the ways in which emic understandings of security have been used by indigenous women to advance their access to justice and more equitable treatment at the same time as confronting the multiple violences and oppressions they suffer as indigenous peoples. For example, within the organization development of the CRIC, an emphasis on the family has provided a means to address gender justice issues in the context of the wider challenges to the security and autonomy of indigenous peoples in the Cauca region. And in the case of the OPIM in Guerrero, the successful legal claim for collective community reparations for Inés Fernández's rape framed an argument about women's and girls' security within the context of militarization in the region. These alternative notions of security and justice emphasize not just women's control over their bodies, but also indigenous people's control over territory and the means of social reproduction for their families and communities.

At best, the kind of research perspective proposed here can contribute to validating alternative epistemologies or ways of being in the world, understanding these as situated ways of theorizing social reality. Yet while we try to meet the imperative that Phillpe Bourgois reminds us of, to "write against inequality" (2006: x), and stay committed to the broad aims of the organizations we work with, this alone does not resolve the multiple ethical and practical challenges of collaborative ethnographic engagement. Our reflections on these came to form an integral part of the project, leading to a chapter coauthored by Aída Hernández Castillo and Adriana Terven that appears here. Our collective reflections over the course of three years yielded a number of conclusions, which are explored at length by Hernández Castillo and Terven. These include (1) the importance of recognizing the heterogeneity of indigenous women's—and indigenous people's—experience, and that of different organizational processes; (2) the need to empirically ground the concept of intersectionality of violence by establishing precise methodological routes that privilege emic positions and different historical specificities; (3) the importance of prior and ongoing dialogue with organizations to establish research priorities and mechanisms for data collection; (4) the value of participatory *diagnósticos*, systematization and intercultural workshops as a means of accompanying organizational processes and generating data; (5) the contribution of testimonies, life histories, and ethnographies to analyzing challenges to improving women's access to justice and security; and (6) the need to explicitly address the difficulties that inevitably arise in the research process as part of the analysis of gendered and intercultural power dynamics. At the same time, the ethical demands of working on violence in contexts often marked by acute physical insecurity and danger form a central part of the reflections offered in many of the chapters.

In short, the research presented in this volume shows how indigenous women have advanced new understandings through their organizational processes, reshaping community, national, and even international law. We believe the adoption of an intersectional perspective challenges us to question an exclusive focus on gender oppression and instead to comprehend the myriad ways in which indigenous women conceptualize and theorize violence, (in)justice, and (in)security from their specific standpoints or contingent positionalities. Such efforts have inevitably involved tensions and conflicts within their families, communities, and organizations, and often considerable personal cost to the women themselves. Yet in recent years indigenous women's organizing across Latin America has transformed debates around gender justice and indigenous peoples. It is impossible to imagine future processes of constitutional or legal reform, or the elaboration of community statutes, that do not take their voices into account. We hope our work will contribute to efforts to build more secure and just futures for indigenous women and men, and for the societies of which they—and we—are part.

NOTES

1. On judicialization and juridification in Latin America, see Sieder, Schjolden, and Angell 2005; Couso, Huneeus, and Sieder 2010.

2. While her research focuses on mestiza, or ladina, Cecilia Menjívar makes a similar argument about the ways in which structural, normalized forms of violence tend to be eclipsed by an emphasis on physical, visible aspects of violence (Menjívar 2011).

3. On postcolonial intersectionality, see Radcliffe 2015.

4. On cultures of servitude, see Ray and Qayum 2009.

5. "[W]e take security to be a culturally, socially, and historically variable political affect that can be parsed as a matter of confronting 'existential threats' to collectives of various orders and scales" (Holbraad and Axel Pedersen 2013: 8).

6. As Thomas Hylland Eriksen and his coauthors note in a recent volume, discussions of human security must take nonmaterial factors such religion, ethnicity, and gender into account. See Hylland Eriksen, Bal, and Salemink 2010.

7. The United Nations Commission on Human Security defines human security as the protection of "the vital core of all human lives in ways that enhance human freedoms and fulfillment" (UN Commission on Human Security 2003: 4).

8. See, for example, Condor Chuquiruna 2009, 2010; Santos and Exeni Rodríguez 2012; Santos and Grijalva Jiménez 2012.

9. For exceptions, see Sierra, Hernández, and Sieder 2013 and Chenaut 2014 on Mexico; for the Andes, see Barrera 2016; Nostas Ardaya and Sanabría Salmón 2009; Franco Valdivia and González Luna 2009; Picq 2012.

10. Amar defines securitization as "the reconfiguration of political debates and claims around social justice, political participation or resource distribution into technical assessments of danger, operations of enforcement, and targeting of risk populations" (Amar 2013: 17).

11. Some organizations have a long track record of negotiating with non-indigenous collaborators and clearly enunciated guidelines—for example, CRIC in Colombia (Rappaport 2005) and the Zapatistas in Chiapas (Mora 2011); however, other groups have less experience or even interest in setting out the parameters for research engagements, particularly when its utility may not be immediately apparent.

REFERENCES

Amar, Paul. 2013. *The Security Archipelago: Human-Security States, Sexuality Politics, and the End of Neoliberalism.* Durham, NC: Duke University Press.

Arias, Enrique Desmond. 2006. *Drugs and Democracy in Rio de Janeiro: Trafficking, Social Networks, and Public Security.* Chapel Hill: University of North Carolina Press.

Arteaga Böhrt, Ana Cecilia. 2013. "'Todas somos la semilla': Ser mujer en la Policía Comunitaria de Guerrero: Ideologías de género, participación política y seguridad." MA thesis, Centro de Investigaciones y Estudios Superiores en Antropología Social, Mexico.

Barrera, Anna. 2015. *Violence against Women in Legally Plural Settings: Experiences and Lessons from the Andes.* New York: Routledge.

Bastos, Santiago, and Quimy de Leon. 2014. *Dinámicas de despojo y resistencia en Guatemala. Comunidades, Estado y empresas.* Guatemala: Editorial Serviprensa.

Belausteguigoitia Rius, Marisa, and María Josefina Saldaña-Portillo, eds. 2015. *Des/posesión: Género, territorio y luchas por la autodeterminación.* Mexico City: UNAM.

Blackwell, Maylei. 2006. "Weaving in the Spaces: Transnational Indigenous Women's Organizing and the Politics of Scale." In Speed, Hernández Castillo, and Stephen, *Dissident Women*, 115–154.

Bourgois, Philipe. 2001. "The Power of Violence in War and Peace: Post–Cold War Lessons from El Salvador." *Ethnography* 2 (1): 5–34.

———. 2006. "Foreword: Anthropology in the Global State of Emergency." In Sanford and Angel-Ajani, *Engaged Observer*, ix–xii.

Brah, Avtar. 2011. *Cartografías de la diáspora. Identidades en cuestión.* Madrid: Traficantes de Sueños.

Calhoun, Craig. 2008. "Foreword." In *Engaging Contradictions: Theory, Politics, and Methods of Activist Scholarship*, by C. Hale, xiii–xxv. Berkeley: University of California Press.

CEPAL. 2013. *Mujeres indígenas en América Latina: dinámicas demográficas y sociales en el marco de los derechos humanos.* Santiago de Chile: United Nations, Centro Latinoamericano y Caribeño de Demografía (CELADE)-División de Población y División de Asuntos de Género de la CEPAL.

Cervone, Emma. 2012. *Long Live Atahualpa: Indigenous Politics, Justice, and Democracy in the Northern Andes.* Durham, NC: Duke University Press.

Chenaut, Victoria. 2014. *Género y procesos interlegales.* Mexico City: El Colegio de Michoacán/CIESAS.

Chirix García, Emma Delfina, and Grupo de Mujeres Mayas Kaqla. 2003. *Alas y Raíces. Afectividad de las mujeres mayas* (Rik'in ruxik' y ruxe'il *Ronojel kajowab'al ri mayab' taq ixoqi'*). Guatemala: Kaqla.

Comaroff, John, and Jean L. Comaroff. 2009. "Reflections on the Anthropology of Law, Governance, and Sovereignty." In *Rules of Law and Laws of Ruling: On the Governance of Law*, edited by B. Beckman, F. von, K. von, and J. Eckert, 31–59. Surrey: Ashgate.

Condor Chuquiruna, Eddie. 2009. *Estado de la relación entre justicia indígena y justicia estatal en los países andinos: Estudios de casos en Colombia, Perú, Ecuador y Bolivia*. Lima, Peru: Comisión Andina de Juristas.

———. 2010. *Experiencias de coordinación y cooperación entre sistemas jurídicos en la región andina*. Lima, Peru: Comisión Andina de Juristas.

Couso, Javier, Alexandra Huneeus, and Rachel Sieder, eds. 2010. *Cultures of Legality: Judicialization and Political Activism in Contemporary Latin America*. New York: Cambridge University Press.

Cowan, Jane, Marie-Bénédicte Dembour, and Richard A. Wilson, eds. 2001. *Culture and Rights: Anthropological Perspectives*. Cambridge: Cambridge University Press.

Crenshaw, Kimberley. 1991. "Mapping the Margins: Intersectionality, Identity Politics, and Violence against Women of Color." *Stanford Law Review* 43 (6): 1241–1299.

Cumes, Aura. 2009. "'Sufrimos vergüenza': mujeres k'iche' frente a la justicia comunitaria en Guatemala." *Desacatos* 31: 99–114.

———. 2014. "La india como sirvienta: Servidumbre doméstica, colonialismo y patriarcado en Guatemala." PhD diss., CIESAS, México City.

Das, Veena, and Deborah Poole, eds. 2004. *Anthropology in the Margins of the State*. Santa Fe: School of American Research Press.

Davis, Angela. 2004. *Mujeres, raza y clase*. Madrid: Akal Ediciones.

de la Cadena, Marisol. 1991. "Las mujeres son más indias: Etnicidad y género en una comunidad del Cuzco." *Revista Andina* 9: 7–45.

ECAP-UNAMG (Equipo de Estudios Comunitarios y Acción Psicosocial; Unión Nacional de Mujeres Guatemaltecas). 2009. *Tejidos que lleva el alma. Memoria de mujeres mayas sobrevivientes de violación sexual durante el conflicto armado*. Guatemala: ECAP-UNAMG.

ECMIA/Chirapaq. 2012. *Violence and Women*. Document presented to the CSW57. Lima: ECMIA and Chirapaq.

Erazo, Juliet S. 2013. *Governing Indigenous Territories: Enacting Sovereignty in the Ecuadorian Amazon*. Durham, NC: Duke University Press.

Faundez, Julio. 2011. "Legal Pluralism and International Development Agencies: State Building or Legal Reform?" *Hague Journal of the Rule of Law* 3: 18–38.

Feldman, Shelley, Gayatri A. Menon, and Charles Geisler. 2011. "Introduction: A New Politics of Containment." In *Accumulating Insecurity: Violence and Dispossession in the Making of Everyday Life*, edited by Shelley Feldman, Charles Geisler, and Gayatri A. Menon, 1–23. Athens: University of Georgia Press.

Figueroa Romero, María de Dolores. 2011. "Comparative Analysis of Indigenous Women's Participation in Ethno-politics and Community Development: The Experiences of Women Leaders of ECUARUNARI (Ecuador) and YATAMA (Atlantic Coast of Nicaragua)." PhD diss., York University, Toronto.

FIMI (Foro Internacional de Mujeres Indígenas/International Indigenous Women's Forum). 2006. *Mairin Iwanka Raya: Indigenous Women Stand Against Violence: A Companion Report to the UN Secretary-General's Study on VAW*. New York: FIMI.

———. 2013. *Manual de Investigación Intercultural. Diálogo de saberes sobre la Violencia contra las Mujeres Indígenas. Investigación Intercultural como herramienta para su abordaje. Aproximaciones metodológicas*. http://www.fimi-iiwf.org/listado_observatorio.php.

Franco Valdivia, Rocío, and María Alejandra González Luna. 2009. *Las mujeres en la justicia comunitaria: víctimas, sujetos y actores*. Serie Justicia Comunitaria en los Andes: Perú y Ecuador. Lima: IDL.

Fukuda-Parr, Sakiko, and Carol Messineo. 2012. *Human Security: A Critical Review of the Literature*. CRPD Working Paper 11. https://soc.kuleuven.be/web/files/12/80/wp11.pdf.

Goldstein, Daniel M. 2004. *The Spectacular City: Violence and Performance in Urban Bolivia.* Durham, NC: Duke University Press.

———. 2012. *Outlawed: Between Security and Rights in a Bolivian City.* Durham, NC: Duke University Press.

Goodale, Mark, and Sally Engle Merry, eds. 2007. *The Practice of Human Rights: Tracking Law between the Global and the Local.* Cambridge: Cambridge University Press.

Goodale, Mark, and Nancy Postero, eds. 2013. *Neoliberalism Interrupted: Social Change and Contested Governance in Contemporary Latin America.* Stanford, CA: Stanford University Press.

Hale, Charles. 2008. "Introduction." In *Engaging Contradictions: Theory, Politics, and Methods of Activist Scholarship*, 1–28. Berkeley: University of California Press.

Hale, Charles R., and Lynn Stephen. 2013. "Introduction." In Hale and Stephen, *Otros Saberes*, 1–29.

Hale, Charles R., and Lynn Stephen, eds. 2013. *Otros Saberes. Collaborative Research on Indigenous and Afro-Descendant Cultural Politics.* Santa Fe: SAR Press.

Haraway, Donna. 1988. "Situated Knowledges: The Science Question in Feminism and the Privilege of Partial Perspective." *Feminist Studies* 14 (3): 575–599.

Hernández Castillo, Rosalva Aída, ed. 2009. *Etnografías e historias de resistencia. Mujeres indígenas, procesos organizativos y nuevas identidades.* Mexico City: CIESAS.

———. 2010. "Violencia de estado y violencia de género: Las paradojas en torno a los derechos humanos de las Mujeres en México." *TRACE* 57: 86–98.

———. 2016. *Multiple Injustices: Indigenous Women, Law, and Political Struggle.* Tucson: University of Arizona Press.

Hill Collins, Patricia. 1990. *Black Feminist Thought: Knowledge, Consciousness, and the Politics of Empowerment.* Boston: Unwin Hyman.

———. 1998. "La política del pensamiento feminista negro." In *¿Qué son los estudios de mujeres?*, edited by Marysa Navarro and Catherine Stimpson, 253–312. Buenos Aires: Fondo de Cultura Económica.

Holbraad, Martin, and Morten Axel Pedersen, eds. 2013. *Times of Security: Ethnographies of Fear, Protest, and the Future.* New York: Routledge.

hooks, bell. 2004. "Mujeres negras: dar forma a la teoría feminista." In *Otras inapropiables. Feminismos desde las fronteras*, edited by bell hooks, Avtar Brah, Chela Sandoval, and Gloria Anzaldúa, 33–50. Madrid: Traficantes de Sueños.

Hylland Eriksen, Thomas, Ellen Bal, and Oscar Salemink, eds. 2010. *A World of Insecurity: Anthropological Perspectives on Human Security.* London: Pluto Press.

Jaramillo, Pablo. 2014. *Etnicidad y Victimización. Genealogías de la Violencia y la Indigenidad en el Norte de Colombia.* Bogota: Ediciones Uniandes.

Lugones, María. 2008. "Colonialidad y género." *Tabula Rasa, Revista de Humanidades* 9: 73–101.

Macleod, Morna. 2011. *Nietas del fuego, creadoras del alba. Luchas político-culturales de mujeres mayas.* Guatemala: FLACSO.

Maguire, Marka, Catarina Frois, and Nils Zurawski, eds. 2014. *The Anthropology of Security: Perspectives from the Frontline of Policing, Counter-terrorism and Border Control.* London: Pluto Press.

McNeish, John-Andrew, and Jon Harald Sande Lie, eds. 2010. *Security and Development.* Oxford: Berghahn Books.

Mella Seguel, E. 2014. "La aplicación del derecho penal común y antiterrorista como respuesta a la protesta social de indígenas Mapuche Durante el periodo 2000–2010." *Oñati Socio-Legal Series* 4 (1): 122–138. http://ssrn.com/abstract=2384498.

Menjívar, Cecilia. 2011. *Enduring Violence: Ladina Women's Lives in Guatemala.* Berkeley: University of California Press.

Merry Engle, Sally. 2006. *Human Rights and Gender Violence: Translating International Law into Local Justice*. Chicago: University of Chicago Press.

———. 2007. "Introduction: States of Violence." In *The Practice of Human Rights: Tracking Law between the Global and the Local*, edited by M. Goodale and S. Merry, 41–48. Cambridge: Cambridge University Press.

Millán, Márgara, ed. 2014. *Más allá del feminismo: Caminos para andar*. Mexico City: Red de feminismos descoloniales.

Mora, Mariana. 2011. "Producción de conocimientos en el terreno de la autonomía. La investigación como tema de debate político." In *Luchas "muy otras": Zapatismo y autonomía en las comunidades indígenas de Chiapas*, edited by B. Baronnet, M. Mora, and R. Stahler-Sholk, 79–110. Mexico City: Universidad Autónoma Metropolitana/CIESAS/ Universidad Autónoma de Chiapas.

Nostas Ardaya, Mercedes, and Carmen Elena Sanabría Salmón, eds. 2009. *Detrás del cristal con que se mira: Órdenes normativos e interlegalidad. Mujeres Quechuas, Aymaras, Sirionó, Trinitarias, Chimane, Chiquitanas y Ayoreas*. La Paz: Coordinadora de la Mujer.

Okin, Susan. 1999. *Is Multiculturalism Bad for Women?* Princeton, NJ: Princeton University Press.

Penglase, R. Ben. 2014. *Living with Insecurity in a Brazilian Favela: Urban Violence and Daily Life*. New Brunswick, NJ: Rutgers University Press.

Perry, Keisha-Khan Y., and Joanne Rappaport. 2013. "Making a Case for Collaborative Research with Black and Indigenous Social Movements in Latin America." In Hale and Stephen, *Otros Saberes*, 30–48.

Picq, Manuela. 2012. "Between the Dock and a Hard Place: Hazards and Opportunities of Legal Pluralism for Indigenous Women in Ecuador." *Latin American Politics and Society* 54 (2):1–33.

Radcliffe, Sarah. 2015. *Dilemmas of Difference: Indigenous Women and the Limits of Postcolonial Development Policy*. Durham, NC: Duke University Press.

Rappaport, Joanne. 2005. *Intercultural Utopias: Public Intellectuals, Cultural Experimentation and Ethnic Pluralism in Colombia*. Durham, NC: Duke University Press.

Ray, Raka, and Seemin Qayum. 2009. *Cultures of Servitude: Modernity, Domesticity, and Class in India*. Stanford, CA: Stanford University Press.

Reguillo Cruz, Rosanna. 2013. "Guarded (In)visibility: Violencias and the Labors of Paralegality in the Era of Collapse." In *Rhetorics of Insecurity: Belonging and Violence in the Neoliberal Age*, edited by Zeynep Gambetti and Marcial Godoy-Anativia, 196–212. New York: New York University Press.

Rivera Cusicanqui, Silvia. 1996. *Ser mujer indígena, chola o birlocha en la Bolivia postcolonial de los años 90*. La Paz: Plural.

Rodríguez-Garavito, C., and B. Santos, eds. 2005. *Law and Globalization from Below: Towards a Cosmopolitan Legality*. Cambridge: Cambridge University Press.

Rousseau, Stéphanie. 2011. "Indigenous and Feminist Movements at the Constituent Assembly in Bolivia. Locating the Representation of Indigenous Women." *Latin American Research Review* 6 (2): 5–28.

Sanford, Victoria, and Asale Angel-Ajani, eds. 2006. *Engaged Observer: Anthropology, Advocacy, and Activism*. New Brunswick, NJ: Rutgers University Press.

Santos, Boaventura de Sousa. 2002. *Toward a New Legal Common Sense*. London: Butterworths.

———. 2006. "The Heterogeneous State and Legal Pluralism in Mozambique." *Law and Society Review* 40 (1): 39–75.

Santos, Boaventura de Sousa, and Agustín Grijalva Jiménez, eds. 2012. *Justicia indígena, plurinacionalidad e interculturalidad en Ecuador*. Quito: Abya-Yala.

Santos, Boaventura de Sousa, and José Luis Exeni Rodríguez, eds. 2012. *Justicia indígena, plurinacionalidad e interculturalidad en Bolivia*. Quito: Abya-Yala.

Sawyer, Suzana. 2004. *Crude Chronicles: Indigenous Politics, Multinational Oil, and Neoliberalism in Ecuador*. Durham, NC: Duke University Press.

Seligmann, Linda. 1993. "Between Worlds of Exchange: Ethnicity among Peruvian Market Women." *Cultural Anthropology* 8 (2): 187–213.

Sieder, Rachel, and John-Andrew McNeish, eds. 2012. *Gender Justice and Legal Pluralities: Latin American and African Perspectives*. New York: Routledge-Cavendish.

Sieder, Rachel, Line Schjolden, and Alan Angell, eds. 2005. *The Judicialization of Politics in Latin America*. New York: Palgrave.

Sieder, Rachel, and María Teresa Sierra. 2010. *Indigenous Women's Access to Justice in Latin America*. CMI working paper. Bergen, Norway: Chr. Michelsen Institute.

Sierra, María Teresa, ed. 2004. *Haciendo justicia: Interlegalidad, derecho y género en regiones indígenas*. Mexico City: CIESAS/Miguel Angel Porrúa.

Sierra, María Teresa, Aída Hernández, and Rachel Sieder, eds. 2013. *Justicias indígenas y Estado. Violencias contemporáneas*. Mexico City: CIESAS/FLACSO.

Speed, Shannon, Aída Hernández Castillo, and Lynn M. Stephen, eds. 2006. *Dissident Women: Gender and Cultural Politics in Chiapas*. Austin: University of Texas Press.

Stephen, Lynn. 2007. *Transborder Lives: Indigenous Oaxacans in Mexico, California, and Oregon*. Durham, NC: Duke University Press.

———. 2011. "Testimony and Human Rights Violations in Oaxaca." *Journal of Latin American Perspectives* 38 (2): 52–68.

———. 2013. *We Are the Face of Oaxaca: Testimony and Social Movements*. Durham, NC: Duke University Press.

Terven, Adriana. 2009. "Justicia indígena en tiempos multiculturales. Hacia la conformación de proyectos colectivos propios: la experiencia organizativa de Cuetzálan." PhD diss., CIESAS, Mexico City.

UN Commission on Human Security. 2003. *Human Security Now*. Geneva: United Nations. http://www.unocha.org/humansecurity/chs/finalreport/.

Weismantel, Mary J. 1989. *Food, Gender, and Poverty in the Ecuadorian Andes*. Philadelphia: University of Pennsylvania Press.

Wilson, Richard A., ed. 1997. *Human Rights, Culture, and Context: Anthropological Approaches*. London: Pluto Press.

PART ONE

Gender and Justice

Mediating State Law and International Norms

1

Between Community Justice and International Litigation

The Case of Inés Fernández before the Inter-American Court

ROSALVA AÍDA HERNÁNDEZ CASTILLO

Based on an analysis of the case of Inés Fernández Ortega versus the Mexican state presented before the Inter-American Court of Human Rights (IACtHR), in this chapter I analyze the ways in which violence, racism, and gender inequalities affect the lives of Mexican indigenous women and determine their lack of access to justice. I also explore how Inés and the women in her organization appropriated human rights discourses and spaces of international justice as tools to denounce the violence, racism, and economic marginalization they and their communities face.

Human rights discourses are deployed in processes of resistance, but they are also being used as new forms of state control of social protest and can encourage neoliberal, individualized conceptions of the person. Here I analyze the complexities associated with processes whereby human rights discourses are *vernacularized* within a context of militarized violence and lack of access to justice. My research is based on collaborative workshops with Inés Fernández Ortega and women and men from her organization that formed part of the elaboration of an anthropological expert report presented to the IACtHR, together with ethnographic research within different national and international spaces for justice associated with the case.

Inés Fernández Ortega, a leader of the Organization of the Me-phaa Indigenous Peoples (OPIM) in Guerrero state, was raped by soldiers from the Mexican army. On March 22, 2002, eleven soldiers from the Forty-First Battalion arrived at Inés Fernández Ortega's home, located in the Barranca de Tecuani community, part of the municipality of Ayutla de los Libres in the state of Guerrero, Mexico. Three of the soldiers entered the room that was being used as a kitchen without the consent of Inés, who at the moment was accompanied only by her four children, who were all under the age of eighteen. The soldiers asked questions in Spanish, which she couldn't answer, after which one of them raped her. Two days after the incident the victim presented a formal allegation to the Attorney General's Office (Ministerio Público of Ayutla de los Libres),[1] which determined that it was not the correct authority to investigate either the unauthorized and illegal entrance to Inés's property or the rape, due to the fact that the accused parties were part of the Mexican army. In May 2002, the local authorities forwarded the case to the military authorities.

As I analyze in this chapter, Inés Fernández Ortega's experience with the Attorney General (Ministerio Público) of Ayutla de los Libres and with the military authorities confirms a tendency towards triple discrimination within the Mexican legal system on the basis of class, race, and gender. She was denied the right to a translator and was examined by doctors who treated her with contempt and ended up "misplacing" the forensic tests they had conducted. After eight years trying to achieve justice in national courts, to no avail, she appealed to the inter-American human rights system.

The IACtHR became not just a space for the search for justice: throughout the lengthy litigation process, collective efforts coalesced and new leaderships were strengthened. Although repressive violence can often have a demobilizing effect, in this case the response was to strengthen local organization and particularly the leadership role of women, who have appropriated human rights discourses as tools for struggle. My analysis focuses on this double process of female victimization and personal reconstruction in the struggle for justice.

Appropriation of International Litigation by Women's Struggles

As a legal anthropologist and a feminist, I face the dilemma of understanding statutory law as a cultural product of liberalism that must be critically analyzed, while simultaneously, as an activist, recognizing the possibilities it offers as a tool to build a fairer life for women. Feminist jurists and anthropologists have extensively analyzed the ways that power works through statutory law to reproduce the ethnocentric and patriarchal viewpoints that have hegemonized Western cultural imaginaries (see Engle Merry 1995; Facio 1992; Fineman and Thomadsen 1991; Hernández Castillo 2004). But they have also shown that in certain contexts law and state justice can be used by women to articulate different forms of resistance (Hirsch and Lazarus-Black 1994; Smart 1989; Sierra and Hernández 2005). In the case I discuss here, international justice had both a restorative effect on the lives of women who have been victims of sexual torture, and a political effect through denouncing gender violence by Mexican state security forces. It also played an important part in promoting legislative reforms in Mexico to limit military jurisdiction.

International law is increasingly becoming a last resort for Latin American women whose human rights are violated by representatives of their states (directly or through omission) and whose demands for justice go unresolved by their national justice systems. In many instances strategic litigation has served to challenge gender discrimination and obtain legislative changes in favor of women's rights. For example, the case of *Maria da Penha v. Brazil*, presented to the IACtHR in 2006, resulted in the approval in that country of one of the most progressive laws on domestic violence anywhere in the region (known as the Maria da Penha Law; see MacDowell Santos 2007). Last, the case of *González et al. v. Mexico*, known as the Cotton Field case because the petition was lodged by the mothers of eight young women whose bodies were found in a cotton field in Ciudad Juárez, Chihuahua, is considered paradigmatic in strategic litigation in favor of women's rights because of the resulting international acknowledgment of the structural causes of gender violence.[2]

While it is true that these paradigmatic cases tend to be positively evaluated by feminist organizations based on their impacts on gender jurisprudence and public policies, we know very little of the concrete effects of processes of denunciation on the women who have had the courage to confront state powers and take their cases beyond national borders. It was this concern that made me hesitate when I was first invited to participate as an expert witness before the IACtHR in the case of Inés Fernández Ortega. I was asked to present an anthropological expert witness report that could help to explain the community impact of sexual violence considering the indigenous cultural context in which the aggression took place. These expert witness reports, also known as anthropological affidavits, are elaborated by specialists and outline the cultural context of the defendant or the plaintiff in any given case. The main objective of these reports is to provide information to the judges on the importance of cultural differences in understanding a specific case.[3] In *Inés Fernández Ortega v. Mexico*, we were required to analyze the impact of this sexual assault and the impunity surrounding the case on the community. We inquired specifically into how the cultural concepts of personhood, violence, and lack of justice influenced how the rape and the latter context of impunity were dealt with.

The Inter-American Commission on Human Rights and the legal representatives of Inés Fernández decided to invite me as an expert witness, taking into consideration my previous academic work on the intersection of indigenous collective rights and gender rights, and my advocacy for a gender agenda that considers the cultural diversity of women in Mexico. But I had many doubts: did she really want to take her case to that international court, or did the human rights organizations that supported her pressure her into "strategic litigation"?

It was with those questions in mind that in March 2009 I first arrived in Barranca Tequani, a Me'phaa community with a population of about five hundred inhabitants in the municipality of Ayutla de los Libres, in the state of Guerrero, where I met Inés Fernández Ortega, a small woman with a piercing look and an inner strength you can feel when she looks you in the eyes. She dispelled my fears, telling me, "I'm the one who wants to present the complaint so that justice is done, so the *guachos* [soldiers] know that they can't get away with it, so my daughters and the girls in the community don't have to go through what I did, so all the women in the region can walk in the mountains without being afraid."[4] Her conviction that the submission at the IACtHR was necessary not only for her but for all Me'phaa women made it clear to me that she was a very different community leader from many others I had met.

Inés's legal representatives from the Tlachinollan Human Rights Center of the Mountain of Guerrero also put her needs and decisions at the forefront of their strategies. For the Human Rights Center the presentation of her case at the IACtHR was not an end in itself, but part of what they call an "integral defense of the person," which places the victims of human rights violations, and not the litigation itself, at the center of their efforts. It was this political outlook on international litigation on the part of Tlachinollan, as well as Inés's resolve to take her complaint outside the country, that convinced me to embark on the long voyage that took me in April 2010 to Lima, Peru, where I participated in the public hearing convened by the Inter-American Court. My role was to inform the judges of the content of the expert report I had elaborated together with the ethnologist Héctor Ortiz in the previous months, which formed part of the documentary evidence presented by Inés Fernández's legal representatives.

One of the objectives of the expert testimony was to demonstrate that the sexual violence suffered by Inés had affected not only her and her family, but also the women of her community and her organization. The elaboration of the report brought me close to Inés and the women in the Organization of Me'phaa Indigenous Peoples (OPIM); I learned not only of their courage, but also of their collective solidarity and communal cohesion. I came to understand that the need for an expert opinion of this type was established not only by the legal representatives, but by Inés herself, who from the very beginning of the process insisted that her rape constituted part of a series of aggressions against her people and her organization, and that it therefore could not be treated in isolation. Her conviction forced her lawyers to argue in favor of community reparations for this case of individual rape, a legal strategy that had never been used before at the IACtHR. It was because of Inés Fernández's steadfast decision to use the court as a space to denounce a whole chain of violence—of which her rape was just one link—that it was necessary to draft the anthropological expert report.

Searching for Justice at the Local Level

After her sexual assault Inés first resorted to her community assembly to ask for support in making a legal complaint, but the support of community authorities was conditional at best and was later withdrawn due to fear of army reprisals. She then went to the state Public Prosecutor's Office (Ministerio Público), where the racism that permeates Mexico's justice system became evident. In common with the situation in most of Mexico's indigenous regions, the attorney general with jurisdiction over Ayutla de los Libres is a mixed-race government official, unfamiliar with the indigenous languages that are spoken in the region (Mepha'a, Tu'un sávi, or Mixteco) and does not have the support of a translator or an interpreter, which is why Inés requested the help of Obtilia Eugenio, a leader of OPIM, to present her allegation. In our interviews with Inés Fernández, she talks about the poor treatment and lack of interest on the part of the judicial authorities, the same authorities who determined that they could not take on the case, due to the fact that the accused parties were part of the Mexican army, which is why they decided to turn it over to the Military Attorney General (Ministerio Público Militar).

A number of studies in Mexico regarding indigenous women's access to state justice have revealed the ways in which gender-discriminatory ideologies and a lack of cultural sensitivity on the part of those who administer justice have affected the relationship between this sector of the population and national law (see Hernández Castillo 2004, 2016; Sierra Camacho 2004). These studies demonstrate that systems of class, gender, and ethnic oppression are mutually constituted and have a direct effect on poor indigenous women's lack of access to legal recourse. Afro-American feminists have proposed an *intersectional* theoretical approach as a means for analyzing how socially constructed categories of discrimination, such as class, gender, race/ethnicity, and generation, interact simultaneously, creating contexts of social inequality (see Crenshaw 1991; Hill Collins 1990). In this sense, Inés's testimony allows us to access the privileged viewpoints of those who have experienced the multiple forms of oppression that characterize Mexican society as a whole.

The simultaneous interaction of these forms of exclusion became evident in the revictimization that Inés suffered when trying to gain recourse to the state legal system. The lack of knowledge of indigenous languages on the part of officials and the high level of monolingualism and illiteracy of the female indigenous population hinder their access to justice. Studies on access to justice indicate that Inés's experience is the norm for indigenous men and women in the state justice system, even though the 2001 reform to article 2 of the Constitution establishes the right of access to a translator and anthropological expert opinion (see OACNUDH 2013). The requirement to provide interpreters is also established in the Federal Penal Code (CPF) and the Federal Code of Penal Procedures (CFPP), but the responsibility for determining what constitutes sufficient fluency in Spanish is left up to the Public Prosecutor (MP), which means that in practice the right to an interpreter depends on what the MP considers "sufficient."

This violation of indigenous people's linguistic and cultural rights is not only the product of a lack of staff and adequate training; it goes hand in hand with degrading and racist treatment by government employees, which in many ways reproduces the racial hierarchies that characterize Mexican society as a whole. In the case of indigenous women, the structural racism reproduced by state institutions is aggravated by gender discrimination, which often revictimizes them by treating cases of sexual violence with an insensibility that takes the form of symbolic violence. This was the case of the forensic doctor who first attempted to attest to the rape of Inés Fernández. When she requested that a female doctor examine her, he responded, "What difference does it make if a man examines you? It wasn't women who raped you."[5]

For ten years Inés traveled the roads of the Costa Chica region of Guerrero in pursuit of justice, suffering the racism and misogyny of government employees. During this *via crucis* she faced death threats, community criticism, family tensions, and the murder of her brother Lorenzo, who had been her main source of support in the lawsuit and who was tortured and executed by "unidentified individuals" in February 2008. Going out to demand justice meant Inés often had to leave her children in the care of Nohemí, her youngest daughter, then a preteen who had to take on the family's responsibilities when her parents traveled to the municipal center of Ayutla de los Libres, to Tlapa, to Chilpancingo, or even to Washington, DC. In her search for justice, Inés gradually built networks of solidarity, finding allies who accompanied them during those nine years, such as members of the Tlachinollan Human Rights Center, Peace Brigades International, and the Mexico team of Amnesty International, among others. Staff from some of these organizations traveled with her to present their cases before the Inter-American Commission on Human Rights in Washington, DC.

Cultural identities and regional history influenced the specific ways in which Inés experienced the rape and her subsequent efforts to seek justice. Inés had started to organize around the rights of women and their communities, and her rape was understood and experienced by her and her family in the light of a historic memory that links the army's presence to the violence and impunity that has dominated the region since the 1970s as a result of the so-called dirty war.[6] Added to this is the more recent memory of the El Charco massacre in 1998,[7] precisely in the municipality of Ayutla de los Libres where OPIM has its headquarters. In the context of this recent history, rape and torture are experienced as part of a *continuum of violence* that has marked the relationship between indigenous peoples in the region and Mexico's armed forces.

The murder of Lorenzo Fernández Ortega, Inés's brother and a member of OPIM in February 2008, together with anonymous death threats against the organization's president, Obtilia Eugenio Manuel, and the issuing of arrest warrants and detentions of five of its leaders in April of the same year spread fear and a sense of vulnerability among OPIM members and residents of the region, reviving memories of a recent past of violence and impunity.

The expert report elaborated for Inés's lawsuit demonstrated how sexual violence is experienced as something affecting the entire community. For

Me'phaa people the individual and the collective are closely related, so that violence experienced by an individual is lived as an offense against the entire community, producing an imbalance within the collective. This imbalance expresses itself as medical pathologies, since events that cause pain manifest themselves in an illness called *gamitú* or *susto* (fright), which has affected several of the women close to Inés. Only justice and the assurance that these events will not be repeated can reestablish the community's equilibrium. As one of the women I interviewed told me, "As long as there is no justice, our spirits are not at peace, there is a lot of fear and we can't sleep in peace, because we know that if what the *guachos* [soldiers] did isn't punished, they can do it again. Lack of justice causes *va jui* and *gamitú*."[8]

An indication of this collective sense of injury is the fact that the reparations Inés requested at the IACtHR are not only for her personal benefit, but also for the girls and women in her organization and her community. These women's testimonies and actions speak of experiences that are lived not as personal offenses, but rather as a part of a *continuum* of violence that has affected their communities and organizations. As a consequence the justice they seek is not limited to imprisonment of their assailants, but includes the demilitarization of their regions, the end of impunity, and legislative reforms that allow real access to justice by women in general and indigenous women specifically. It was these reparations I had to justify in the IACtHR, my first experience in international litigation.

The Hearing before the IACtHR—An Ethnographic Approach to International Litigation

While it is true that legal anthropology has shown a particular interest in ethnographies of dispute processes in spaces of community justice (see Collier [1973] 1995; Moore 1996; Nader 1978, 1990; Sierra Camacho 1992, 2004) and, to a lesser extent, in the spaces of state justice (see Barrera 2012; Baitenmann, Chenaut, and Varley 2008; Engle Merry 2000; Latour 2002), there are very few ethnographic descriptions of the "cultural rituals" that develop in the spaces of international justice.[9]

Some authors have shared their theoretical reflections regarding experiences of cultural expert work in spaces of international justice (see Hale 2006; Anaya and Grossman 2002) or in the UN gatherings where women's rights are discussed (Engle Merry 2006), pointing to the cultural dimension of discourses and practices produced in such spaces. However, the idea appears to prevail that so-called indigenous law and community justice are full of "culture," while international law and its justice procedures are simply "transparent" expressions of the exercise of law. In this section I approach international litigation as a space of dispute where cultural models and power relations manifest themselves among all the actors participating in a legal *performance*. Following Leticia Barrera's methodological proposal, I assume that "hearings are not discrete acts, but choreographed events calculated to create an effect, and they involve discourse repertoires that are oriented toward the interests of the audience to which they are addressed" (2012: 141). The participants in this particular *legal performance* at the IACtHR included not only the parties involved, but also a wider audience of law students, members of human rights organizations, indigenous women organized against military violence, and feminist groups.

The court was established in 1979 as an autonomous judicial institution of the Organization of American States, with the purpose of applying the American Convention on Human Rights and other international treaties.[10] It is a space of international justice that aims to monitor and sanction member states that violate human rights. The court is headquartered in San José, Costa Rica, where that country's government donated a space that would serve to hold all hearings. However, as of May 2005, the court decided to hold itinerant sessions in the various member states in order to publicize the work of the inter-American human rights system. The trial of *Inés Fernández Ortega v. Mexico* took place at the Palace of Justice in Lima, Peru, a gray, granite, neoclassical structure built in 1939, a symbol of judicial power in Peru. Two white marble sculptures of lions frame the entrance and give the building an air of grandeur that contrasts with the squalor of some of the streets in Lima's historic center.

The three experts who would declare on behalf of Inés's legal representatives arrived at the building on April 15, 2010: the Colombian psychologist Clemencia Correa, the Peruvian lawyer Marcela Huaita, and myself as the team's cultural anthropologist. Inés's legal team was composed of the lawyers Vidulfo Rosales, Alejandro Ramos, and Jorge Santiago Aguirre, and the anthropologist Abel Barrera Hernández, from the Tlachinollan Human Rights Center; and, from the Center for Justice and International Law (CEJIL), the lawyers Gisela de León and Agustín Martín. Inés's advanced pregnancy had prevented her from traveling to Lima, and the court had declined the team's petition for her to be substituted by the OPIM's president, Obtilia Eugenio, who had served as her translator since her first complaint to the Public Prosecutor's Office in Ayutla de los Libres. We were all aware of the power of Inés's spoken testimony, and her absence increased her legal representatives' concern. Her description of events, and that of her husband Fortunato Prisciliano Sierra and her daughter Noemí as witnesses, was presented before a Notary Public in Guerrero and handed in writing to the court (a format legally known as an affidavit). The strength of Inés's voice filled the courtroom through a video presented at the beginning of the hearing.

Upon entering the Palace of Justice, the first thing that caught our attention was the presence of a large group of Peruvian indigenous women dressed in traditional outfits who waited patiently for the hearing to begin. We later learned that they were members of the National Coordination of Women Affected by the Internal Armed Conflict and the National Federation of Peasant, Artisan, Indigenous, Native and Salaried Women, organizations that have been supporting women victims of sexual violence of Peru's twenty-year internal armed conflict (1980–2000). Several of the women approached me after the hearing and spoke with emotion of how important it was for them that an indigenous woman like themselves would dare to confront the army and take her government to an international court; Inés Fernández's example motivated them to think of the IACtHR as a space to look for justice. Two of them handed me brief written messages for Inés expressing their admiration.

The presence of these peasant women, most of them Quechua speakers, made the space of the court feel like a place of the people, contrasting with the formality of the bench and the overall environment of the Palace of Justice itself. Since it was a public hearing, several law schools took their students to witness the first international trial carried out by the Inter-American Court in Peruvian territory. The spectators' bustle turned to silence when the seven judges entered: five men—Leonardo A. Franco, Manuel E. Ventura Robles, Alberto Pérez Pérez, Eduardo Vio Grossi, and Alejandro Carlos Espinosa—and two women—Margarette May Macaulay and Rhadys Abreu Blondet. Their black and red togas gave the ritual a solemnity that reminded me of the public defense of theses in European universities. The paraphernalia of the ritual emphasized the distance separating the judges from the people witnessing the trial. The Quechua women, for whom Inés's case resonated with their own memories of military violence, were silent witnesses to a justice ritual that had little to do with the forms of community justice in which many of them had participated.

As an expert witness who would present an oral opinion to the court, I could not be present at the entire hearing, so I was led to a small room in the back of the building where I nervously awaited my turn to speak. Before leaving the courtroom I was able to witness the ostentatious arrival of the delegation representing the Mexican state, composed of more than twenty government officials in addition to the legal team.[11] The public officials were accompanied by a group of aides who carried about twenty boxes of documents. This extensive delegation with their "mysterious" documents contrasted with Inés's team of five lawyers with portfolios in their hands. We later learned that the documents were simply reports on the various programs on "transversalization of the gender perspective" promoted by the Mexican government in its public policies, which were presented as "proof" that the state is concerned about women's rights.

The distribution of both teams in the space of the trial proceedings, the ways in which they communicated internally, and the manner in which they addressed the magistrates demonstrated the power inequalities between the representatives of the state and those of Inés. The government's legal team opted for a strategy that began with a partial recognition of the responsibility of the Mexican state for the crimes of omission and delay in the administration of justice. Without presenting witnesses or experts to support its defense, the team began its participation in the hearing by stating that the Mexican state acknowledged

> First, that the absence of specialized medical care for Mrs. Fernández Ortega, which should have included the psychological and not merely the physical aspect, and which should have been provided immediately, constitutes a flagrant violation of Article 8.1 of the American Convention. Second that the destruction of the scientific evidence taken from the victim also constituted a flagrant violation of Article 8.1 of the American Convention. Third, that despite the efforts made by the authorities, there have been delays and absence of due diligence in the investigations; therefore, there have been different violations to Articles 8.1 and 25 of the American Convention and, consequently, also of Article 5.1 thereof, with regard to the mental integrity of Mrs. Fernández Ortega. This is . . . the state's acknowledgement of international responsibility for violations of the American Convention . . . that it has come here to present today . . . so that the Court may order the reparations required by international law and by its jurisprudence.[12]

This acknowledgment excluded the direct responsibility of the Mexican army for the sexual torture of Inés, and the impact that "military institutional violence" had on her family and community during these ten years, as well as the violations of the Inter-American Convention on the Prevention, Punishment, and Eradication of Violence against Women (Convention of Belém do Pará) and the Convention against Torture and Other Cruel, Inhuman or Degrading Treatment or Punishment, which these acts implied. In other words, although the state began the trial by acknowledging its responsibilities, the Tlachinollan and CEJIL team still had much to demonstrate to obtain the conviction expected by Inés.

When my turn came to speak, the other two expert witnesses had already given their declarations and I was unaware of how the hearings had proceeded up to that point. I began my declaration with a presentation lasting about twenty minutes, where I summarized the main arguments contained in our expert report, based on field research and interviews with Inés, her family, and members of her community. In the report we discussed (1) the impact of the rape of Mrs. Fernández Ortega on the indigenous community of Barranca Tequani, and especially the impact on the women; (2) the alleged harm to the social fabric of the community and the alleged impunity in the case; and (3) possible measures for reparations.[13]

The judges' questions had to do with clarifications of parts of the document presented and the oral testimony I had just given. Judge Margarette May Macaulay, an Afro-Caribbean magistrate from Jamaica, seemed to be best acquainted with the expert report and later confronted the Mexican state's legal representatives most emphatically. While all the judges followed a pre-established protocol and consistently based their questions on previously presented documentary evidence, Judge Macaulay was clearly committed to Inés's case. Her trajectory as a defender of women's rights and promoter of legislative reforms against domestic violence and sexual harassment in her own country meant she approached the case with a level of cultural and political capital that the other judges seemed to lack. After the hearing I learned that she was a member of the steering committee of the Caribbean Association of Feminist Research and Action. The presence of judges like Macaulay in the IACtHR is in part a consequence of the involvement of the Latin American feminist movement in the inter-American human rights system.

While it is true that the gender sensitivity of some of the judges may have helped bring about the guilty verdict that was ultimately obtained, the cultural arguments did not resonate to the extent I had anticipated in either the discourse of Inés's legal representatives or the recapitulations by the members of the court. To my surprise, neither CEJIL nor Tlachinollan's lawyers incorporated the arguments presented in our cultural expert report regarding the community impact of Inés Fernández's rape in their final statements. In the workshops in Guerrero, Inés and members of OPIM had strongly insisted on the demand for demilitarization of the region as a *guarantee of no repetition*. Based on this collective reflection we included in the expert report, under reparations demanded, a clause that stated,

> The removal of military forces from the region is seen by many residents as an indispensable measure to guarantee no repetition. The very presence of military forces without the corresponding application of current international legislation regarding armed conflicts creates a situation of ambiguity which means that neither the military officers nor the residents of the region know whether the population is recognized as civilians or as non-belligerent forces. This results in mutual mistrust that fosters conflicts and hence human rights violations. This ambiguity could be resolved by the Mexican state's acknowledgement of the capacity of indigenous communities to decide on fundamental aspects that concern them according to their culture, as stipulated in Article 2 of the Mexican Constitution regarding autonomy, and in Article 6 of Convention 169 regarding the right of consultation. (see Appendix 1 in Hernández Castillo 2016)

This argument was not incorporated into the oral statements presented by Inés's legal representatives. We later learned that it had initially been included in their written statements, but they eventually decided to leave it out because they calculated that there was little chance that it would be accepted by the court. This omission made me question the importance that human rights activists themselves give to cultural expert opinion.

Five months later, on August 20, 2010, the court released its final judgment, declaring that Inés Fernández Ortega had been raped and tortured by members of the Mexican army in a context of poverty, discrimination, and what the court termed "military institutional violence." The court's decision itself was a form of reparation, since it finally acknowledged the legitimacy of her complaints after so many years of struggle. The judgment consists of sixteen resolutions, in which the judges demand that reparations be made by punishing the guilty; publicly acknowledging the state's responsibility; modifying and implementing public policies that promote and facilitate indigenous women's access to justice; implementing reparations at the community level such as the construction of a women's rights center and a shelter; implementing legislative reforms that limit military jurisdiction and that establish that human rights violations committed by military personnel must be tried in civilian courts; providing educational support for Inés's children and medical and psychological care for them and their families; and monetary compensations for Inés and her close relatives who were affected by the violence.[14] The judgment makes a number of mentions of our expert report (paras. 243, 244, and 267–270) and acknowledges the importance of the cultural context for determining reparations.[15]

In spite of my initial skepticism due to the scarce attention that was paid to the cultural expert opinion in the oral statements during the trial, the judgment demonstrated that international law is gradually beginning to integrate cultural context into its interpretation of the human rights of indigenous peoples. While it is true that in several previous cases the court had mandated community reparations, these had always been in situations of collective impacts on peoples or communities.[16] This was the first case where the violations of the human rights of an individual resulted in a judgment in favor of community reparations. Inés's concern that her case be judged in the context of a history of violence suffered by her people and that measures be taken to end that *continuum* of violence seemed to have been at least partially addressed in the court's judgment.

The Ritual of Forgiveness?
Public Acknowledgment of Responsibilities

The Act of Public Acknowledgment of Responsibilities by the Mexican State for the case of Inés Fernández took place on March 6, 2012. Inés had refused to travel to Mexico City to receive the government's apology, rather demanding that the act whereby the Mexican state would publicly acknowledge its responsibility be held in the municipal center of Ayutla de los Libres, and that the special guests be her colleagues from the various organizations in the region.

Surrounded by their many bodyguards and security details, the state's representatives arrived at the main square of Ayutla de los Libres: Secretary of the Interior Alejandro Poiré, Attorney General of the Republic Marisela Morales, the governor of the state of Guerrero, Ángel Aguirre, the Director of Human Rights of the National Defense Secretariat, General Rafael Cázares Anaya, and a dozen other lower government officials who competed with each other to occupy the first rows of seats so they could appear in the photos. On the podium beside Ines were her husband, Fortunato Prisciliano Sierra, the president of OPIM, Obtilia Eugenio, and the director of Tlachinollan, the anthropologist Abel Barrera. The two faces of contemporary Mexico were present on that stage, making no eye contact and with their backs almost turned to each other, manifesting the class and race barriers that divide these two worlds. The face of power allowed no emotion to surface, and the face of Inés, the defiant face of resistance, was supported by the cheers of the peasant men and women who had traveled from distant parts of the coastal and mountain regions of Guerrero to witness the public act. Among the audience were the authorities of the Community Police of Guerrero, peasants from Atoyac de Álvarez and from Xochistlahuaca, students from the Rural Teacher's School of Ayotzinapa, and opponents of the La Parota Reservoir, among others.[17] Inés addressed all of them in Me'phaa with a warning:

> Listen to me all of you, men, women, and children: government officials, even if they say that they're on your side, they will not keep their promises. Do not believe them. They committed this crime against me because we are poor. And not only against me, against other people as well. . . . The governor, even though he is here today, will not comply. That is why I had to look for justice elsewhere, because here they ignored me. He must tell us today what he can and cannot do. The government doesn't let us organize. Soldiers stop us from moving around freely in our communities. They are always nearby, sometimes in civilian clothes, not necessarily in uniforms. At this very moment they are here amongst us. (transcription of the translation of Inés Fernández Ortega's speech in the Public Act of Acknowledgment of Responsibilities, March 6, 2012, Ayutla de los Libres)

The loudspeakers in the square continued to broadcast the resonant voice of Inés's translator. I felt chills when I heard her say "they are here amongst us," realizing that there were many armed men in civilian clothes in the audience, identified by OPIM colleagues as members of paramilitary groups linked to the mayor of Ayutla, Armando García Rendón. Once again, Inés raised her voice to denounce the charade that was taking place by presenting a public apology without imprisoning the people responsible for her rape and their accomplices, who moved about freely in Ayutla's main square.

From Victim to Human Rights Defender

During the ten years since she was raped, Inés has chosen to remain in Barranca Tequani, even though a part of her community has criticized and turned their back on her. In her testimonies she narrated how at first the community organized to expel the military from their communal lands, where they had set up camp. However, over time this social cohesion broke down because of differences over strategies to confront the threat posed by the army. In one interview, Inés said, "Before I was raped, the community was united, but the government and fear divided us. Alfonso Morales, one of the people who works for the Army, told the women that they shouldn't accuse the *guachos* [soldiers] because they would get in trouble. They are afraid that the same thing that happened to me will happen to them, and because of that they no longer want to support me or organize themselves."[18]

However, communal links of solidarity among those who agree with Inés's call for justice were reconstituted in the collective space of OPIM, where she found the support denied to her by some of her colleagues from Barranca Tequani. "OPIM is now my family and my community, they suffered injustice with me, they are like my father and mother."[19] The support of other women in OPIM has enabled Inés to reassume her local leadership role and begin discussing the terms of implementation of the IACtHR's reparations judgment.

Inés has decided to share her story with whoever wants to hear it. As a result, her testimony is available on the Internet through a documentary titled *Mirando hacia adentro: la militarización en Guerrero* (Looking Within: Militarization in Guerrero), where she tells not only of the violence she has suffered, but also of her experiences in the struggle for justice.[20] Inés Fernández's colleagues Cuauhtémoc Ramírez, Valentina Rosendo Cantú, Andrea and Obtilia Eugenio, Fortina Fernández, and Orlando Manzanares have united to denounce the prevailing violence against women and impunity of the perpetrators.

The gender violence revealed in Inés testimony has occurred at the same time as the government's ratification of international conventions in favor of women's rights and the implementation of legislative reforms that supposedly foster "the elimination of all forms of violence against women." It is in this context of impunity that Inés demanded justice in the name of all those other women who have opted for silence out of fear. For Inés, justice means not just jailing the soldiers who raped her, but stopping counterinsurgent violence in the Me'phaa region, demilitarizing the communities, and providing security so that children can walk the mountain roads without being assaulted. A specific demand was to have a shelter in the municipal seat of Ayutla de los Libres, so that their daughters would not have to work as live-in domestic servants in the homes of mestizos when they go to the municipal capital to attend school. The center envisaged by the members of the OPIM would enable young people to learn about their rights and become human rights promoters, challenging racism and misogyny in the state justice system. These were some of the demands that grew out of the collective workshops to discuss the community reparations to be requested of the court.[21]

During the public act of acknowledgment of responsibilities, Inés added a new demand to her list of community reparations. She personally handed the Secretary of the Interior a document previously drafted by OPIM demanding the implementation of a development plan for the region. By referring to the problems of extreme poverty and marginalization that furnish the context for the lack of access to justice and health services, Inés took advantage of the high-ranking government official's arrival to denounce the persistence of not only military and paramilitary violence, but also structural violence. In the event, this supposed "development plan" turned out to be a double-edged sword, since it enabled state and federal government officials to legitimize themselves in the eyes of the local population by handing out limited resources for micro projects. Some leaders in the region speak of the "danger of the goats," since funds are being delivered to purchase farm animals as a way of building new loyalties to the government. The time-honored policy of co-optation that had characterized PRI administrations for over seventy-five years returned with the presidency of Enrique Peña Nieto and, in Guerrero, with the government of former PRI member Ángel Aguirre Rivero, then governor for the Party of the Democratic Revolution.[22] Organizations are facing new challenges with the increasingly violent presence of organized crime, which provides the justification for militarizing the region and deepens a policy of co-optation that puts their autonomy at risk.

Although the soldiers who participated in the sexual assault were eventually jailed, most reparatory measures continue to be unfulfilled. The government has complied (albeit after the established deadlines) only with the stipulation to publish the judgment, publicly acknowledge responsibilities, and attend to some of the measures of compensation, expenses, and costs determined by the IACtHR. International litigation generated numerous contradictions: on one hand, the judgment helped strengthen the OPIM and, more specifically, Inés's leadership at the local level; on the other, it justified greater subsequent intervention in the region's organizational dynamics by state agents. However, the process that followed the court hearing allowed Inés and the female members of OPIM to reflect collectively on the roots of the violence affecting their lives and the lives of their daughters, and on the strategies needed to confront it. Inés's voice has been multiplied by the women in her organization, who have taken their experiences to Washington, DC, Spain, Cuetzalan Puebla, the Community Police of Guerrero, Tlaxcala, and various forums in Mexico City, where they have denounced the use of sexual violence as a form of torture and the impacts of militarization in the Mountain and Costa Chica regions of Guerrero.

Thanks to her efforts and her courage in demanding justice, Inés Fernández, together with Valentina Rosenda Cantú and Tita Radilla—daughter of a peasant leader murdered during the "dirty war"[23]—was able to get IACtHR to declare the Mexican state guilty, forcing it to modify the Code of Military Justice and limit military jurisdiction.[24] After these historic cases, human rights violations by military personnel can no longer be tried by military public prosecutors, but must go through the civilian justice system. In the current context of militarization in the name of the "war on drugs," it is essential that military officers are unable to hide human rights violations in their networks of complicities.[25] The human rights reform approved by the Mexican federal legislature in June 2011 is closely related to these three cases. Thanks to those women's struggles, the human rights agreements ratified by the Mexican state have been incorporated into the Mexican Constitution, strengthening the legal framework for access to justice for all Mexicans.[26]

Inés Fernández's insistence on including all the women of her organization as beneficiaries of the court's sentence set a precedent in international litigation, since it was the first time that it was acknowledged that the harm done to an individual (in this case the rape of Inés) could affect her entire community when that person's cultural context is taken into account in order to understand how gender violence is experienced and how justice is imagined.

In spite of the Mexican state's dilatory tactics in implementing the sentence, Inés and the women in OPIM have continued with their processes of organization and reflection, discussing the objectives and structure of the Community Center for the Rights of Me'phaa Men and Women that they plan to build as part of the reparations ordered by the court. As part of this process, they have approached other indigenous women fighting for women's rights based on their own culture, such as the women in the Community Police of Guerrero and Nahuatl women from the Cuetzalan Indigenous Women's Home of Puebla.[27] If the purpose of the use of sexual violence as a form of torture was to terrorize and demobilize women, the courage and communal solidarity of the women in OPIM have challenged these counterinsurgency strategies. Rather than eliminating indigenous leaderships, the effect has been the emergence of new women's rights defenders who, like Inés, speak out not only to denounce personal experiences of violence, but also to demand justice for all those whose lives are affected by militarization and violence by government security forces.

Conclusions

It is not my place to evaluate the negative or positive impact that Inés's decision to publicly denounce her rape has had on her life; only she can know whether the risks she has taken have been compensated by the court's judgment, by the declaration of "most sincere apologies" pronounced by the Secretary of the Interior, or by the conviction that her voice has become the voice of many other silenced women. Only she knows "what is in her heart," but from the little I have come to know her, I am sure that her answer would not be simple.

Following the public act of acknowledgment of responsibilities described in this chapter, the context of militarization and paramilitarization in Guerrero has worsened. In February 2013, two hundred members of the Mexican army entered Barranca Tequani without requesting the permission of the community's authorities, spreading fear and insecurity among the region's residents (see *La Jornada de Guerrero*, February 7, 2013). The creation of self-defense groups in Ayutla de los Libres in early 2013 united in the Union of Peoples and Organizations of the State of Guerrero (UPOEG) greatly complicated the political landscape. Leaders of the OPIM leaders denounced the UPOEG as being infiltrated by paramilitaries responsible for the murder of Inés's brother. Although they acknowledge the inefficiency of the state's security forces and their frequent complicity with organized crime, the OPIM has been highly suspicious of the self-defense groups that emerged in numerous municipalities of Guerrero from 2013 onward.[28] In this complex context of militarization and paramilitarization, the construction of a Community Center for the Rights of the Me'phaa People has constituted a considerable challenge. Although Inés and the OPIM women were able to purchase a plot of land in Ayutla de los Libres and a symbolic ceremony was held to set the first stone, collective planning has been interrupted due to the lack of security.

On a personal level I was greatly enriched by the teachings of Inés and the OPIM, their courage, their sense of collective solidarity, and their ways of "knowing and being in the world." During the past decade the so-called "transversalization of the gender perspective in public policies" has had very little impact on ordinary people's access to justice. A feminist agenda is partially incorporated or, at worst, simply tolerated, when its struggle is circumscribed to the space of the family. Yet for indigenous women, state violence is also characterized by racism; the failure of the state justice apparatus to recognize their language or cultural context increases their invisibility and hence their vulnerability. The erasure of their experiences signals old and new forms of colonialism. The voices of women like Inés Fernández denounce and unveil neocolonial strategies that use sexual violence as a tool for counterinsurgency.

ACKNOWLEDGMENTS

A previous version of this chapter was published in my book *Multiple Injustices: Indigenous Women, Law, and Political Struggle* (University of Arizona Press, 2016). In that longer version I included the case of Valentina Rosendo Cantú. Here I focus on the case of Inés Fernández Ortega, for the obvious reason that I developed the cultural report surrounding her case, but her case has been closely related to that of Valentina, a member of the same organization who was also raped by the military one month previously.

NOTES

1. In most common law jurisdictions, the attorney general is the main legal advisor to the government, and in some jurisdictions he or she may also have executive responsibility for law enforcement and public prosecutions or even ministerial responsibility for legal affairs more generally.

2. Inter-American Court of Human Rights 2009a.

3. For an English version of the Expert Witness Report for *Inés Fernández Ortega v. Mexico*, see Appendix 1 of Hernández Castillo 2016.

4. Interview with Inés Fernández, Barranca Tequani, March 13, 2009, translated by Andrea Eugenio.

5. Ibid.

6. For a description of the impact of the "dirty war" in the state of Guerrero, see Comisión de la Verdad del Estado de Guerrero 2014. A historical analysis of guerrilla movements in Guerrero and state violence can be found in Bartra 1996.

7. The massacre of El Charco took place on June 7, 1998, in the municipality of Ayutla de los Libres, Guerrero, when members of the Mexican army murdered eleven peasants as they slept in the local elementary school, after participating in a community assembly to discuss production projects. The army accused the peasants of being guerrilla fighters.

8. Interview with María Sierra Librada, Barranca Tequani, March 13, 2009.

9. For notable exceptions, see Maxine Clark 2009 and various contributions to Maxine Clark and Goodale 2009.

10. The American Convention on Human Rights has been ratified by twenty-five American nations: Argentina, Barbados, Bolivia, Brazil, Chile, Colombia, Costa Rica, Dominica, Dominican Republic, Ecuador, El Salvador, Grenada, Guatemala, Haiti, Honduras, Jamaica, Mexico, Nicaragua, Panama, Paraguay, Peru, Suriname, Trinidad and Tobago, Uruguay, and Venezuela. This regional treaty is mandatory for all the signatory states and is the result of a process that began at the end of World War II, when the nations of the Americas met in Mexico and decided that a declaration on human rights should be drafted in order to be eventually adopted as a convention. That declaration, the American Declaration of the Rights and Duties of Man, was approved by the Organization of American States member states in Bogota, Colombia, in May 1948. See http://www.oas.org/dil/treaties_B-32_American_Convention_on_Human_Rights. htm.

11. The IACtHR judgment reports the following participants for the Mexican state delegation: Juan Manuel Gómez Robledo, Assistant Secretary for Multilateral Affairs and

Human Rights of the Secretariat for Foreign Affairs; Alejandro Negrín Muñoz, Director General of Human Rights and Democracy of the Secretariat for Foreign Affairs; Rogelio Rodríguez Correa, Deputy Director for International Affairs of the General Directorate of Human Rights of the National Defense Secretariat; Yéssica de Lamadrid Téllez, Director General for International Cooperation of the Office of the Attorney General of the Republic; Carlos Garduño Salinas, Deputy Director General of the Unit for the Promotion and Defense of Human Rights of the Secretariat of the Interior; Jorge Cicero Fernández, Head of the Mexican Foreign Ministry in Peru; Rosa María Gómez Saavedra, Secretary for Women's Affairs of the state of Guerrero; María de la Luz Reyes Ríos, Director General of the Ombudsman of the General Secretariat of the government of the state of Guerrero; José Ignacio Martín del Campo Covarrubias, Director of International Litigation on matters relating to human rights of the Secretariat for Foreign Affairs; Luis Manuel Jardón Piña, Head of the Litigation Department of the Legal Office of the Foreign Ministry; Katya Vera, Head of International Litigation on matters relating to human rights of the Secretariat for Foreign Affairs; and Guadalupe Salas y Villagomez, Deputy Director General for Policy of the Office of the Special Prosecutor for Crimes of Violence against Women and Human Trafficking.

12. Participation of the Mexican state's legal representative at the Inter-American Court of Human Rights, at its XLI Extraordinary Period of Sessions in Lima, Peru, April 15, 2010.

13. These were the three topics that the Inter-American Commission on Human Rights requested that we develop in our expert report.

14. See Inter-American Court of Human Rights 2010a, 2010b.

15. See Inter-American Court of Human Rights 2010a.

16. See Inter-American Court of Human Rights 2004, 2005.

17. Three months after the Acknowledgment of Responsibilities by the Mexican government in the case of Inés Fernández on December 12, 2011, the students of the Rural Teacher's School Raúl Isidro Burgos, better known as Escuela Normal Rural de Ayotzinapa, blocked the highway that connects Mexico City to Acapulco, demanding government support for their institution. The ensuing confrontation with the federal and state police resulted in the deaths of Jorge Alexis Herrera Pino and Gabriel Echeverría de Jesús. This led to renewed student demonstrations in Chilpancingo and Mexico City, supported by nongovernmental organizations for the defense of human rights, demanding a political trial against Ángel Aguirre Rivero, the governor of the state for the PRD party. A few days after the events, the state attorney resigned, stating that the scene of the students' murder had been accidentally contaminated. Three years later a new case of government repression against the students of Ayotzinapa took place. On the evening of September 26, 2014, a group of students from that institution hijacked buses in order to participate in demonstrations in Mexico City. Officers with the municipal police of Iguala, allegedly in complicity with members of the criminal organization Guerreros Unidos, attacked the group of students on the orders of José Luis Abarca Velázquez, then mayor of Iguala. The event culminated in the abduction of forty-three students, and a total of six people were murdered, including students and other civilians, and twenty-five people wounded. The news of this aggression shocked people around the world, and international human rights organizations demanded that the Mexican state conduct a thorough investigation and punish the material and intellectual authors of these crimes.

18. Inés Fernández interview.

19. Ibid.

20. See https://www.youtube.com/watch?v=k9pOrnYJQNM.

21. Minutes of the Workshop on Community Reparations organized with Inés Fernández and OPIM members in Ayutla de los Libres, February 2009.

22. Ángel Aguirre was governor of the state of Guerrero between April 1, 2011, and October 23, 2014, when he was asked to resign in the wake of the case of the students abducted from Ayotzinapa and murdered in Iguala (see note 17).

23. Rosendo Radilla was a social leader from the municipality of Atoyac de Álvarez, Guerrero, who worked for his people's health and education and was elected mayor. On August 25, 1974, he was illegally detained at a military checkpoint and was last seen in the former Military Headquarters of Atoyac de Álvarez, Guerrero. Thirty-four years later, his whereabouts remain unknown. His daughter, Tita Radilla, took the case to the IACtHR and obtained a guilty verdict against the Mexican state.

24. See Inter-American Court of Human Rights 2009b.

25. This constitutional reform has met with considerable resistance from military powers. For an analysis of the challenges implied in transferring cases of human rights violations committed by the army to civilian jurisdiction, see chapter 8, by Mariana Mora.

26. For the full text of the 2011 constitutional reform, see http://www2.scjn.gob.mx/red/constitucion/inicio.html or Fix-Zamudio 2011.

27. See chapter 4, by María Teresa Sierra, and chapter 2, by Adriana Terven Salinas.

28. See *La Jornada de Guerrero* (February 7, 2013), http://www.lajornadaguerrero.com.mx/2013/02/07/.

REFERENCES

Anaya, James, and Claudio Grossman. 2002. "The Case of Awas Tigni v. Nicaragua: A New Step in the International Law of Indigenous Peoples." *Arizona Journal of International and Comparative Law* 19 (1): 2–15.

Baitenmann, Helga, Victoria Chenaut, and Ann Varley, eds. 2008. *Decoding Gender: Law and Practice in Contemporary Mexico.* New Brunswick, NJ: Rutgers University Press.

Barrera, Leticia. 2012. *La Corte Suprema en Escena. Una Etnografía del Mundo Judicial.* Buenos Aires: Grupo Editorial Siglo XXI.

Bartra, Roger. 1996. *Las redes imaginarias del poder político, nueva edición corregida, revisada y aumentada.* Mexico City: Océano.

Collier, Jane. [1973] 1995. *El derecho Zinacanteco: procesos de disputar en un pueblo Indígena de Chiapas.* Mexico City: CIESAS/UNICACH.

Comisión de la Verdad del Estado de Guerrero. 2014. "Informe Final de Actividades." http://desinformemonos.org/PDF/InformeFinalCOMVERDAD.pdf.

Crenshaw, Kimberlé W. 1991. "Mapping the Margins: Intersectionality, Identity Politics, and Violence Against Women of Color." *Stanford Law Review* 43: 1241–1299.

Engle Merry, Sally. 1995. "Gender Violence and Legally Engendered Selves." *Identities* 2 (1–2): 49–73.

———. 2000. *Colonizing Hawai'i: The Cultural Power of Law.* Princeton, NJ: Princeton University Press.

———. 2006. *Human Rights and Gender Violence. Translating International Law into Local Justice.* Chicago: The University of Chicago Press.

———. 2011. "Derechos Humanos, Género y Nuevos Movimientos Sociales: Debates Contemporáneos en Antropología Jurídica." In *Justicia y Diversidad en América Latina. Pueblos Indígenas ante la Globalización*, edited by Victoria Chenaut *et al.*, 261–291. Mexico: CIESAS/FLACSO.

Facio, Alda. 1992. "El derecho como producto del patriarcado." In *Sobre patriarcas, jerarcas, patrones y otros varones*, edited by Alda Facio and Rosalia Camacho. San José, Costa Rica: ILANUD.

Fineman, Martha, and Nancy Thomadsen, eds. 1991. *At the Boundaries of Law: Feminism and Legal Theory*. New York: Routledge.

Fix-Zamudio, Hector. 2011. "Las Reformas Constitucionales Mexicanas de Junio del 2011 y sus Efectos en el Sistema Interamericano de Derechos Humano." *Revista Interamericana de Derecho Público y Administrativo* II: 232–255.

Hale, Charles R. 2006. "Activist Research v. Cultural Critique: Indigenous Land Rights and the Contradictions of Politically Engaged Anthropology." *Cultural Anthropology* 21: 96–120.

Hernández Castillo, Rosalva Aída. 2004. "El derecho positivo y la costumbre jurídica: Las mujeres indígenas de Chiapas y sus luchas por el acceso a la justicia." In *Violencia contra las mujeres en contextos urbanos y rurales*, edited by Marta Torres Falcón, 335–379. Mexico City: El Colegio de México.

———. 2016. *Multiple Injustices: Indigenous Women, Law, and Political Struggle*. Tucson: University of Arizona Press.

Hill Collins, Patricia. 1990. *Black Feminist Thought: Knowledge, Consciousness and the Politics of Empowerment*. Boston: Unwin Hyman.

Hirsch, Susan, and Mindie Lazarus-Black, eds. 1994. *Law, Hegemony and Resistance*. New York: Routledge.

Inter-American Court of Human Rights. 2004. *Plan de Sánchez Massacre v. Guatemala*. Judgment of November 19, 2004. Series C, no. 116, para. 86. http://www.corteidh.or.cr/docs/casos/articulos/seriec_116_ing.pdf.

———. 2005. *Moiwana Community v. Suriname*. Judgment of June 15, 2005 (Preliminary Objections, Merits, Reparations and Costs), series C, no. 124, para 194. http://www.corteidh.or.cr/docs/casos/articulos/seriec_124_ing.pdf.

———. 2009a. *González et al. ("Cotton Field") v. Mexico*. Judgment of November 16, 2009. http://www.corteidh.or.cr/docs/casos/articulos/seriec_205_ing.pdf.

———. 2009b. *Radilla-Pacheco v. Mexico*. Judgment of November 23, 2009. http://www.corteidh.or.cr/docs/casos/articulos/seriec_209_ing.pdf.

———. 2010a. *Fernández Ortega et al. v. Mexico*. Judgment of August 30, 2010. http://corteidh.or.cr/docs/casos/articulos/seriec_215_ing.pdf.

———. 2010b. *Rosendo Cantú et al. v. Mexico*. Judgment of August 31, 2010. http://corteidh.or.cr/docs/casos/articulos/seriec_216_ing.pdf.

Kelsall, Tim. 2013. *Culture under Cross-Examination: International Justice and the Special Court for Sierra Leone*. Cambridge: Cambridge University Press.

Latour, Bruno. 2002. *La Fabrique du droit. Une ethnographie du Conseil d'Etat*. Paris: La Découverte.

MacDowell Santos, Cecilia. 2007. "Transnational Legal Activism and the State. Reflections on Cases Against Brazil in the Inter-American Commission of Human Rights." *Sur International Journal of Human Rights* 7: 29–61.

Maxine Clark, Kamari. 2009. *Fictions of Justice: The International Criminal Court and the Challenge of Legal Pluralism in Sub-Saharan Africa*. New York: Cambridge University Press.

Maxine Clark, Kamari, and Mark Goodale, eds. 2009. *Mirrors of Justice: Law and Power in the Post–Cold War Era*. Cambridge: Cambridge University Press.

Moore, Henrietta. 1996. *Antropología y Feminismo*. Valencia: Editorial Cátedra.

Nader, Laura. 1978. *The Disputing Process: Law in Ten Societies*. New York: Columbia University Press.

———. 1990. *Harmony Ideology: Justice and Control in a Zapotec Mountain Village*. Stanford, CA: Stanford University Press.

OACNUDH (Oficina del Alto Comisionado de las Naciones Unidas para los Derechos Humanos). 2013. *Informe del diagnóstico sobre el Acceso a la justicia para los indígenas en México: Estudio de caso de Oaxaca*. Mexico City: OACNUDH.

Santos, Boaventura de Sousa, and César Rodríguez-Garavito, eds. 2005. *Law and Globalization from Below: Towards a Cosmopolitan Legality*. Cambridge: Cambridge University Press.

Sieder, Rachel. 2013. "Subaltern Cosmopolitan Legalities and the Challenges of Engaged Ethnography." *Universitas Humanística*, no. 75: 219–247.

Sierra, María Teresa, and Rosalva Aída Hernández. 2005. "Repensar los derechos colectivos desde el género: Aportes de las mujeres indígenas al debate de la autonomía." In *La Doble Mirada: Luchas y Experiencias de las Mujeres Indígenas de América Latina*, edited by Martha Sánchez, 93–118. Mexico: UNIFEM/ILSB.

Sierra Camacho, María Teresa, ed. 1992. *Discurso, cultura y poder: el ejercicio de la autoridad en pueblos ñhahñús del Valle del Mezquital*. Mexico City: CIESAS-Government of the State of Hidalgo.

———, ed. 2004. *Haciendo justicia. Interlegalidad, derecho y género en regiones indígenas*. Mexico City: CIESAS-Porrúa.

Smart, Carol. 1989. *Feminism and the Power of Law*. New York: Routledge.

Tlachinollan/CEJIL. 2011. *Supervisión de cumplimiento de sentencia, observaciones al primer informe estatal (CDH-12.580/152)*. San José, Costa Rica, November 19.

2

Domestic Violence and Access to Justice

The Political Dilemma of the Cuetzalan Indigenous Women's Home (CAMI)

ADRIANA TERVEN SALINAS

When I began my fieldwork at Cuetzalan Indigenous Women's Home—CAMI (Casa de la Mujer Indígena de Cuetzalan), I told Oligaria, a Nahua woman and a member of CAMI, that I wanted to meet the promoters and ask them about their work. Oligaria worked with me as part of an activist/scholar team. One day when the promoters were meeting, Oligaria asked them to participate in an interview. We settled in one of the rooms; I took out the questions that we had drafted together and placed a digital camera on the table beside my notebook. The promoters came forward one by one, and Oligaria explained to them in Nahuat what we were about to do. All of them agreed to be videotaped. They were women between the ages of thirty-seven and fifty, most of them in native dress. They began by stating which community they came from and then spoke of their own experiences of mistreatment, which seemed to be the connection that linked them to their work at CAMI supporting women victims of violence. They subsequently talked about the cases they had worked on.

When asked about the main reasons why Nahua women do not denounce domestic violence, they all agreed that it was out of shame. Those comments—and their willingness to be videotaped—suggested to me that the promoters were a group of women very different from others, in the sense that they could speak openly about situations of violence, situations that tend to be regulated by family and community in ways that limit women's power to talk about and denounce them. This first meeting raised a number of questions: What role did the narration of experiences of mistreatment play in their development as women's rights promoters? How were their narratives constructed when they dealt with topics regulated by local gender norms, especially since the word "violence" does not exist in Nahuat? How does reflection on personal and collective memories facilitate the narration of experiences of violence in the present in a way that is recognized by other indigenous women?

These questions motivated me to analyze processes of construction of the intersubjective world—shared knowledges that are transformed and confirmed in everyday interactions—and their objectification in testimonies that permit that intersubjective world to be externalized (Schütz and Luckmann 1973; Berger and Luckmann 2005), and, in this case, that allows for the construction of a strategy for tackling violence. Therefore, the descriptions of experiences and situations do not require the usage of concepts such as violence, sexual abuse, or harassment due to the nonexistence of these terms in the women's own vocabulary. In order to explain violent aggression, for example, they apply diverse semantic fields such as "he reached me" (*me alcanzó*), "he followed me" (*me siguió*), or "he pursued me" (*me correteó*). It is from the testimonies that CAMI women have re-created local concepts around violence that include notions of gender, ethnicity, and culture, intersubjectively building a context-specific frame for tackling violence.

In this chapter I examine the processes whereby Nahua women in CAMI, in Cuetzalan in the Mexican state of Puebla,[1] construct a concept of violence, considering first and foremost that the fight against violence toward women, understood as a specific field of attention, is an element external to Nahua practices. Its constitution therefore demanded analysis of the interrelationship between discourses on women's rights, funding, local demands, social partici-pation, and differentiated cultural meanings.

CAMI's constitution is understood here as a multidimensional experience where we can observe, on one hand, a macro dimension that corresponds to the international scenario of the 1980s and 1990s, when issues like the eradication of violence against women and the recognition of cultural diversity gained prominence; and, on the other, a midrange dimension that comprises the passage from the international to the national agenda and the promo-tion of civil society as the means for generating social change. It is in this context that we can understand CAMI's creation in 2003 by Mexico's National Commission for the Development of Indigenous Peoples (CDI), the Secretariat of Health, and the United Nations Development Program, in collaboration with local organizations like the nonprofit Center for Advising and Development among Women (CADEM) and the Social Solidarity Association Maseualsiuamej Mosenyolchicahuanij.

Finally, regarding the micro dimension, a coming together of processes has led Nahua women to gradually make known their situation of risk and vulnerability, allowing them to develop a specific field for intervention: that of domestic violence. This construction has happened through a gradual integration of experiences of mistreatment, subordination, oppression, and exclusion, understood from the perspectives of new national and global dis-courses, as well as activities related to their participation in local and regional organizations. CAMI can be understood as the materialization of an interest in providing attention to women victims of domestic violence. It is a space that brings together indigenous women with a long experience working in various organizations in the region.

What women in CAMI currently define as "violence" corresponds to certain experiences and situations that can be successfully denounced and addressed in legal terms. By locating CAMI's experience in a multidimensional context, I ask how international discourses on women's rights and the eradication of violence affect the construction of the field of attention in CAMI, as well as the impacts that Mexican state institutions may have on those processes. In addition to these questions, I provide a critical examination of CAMI's work: although they have been successful in positioning the issue of domestic violence within Nahua families and communities, and have even been able to work together with municipal institutions, the anticipated social transformations have not been achieved.

This fact led us to complicate the analysis of the concept of violence at CAMI, understanding it as a category with a dual character: on one hand, it allows Nahua women to reveal and denounce situations of abuse; on the other, it seems to function as a mechanism that ensures the persistence of existing power relations. In this latter sense, attention to certain expressions of violence, especially those that do not upset structural power and market inequalities, is widely supported by state, private, and funding institutions as well as local agents, as is the case with domestic violence. By contrast, cases related to land, property, and employment are not generally perceived as putting women's lives at risk: here, as I will show in this chapter, discursive and institutional mechanisms end up reproducing indigenous women's exclusion within the organizations themselves. In what follows I examine the complex construction of the concept of violence in the work of organized Nahua women in Cuetzalan, Puebla, understanding this as a process that integrates various experiences based on the trajectories of the women in CAMI and other organizations, generating in turn new senses and uses. I explore the tensions for CAMI's project between the possibilities and limitations inherent in the concept of violence, raising the possibility of conceiving understandings of violence distinct from those currently institutionalized in the legal field in Cuetzalan and asking what place they occupy in the work of the women at CAMI.

The Construction of a Concept of Violence

The creation of the CAMI in Cuetzalan has been studied by Mejía (2010) and Terven (2009). The original project was focused on women's health; by the early 2000s a new strategy emerged prioritizing legal support as a means of addressing the issues affecting indigenous women. Through the CAMI integral support mechanisms were developed (psychological care, workshops for reflection, counseling, mediation, and legal defense), and the institution was reorganized into four operational areas: general coordination, emotional assistance, health care, and legal. They also created a group of promoters:

> The promoters are indigenous women from various communities in the municipality, colleagues who have been trained on women's rights here at the CAMI, and they are the ones who support us in the communities when a woman has a problem; since they're already well known, they bring them here, many [of the women with problems] don't speak Spanish, so they accompany them. They follow up their case and bring them to the workshops for reflection. They also give workshops on women's rights, violence, and women's sexual and reproductive rights. (Angélica Rodríguez in Terven, 2009: 179)

Finally, during this period the CAMI acquired a house in the center of the town of Cuetzalan, the second property in the municipal seat owned by indigenous women. This first space in the municipal center acquired by indigenous women was the land for the construction of the Taselotzin Hotel, a project of Maseualsiuamej. Mejía (2010) narrates the difficulties they faced to acquire the land, since both the City Council and private owners hindered the sale because they did not think that indigenous women should own property in the town. They also encountered problems later during the construction, such as road-blocks to prevent building materials from reaching the construction site.

These changes facilitated organizational processes for the promotion of women's rights and the fight against domestic violence. CAMI members gained abilities to talk about situations of violence; they also spread information through workshops in the communities and radio programs (in Spanish and Nahuat) on the local indigenous radio station, which has resulted in an increase in the number of denunciations presented to CAMI (12 in 2003 starting in October; 83 in 2004; 70 in 2005; no data available for 2006; 87 in 2007; 87 in 2008; 112 in 2009; 116 in 2010; and 42 from January to May 2011). Finally, in 2007 CAMI was constituted as a nonprofit organization in order to gain access to other funding agencies; if the organization had remained as a community committee, it could use only resources from the government commission for the development of indigenous people (CDI).

Regarding the construction of the concept of violence as the way to denounce situations of abuse against Nahua women, a number of processes led CAMI's members to reflect on their position and their condition within their family and community. While high levels of mistreatment, abuse, and oppression in the domestic realm meant domestic violence was the organization's main priority,[2] the construction of the concept as such has involved a process that gradually introduced different situations that have been defined as violence, which are directly related to the organizational experiences of Nahua women in Cuetzalan.

One of the key means to define and enunciate situations of abuse is the narration of events of mistreatment, a strategy that women in CADEM have promoted since the late 1980s with the women who currently make up Maseualsiamej. Working with testimonies has been a fundamental resource in denouncing women's human rights violations, since, according to Crosby and Lykes (2011), narrating experiences entails a complex political, cultural, and gender construction. In other words, it is not a neutral act, but rather an inherently relational process whereby we narrate for different people with multiple intentions. In that sense, working with testimonies allows the transfer of experiences such as discourse to denounce violence by bringing back memories as well as socially and culturally shared references, expressed in such a way that they can be recognized by others, for instance by other indigenous women who identify themselves with the narrators. As does Mariana Mora in chapter 8, I understand testimony as action: "Testimony aspires not only to interpret the world, but also to change it" (Beverley 2004: xvi).

In short, the construction of knowledge has a transformational effect on the narrator and the people who listen to her. Sommer (1998) points out that the individual testimony represents the group, since the narrator speaks from within her community. In this way, the transformation assumes an ethical posture regarding what to do with that information (Géliga and Canabal 2013). Hence, testimonies recount memories through an intersubjective process whereby knowledges are transformed and confirmed in everyday interactions between different actors, materializing in oral or written expressions or drawings (Schütz 1974). The narration of abuse by CAMI's members constitutes the endpoint of a process whereby the objectification of experiences integrates political positions on gender, ethnicity, and culture, constructing them as promoters and vehicles for transmitting other women's grievances.

In our research we were interested in exploring the relationships between the various processes of construction of the concept of violence and the narration of experiences of abuse. In this regard, we tried to determine to what extent the concept of violence is related to idioms whose meaning tends to harm or victimize women or, on the contrary, to foster their transformation from victims to survivors (Crosby and Lykes 2011). The concept of violence as such does not exist in Nahuat, and yet the term is widely used by CAMI's members. We consider whether this concept is able to categorize women's experiences located in specific cultural contexts and norms; to what extent it allows them to refer to situations of abuse, thus avoiding the shame of speaking in their native tongue of what is culturally forbidden; and how it articulates with the semantic fields themselves.

> My name is Oligaria Saldaña Bautista, from the community of Ayozina-
> pan. . . . There was a meeting in my community one year on the 8th of
> March, International Women's Day, and it was there that I was invited to

participate as a promoter . . . and so I continued learning and getting involved with the rights of women and indigenous peoples, and it really caught my attention because I was one of the women who also experienced violence . . . so there we started to realize that it was necessary for us to speak out, well, we started to see the needs of the women who experienced violence, but not only those of us who lived through violence, but for the other women who suffered that type of violence. . . . I had several problems with violence because my husband used to beat me, he drank and he beat me, and I worked in the first education program and I had to go give talks . . . and since I still lived with his grandparents, they were my grandparents-in-law, and my grandmother-in-law was something special, she still has the old mentality where women are for the home, and if I went out it was because I was lazy and I liked hanging out on the street and she said she didn't know what I did going out, and she put ideas in her grandson's head and when I came back there were problems. . . . So I put up with that for two or three years, I never made up my mind to file a complaint, whenever I left the house I would go to my mother's or my godmother's and I would be there and later he would go look for me . . . it was for another reason I decided not to be there anymore, because my husband had gone to the city to work. . . . I had to cook and make the tortillas . . . and I was alone and my grandfather-in-law was there in the stable . . . so I made his food and he arrived and started to ask me, he started to talk to me and asked me what did my grandson say, will he come back? Well, he didn't say anything, he was mad when he left; so he came near me, he thought it was going to be easy, he said don't worry, let yourself go with me, he said, I'll give you a kiss, so that was what made me get angrier, I told him I'm not going stay here, I told him no, I'm not here for that. (Interview, June 2011)

Oligaria's testimony introduces a number of elements: one has to do with her training as a promoter, during which she identifies with other women by getting to know their experiences, thus understanding her relationship with her husband as one of violence and realizing the importance of narrating situations of mistreatment as a way to support other women. The language she used in this testimony, rather than one of victimization, is that of an actor with agency; hence she objectifies her memories as situations that can be coped with. Another point worth highlighting has to do with the way in which she narrates more specific events; there we see the use of referents from her own semantic fields rather than from rights or legal discourses. When she says that they told her that she liked to hang out on the street (*le gusta andar en la calle*), she refers to the control they exerted over her body, sexually speaking; likewise, when she says that her grandfather-in-law "asked her" (*la pidió*) and told her "let yourself go with me" (*déjate conmigo*), she is using expressions translated from Nahuat to refer to sexual harassment. This issue, further examined below, demonstrates how cultural references prevail over extraneous ones in the narration of experiences of abuse.

Another issue has to do with cultural gender orders. Oligaria criticizes her grandmother-in-law's "old mentality," thus confronting the norms and customs that oppress women. In this sense she differs from other women who do not participate in organizations and who tend to frame their denunciations from their position in socially accepted gender orders. This is evident from studies in Cuetzalan before the CAMI was established,[3] which analyze the reproduction of gender roles and identities and their influence on access to justice, how complaints are presented and the arguments used, and the ways in which community authorities respond to the cases. Sierra noted that "while women are able to express their complaints and receive attention from authorities, they are constantly confronted with sex/gender models that legitimize men's authority and their rights over their wife" (Sierra 2004c: 169).

In the context of these gender values, women's demands are not well addressed, since they are generally considered guilty of causing the acts of violence against them. Community authorities initially tend to discourage women from filing a complaint, attempting to convince them that their denunciation is unimportant and urging them to rethink their own behavior. If the woman insists, demonstrating that she did not provoke the crime in question, authorities tend to request that her reputation be investigated before giving credence to her complaint (Vallejo 2000).

Another place where such gender ideologies are evident is the "agreements of compliance" (*actas de conformidad*) drawn up by the community authorities, which usually contain the following recommendation: "the woman must care for her husband as is her obligation, feeding him at the right time and refraining from confronting him when he is drunk, in order to avoid conflicts" (Martínez and Mejía 1997: 77). At the same time, men are requested not to repeat the aggression, but without any effective guarantees to ensure compliance. According to these studies, the result is that in order to have a right of defense women must demonstrate that they have complied with the established gender ideal, in contrast to their husbands.

More recent cases involving women who have had no contact with local women's organizations are also characterized by the absence of arguments related to gender orders, as well as the absence of any concept of violence deployed to name situations of abuse. During our research we documented a case of sexual abuse that occurred within the domestic group among first cousins. The victim, a nineteen-year-old woman, was living at the home of her paternal uncle and aunt. One of their sons, aged twenty-two, repeatedly sexually abused her; this erupted into a conflict when she became pregnant.

The complaint was presented at the Indigenous Court in Cuetzalan. On the plaintiff's side, the victim and her mother were present; on the defendant's side, the aggressor (the victim's cousin) appeared with his father and mother (the victim's uncle and aunt). Of particular interest here are the arguments presented by the plaintiff and the defendant, which aimed to demonstrate that the victim and the assailant had complied with expected behavior according to prevailing sex/gender norms. Also noteworthy is the fact that no referents were available to talk about what happened as sexual violence.

Victim's aunt: He's my son but he didn't do anything, they're only blaming him, I raised my children but I've made sure they don't do anything wrong, one of them is married and they have a child, but with his wife, not with another woman. . . . Yes, how do they dare blame my son, if the girl used to go out at night? Her mother should have looked after them, she shouldn't let them go out at midnight.

Victim: What he says isn't true, because every time we were alone he sent the kids out to play so he could be with me. He always did that, wherever I was doing something he would go and reach me. I already explained how things were, he reached me wherever I was. I'm telling the truth. He would go reach me when my aunt wasn't around. I would go eat at my house because my mother called me and he would come after me.[4]

As we can see, the victim resorted to expressions like "he reached me" (*me alcanzaba*) or "he came after me" (*me seguía*) to name sexual abuse, demonstrating the absence of concepts such as rape or sexual abuse as terms used to define violent events; instead, what we see is a translation of her own semantic fields, which in turn reflect prevailing gender norms and prohibitions on speaking about such matters. With this, however, we do not mean to imply that organized women are the only ones to use these concepts; even CAMI's promoters adopt such linguistic mechanisms. For example, one promoter referred to the crimes committed against women in her community in the following terms: "The other day I heard that a girl was also pursued [*la corretearon*; i.e., raped] on the road, and apparently she didn't go to the public prosecutor's office" (Testimony of a promoter, 2010). In her testimony, Oligaria also uses expressions such as "he started to ask me" or "let yourself go with me" to refer to sexual harassment by her grandfather-in-law. Although both the promoter and Oligaria are aware of the concepts referring to various modalities of violence, when mentioning this type of situation they tended to translate from Nahuat to Spanish. Even though CAMI introduced mechanisms and training for presenting legal denunciations, Nahua cultural referents tend to prevail over extraneous discourses.

Categorizing situations as different kinds of violence is something we observed as a process among organized women, who gradually started to reinterpret various expressions of abuse, mistreatment, exclusion, and oppression. Hence the tension generated within the family group between the control over women's activities—exerted mostly by men—and women's interest in doing something different, which, together with their training in women's rights, led them to construct their specific field of attention: domestic violence. This categorization has allowed them to introduce non-Nahua referents in order to file complaints, which, it should be noted, are encouraged and legitimized by various state institutions in Cuetzalan, such as the Puebla Women's Institute, the Department of Family Integration, the Secretariat of Health, the Municipal Court, the Public Prosecutor's Office, the Attorney General's Office, and the state's Human Rights Commission.

The possibility of naming these expressions of abuse and coercion as violence and of being widely supported has its origins in the 1980s and 1990s, when the eradication of violence against women was prominent in international agendas. These were translated into a national agenda in Mexico, as in other countries, through various processes including the signing of conventions and agreements, the implementation of constitutional reforms, the creation of institutions, and the integration of these issues within government development plans, something Schild (2013) has termed the feminization of social policies in Latin American countries. This context favored the promotion of certain discourses about respect for cultural differences and gender equality, and also facilitated funds from international and government institutions to address those issues. This encouraged organizational and participatory initiatives by civil society, with the creation of a large number of nonprofit organizations (*asociaciones civiles*), social solidarity associations, and community committees.

During the 1990s both Masehualsiuamej, constituted as a "social solidarity association," and the nonprofit CADEM promoted projects combining women and development, taking advantage of the availability of state, national, and international funds.[5] With the aim of mitigating poverty by gaining access to better economic options, the women at Masehualsiuamej obtained funds for commercialization of handicrafts, pig and chicken farms, housing, *nixtamal* mills (for corn grinding), and community tortilla factories. In 1997, again with international funds, they carried out an innovative large-scale project: the construction of the Taselotzin Eco-tourism Hotel, the first hotel managed by indigenous women in the region and in the state of Puebla.

Nahua women's participation in these productive projects confronted them with relations of male domination, in the sense that for the first time they were able to correlate their family experiences of control and oppression with discourses of gender equality promoted by various institutions and actors. (According to prevailing sex/gender norms, women were not allowed to go out alone, to associate with men who were not part of the family, such as members of government institutions, or to administer their own resources, much less to travel outside the region to sell their arts and crafts.) In this respect, indigenous women's organizations in Cuetzalan had the support of the state, international agencies, scholars, and feminist civil society organizations, which provided training and assistance in resource and project management. CAMI's concept of domestic violence can be understood as a localized construct related to the intersubjectification of experiences among Nahua women, but also as a broadly globalized concept, subject to international and national trends that define the types and modalities of violence. These definitions, as well as the measures for their prevention and punishment, are incorporated into associations' agendas through different means, such as the management of programs by organizations, as is the case of the leadership course offered by the NGO Semillas, which has supported members of CAMI.[6]

Despite all of this, the concept of violence used by CAMI has little to do with the provisions set out by the international organizations and government programs that surround the project. Rather than speaking of different types of violence (psychological, physical, patrimonial, economic, and sexual) as defined by the Law of Women's Access to a Life Free from Violence (approved by the Mexican Congress in early 2007), a more complex construction is evident that begins with identifying experiences of abuse located in the domestic realm, which serves as a starting point for subsequently incorporating other experiences, as we shall see below.

Regarding the use of the concept of violence related to the family environment, testimonies by CAMI promoters made recurrent references to the domestic space as the place where women suffer *violence*:

> I'm supporting the women who suffer violence, and well, also sometimes the women who are still young and are really mistreated by their parents or their uncles. (Testimony of a promoter, 2010)

> As a promoter we support [women], in my community I go to the women who suffer . . . domestic violence. (Testimony of a promoter, 2010)

> I tell you I suffered violence because my husband didn't let me speak with anyone about what was said at home. (Testimony of a promoter, 2010)

Likewise, situations of domestic violence and the use of this specific concept prevail in CAMI's case files.[7]

> The woman came to the CAMI. She says she needs help because she left her parents-in-law's house because she suffered a lot of violence from her spouse and her parents-in-law and her brothers-in-law. (File, October 3, 2007)

> The woman came to the CAMI saying that last Saturday her spouse Fidel hit her and she left her house and it isn't the first time he mistreats her,

since she has always suffered violence. She requests that they summon him to speak with him, and that they tell him that if he wants to live with her, he should stop beating her. (File, May 12, 2008)

The woman came to the CAMI to ask for help, saying that since she married her husband, one year after they were married he beat her and has successively beat her. The woman says that the man has a grocery store and he doesn't let her go anywhere, if he arrives and she leaves the house he beats her, he is [also] very violent, verbally. (File, July 6, 2009)

Narrating situations of violence in the domestic space by naming them as such allows the promoters and CAMI staff to present cases in such a way that they can be addressed. It is important to understand this progression as a process of symbolic and cognitive appropriation, whose complexity becomes evident when the women speak of their inability to signify experiences of abuse—everything that cannot be said because of shame or because it is a forbidden topic. In this sense, CAMI's definitions of situations of violence and the dynamics for their attention entail understanding Nahua sex/gender norms, local structural conditions, the use of the Nahuat language, Nahua worldviews, the relationships between culture and nature, and the use of indigenous and state law. From this standpoint we can speak of localized forms of violence and the possibility of designing interventions that are adequate for the specific context—a topic with which I conclude this chapter. In common with other organizations in Mexico and Latin America (Sieder and Sierra 2010), the experience of CAMI in Cuetzalan demonstrates indigenous women's ability to reconceptualize hegemonic discourses, such as "human rights," "women's rights," or "cultural rights," and to appropriate dominant practices such as public policies, government programs, or training initiatives by various institutions.

However, as in other cases, achievements in terms of the transformation of gender, political, economic, and social power relations are minor, with impacts circumscribed to certain groups or, in the best-case scenario, perceived as a long-term process. Only some members of CAMI and Maseualsiuamej have managed to achieve changes in gender relations within their families and, to a lesser extent, in community and municipal economic and political relations. Yet while CAMI's attention focuses on the domestic field, the problems faced by Nahua women are composed of a plurality of violences, indicating the need to broaden the scope of analysis beyond the domestic realm. Hence, CAMI offers an opportunity for understanding the ways in which discursive and international mechanisms can reproduce women's exclusion within indigenous women's organizations themselves. In what follows I discuss the dual character of the concept of violence, which, on one hand, allows situations of abuse to be revealed and denounced and, on the other, functions as a mechanism to ensure the persistence of established structural relations of power.

Domestic(ated) Violence and the Permanence
of Structural Power Imbalances

Analyzing the use of violence as a concept reveals the (re)organization of civil society and the emergence of new women's collectives, which have allowed women to gain greater influence within economic, political, and legal spaces in the municipality. But it has also revealed the mechanisms that lead to the persistence of structural relations of power and domination. CAMI is mainly focused to address the violence suffered by Nahua women in the domestic space and, to a lesser extent, in the community or in the municipality. The construction of this specific field of action, concentrated in the domestic sphere, hinders an understanding of how other expressions of abuse involving spaces and actors beyond this sphere take place. Therefore, it is precisely in the distinction between the private and the public that the mechanisms that reproduce power relations are located. Hence in our research, Oligaria and I explored conflicts related to employment, land, and property involving both indigenous and mestizo players. There is not one single case categorized as an employment issue in CAMI's files from 2007 to May 2011; nonetheless, indigenous women work as cooks, waitresses, and housemaids in the growing tourism industry in the municipal seat of Cuetzalan, or as *intendentes* in the municipal government.[8] Salaries are extremely low (between thirty and fifty pesos per day), and there are reports of nonpayment or refusal to allow time off for holidays, not to mention spontaneous layoffs and lack of benefits. It is important to note that denouncing workplace abuses would necessarily involve non-indigenous actors, political domains, and economic—especially commercial—interests at the local, state, and national levels.[9]

Circumscribing violence to the domestic and community realms, where the main participants are Nahua residents, effectively creates a dividing line between indigenous and non-indigenous conflicts, relegating to invisibility those that involve both, thus contributing to the perpetuation of unequal power relations and abuses in the workplace. Interestingly, the various municipal government bodies in Cuetzalan that support the fight against violence toward women also focus on the domestic realm without publicizing or paying attention to other forms of abuse, such as those that are employment-related. This leads us to consider the field of attention of *domestic(ated) violence* as one that addresses certain denunciations of abuse and subordination, as long as they do not antagonize the economic interests of the mestizo population. We found two cases related to land in CAMI's files—one of them filed as "Inheritance management" (December 2, 2009) and the other one as "Advice on a plot of land" (February 1, 2010). Beyond the fact that CAMI is not legally qualified to address cases related to land or property rights, what surprised us was the lack of legal referents for their enunciation.

ISSUE: Inheritance management. 2 Dec. 2009

Mrs. Alejandra says that 16 years ago they promised to give her a plot of land located in La Loma, named Nantzicuojta Yohualichan. This plot belonged to her grandmother, later it was in the possession of an aunt called Fernanda, widow of Brayan, who was the one who told her that she would bequeath the plot to her, but since the Rivas brothers took possession of the house and the land they evicted Mrs. Fernanda and left her homeless. Now Mrs. Alejandra wants to recover at least part of the plot, since she says that she took care of her aunts and uncles until they died, and from the latter she even has death certificate; she asks for help.

Procedure: CAMI's lawyer explained she should go to the Citizen's Attorney of the Attorney General's Office (PGR).

ISSUE: Advice on a plot of land. 1 Feb. 2010

The aforementioned woman came to the CAMI to request advice, since she claims that her husband bought a plot of land from his brother, but now the brother wants to take the plot. The husband has the deed showing that his brother sold him the lot, the only detail is that the woman does not appear in the deed as his wife.

Procedure: CAMI's lawyer explained to her that there is no problem, because the deed is written and notarized, and that the brother can do nothing because he already sold it.

The first case was taken to the Citizen's Attorney of the Attorney General's Office, which is in charge of formalizing deeds of property; in the second case, although it was noted that the woman is not included in the deed, she was informed only that everything is in order. In this respect we perceive what Gómez (2000) points to regarding the differentiated impacts and interlegal power effects that legal provisions have on indigenous peoples, in other words, the discrepancy between government-issued deeds and the orality of customs regarding land distribution and use. In these cases, official deeds take precedence over local customs. In the first case, inheritance of the house and land seems to be decided in favor of the deed holders rather than the relative who took care of the owners until their death. In the second case, custom considers the man as the only landowner.[10] In both cases, women's vulnerability and insecurity in terms of having a place to live seem not to be expressible as such.

When reviewing CAMI's files, we found other cases involving problems related to land, but they were categorized as other issues, such as advice (March 14, 2007; March 31, 2008; April 11, 2008; July 7, 2008; February 3, 2009; April 14, 2009; May 29, 2009; February 22, 2010), legal aid (June 29, 2009), defamation

(May 17, 2007), family disputes (June 22, 2007), no issue (July 25, 2007), advice on alimony (August 16, 2007), and psychological and physical violence (August 12, 2009). Below we examine some of these cases, which indicate a lack of referents to address problems that consist of nondomestic(ated) forms of violence.

Advice on Alimony (16 Oct. 2007)

The woman came to the CAMI and declared that she previously reached an agreement with Mr. Octavio, whereby he agreed to register the baby, pay alimony, give him the [agricultural] produce of a plot of land, and put the deed of property in the name of the minor, Ricardo. It is this last point which he has not complied with.

Although it is noted that the deed of property was not executed as agreed, the case is categorized under Alimony.

Advice 7 Jul. 2008

The woman came to the CAMI to ask for advice, stating that although a lawyer is handling her case she sees no progress. She says that her husband and her son are selling the land and they want to sell the house where she is living; she says that if they sell it she will have nowhere to go.

Procedure: She is informed about CAMI's organization and procedures and advised to go to the Public Prosecutor's Office to check whether her case has been forwarded to that agency and to see how the investigation is progressing or whether they have closed the case.

The case was sent to the Public Prosecutor's Office, even though the land conflicts were confined to the family (between the woman and her spouse and son); here the solution deemed most appropriate was the legality of the state.

While conflicts over land ownership seem to pass unnoticed, the lack of referents among CAMI's members to address these and employment problems signals the gaps created by the institutionalization of domestic(ated) violence. This compounds difficulties in signifying experiences of abuse, affecting the attention given to cases characterized by a plurality of violences. By not being addressed, these situations reproduce power relations and the subordination of Nahua women in the family and in the community. They also reproduce unequal power relations between the legality of the state and indigenous law, and between the indigenous and non-indigenous population. One case among those we monitored allowed us to analyze this issue in greater depth, demonstrating precisely the ways in which the problems women face involve various situations of abuse and mistreatment, manifesting the limits of "domestic(ated) violence."

The case in question was presented as one of domestic violence.[11] Three women arrived at CAMI, the mother and two sisters-in-law of the victim, who had been brutally beaten by her husband the previous night. Ana had left her house, and Paco caught up with her and beat her with a belt, kicking her while she was on the floor. Her screams led a female neighbor to come out and try to stop Paco, who threatened her and tried to beat her as well. When Sofía (Paco's sister) managed to wrest the belt from him, Paco threatened to kill them; they said he was completely out of control. At that moment Ana tried to escape by crawling away, but Paco grabbed her by the hair, slammed her on the floor, and dragged her into the house. Sofía and the neighbor went to fetch the police. When they arrived at Paco's house, Ana had changed her clothes—the ones she had on before were covered in blood. She refused to come out and from inside the house she told the policemen that everything was alright, covering her face with her blouse. The policemen left.

Violent events like this, which are quite common, are so dramatic that they grab all the attention and rage of the women at CAMI, who in addition identify very closely with the victims, since many of them lived through similar experiences. However, the focus on domestic violence under the duality of assailant/assaulted ultimately limits the possibilities of addressing conflicts composed of multiple forms of violence.

The next day, Sofía, Marcela (Sofia and Paco's sister), Ana's mother, and a promoter from CAMI whom they had contacted decided to fetch Ana and file a complaint. Marcela told Ana to come out of the house; Paco was there, and they did not want him to hear that they were going to file a complaint. But Ana refused to come out. Back in Cuetzalan, the women said that Paco had probably threatened Ana, an issue that, as has been noted in CAMI, is one of the factors that keeps women from denouncing violence. They commented that it was not the first time that he had beaten her and that on a previous occasion he hit her so hard that he broke a broom on her back. Sofía, Marcela, and Ana's mother insisted on filing a complaint since Paco had a previous history of violence, and they said that if he did it again they would take him straight to Zacapoaxtla (the district court), although without Ana's presence the complaint could not in fact be filed. They took the bloody blouse as proof and, together with CAMI's lawyer and promoter, said they would figure out what to do.

They went to the Public Prosecutor's Office, where the agent told them that, without the victim, nothing could be done. They then had the idea of having Sofía file the complaint as a victim of Paco, who tried to hit her and threatened her, and to summon Ana as well. But the summons would take three days, and it was urgent to bring Ana before her injuries became less visible.

They then thought of asking her to go to the shelter to receive medical treatment and, once there, to convince her to file the complaint. They returned to the community. The window of Ana's house was closed and the door was locked; they knocked and the door was opened by Ana's four-year-old daughter, who was then scolded by Ana for opening the door. Paco was not home.

Ana was lying down on the bed, and CAMI's promoter asked her what she was doing.

"Nothing, I'm just lying down," she said.

"What happened to you yesterday," she asked.

"Paco beat me."

"Why do you let him beat you, you're going to let him kill you, now you can't get up, and what about your children?" Ana started to cry. "Come to the shelter."

"No."

Sofía said, "Go to the shelter, they'll help you."

Ana answered, "You want me to go and you want Paco to go to jail so you can keep the house."

The promoter said that they were only going to attend to her injuries, and after a while she convinced Ana and they took her to the shelter. Once there, they were unable to convince her to file the complaint.

Later, inquiring with Paco's sisters Sofía and Marcela, we started to realize that the problem that affected them directly had to do with the house and the plot of land that had been partially taken over by Paco with the approval of their father, now deceased. Sofía and Marcela had been left with no property; however, they had not explicitly denounced the situation, nor had they demanded their right to inherit part of the land. Paco and Ana knew that they wanted the house, as Ana indicated when they tried to convince her to go to the shelter.

This case demonstrates how situations composed of multiple conflicts are confined to the category of domestic violence, especially between consorts; this became evident in the way in which Sofía and Marcela used the situation of violence between Paco and Ana to try to regain access to the house. The family members knew that Paco had already been arrested for domestic violence and that a repeat offense would land him in jail, hence their insistence on filing the complaint, hoping that with his imprisonment his relationship with Ana would end and she would return to her family. Sofía and Marcela had called on Ana's mother to help them support her daughter to confront the abuse she was suffering, and she told Ana to leave Paco and return to her home; this way, the house and the land would become vacant. While Ana seemed not to want to resolve her problem with Paco, she finally decided to go to the shelter, demonstrating a certain need to be in a safe place. Ana strongly refused to file the complaint, but she later asked Paco to build a small home for her and their children. As we observed some time later, Ana knew that if Paco went to jail she would also lose her home. She did not want to stay with Paco, but neither did she want to return to her mother's house. Ana also wanted the part of the land that was due to her because she was the mother of Paco's children.

This case reveals how the operational concept of violence developed at CAMI does not allow Sofía, Marcela, or Ana to claim their right to the house and land, even though the prevailing situation significantly threatens their survival. This ends up reproducing male domination over land and property, reifying certain relationships of subordination and exclusion of women in the domestic sphere. The case also allowed us to observe a strategic use of the notion of violence by Sofía and Marcela, who tried to denounce those acts that could be enunciated as violence, well aware as they were of the legal procedures and support provided by state agencies for such cases.[12] Jailing Paco would have been advantageous for Sofía and Marcela in terms of access to the house and land but not for Ana, signaling a degree of ambiguity surrounding the issue of denouncing and addressing domestic violence.

Ultimately, the concept of violence deployed by indigenous women of the CAMI has a limited capacity to address conflicts other than those corresponding to the assailant/assaulted duality. Nonetheless, institutional understandings of violence are not static or closed; since they are linked to the experiences and trajectories of the women at CAMI, new meanings and uses can be generated.

Conclusions

In this chapter I have explored domestic violence as a two-sided concept, signaling its capacity to reveal and denounce situations of abuse but also its function as a mechanism that perpetuates structural inequalities. I have analyzed the tensions this duality implies for the CAMI project, exploring the challenges faced by organizations in their efforts to transform power relations. Nahua women activists at the CAMI narrate situations of abuse to enunciate and denounce violence against women. Through these narrations, experiences of abuse become objectified, incorporating more political positions on gender, ethnicity, and culture. Women at the CAMI address issues that are regulated by local gendered cultural norms, and they have achieved significant victories by taking complaints to various justice institutions. At the same time, constant references to the domestic space as the place where women suffer violence results in a narrow conceptualization of violence, with a limited capacity to account for conflicts that take place outside the strict assailant/assaulted duality in the space of the family and, to a lesser extent, the community. This state of affairs is reinforced by the various municipal institutions in Cuetzalan that support the fight against domestic violence, but pay little attention to conflicts over property rights or those that involve both indigenous and mestizo players.

I have used the concept of "domesticated violence" to refer to situations of abuse that do not threaten the economic interests of the mestizo population, positions of power or gender, or (inter)ethnic relations, including the subordination of indigenous legal forums to state justice institutions. However, this analysis has also shown how the CAMI has, in practice, developed a concept of violence that integrates Nahua culture, local structural conditions, the Nahuat language, and indigenous law, as well as state law and the agendas of other organizations and funding agencies. This can be seen in the narrations of abuse explored in this chapter, where cultural referents and semantic expressions from Nahuat prevail. Such a hybrid understanding of violence against women has allowed other Nahua women and state authorities to identify with the narrators.

Exploration of a range of cases brought to the CAMI reveals the limits of their operational concept of violence in terms of its capacity to refer to conflicts, in this case those that defy regulatory beliefs (Lazos and Paré 2000), praxis schemes (Descola 2001), and their relationships with people's survival and the reproduction of nature. How, for example, might we speak of the harm effected by the use of herbicides, which kill herbs, mushrooms, and edible insects, increasing people's dependence on money and the food market? Monetization now extends to practically all aspects of life in the communities. Issues of local concern include government programs, the introduction of single-crop farming to replace the *milpa* (corn, squash, tomato, and beans), and the extensive use of herbicides that kill the brushwood. Thus the wide variety of wild plants and animals that was formerly collected and hunted, as well as the *milpa*, are no longer the main sources of sustenance for indigenous families. The practices related to those activities are no longer part of young people's lives, and therefore local ethno-ecological knowledge is being lost, as are beliefs that nurture the relationship between nature, people, and spirits. The presence and increase of various illnesses were also mentioned as a result of changes in the diet and the lack of herbal medicines and spiritual healing, with locals often concluding that the older generations lived better than people do now.

All of these situations are perceived as very significant grievances, indeed much more so than prevailing notions of domestic violence and related official discourses. Yet the attention provided by the women at the CAMI not only incorporates an understanding of Nahua sex/gender norms, local structural conditions, the use of the Nahuatl language, and the mind-sets of state institutions, but may also begin to explain other forms of abuse that involve Nahua worldviews and their relationship to culture and nature. The experience of the CAMI in Cuetzalan is a work in progress, where administrative procedures and institutional regulations contend and negotiate with other ways of understanding grievances. The challenge is how to enunciate and denounce these situations so that they can be part of strategies to transform relations of power and subordination.

NOTES

1. The municipality of Cuetzalan del Progreso is located in the Northern Sierra of the state of Puebla, Mexico, and is inhabited mainly by Nahua indigenous peoples.

According to the 2010 census, it has a total population of 47,433 inhabitants, 30,738 of them older than five years who speak an indigenous language, especially Nahuat.

2. A number of studies address the issue of violence and indigenous women in the municipality of Cuetzalan. See Alberti 1996; D'Aubeterre 1996; González 1996a, 1996b; Martínez and Mejía 1996, 1997; Mejía 2008; Sierra 2004a, 2004b, 2004c; Vallejo 2000, 2004; and Villa and Mejía 2006.

3. See González 1996a, 1996b, 1996c; Martínez and Mejía 1997; Sierra 2004a, 2004c; and Vallejo 2000.

4. Fragment of a case conducted in Nahuat at the Indigenous Court. Translation by Cristina Tellez from San Miguel Tzinacapan.

5. CAMI began as a community committee to administer social development funds from the federal government's Commission on Indigenous Development.

6. Semillas is part of two international networks: the Women's Funding Network and the International Network of Women's Funds.

7. We randomly selected cases between 2007 and 2011.

8. *Intendentes* are employees in charge of cleaning offices, waiting rooms, bathrooms, and outside areas.

9. In Cuetzalan, hotels and restaurants are owned by local caciques and entrepreneurs mainly from the cities of Puebla and Mexico City. Only the Taselotzin and Tosepancalli hotels are owned by indigenous organizations.

10. In the case of Cuetzalan, land is transferred patrilineally to the male child, a pattern that responds to the organization of conjugal residence according to patrilocality.

11. Pseudonyms are used to refer to the people involved in this case.

12. In a workshop with women who do not belong to any organization, different situations of abuse were presented, and the women were asked to explain how they would resolve them and whose support they would seek. The workshop revealed extensive knowledge of the options for addressing cases of family violence.

REFERENCES

Alberti, Pilar. 1996. "La violencia en el ciclo de vida y la percepción de las mujeres." In Soledad González, *La violencia doméstica y sus repercusiones*, n.p.

Berger, Peter, and Thomas Luckmann. 2005. *La construcción social de la realidad*. Salamanca: Universidad de Salamanca.

Beverley, John. 2004. *Testimonio: On the Politics of Truth*. Minneapolis: University of Minnesota Press.

Crosby, Alison, and M. Brinton Lykes. 2011. "Mayan Women Survivors Speak: The Gendered Relations of Truth-Telling in Postwar Guatemala." *International Journal of Transitional Justice* 5: 456–476.

D'Aubeterre, María Eugenia. 1996. "Sexualidad y violencia." In Soledad González, *La violencia doméstica y sus repercusiones*, n.p.

Descola, Philipe. 2001. "Construyendo naturalezas. Ecología simbólica y práctica social." In *Naturaleza y sociedad. Perspectivas antropológicas*, edited by Philipe Descola and Gísli Pálsson, 101–123. Mexico City: Siglo XXI.

Géliga, Jocelyn, and Inés Canabal. 2013. "Las rupturas de la investigación colaborativa: Historias de testimonios afropuertorriqueños." In *Otros Saberes. Collaborative Research on Indigenous and Afro-Descendant Cultural Politics*, edited by Charles Hale and Lynn

Stephen, 154–179. Santa Fe: School for Advance Research Press, Latin American Studies Association.

Gómez, Herinaldy. 2000. *De la Justicia y el Poder Indígena*. Colombia: Universidad del Cauca.

González, Soledad. 1996a. "La violencia captada por los prestadores de servicios de salud: curanderos, parteras y médicos." In Soledad González, *La violencia doméstica y sus repercusiones*, n.p.

———. 1996b. "La violencia doméstica como problema de estudio." In Soledad González, *La violencia doméstica y sus repercusiones*, n.p.

———, ed. 1996c. *La violencia doméstica y sus repercusiones para la salud reproductiva en una zona indígena (Cuetzalan, Puebla)*. Mexico City: Mexican Association of Population Studies.

Lazos, Elena, and Luisa Paré. 2000. *Miradas indígenas sobre una naturaleza entristecida. Percepciones del deterioro ambiental entre nahuas del sur de Veracruz*. Mexico City: IIS-UNAM, Plaza y Valdez.

Martínez, Beatriz, and Susana Mejía. 1996. "El sistema judicial y la violencia hacia las mujeres." In González, *La violencia doméstica y sus repercusiones*, n.p.

———. 1997. *Ideología y práctica en delitos cometidos contra mujeres: el sistema judicial y la violencia en una región indígena de Puebla*. Mexico City: Colegio de Postgraduados.

Mejía, Susana. 2000. "Mujeres indígenas y su derecho al desarrollo sustentable desde una perspectiva de género: el caso de las Masehualsiuamej mosenyochcauanij." In *Actas del XII Congreso Internacional de Antropología Jurídica*, edited by Milka Castro, n.p. Chile: Universidad de Chile, Universidad de Tarapacá.

———. 2008. "Los derechos de las mujeres nahuas de Cuetzalan. La construcción de un feminismo indígena, desde la necesidad." In *Etnografías e historias de resistencia: Luchas de las mujeres indígenas de América Latina*, edited by Aída Hernández, 453–502. Mexico City: CIESAS.

———. 2010. "Resistencia y acción colectiva de las mujeres nahuas de Cuetzalan: ¿construcción de un feminismo indígena?" PhD diss., UAM-X, Mexico City.

Schild, Verónica. 2013. "Care and Punishment in Latin America: The Gendered Neoliberalization of the Chilean State." In *Neoliberalism Interrupted: Social Change and Contested Governance in Contemporary Latin America*, edited by Mark Goodale and Nancy Postero, 195–224. Stanford, CA: Stanford University Press.

Schütz, Alfred. 1974. *El problema de la realidad social*. Buenos Aires: Amorrortu Editores.

Schütz, Alfred, and Thomas Luckmann. 1973. *The Structures of the Life-World*. Evanston, IL: Northwestern University Press.

Sieder, Rachel, and María Teresa Sierra. 2010. *Indigenous Women's Access to Justice in Latin America*. CMI working paper. Bergen, Norway: Chr. Michelsen Institute.

Sierra, María Teresa. 2004a. "De costumbres, poderes y derechos: Género, etnicidad y justicia en regiones indígenas de México." Paper presented at the Law and Gender in Contemporary Mexico seminar, University of London School of Advanced Studies, Institute of Latin American Studies.

———, ed. 2004b. *Haciendo justicia. Interlegalidad, derecho y género en regiones indígenas*. Mexico City: CIESAS-Porrua.

———. 2004c. "Interlegalidad, justicia y derechos en la sierra norte de Puebla." In María Teresa Sierra, *Haciendo justicia*, 115–186.

Sommer, Doris. 1998. "Not Just a Personal Story." In *Women's Testimonios and Plural Self. In Life/Lines: Theorizing Women's Autobiography*, edited by Bella Brodzki and Catharine Schenck, 107–130. Ithaca, NY: Cornell University Press.

Terven, Adriana. 2009. "Justicia indígena en tiempos multiculturales. Hacia la conformación de un proyecto colectivo propio: la experiencia organizativa de Cuetzalan." PhD diss., CIESAS, Mexico City.

Vallejo, Ivette. 2000. "Mujeres maseualmej y usos de la legalidad: conflictos genéricos en la sierra norte de Puebla." Master's thesis, CIESAS, Mexico City.

———. 2004. "Relaciones de género, mujeres nahuas y usos de la legalidad en Cuetzalan, Puebla." In María Teresa Sierra, *Haciendo justicia*, 187–236.

Villa, Rufina, and Susana Mejía. 2006. "Rufina: bordadora de sueños, hilvanadora de vidas, tejedora de esperanzas." In *Historias a dos voces: testimonios de luchas y resistencias de mujeres indígenas*, edited by Aída Hernandéz, 137–160. Mexico City: Gobierno de Michoacán, Instituto Michoacano de la Mujer.

3

Between Participation and Violence

Gender Justice and Neoliberal Government in Chichicastenango, Guatemala

RACHEL SIEDER

How do neoliberal paradigms of governance and development shape indigenous women's attempts to confront violence? In recent years, organizational initiatives in Guatemala to combat gender violence have occurred against the backdrop of government agendas to strengthen women's participation and development at village and municipal levels, and new national policies aimed at combatting violence against women. In this chapter I analyze the effects of development-related social policies and decentralizing reforms on efforts to increase gender justice from indigenous women's standpoints and perspectives, specifically the efforts of Maya K'iche' women in the municipality of Chichicastenango to develop strategies to combat discrimination and violence in their families and communities. Based on ethnographic research carried out accompanying the Municipal Women's Council (Junta Directiva Municipal de Mujeres—JDMM) between 2010 and 2013, I analyze the emergence of an agenda for indigenous women within municipal politics, the languages and techniques used in this field of action, and the initiatives undertaken by a group of Maya-K'iche' women community leaders to confront gender violence from within those spaces. My main objective is to consider the ways in which these recent processes of political and administrative reorganization affect possibilities for achieving what Maya-K'iche' women define as greater gender justice. I suggest that dominant schemes to decentralize development, aimed at increasing the "participation" of indigenous people, have in practice constrained the spaces where the *pobladores* of Chichicastenango can create visions of development with gender justice according to their own cultural and epistemological frameworks.

"Decentralization-participation-development" constructs that subcontract responsibility for social development to so-called civil society are a recurring feature of neoliberal governance. While representing a new phase in the transnationalized field of development, these public policy models signal the continuity of the notorious depoliticization that characterized the postwar period, something James Ferguson referred to as the "anti-politics machine" (1994).[1] As Julia Elyachar shows in her study of NGOs and microcredit in Egypt, new hybrid forms of power involving the state, international organizations, and NGOs are premised on the reconstruction of the social networks and practices of the poor (2005: 4–5). These reconstructions imply in turn the creation of new subjectivities and forms of self-regulation to generate specific kinds of behavior among target populations, now explicitly deemed "agents" of social development programs (Schild 2000: 288). This shift creates opportunities for new political and social linkages, but also reinforces structural patterns of exclusion as the neoliberal subject is exposed to greater risks. A significant part of the responsibility for development now falls on the poor, who have effectively become the fetish of neoliberal social policies.

The concept of gender has played a central role in this reorganization of dominant development paradigms. The institutionalization—or "mainstreaming"—of gender perspectives reflects the global codification of women's rights since the approval of the Convention on the Elimination of All Forms of Discrimination against Women (CEDAW) by the UN General Assembly in 1979 and the Beijing processes in the 1990s. As Verónica Schild observes, "Today, women as agents are at the heart of the efforts to transform those who are 'excluded' from the benefits of an empowered life in the market, into active, responsible citizens" (2000: 277–278). In Guatemala, the peace agreements emphasized the need to address the structural discrimination affecting indigenous peoples, and particularly indigenous women.[2] Approximately 77 percent of indigenous women in Guatemala live below the official poverty line. Although female literacy rates have improved since the early 1990s, in 2007 some 58 percent of indigenous women were illiterate, compared to 38 percent of indigenous men (DEMI 2007: 28). Women earn less than men, and the vast majority of them work in the informal sector. After the end of the armed conflict, a number of techniques were used to address what in global terms is defined as "poverty," including the decentralization of development efforts to improve citizens' participation. At the same time, different measures were enacted to "empower" women, including the creation of institutions and training programs in rights to combat exclusion and gender violence. The peace agreements led to the setting up of a National Women's Forum and the Office for the Defense of Indigenous Women (DEMI). In 2000 the Presidential Secretariat for Women was created, charged with overseeing the drafting and implementation of "transversal policies for the advancement and development of Guatemalan women" (Mendizábal and Asturias de Castañeda 2010). Gender mainstreaming meant "indigenous women" became an important category in development policies with a presumed emphasis on cultural diversity.

This chapter is structured as follows. The first section analyzes the decentralization laws and organizational histories of community development in Chichicastenango in an attempt to uncover the effects of national political and legal reorganization. In the second part I focus on the intersections between policies to decentralize development and policies toward women, and the efforts of local Maya-K'iche' leaders in Chichicastenango's Municipal Women's Council (JDMM) to strengthen a local gender agenda. I subsequently reflect on the different channels and mechanisms deployed by the leaders and women in the hamlets to "name, frame, and claim" their grievances, and point to the broader limits that prevailing forms of electoral politics pose to indigenous women's intersectional framings and demands for justice.

Disputing Community, Authority, and Participation

Approximately 98 percent of the inhabitants of Chichicastenango in the department of Quiché in Guatemala's central highlands are Maya K'iche', and K'iche' is the mother tongue of 93 percent. Most of the population survives through small-scale agriculture, handicrafts, commerce, or remittances from relatives in the capital or the United States, although with more than 68 percent of residents below the official poverty line, it is one of the poorest municipalities in the country. Southern Quiché suffered bloody military counterinsurgency campaigns during the armed conflict. The liberation-theology-influenced Catholic Action had trained catechists in the villages beginning in the late 1960s; the crisis of subdivision of family plots and the dispossession of communal lands turned the region into one of the bases for the Committee of Peasant Unity, which then became the support base for the Guerilla Army of the Poor (McAllister 2003; ODHAG 1998: 188). Military offensives in the early 1980s against southern Quiché and the neighboring department of Chimaltenango led to massacres in villages thought to be linked to the guerrillas, such as Patzibal, Camanchaj, Chicuá, and Chupol (ODHAG 1998: 42–43, 174). The army subsequently militarized the villages, forcing the male population to join the counterinsurgent Civilian Defense Patrols (PACs). The legacy of violence left behind by the armed conflict and the political and social ruptures it created persist decades later: in some communities there is still a notorious "anti-state" culture, while others are more aligned with official structures of power. Processes and experiences of community social organization are diverse but also highly atomized and fragmented, marked by conflict, mistrust of state institutions, and a constant dispute for political leadership.

After the war Chichicastenango became a center for international development cooperation and a showcase for "rights-based development" and "postconflict peace building." K'iche' women, many of them young professionals, played an important role in a tight network of NGOs and local civic associations, most focusing on rights and local development issues through training, awareness raising, and accompaniment. Local chapters of national indigenous people's movements, such as the CONAVIGUA widows' association and local community development organizations Majawil Q'ij (New Dawn), Ixmucané, and the Association for Community Development (ASDECO), combined human rights and gender rights norms and Maya epistemologies and values in their approaches. At the same time, rural communities and the poor who inhabit them became the main objective of postwar policies prioritizing "the communal/local" and mobilizing "social capital" for social development.[3] This fostered a refunctionalization of certain traditional authorities, such as the auxiliary mayors (*alcaldes auxiliares*)—village-level representatives of the municipal mayor were also part of the state's politico-administrative system. As Tania Li reminds us, when we analyze various "improvement schemes" proposed from the centers of global and national power, it is vital to scrutinize their rationalities, calculations, and effects (2007). Although the decentralization reforms were built on existing structures of authority and leadership in the villages, they also gave rise to a new field of power. The auxiliary mayors were legally recognized as the lowest level of executive power, yet they also constituted an instance of nonstate power, forming part of a complex web of Maya spiritual, religious, and civilian authorities that were being reconstituted in some of the rural cantons of Chichicastenango in the wake of the armed conflict. Yet rather than seeing them as moral and ethical authorities within their communities, the new legislation conceived of the auxiliary mayors and the different village-level improvement committees as "agents of development" who thenceforth became an integral part of the state's operation.[4] Elyachar has questioned the notion of "empowerment" of the poor, noting that "the poor, of course, didn't live in a power vacuum. The idea that they had to be empowered implied that a new form of power was entering their lives and that the power they had was being taken away" (2005: 215). This logic, which Elyachar calls "dispossession through empowerment" (2005: 217), was evident in processes that developed in Chichicastenango after the approval of the decentralization reforms.

The Decentralization Law, the Municipal Code, and the Law on Urban and Rural Development Councils approved in 2002 represented the materialization of commitments made in the peace agreements.[5] Together they constituted a new legal framework to allow for "citizen participation" in the elaboration—or at least in the implementation—of development-related public policies. In practice, they imposed a certain type of "citizen participation" on the rural indigenous population, as well as other innovations related to the organization and remit of municipal governance and administration, forms of association, provision of services, and municipal finances. The Municipal Code allowed for consultations with "traditional" authorities of indigenous communities according to their criteria or customs when the issues at stake affected their rights and interests.[6] However, the Decentralization Law simultaneously created a series of new authority structures at the department, municipal, and rural village levels: the so-called Development Councils.[7] These were described as a means for "democratic planning for development"; their stated objectives included "to organize and coordinate public administration through the formulation of development policies, funding plans and projects, and the promotion of private and public inter-institutional coordination." At village level, the councils are called Community Development Councils or COCODEs and are composed of the community mayor, who heads them, and up to twelve representatives. According to the law, the COCODE "is constituted by the community assembly, which is composed of the residents of a single community, according to its own principles, values, norms, and procedures. The coordination body is presided over by its community mayor and up to a maximum of 12 representatives elected in a general assembly, whose responsibility is to coordinate, implement, and conduct social audits of the projects or works prioritized by the community."[8]

It was argued that COCODEs would constitute a way to build development "from below." However, in practice they have little control over national development policies, which are designed in the centers of national and international political power and implemented in top-down fashion. Nor do they have control over municipal funds, which tend to be tightly controlled by the elected municipal mayors and councils. In line with the Decentralization Law, the 87 COCODEs in the villages or *cantones* of Chichicastenango are grouped into a second tier of political and administrative organization, with the municipality divided into eight "micro-regions" each containing several COCODEs.[9] The representatives of these micro-regions—the vast majority of whom are men—compose a municipal board that represents the villages in the Municipal Council for Development Planning (COMUDE), the forum where municipal development policies are decided. Some local development associations, NGOs, and representatives of government institutions such as the Human Rights Ombudsman's Office (PDH) also participate in the COMUDE.

In the years after the finalization of the peace agreements in 1996, a number of local associations for development arose in Chichicastenango, supported by some national NGOs and international cooperation agencies such as NOVIB from the Netherlands, IBIS from Denmark, and ASDI from Sweden. Two of the most important were the Coordination of Associations and Organizations for Integrated Development (CASODI) and ASDECO.[10] ASDECO was originally part of CASODI, but became independent in 1996 as an association of fourteen communities. Both worked to strengthen local power, community organization, leadership development and training, interinstitutional coordination between the villages, and the elaboration of self-managed community projects. Differences between them reflected historic and political fractures and tensions in Chichicastenango, as well as contrasting understandings of "development" and politics. ASDECO is an association of communities from a subregion in the south of the municipality (initially fourteen and then seventeen *cantones*) with a history of opposition to the state during the armed conflict. It aimed to foster the holistic, self-managed development of Maya K'iche' communities by strengthening traditional indigenous authorities and focusing on the specific rights of indigenous peoples, although it also participated in new structures such as the COCODEs. As Macleod and Xiloj Tol noted, ASDECO "gives a great deal of importance to recovering Mayan institutionality, understood as organizational forms and traditional authorities (indigenous mayoralties, or *alcaldías indígenas* and community assemblies), decision-making styles (consensual and collective), and conflict resolution methods (negotiated between the parties), based on Mayan principles such as respect, service to the community, advice and equilibrium, among others" (2011: 468).

These traditional forms of indigenous institutionality had been undermined by Catholic Action's influence in the 1970s and then were so drastically affected by the armed conflict that they had stopped functioning altogether in many villages. In the 1990s the institution of the *alcaldías indígenas*—a supracommunal structure of traditional indigenous authorities that assembles approximately three hundred people, including auxiliary/community mayors and village elders or *principales*—was reinstated. The *alcaldía indígena* was not so closely linked to the community development bodies created by the new decentralization laws and indeed presented itself as an "ancestral" form of Mayan authority.[11] ASDECO supported the structure of the *alcaldía indígena* and worked with them to strengthen the role of the community mayors, the revitalization of indigenous law, and nonpartisan indigenous community authorities: "Community authorities participate in the organizational system promoted by ASDECO, but an increase in their participation and strengthening of their political vision is required so they can oversee the use of resources administered by state bodies and non-governmental organizations" (ASDECO 2011: 12).[12]

In contrast, in the 2000s CASODI's efforts were focused on strengthening the new structures of decentralized government—the COCODEs, the microregions, and the COMUDE, in coordination with the new Municipal Planning Office. Instead of emphasizing the "recovery" or strengthening of traditional Mayan authorities, CASODI focused its efforts on a process of participatory planning in dialogue with the elected municipal government in order to influence municipal development plans. In effect, ASDECO had the same demands, but from a different organizational perspective that emphasized the institutionality that they considered to be truly "Mayan." In July 1999 and with the support of national NGO Legal and Social Services, CASODI carried out a process of consultation to identify solutions for local needs and strengthen intercommunal links and channels of communication with the municipal authorities. CASODI systematized and presented the results as a proposal for municipal development to which all the candidates running for the office of municipal mayor subsequently pledged their commitment (CASODI 2003: 10). In November 1999 Manuel Sut Lucas was elected municipal mayor for the Guatemalan Republican Front (FRG), the party led by former military dictator General Efraín Ríos Montt. The FRG's municipal administration in Chichicastenango had close ties to former members of the PACs, which had been a central element of the counterinsurgency strategy. The FRG party—which controlled the presidency of the republic from 2000 to 2003 under the administration of Alfonso Portillo— relied on clientelist policies centered on the municipal mayor. While various groups, civic associations, and NGOs did participate in Chichicastenango's development planning during the first half of the 2000s, both Sut Lucas and the political parties in the municipal council preferred to centralize and personalize the administration of local government. They particularly mistrusted local NGOs and civic organizations, many of which had emerged from processes close to the guerrilla insurgency of the 1980s.

Significant tensions emerged between the *alcaldía indígena* and the municipal mayor, each of them questioning the other's legitimacy and authenticity as "indigenous" representatives. In previous decades, municipal mayors had always been from the non-indigenous *ladino* elite and the *alcaldía indígena* had functioned as a space to resolve disputes and issues affecting the majority K'iche' population. However, in the years after the armed conflict political parties attracted more indigenous candidates for municipal elections, and today more than two-thirds of mayors in the 334 municipalities are non-mestizo. ASDECO supported the *alcaldía indígena* as part of its policies to strengthen Mayan culture. However, the municipal mayor perceived the training programs offered by ASDECO to community mayors as a challenge to the power of the municipal corporation. José Tiriquiz Tiniguar, elected mayor for the FRG in 2003, saw community mayors as part of the municipal government structure and demanded they report directly to him. As Macleod and Xiloj Tol observed when writing about the situation in Chichicastenango in 2006, "The difference in conceptions—between being the municipal mayor's right-hand man or even 'messenger,' . . . or being the community mayor [and] the authority in his own community [as defined by] a bottom-up understanding of democracy—is at the heart of the conflict between the *alcaldía indígena*/ASDECO and the municipal corporation" (2011: 476). Accusations later surfaced to the effect that ASDECO was trying to "control" traditional authorities. These conflicts over the nature of communal authorities and local development provide the background for understanding women's organization in Chichicastenango to combat violence and demand greater gender justice according to their own standpoints and perspectives.

Decentralization, Gender Violence, and Women's Participation

Some of the highest levels of violence against women in the hemisphere meant that gender violence became a central issue for international agencies operating in postwar Guatemala, sparking a number of legal and institutional reforms. Guatemala ratified the CEDAW in 1995 and was one of the first countries to sign up to the Inter-American Convention on the Prevention, Punishment, and Eradication of Violence against Women in 1994 (known as the Convention of Belém do Pará). The Law against Femicide and Other Forms of Violence against Women, in force since May 2008, characterized murders of women as femicide for the first time and mandated important changes to the Penal Code (those convicted of femicide had to serve custodial sentences and were denied parole). Laws were approved to prevent sexual violence, exploitation, and trafficking, and to provide universal access to family planning services. The Optional Protocol to CEDAW was ratified, and a National Coordination for the Prevention of Domestic Violence and Violence against Women was created. Collaborative efforts between government and civil society were also promoted to increase public awareness of gender discrimination and violence against women. At the departmental level, a representative of the Presidential Secretariat for Women (SEPREM) attempted to coordinate central government's policies and initiatives for women,[13] and at the municipal level the COMUDE had a Women's Sub-Commission that was in charge of ensuring that municipal development planning was consistent with national policies toward women.[14]

In Chichicastenango, civic associations such as ASDECO and CASODI underscored the need to develop innovative strategies to support greater gender equity and women's participation within a framework promoting the identity and collective rights of indigenous peoples. Within their own institutional structures they practiced affirmative action by employing Maya K'iche' women in leadership positions. Several civic organizations in the municipality led by women began developing methodologies to transform gender relations in rural villages (Sieder and Macleod 2009). ASDECO promoted the organization of women and young people, working in small groups at the community level on issues such as self-esteem and always emphasizing Maya K'iche' identity, culture, and worldviews. This methodology allowed them to address issues such as domestic violence, women's lives and sexuality, racism and discrimination, affects, individual and collective histories, and reproductive health. In conjunction with other local community development organizations (such as Ixmucané, which promotes holistic health services for Mayan women), they accompanied village midwives, traditionally seen as an authority providing advice for indigenous couples. According to a number of the women associated with ASDECO, these processes of accompaniment did not imply direct interventions in domestic conflicts, nor were they designed to combat "gender violence" in crisis situations. Rather, they were conceived as part of holistic efforts to prevent violence in order to "generate conditions of dignity for women and strengthen their self-confidence" (ASDECO 2011: 13). Community associations also promoted education, community health, and micro-credit projects for women to augment their family incomes, for example by providing seed money for domestic textile production or small-scale agriculture. By strengthening indigenous authorities, indigenous law, and women's self-esteem, the women of ASDECO hoped to have an impact on gender justice by validating and rein-forcing Maya K'iche' identity and culture.

The priority afforded in the national development agenda to poverty and violence against women failed to translate into effective actions in practice. The administrative and political scheme of decentralization did not favor gender equity in Chichicastenango. In fact the creation of the COCODEs strengthened male leaderships at the village level, sometimes interrupting processes that civic associations had been supporting to encourage female and youth com-munity leadership.[15] COCODE representatives were expected to participate in community assemblies and know how to read and write, both aspects that cur-tailed women's participation. According to the director of the PDH in Quiché, the creation of the COCODEs also had a negative impact on the possibilities of denouncing cases of domestic violence: "There was a time when people did make formal complaints about domestic violence, but now they don't. Why? I discovered that the COCODEs have had a great deal of influence. COCODEs do address the issue of domestic violence, but they tend to resolve it in a way that favors men. . . . Some COCODEs have told women: 'don't say anything in courts or council meetings, because we resolve domestic violence here in the commu-nities, no one else can find out'" (Interview with Aida López Cordero, July 2013).

Municipal mayor José Tiriquiz Tiniguar (who served two terms—for the FRG from 2004 to 2007 and for the Unidad Nacional de la Esperanza, UNE, from 2008 to 2011) supported women's participation in municipal develop-ment planning. As stipulated in the Decentralization Law, women representa-tives were elected to the various village committees and also took part in the second-tier structures of the micro-regions. In 2008 nine women were elected in a regional assembly to represent the various micro-regions, constituting the JDMM. Three of the women leaders elected to the JDMM were also leaders in the network of women organized by ASDECO in the seventeen communities that formed part of the association. Elections were held again in 2011, and some of the women were reelected for a second term. The Decentralization Law stipulates that the JDMM participate in the Regional Development Council or COMUDE to represent women in the micro-regions, alongside representa-tives from various NGOs, civic organizations, and several government agencies, such as the PDH—then represented by Aída López Cordero, who had strongly supported local initiatives to tackle gender violence. The leaders of the JDMM tried to obtain various projects and assistance for women in their microregions through these official structures. In addition to participating in the COMUDE, their main point of contact in the municipal corporation was the Municipal Women's Office (OMM), charged with promoting women's participation and gender equity in municipal development planning and promoted by central government as a measure that would improve women's security and reduce gender violence.[16] In 2011 the person in charge of the OMM was Magdalena. A graduate in business administration, she had formerly held another administrative position in the municipality and was one of many female K'iche' professionals employed in the structures of local government, civic associations, and NGOs in the town.[17] By contrast, most of the nine representatives of the micro-regions assembled in the JDMM had only elementary schooling, were monolingual in K'iche' or spoke little Spanish, and lived off agriculture, the sale of handicrafts, or petty commerce. None of them were paid a salary for their participation as representatives of their micro-regions, although the OMM did provide travel expenses and food when they had to attend meetings. Yet despite Mayor Tiriquiz's proclaimed support for women's participation in the COCODEs and COMUDE, in practice they had little access to municipal funds and were often unable to attend planning meetings due to lack of resources.

By 2010 the process of participatory planning in Chichicastenango's COMUDE and its Women's Sub-Commission had created the first Municipal Gender Policy in Guatemala, whose main objective was to incorporate a gender perspective into local development planning. The JDMM leaders were extremely proud of this milestone in municipal politics and continuously referred to it as "our document" or "our gender program": "We keep working and struggling because we have obtained projects for women and now we also have our Municipal Gender Policy. . . . We were able to get the support of the municipal mayor. Now we have to knock on doors to ensure that all of the points [set out in the document] are implemented" (Luz María, September 2011).

The Municipal Gender Policy was divided into seven sections: Education with Cultural Pertinence; Holistic Health for Women; Culture; Natural Resources, Land and Housing; Economic and Productive Development; Social and Political Participation; and Security and Non-Violence. The process of elaborating the document was very important for the women leaders of the JDMM, although the influence of NGOs and civic associations meant the wording and language at first sight appeared to be very far from the ways they talked about their concerns. The section on Security and Non-Violence focused on domestic and gender violence and set out the following objectives:

- Implement programs to orient and accompany women victims of domestic and gender violence in the process of filing a complaint
- Provide psychological, medical, and legal attention to women victims of violence

- Develop programs that increase men and women's awareness about the causes and effects of domestic and gender violence
- Implement training programs for adolescent and adult women about their rights to a life free of discrimination, violence, and racism
- Create and implement informational programs in K'iche' and Spanish about the mechanisms available to denounce all acts of violence against women
- Implement training programs for local justice officials about national and international mechanisms for the protection of women's rights
- Inform the general population about the laws that punish discriminatory practices (Política Municipal de Género, Chichicastenango, 2011)

The document placed a strong emphasis on legal instruments and rights training. This reflected many years of organization to defend human rights in Quiché, but also demonstrated the influence of dominant paradigms to combat violence against women that focused on legal reforms and state justice institutions—something similar to tendencies observed by Adriana Terven in chapter 2, on Cuetzalan, Puebla. Reflecting such frameworks, this section of the Municipal Gender Policy insisted on the need to improve women's access to state justice and to accompany them in the process of filing formal complaints before the legal authorities. Yet although women suffer many types of gender violence, such as physical and psychological abuse (most of it at the hands of their male consorts), incest, sexual abuse, and rape, very few cases are reported, and sexual violence is almost never formally denounced (ASIES/OACNUDH 2008).[18] The majority are monolingual or have very limited use of Spanish, and there is almost no access to services of state justice in K'iche'. As Terven underlines, narration is central to communicating experience and elaborating intersubjective understandings of violence, yet this is impossible when interlocutors lack the means for communicating. In Guatemala approximately 50 percent of indigenous women older than fifty years, 40 percent of those between thirty-one and fifty, 33 percent of those between sixteen and thirty, and 40 percent of those younger than fifteen are monolingual, with percentages higher in rural areas (PNUD 2005). Even when they do speak Spanish, most women victims of violence lack sufficient economic resources or family support to file an official complaint. Doing so inevitably requires several trips to the departmental capital of Santa Cruz del Quiché (half an hour by bus from the town center of Chichicastenango), with all the costs in terms of money and time this implies. Cases tend to progress extremely slowly, with few guarantees of a conviction, and even when women do obtain a favorable sentence, such as an order for child support payments, my observations indicate that state authorities make no efforts to enforce these resolutions.

At the start of 2011 I began to explore collaborative research with the nine K'iche' female community leaders of the JDMM, together with Lidia Osorio, a K'iche' social worker from the town of San Antonio Ilotenango who had worked with them for the previous three years on an NGO project to strengthen their participation in municipal planning. In our initial discussions the women leaders said they had emphasized strengthening female leadership within the villages, but had perhaps neglected the issue of domestic and sexual violence. Women in their communities often called on them for help, but they had received little training on the issue. I was interested in knowing what strategies they would pursue to implement the ambitious Municipal Gender Policy, especially given the lack of municipal resources. The women said what they most needed were funds, projects, and training, effectively reflecting prevailing idioms and practices of working for gender justice in Chichicastenango. Many had long participated in activities organized by CONAVIGUA and ASDECO, and those organizations' gender training programs had offered opportunities to increase their knowledge and for self-confidence. Several affirmed the importance of training programs (*capacitaciones*) "because it's where women learn and become strong." These processes were evident, for example, in the life history of Luz María, a community leader from the village of Chumanzana:

> I no longer have a father. Thirteen years ago he died because of alcohol and he never sent me to school. But I learned how to read at the Literacy Program, and CONAVIGUA [the indigenous widows' association] also helped me, and only that way did I learn how to read a bit and to write. When I started to work for the community I had problems with my mother because she said that women are only for the kitchen and to have children, she also said that a woman shouldn't go out onto the streets because men can harm her. Because of that it wasn't very easy to participate in the women's committee, and then CONAVIGUA arrived and they didn't provide economic projects, just training, and there they gave us strength because they taught us that women have the right to participate. Only then was my mother convinced, and then the community elected me to be part of the women's committee and I told my mom and she supported me, and that's how I started to work. (Luz María, September 2011)

The Participatory Evaluation (*Diagnóstico Participativo*)

The JDMM leaders proposed that Lidia and I carry out what they called a *diagnóstico* or evaluation about violence against women in the municipality. They told us that when women in their villages came to them with this type of problem they could do little more than listen and give them moral support. They reasoned that if they had a document that specified local problems related to domestic and sexual violence they would stand a better chance of obtaining resources for training projects, reflecting the fact that a *diagnóstico* of some sort is usually elaborated by funding agencies or their counterparts prior to the approval of any project. We agreed it was important to understand what women did when they suffered gender violence, and specifically who they took their complaints to: Their families? Village authorities? Religious or spiritual leaders? Or state justice services, such as DEMI, the PDH, or the Public Prosecutor's Office, all of which were located in the departmental capital of Santa Cruz? We worked together to develop a script of questions and fine-tune interview techniques. Subsequently, over a period of six months, Lidia accompanied JDMM leaders Rosa, Candelaria, Ana María, Luz María, and Virginia to their different villages to carry out in-depth interviews with twenty-four women victims of violence, all of them conducted in the K'iche' language.[19] We also transcribed the life histories of several members of the JDMM. The women usually didn't speak publicly about their own stories as victims of violence fearing this would expose them to gossip, but their life histories revealed this experience had marked several of them. After the materials were translated into Spanish and transcribed, Lidia and I worked on a preliminary analysis of the data to be discussed in a workshop. We also agreed that in a second phase of the research we would organize some sort of workshop or training course for the women who had shared their testimonies for the *diagnóstico*, as the JDMM requested.

Our sample was small but pointed to an almost complete lack of options for women suffering domestic or sexual violence, confirming what had been documented in other studies on women's access to justice in Quiché (ASIES/OACNUDH 2008; Consorcio Actoras de Cambio 2009; ECAP-UNAMG 2009). Inspired by intersectional perspectives, we wanted to highlight the multiple forms of structural violence that indigenous women faced rather than focusing only on male violence toward women. Through our analysis of the testimonies and discussions with the JDMM together we developed a series of categories for the causes of gender violence in Chichicastenango; among them were poverty, gender ideologies and expectations, the bad image of single mothers, the impacts of the armed conflict, and migration to the United States. Poverty and women's economic dependence on men were evident in all the testimonies. A typical case was that of a woman abandoned by her husband, who failed to provide economic support for their children: "I'm a single mother and have nowhere to live. I'm staying here on my brother's land because my mother left all the land to my brother and she doesn't want to give me any because she says that I'm a woman and I don't have the right to it." The women's testimonies of psychological and physical violence pointed to jealousy, gossip, accusations of infidelity, infidelity, and alcoholism. As other chapters in this volume signal, gender ideologies justifying violence against women were reproduced not only by men but also by other women, frequently members of women's own families: "I suffered a lot and I wanted to go home to my mother and father but I remembered that she had told me that if I returned home she would throw chili pepper [in my face] because I had to put up with my husband." Women tended to seek the intervention of other family members on their behalf. Sometimes they sought justice with the village authorities, but many were too afraid or ashamed. This was worse in cases of sexual violence or coercion. The family of a young woman who became pregnant by a neighbor complained to community authorities, but the young man denied paternity. When asked what the consequences of seeking justice had been, she said, "The whole community found out what [he] did to me. I felt ashamed. The whole community is talking about me. Instead of helping me that makes me very sad."

The experiences of violence shared by the women reflected understandings that went well beyond the definitions of gender violence established in national legislation or the operational plans of official programs of interinstitutional coordination. They pointed to socioeconomic exclusion, the effects of the armed conflict on families in the region, and the discriminatory ideologies that prevailed despite improvements in indigenous women's political participation and education. Rights training or better access to state justice institutions alone could not resolve these structural and historic problems. Our *diagnóstico* tried to reflect the breadth of the testimonies and analyze the steps taken by women themselves, including appeals to their relatives, female leaders in their communities, or communal authorities. They also sought rights training from local civic associations or became active in women's organizations.

Healing Workshops (*Talleres de Sanación*)

Although some of the incidents or experiences narrated had occurred several years previously, the women still felt a great deal of pain, sadness, and suffering, and the JDMM leaders wanted some sort of training course or workshop for those who had shared their testimony. Some had previous knowledge of healing therapies through their community work with ASDECO. We contacted several women with experience in healing workshops (*talleres de sanación*) and eventually contracted the services of Petronila, a local K'iche' spiritual leader and healer who had worked for many years with victims of the internal armed conflict and young victims of domestic and sexual violence. Each day we would take paper, crayons, cushions, music, and bags with aromatic herbs to a house in each village. Around eight to ten women participated each time, and the workshops were private and quite intimate, in part because they took place in the women's own homes or those of their neighbors rather than in the communal halls generally used for meetings. Paula, the daughter of Candelaria from Patzibal, organized play sessions for small children to keep them occupied. Sometimes Lidia and I participated, other times we sat outside in the patio, making lunch or herbal infusions to offer everyone throughout the day. Petronila invited the women to reconstruct their life stories through playacting, drawings, or narration. She stressed that "what's important is to bring [the pain] out, but with a different name." Group reflection was focused on ideas of intergenerational suffering and the effects of different types of violence, something Petronila called "chains of pain," which she said had to be broken. "We talk to be able to cure ourselves. It's strange, but violence affects us this way." She also worked a lot with so-called ancestral treatments, different techniques to work with energies that included massage, breathing, herbal and plant infusions, offerings, and various techniques to express feelings and release negative energies. Sometimes we all did physical exercises together like running on the spot or dancing, which usually prompted peals of laughter. We also spent considerable time each day combing the nearby paths and hedges looking for different plants and herbs. Often women were particularly interested in Petronila's knowledge of herbal cures for certain medical conditions or feelings. As Tomasa told us one day, "we didn't expect this kind of capacitación, it's very useful for us." The question of guilt, responsibility, and punishment for the suffering and violence the women had endured was dealt with indirectly. As Petronila emphasized, "someone who committed a grave wrong should be sanctioned. But that in order for it to have longer lasting consequences the person really needs to accept their wrong and want to change. And that's a long process." The workshop dynamics highlighted the distance between legal rights discourses and judicialized forms of seeking justice through formal, public complaints, and more specific, localized, and personal ways of understanding harm and reparation. These two aspects are not mutually exclusive: women can file a formal complaint with the appropriate state institutions, but also seek forms of healing—in this case ancestral therapies and techniques, now reframed as methodologies for workshops on gender violence.[20]

Limits of the Search for Gender Justice: Between NGOism and Political Clientelism

Chichicastenango's volatile political context had a considerable impact on the JDMM. Throughout the 2000s national political parties adapted to the new political opportunities afforded by the paradigms of decentralization, citizen participation, and the new antipoverty social policies. Party structures extended to village level, politicizing the selection of communal authorities, an effect of decentralization reforms Xavier Albó noted in Bolivia during the 1990s (2002). This had a negative impact on possibilities for confronting domestic violence: "The electoral process lasts two or three years. . . . They start with the campaigns and all of that, and that has a big influence. If a community leader is violent at home but is helping [a person] in his [political] party, then nothing is said or women are told: 'you mustn't do anything, because these leaders are working.' I saw how this also contributed to a decrease in denunciations by women."[21]

Clientelist practices in municipal politics became more accentuated as decentralization laws and antipoverty programs fostered the creation of different organized groups in the *cantones*, heightening disputes for political control at all levels. Mayor Tiriquiz Tinuguar saw local women's committees primarily as a means to improve his vote, while Sebastián Xon Cortez, his main opponent in the 2011 campaign for municipal mayor, used his own position as local head of the nationwide cash transfer program Mi Familia Progresa (MIFAPRO) to garner the female vote. During the months prior to the September 2011 election, JDMM leaders and the OMM were occupied with Tiriquiz's campaign. Zenaida, JDMM's president, ran for the municipal council on Tiriquiz's UNE slate. Rumors circulated that Xon Cortez intended to disband the JDMM if he won the elections and replace the existing leaders with his political allies in the villages, linked to the structures of MIFAPRO. In September the La Manzana civic committee secured a majority on the new municipal council and Xon Cortez was elected mayor.[22] Combined with the uncertainty created by the victory of former General Otto Pérez Molina for the Patriot Party in the September 2011 presidential election, these events effectively paralyzed the JDMM's organizational work for several months. The COMUDE failed to meet, and the new government announced it would carry out a thorough audit to analyze accusations of corruption during the Colom administration, meaning funding flows to the municipalities were effectively suspended. Magdalena was removed as head of the OMM, and the woman appointed to replace her was initially unaware of the Municipal Gender Policy, which was delivered to her in person by the women leaders of the JDMM. The JDMM was not able to resume its work on gender violence until mid-2012, this time with a series of meetings and activities organized together with Lidia and Aída López Cordero from the PDH. In October 2012 they organized a workshop on the "steps for making a complaint" (*ruta de denuncia*), where each female JDMM representative was accompanied by a woman from her village. In accordance with state policies to stop violence against women, the aim was to train local leaders about the measures they could take to help women file a complaint with the various state authorities. In the workshop women dramatized situations of gender violence while Aída explained their rights and the functions and responsibilities of the various government bodies, among them the National Civilian Police's Office for Attention to Victims,[23] DEMI, the PDH, the Justice of the Peace or local court, the National Institute of Forensic Sciences, and the Public Prosecutor's Office. Other agencies or organizations that could provide support in crisis situations, such as the local health clinic, the woman's own family, and the Center for Integral Attention to Women Survivors of Violence in Santa Cruz del Quiché, were also mentioned.[24] The women appreciated the information given in the workshop and the space to meet and share their experiences and reflections. However, their commentaries also revealed a clear understanding of the obstacles they face when trying to file a complaint with the state justice system:

> Sometimes men pay bribes to the employees [of the state justice system].
>
> Women who suffer violence have no money.
>
> They don't speak K'iche' in the mediation procedures.
>
> They discriminate against us because of our clothing.
>
> We don't have the courage to denounce, we're afraid men will take their revenge on us.

Their proposals also went beyond simply filing complaints with state institutions:

> Organize ourselves as women.
>
> Look for more training.
>
> Support victims with advice about how to make complaints.
>
> Attention to victims should be given by women.
>
> Train the men.

During the 1990s and 2000s civic associations such as ASDECO and Ixmucané had developed innovative proposals for addressing gender violence and injustice based to a large extent on strengthening the ancestral Maya K'iche' institutions and norms and holistic perspectives on health based on Mayan worldviews. However, dominant schemes of decentralization/participation in development and for combatting violence against women tended to keep the focus on state institutions. They also placed more emphasis on denouncing situations of acute crisis than on building and strengthening community and family-based mechanisms to prevent gender violence. Another important structural aspect is the problematic legacy of economic dependence on international development cooperation agencies and NGOs. Even the most innovative organizations such as ASDECO depended almost entirely on international funding in order to maintain their training programs and scholarships. After the 2011 elections, CASODI and ASDECO were left with practically no budget and were unable to support the work of the JDMM. Many of the workshops, training programs, and even support in filing legal complaints depended on external funds to finance projects. Other initiatives such as the plan to build a shelter for women and children in acute situations of domestic violence could not be implemented because of the chronic lack of resources affecting local organizations and associations (in this case, the government donated the land but expected NGOs to fund the shelter's operational expenses). In addition, after the end of the war it became common practice to make small cash payments in exchange for participation in activities or organizational processes, particularly those promoted by the state. ASDECO and CASODI had long identified this as problematic (CASODI 2003: 8), yet extreme poverty made it difficult to escape this systemic logic, presenting complex challenges for local organizational processes.

The Political Outcome of 2013

In January 2013 the municipal mayor's office in Chichicastenango was sacked by enraged villagers who accused the new mayor of misappropriation of funds. Rumor had it that Xon Cortez had received a large amount of money to improve a road, but the work was never carried out. The protestors not only pillaged the mayor's office, taking computers and other items; they also burned down his house. Xon Cortez had to leave town for several days while the central government sent in the National Civilian Police to restore order. Supporters of former mayor Tiriquiz were blamed for the disorder. The JDMM did not escape this political polarization. Because of the rumors that Xon Cortez wanted to disband the JDMM, the women leaders had confronted him at several meetings after his electoral victory. Subsequently, Zenaida and others, together with leaders from the municipal board of directors of the COCODEs who had supported Tiriquiz in his electoral campaign, were accused by Xon Cortez and his followers of having participated in the disturbances. They were summoned to the Public Prosecutor's Office to give their testimonies, although criminal charges were subsequently dropped. Political divisions and clientelism had effectively paralyzed the work of the JDMM. Under such conditions it was very difficult to advance the Municipal Gender Agenda. Rather, efforts focused on how to preserve the space for women's organization and participation.

Conclusions

Indigenous women's possibilities to frame their own organizational forms and demands depend on specific historical and political contexts, and their personal and collective trajectories. They also depend on prevailing schemes for improvement and forms of politics. In postwar Chichicastenango, discourses on indigenous people's rights, human rights, and women's rights were reappropriated and resignified within a dense network of community organization. New ideas circulated emphasizing women's right to live without violence and demanding that their dignity as human beings be respected; in some cases these were linked to discourses on Mayan identity highlighting the importance of respect and protection toward women. The shift toward "gender main-streaming" in public policies and the official focus on violence against women throughout the 2000s created new possibilities for developing a gender agenda at municipal level. Some analysts have pointed to Chichicastenango as a successful case where "civil society" was able to ensure its participation, in contrast to other municipalities where COMUDEs were entirely controlled by the mayor and the political parties that dominated the municipal council (Barrientos 2007). However, although local civic organizations did play a role in municipal development planning, the situation was more complex. Maya K'iche' women activists found themselves between a neoliberal development culture that emphasized their "participation" and more naked clientelist dynamics. Yet by combining their individual and collective experiences in different organizational processes over time and aligning themselves with local power holders, women leaders of the JDMM were able at least partially to advance an agenda to combat gender violence, an issue that is particularly difficult to address. In parallel with their use of discourses and mechanisms focusing on rights and state institutions, they also emphasized the intersectionality of violences affecting women and deployed other languages and ways of working, such as healing workshops focused on physical and emotional well-being. Instead of emphasizing "participation" alone, women's narratives continuously underline the structural inequalities that hinder their chances for a better present and future, pointing in turn to legacies of prior processes of community organization. After the war, "the local" became a fetish, but the control of public finances and policies remained in the hands of the national and international elites. Models of postwar participation centered on community and municipal development made no mention of the economic redistribution that was at the heart of the revolutionary project when entire villages in Chichicastenango demanded not only political but also economic and cultural citizenship.

NOTES

1. James Ferguson showed how the expansion of development programs to rural areas extended the bureaucratic reach of the state while depoliticizing poverty, the actions of the dominant elites, and the state itself (Ferguson 1994).

2. The peace agreements focused on guaranteeing basic human rights and the rights of the indigenous population, and in particular of indigenous women. The Agreement on the Identity and Rights of Indigenous Peoples (1995) included specific commitments to protect and promote the social and political participation of women as part of the broader guarantees to respect the collective rights of indigenous peoples to exercise greater autonomy. The Agreement on Socio-Economic Matters and the Agrarian Situation (1996) committed the government to promote gender equity and the economic participation of indigenous women.

3. The concept of social capital has been a central element of neoliberal social policies. In Latin America, the World Bank in particular has promoted "ethno-development" premised on indigenous peoples' "social capital" (see Andolina, Laurie, and Radcliffe 2009).

4. The improvement committees had their origins in the counterinsurgency policies of the 1980s; the army played a central role in organizing and coordinating development activities in conflict areas. Regarding the history of development councils prior to the 2002 reforms, see Macleod (1997).

5. The Agreement on Socio-Economic Matters and the Agrarian Situation appointed the Development Councils (which had existed previously but were suspended in 1988) as the mechanism to promote citizen participation in development.

6. According to the 2002 Municipal Code, the Municipal Council must recognize auxiliary mayors (now renamed community mayors) as representatives of indigenous communities, according to their uses, norms, and traditions. The auxiliary or community mayor is ratified in office by the municipal mayor based on the respective community's appointment or election according to its traditional norms. Auxiliary or community mayors represent the municipal authorities and are the link or communication channel between municipal authorities and the community's residents.

7. The Decentralization Law reflected ideas dominant in development frameworks in the postwar years, such as participatory democracy, cultural pluralism, and gender equity.

8. Congreso de la República de Guatemala, Ley de los Consejos de Desarrollo Urbano y Rural, decreto 11–2002, arts. 13 and 16.

9. To facilitate the operation of community councils in municipalities with many communities, a second-level community development council can be created, with the participation of more than twenty community development councils.

10. Both associations had their origins in the Foundation for Educational, Social and Economic Development, headquartered in Chichicastenango.

11. Dating to the nineteenth century, Guatemalan municipalities were characterized by the existence of two separate mayoralties, one indigenous and one ladino (non-indigenous mestizo). Indigenous mayoralties (*alcaldías indígenas*) continue to exist in Chichicastenango, Sololá, Totonicapán, and other municipalities throughout the country. Their form of authority derives from the traditions, customs, and worldviews of Mayan communities (Barrientos 2007: 77).

12. ASDECO also supported training for *chonabs*, the wives of the male authorities who made up the *alcaldía indígena* (ASDECO 2011: 20).

13. SEPREM was created as the Secretariat of the Presidency of the Republic, part of the executive branch. As an entity at the highest level of government, its main purpose is to advise and support the president about programs and projects to implement public policies for women's development that promote conditions of equity between men and women, in accordance with the social and cultural diversity of the nation (Acuerdo Gubernativo no. 130–2001, Reglamento Orgánico Interno de la Seprem, 9).

14. Article 176 of the 2002 Municipal Code states, "The concept of gender equity is understood as non-discrimination between both sexes according to . . . Article 4 of the Constitution." SEPREM advocated the mandatory inclusion of a municipal women's commission, but Congress changed this to include the family and children so that each municipal council must now have a Commission on the Family, Women, and Children.

15. In 1997 ASDECO promoted women's organizations, creating association groups in the communities to work on health issues; since 2000 they have promoted the

development of women's networks and the promotion and training of female leaders. A female board of directors was created, composed of seventeen representatives from each of the community networks (ASDECO 2011: 26).

16. In March 2013, the Presidential Secretariat for Women (SEPREM) and USAID announced a plan to strengthen eleven municipal women's offices in several municipalities. This was in tune with the policy of the government of former General Otto Pérez Molina (2012–2016) to establish "municipal agreements for security with equity" in order to "develop proposals and mechanisms for the prevention of violence against women at the municipal and community levels." Eleven locations were selected for this pilot project due to their high levels of violence against women ("SEPREM y USAID Fortalecen Oficinas Municipales de la Mujer," http://www.seprem. gob.gt/noticia.php?noticia=455).

17. Apart from those of elected state officials, all names have been changed.

18. Domestic violence is the most common reason indigenous women go to the police or state legal institutions. In 2004, 136 of the 147 cases of domestic violence processed by the courts were against women, 119 of them indigenous women. In 2005, 149 out of 226 reported cases of domestic violence were against indigenous women (DEMI 2007: 35–36).

19. Initial visits were only for the purpose of getting to know the women who had offered to give their testimonies. The recorded interviews were carried out only after several meetings, and they generally took place at the women's homes or those of a neighbor or relative. Lidia and I discussed the interviews, constantly adjusting the questions and the format. Our starting point was this: "How would you describe your problem? What did you do to resolve it? Who did you go to? What were the results?" When narrating "the problem," the women, especially the older ones, often told Berta their life story. The interviews were difficult, since the women's experiences were sad and traumatic, and Lidia often felt angry or frustrated, unable to provide more support. A workshop for the research team with a Colombian psychologist helped us to emphasize the validation of the experience and agency of survivors of violence, and also to reflect on how to process our own reactions.

20. See ASDECO 2011 for a detailed explanation of some of the healing techniques used in workshops in Chichicastenango.

21. Interview with Lic. Aída López Cordero, Human Rights Attorney's Office, Quiché, July 24, 2012.

22. According to current electoral legislation, candidates can be elected to the presidency or to the national congress only through a legally registered political party. However, in the case of municipalities, candidates for mayor and the municipal corporation may seek election through local civic committees.

23. In 2009, equipment and personnel were provided for an Office for the Attention to Victims at the headquarters of the National Civilian Police in Santa Cruz del Quiché.

24. The Centers for Integral Attention to Women Survivors of Violence (Centros de Atención Integral para Mujeres Sobrevivientes de Violencia, CAIMUS) were established in 2008 and are administered by the Guatemalan Women's Group (GGM), an NGO. The CAIMUS were included in the National Plan for the Prevention of Domestic Violence and Violence Against Women (PLANOVI 2004–2014) as an alternative response from feminist and women's organizations to address, prevent, and eradicate gender violence.

REFERENCES

Albó, Xavier. 2002. "Bolivia: From Indian and Campesino Leaders to Councillors and Parliamentary Deputies." In *Multiculturalism in Latin America: Indigenous Rights, Diversity and Democracy*, edited by Rachel Sieder, 74–102. New York: Palgrave Macmillan.

Andolina, Robert, Nina Laurie, and Sarah Radcliffe. 2009. *Indigenous Development in the Andes. Culture, Power and Transnationalism*. Durham, NC: Duke University Press.

ASDECO (Asociación de Desarrollo Comunitario). 2011. "Sistematización de la metodología 'Reconocimiento de nuestro ser.'" Unpublished document.

ASIES/OACNUDH. 2008. *Acceso de los pueblos indígenas a la justicia desde un enfoque de derechos humanos: Perspectivas en el derecho indígena y en el sistema de justicia oficial*. Guatemala: ASIES/OACNUDH.

Barrientos, Claudia Inés. 2007. *Participación ciudadana y construcción de ciudadanía desde los Consejos de Desarrollo. El caso de Chichicastenango*. Guatemala: Flacso-Guatemala.

CASODI. 2003. *Poder local, participación y descentralización. Lecciones aprendidas de CASODI*. Guatemala: CASODI/INCIDE/MAGA/RUTA, Editorial Serviprensa.

CEH (Comisión para el Esclarecimiento Histórico). 1999. *Guatemala: Memoria del Silencio. Tz'inil Na'Tab'Al*. Guatemala: Publicación de la Oficina de Servicios para Proyectos de las Naciones Unidas.

Consorcio Actoras de Cambio. 2009. *Rompiendo el silencio. Justicia para las mujeres víctimas de violencia sexual durante el conflicto armado en Guatemala*. Guatemala: FyG Editores.

DEMI. 2003. *Primer Informe: Situaciones y Derechos de las Mujeres Indígenas en Guatemala. Nabe' wuj ke ixoqib*. Guatemala: DEMI.

———. 2007. *Segundo Informe: El Acceso de las Mujeres Indígenas al Sistema de Justicia Oficial de Guatemala, Ukab' wuj ke ixoqib.'* Guatemala: DEMI.

ECAP-UNAMG (Equipo de Estudios Comunitarios y Acción Psicosocial; Unión Nacional de Mujeres Guatemaltecas). 2009. *Tejidos que lleva el alma. Memoria de mujeres mayas sobrevivientes de violación sexual durante el conflicto armado*. Guatemala: ECAP-UNAMG.

Elyachar, Julia. 2005. *Markets of Dispossession: NGOs, Economic Development, and the State in Cairo*. Durham, NC: Duke University Press.

Ferguson, James. 1994. *The Anti-politics Machine: "Development," Depoliticization, and Bureaucratic Power in Lesotho*. Minneapolis: University of Minnesota Press.

Li, Tania Murray. 2007. *The Will to Improve: Governmentality, Development, and the Practice of Politics*. Durham, NC: Duke University Press.

Macleod, Morna. 1997. *Poder local: Reflexiones sobre Guatemala*. Oxford: Oxfam UK and Ireland.

Macleod, Morna, and Josefa Xiloj Tol. 2011. "Justicia, dignidad y derechos colectivos. Acompañando a las comunidades y a la Alcaldía Indígena de Chichicastenango." In *Justicia y diversidad en América Latina. Pueblos indígenas ante la globalización*, edited by Victoria Chenaut, Magdalena Gómez, Héctor Ortiz, and María Teresa Sierra, 465–485. Mexico City: CIESAS.

McAllister, Carlota. 2003. "Good People: Revolution, Community, and *Conciencia* in a Maya-K'iche' Village in Guatemala." PhD diss., Johns Hopkins University, Baltimore.

Mendizábal, Beatriz, and Mercedes Asturias de Castañeda. 2010. *Políticas públicas sobre mujeres y equidad de género 1985–2009*. Guatemala: Programa de las Naciones Unidas para el Desarrollo.

ODHAG (Oficina de Derechos Humanos del Arzobispado de Guatemala). 1998. *Guatemala Nunca Más. III. El Entorno Histórico*. Guatemala: ODHAG.

PNUD (Programa de las Naciones Unidas para el Desarrollo). 2005. *Diversidad Étnico-Cultural: La Ciudadanía en un Estado Plural. Informe Nacional de Desarrollo Humano.* Guatemala: PNUD.

Schild, Verónica. 2000. "Neo-liberalism's New Gendered Market Citizens: The 'Civilizing' Dimension of Social Programmes in Chile." *Citizenship Studies* 4 (3): 275–305.

Sieder, Rachel, and Lidia Osorio de Cumatz. 2011. "Diagnóstico sobre Mujeres, Violencia Intrafamiliar y Acceso a la Justicia en Chichicastenango." Unpublished document.

Sieder, Rachel, and Morna Macleod. 2009. "Género, Derecho y Cosmovisión Maya en Guatemala." *Desacatos* 31: 51–72.

PART TWO

Indigenous Autonomies and Struggles for Gender Justice

4

Indigenous Autonomies and Gender Justice

Women Dispute Security and Rights in Guerrero, Mexico

MARÍA TERESA SIERRA

This chapter documents the process whereby women in the Community Police of the state of Guerrero have discussed gender justice and created a space for their participation in one of the most emblematic indigenous institutions in contemporary Mexico. Based on a collaborative research project, the text explores the cultural significance of women's grievances and complaints when discussing their customs and claiming their rights. It also highlights the trajectory of a group of outstanding women leaders, revealing the challenges they face when confronting a deeply rooted patriarchal order within their communal institution. In contrast to liberal understandings of women's subordination that homogenize gender inequalities, my analysis highlights the contextual and culturally constructed nature of female oppression and underlines the need to understand it in order to promote women's rights. By decentering discourses on indigenous law (*justicia propia*) through a gender perspective, women's demands confront colonial and racist discourses that often disqualify experiences of indigenous autonomy for their presumed exclusion of women. At the same time this decentering also questions hegemonic male narratives about the Community Police in Guerrero, which have rendered women's participation invisible. It also confirms that, for indigenous women, gender rights are strongly intertwined with the collective rights of their peoples. Through their practices, women contribute to a liberating vision of communal justice and indigenous rights distinct from western feminist conceptions of agency and emancipation.

> When they called me because of a crime committed by a young woman from Pueblo Hidalgo . . . the crime of infanticide . . . [the Community Police authorities] summoned a female representative from each organization . . . to a meeting. They wanted to hear the women's ideas. What

are we going to do with the woman who committed that kind of crime? What would you do? As women, how do you understand this case? Several of us participated. (Carmen Ramírez, justice promoter, San Luis Acatlán, Guerrero)

This is how Carmen Ramírez, a Me'phaa woman from Pueblo Hidalgo, municipality of San Luis Acatlán, Guerrero, narrated her involvement with the Regional Coordination of Communal Authorities (Coordinadora Regional de Autoridades Comunitarias—CRAC), when they decided to seek women's help with serious cases involving female detainees. This occurred shortly after the CRAC's decision to take on the task of administering justice and not just to provide security for the communities.[1] With direct and forceful words, Carmen recalled these events and recounted the reasons why women became involved in the institution from its inception. The need to respond to a complex issue related to the death of a newborn baby led to women's active participation in the *comunitaria*'s justice and security institutions.[2]

Some of the crimes the CRAC authorities confronted were not easily assessed from an exclusively male standpoint; by inviting women to participate in the task of administering justice, they opened alternatives to ensure that crimes committed by women were judged taking into account the context that led them to commit the crime. It has been far from easy to earn a place in this hypermasculine institution, where gender ideologies naturalizing women's subordination prevail. Nonetheless, women have not hesitated to respond to authorities' request for support in justice-related tasks, thus revealing their strong identification with the autonomous justice and security system itself.

Why do women devote themselves to the *comunitaria* even if male dominance prevails? How were they able to open a space for women's participation in an institution that has traditionally excluded them from collective decision making? How do they conceptualize gender violence, and in what sense does the discourse of rights provide them with alternatives to confront subordination? To what extent do women's trajectories in the *comunitaria* reveal the tensions between gender rights and collectives' rights? And, finally, what kind of security and justice constructs do these women elaborate, and what are their connections to the cultural and political imaginaries of indigenous people's autonomy?

In this chapter, I place the agency of indigenous women at the center of my analysis. My examination of this emblematic, pluri-ethnic experience of indigenous autonomy in Mexico pays close attention to language and cultural styles, analyzing the forms and local meanings of gender violence and women's responses to this. In their practice women continuously dispute male-established notions of rights, justice, and security within the institution. Their appeals to communal justice have opened new venues to vent their grievances without necessarily challenging the established gender order. It is impossible to understand the commitment of Me'phaa, Na'savi, and Mestizo women without taking into account the economic marginalization and social inequality that characterizes indigenous communities of Guerrero. At the same time, women's demands become legible only in the context of the collective dynamics and cultural traditions in which they are signified. Within these parameters women have been defining what "good treatment" means to them, which involves forms of life with greater dignity and less violence. Such notions challenge liberal views of gender justice (Molyneux and Razavi 2002) and demand an intersectional standpoint (Crenshaw 1991) to document the cumulative character of women's subordinations—gender, class, ethnicity—and to explore how women experience them. Speaking of indigenous women's rights therefore necessarily implies reconstructing the imaginaries they evoke in specific contexts.

Given the Community Police's uniqueness as an institution that exercises jurisdiction and de facto autonomy, indigenous women's efforts to open up spaces for gender rights endorse an emancipatory potential for the institution as a whole (Santos 2010). This involves an "ecology of knowledge"[3] that contributes to destabilizing patriarchal order and to challenging essentialist notions of indigenous law—the so-called *usos y costumbres*—seen as unchangeable traditions.

By examining this experience in dialogue with similar processes that have arisen in other parts of Mexico and Latin America (Lang and Kucia 2009; Sierra 2009; Sieder and McNeish 2012; FIMI 2006; Hernández and Canessa 2012; and the chapters in the present volume by Cervone and Cucurí, Lozano, and Arteaga), it is possible to identify the traits of specific forms of gender justice emerging in the context of indigenous people's autonomous processes. This chapter is based on the results of a collaborative research I developed with female justice promoters of the CRAC-PC in San Luis Acatlán, Guerrero, Mexico (2007–2011). It is structured as follows: I begin with a brief reflection on the collaborative work I did to support women's organization within the *comunitaria*. I then focus on two aspects that show different domains of women's agency regarding the promotion of women's rights: first, the engagement of these women, the justice promoters, in a Participatory Evaluation (*Diagnóstico*) to identify indigenous women's cultural constructions of grievance and their relation to gender violence, rights and access to justice. The aim of this evaluation was to establish the framework for a gender justice agenda within the CRAC. Second, I analyze the experiences of two justice promoters in order to highlight what it means for women to become an authority in this institution and the challenge they face throughout this process. Finally, I reflect on my personal experience in this collaborative work and its contribution to discussing indigenous women's rights and debates on community justice. Overall I aim to highlight the political and cultural significance of gender justice constructed within an emblematic experience of indigenous autonomy in Mexico.

Collaborative Research to Promote
Gender Justice: Methodological Notes

In March 2007, three women and four men were elected by a regional assembly
to participate in the administration of justice at the highest level of the *comunitaria*, the Regional Coordination of Community Authorities (CRAC) in San
Luis Acatlán, at that time the organization's only Casa de Justicia or House of
Justice. Carmen Ramírez Aburto, Teófila Rodríguez, and Catalina Rodríguez followed in the footsteps of Felicitas Martínez, the first female coordinator of the
comunitaria, all of them Me'phaa women. It was in this context that the CRAC's
coordinators, men and women, asked me to support women's organization
within the institution.[4] The background to this proposal was the initiative of
a group of women who in 2005 had created a commission to defend women's
rights. The chance to support this process was an extraordinary opportunity
for me, since it converged with my own research interests on gender justice
in the *comunitaria*. We discussed the importance of developing a collaborative project that began by identifying the problems experienced by women
in their communities and then went on to organize workshops about their
rights. I wanted to avoid imposing an external gender agenda, but at the same
time to take into account advances in national and international normative
frameworks conceived to guarantee a life free of violence for women.[5] I agree
with Macleod (2011: 174), who emphasizes the need to pay attention to the
manner in which these topics are addressed in order to avoid partial views of
the problems experienced by indigenous women. It was therefore essential
to distance ourselves from the vertical workshop styles with which women's
rights and topics related to gender violence in indigenous regions tend to be
promoted, which usually impose a liberal gender agenda without taking into
account the cultural and social contexts of women in the communities. We
decided to move in two directions: first, to create a group of promoters who
would be trained about gender rights and who would actively collaborate in
the participatory evaluation;[6] and second, to promote women's organization in their communities and workshops to be conducted by the promoters
themselves. Although men were not the main actors, several of them actively
contributed to this process and, most importantly, the CRAC's authorities supported our efforts, which was essential for carrying out the workshops in the
communities.

I have analyzed this process in other documents and in a video (Sierra
2013a), all of them resulting from the collaborative research project undertaken
with the justice promoters.[7] This chapter is based on the information derived
from this collaboration and highlights what this experience reveals about
debates surrounding community justice and security from the viewpoint of
indigenous women and their efforts to act on them.

Discussing Customs, Rights, and Women's
Access to Justice: A Participatory Evaluation

One of the main goals of the collaborative project was to discover, from the women's own standpoint, which grievances were most relevant, which paths they followed to address them, and the notions of rights and justice involved. The interest was to identify the cultural constructions of gender subordination that influence women's possibilities for accessing community justice. To this end, we conducted a participatory evaluation with a gender focus based on a model of popular education.[8]

The evaluation was a very productive way to reconstruct women's positions and outlooks on community life. Given the relevance of the methodology, I examine here some of the procedures and central issues addressed during the workshops, highlighting the dynamics that motivated women's interventions to talk about their problems. The active participation of the promoters was central to this endeavor.[9] The evaluation was carried out in two of the *comunitaria*'s founding communities: the Na'savi community of Buenavista, in the municipality of San Luis Acatlán, and the Me'phaa settlement of Santa Cruz del Rincón, in the municipality of Malinaltepec. Two workshops were organized in each community: one for the evaluation itself and another one to discuss the results.[10] A final workshop was carried out on March 10, 2009, at the CRAC headquarters in San Luis Acatlán specifically for the *comunitaria*'s authorities, that is, the regional coordinators and commanders, the councilors or past authorities, as well as community police officers.

The evaluation focused on three broad topics previously discussed with the promoters: customs, rights, and access to justice. These issues provided the basis for reconstructing understandings and practices that place women in a vulnerable condition, allowing us to identify grievances and to reflect on what having rights and access to justice meant for them. A detailed presentation of the results is beyond the scope of this chapter (see Corzo, Cruz, and Sierra 2009), but in order to exemplify the dynamics, I present the workshop held in one of the communities, the *ejido* of Buenavista.[11]

Evaluation and Workshop at Ejido de
Buenavista, San Luis Acatlán: Bad Customs

We arrived at the Buenavista community headquarters (*comisaría*) on January 31, 2009, to conduct the first workshop. We presented ourselves before the local authority (the *comisario*), who received us respectfully, confirmed his support, and showed us the space reserved for the activity: a large room on the ground floor of the *comisaría*, with columns on one side and a spectacular view of the mountains on the other side, open to the patio where the community's assemblies take place. While we waited to be received, the *comisario* was hearing the complaint of a woman who accused her husband of taking the document that allowed her to receive her monthly payments from the government's antipoverty program, Oportunidades.[12] As is typical in this community, the conversation between the authority and the women took place in the Tu'un Savi (Mixteco) language. In fact this case reflected precisely the subject of the workshop, so we decided to invite the woman to the two-day meeting, to which she agreed.

Buenavista is a Na'savi community, head of one of the most organized *ejidos* in the Mountain region, with considerable participation in the Community Police. This community was also the birthplace of renowned leaders of indigenous organizations such as the Consejo Guerrerense 500 Años de Resistencia Indígena (Guerrero Council 500 Years of Indigenous Resistance) and the Community Police itself, which is indicative of a long-standing organizational tradition. The workshop was attended by twenty-two women from the community of Buenavista and from nearby communities belonging to the *ejido*. We were surprised by the presence of five men from different communities, three of them *comisarios* from Jicamaltepec, Cerro Zapote, and Llano Silleta, members of the Buenavista *ejido*, who participated in the entire workshop, in contrast to the Buenavista *comisario*, who was not present. They had apparently turned up to accompany their wives and to find out which topics we would cover. We interpreted their presence as indicative of male caution, but it was also revealing of masculine control, which sought to keep watch over what women say. We initially feared that their presence would affect the workshop dynamics, and in a way it did create a bias in terms of the emphasis given to some points over others; however, I was surprised at the women's forcefulness and their determination not to be censored and to speak their mind. In the end, the men's participation enriched the discussions and allowed their viewpoints to be known regarding topics of great relevance to both women and men, although the women's standpoint prevailed. Most of the participants were not Spanish speakers, which meant that the promoters had to translate to Tu'un Savi and make efforts to generate trust in the dialogue. The workshop lasted two days, time enough to facilitate communication and the participation of both women and men. After discussing the general issues that make women's life difficult in the communities—problems related to health, education, lack of income, poor roads, and so on[13]—they identified three important topics to be examined in depth: (1) bad customs, (2) men do not allow women to participate, and (3) justice benefits men.

I examine here the topic of "bad customs" because it refers to women's principal concerns regarding their personal integrity within the family and the community. Three aspects of "bad customs" were underscored: (1) men think they can have many women, (2) bad customs such as witchcraft, and (3) gossip between the families and among women. These points refer to very delicate issues for women and men, which led to a lengthy discussion.

Men think they can have many women. It is usual to find men with more than one family, sometimes in the same community, although officially married to only one woman. A number of the cases that reach the CRAC at the Casa de Justicia of San Luis Acatlán are related to this topic. Instead of accusations against husbands for infidelity, the main complaint has to do with men abandoning their families and refusing to provide for their children, often in conjunction with domestic mistreatment. The case of Martina—the woman whose complaint we had heard at the *comisario* office—illustrates the chain of vulnerabilities and forms of violence to which indigenous women are exposed; these are concomitant with male domination and the marginal conditions experienced by families in communities. Martina had five small children, one of them a newborn. She said her husband constantly mistreated her and threatened to kick her out of their home, which was her in-laws' house, while he spent time with another woman outside the community without providing for their children, thus forcing her to live in very difficult conditions. But what made her decide to present her complaint to the Buenavista *comisario* was the fact that her husband took the document entitling her to government support through the Oportunidades antipoverty program, thereby denying her the cash benefits for her five children.

In other words, it was economic necessity as an abandoned woman with five children to provide for that motivated Martina to present her complaint to the authorities and eventually to share it with us. During the workshop she explained her case in Tu'un Savi, which led the promoters to speak of her situation and the defenselessness experienced by women like her, who—according to Paula—"don't know how to defend themselves, don't know their rights." In this case, Martina wanted her husband to pay alimony for her children and to return the Oportunidades identification document. She had already complained to the local *comisario* in the community of Río Iguapa, where she lives, and later to the *comisario* of Buenavista, the *ejido*'s seat, but they had failed to solve her problem. It was interesting that the men present at the workshop were aware of her case and mentioned a large number of abuses committed by her husband that had gone unpunished, thus indirectly criticizing both communities' authorities for their inaction. Given their unresponsiveness to her plight, they suggested that she take her complaint to the CRAC's headquarters in San Luis Acatlán, an idea that was strongly supported by the women promoters. The next day, Martina finally took her case to the CRAC. While this did not bring about significant changes in her situation, it did at least put greater pressure on her husband to refrain from mistreating her. This explains women's insistence on arguing that for "men to have other women" is a "bad custom." For Apolonia, a justice promoter, this also means "women don't know their rights" and that authorities "don't administer justice right and benefit men." Although Martina did not actually know her rights, the fact that she presented her complaint to the authorities and dared to make her case public in the workshop revealed her courage in seeking a solution to her situation, which triggered the women's support.

Another issue discussed was the bad custom of "bewitching" women who "meddle in other people's affairs by supporting other women." This tends to happen when women, such as the promoters themselves, accompany other women victims of violence to present a complaint and as a result are the object of gossip. "Bewitching" (echar brujo) is a deep-rooted practice in these communities that functions as a mechanism of internal control and dissuasion. This explains the promoters' proposal that they be officially recognized by the community's assembly in order to avoid being harassed. As an example, Apolonia recounted the time when a neighbor threw rocks at her house because she had accompanied his wife to the authorities. Paula also narrated the harassment she suffered after accompanying a neighbor who had been beaten: "they told us, who are you, you're not authorities [to get involved] . . . they drove by in a pickup truck, shouting at Paty, Apolonia, and me: Those women are busybodies!" These recurring complaints reflect the fact that women who dare accompany other women victims of violence are highly vulnerable if they do not have the support of communal authorities.

Gossip was also a priority in discussions in both communities, identified as a "bad custom" that severely harms families because it usually aims at slandering women, creating mistrust and violence. The issue of gossip led to intense participation by both men and women to discuss what Enedina called chismerío ("tittle-tattle") about women who go out to participate, as can be observed in the following interaction between Bonifacio and Apolonia:

B: [Men] give them freedom . . . and the women don't appreciate it because other men come and they start speaking nicely to them and then they go off somewhere [with them]. . . .

A: I have to speak up here, part of what Bonifacio says is right and part is wrong. What he's saying, well it depends on the woman if your husband gives you the freedom to go to meetings. . . . But it depends on you, one thing is freedom, another is licentiousness . . . it depends on you . . . you have to respect your husband if there's good love and care, you have to respect him.

Here women's "bad behavior" is identified as licentiousness, which makes people speak badly of them. This kind of gossip disqualifying women who leave the confines of their homes to participate in community affairs elicited a firm response from Apolonia, who is not only a midwife, but also since 2011 the coordinator of the Indigenous Women's Home (CAMI)[14] in San Luis Acatlán and as such has personally experienced this kind of gossip. The interaction also reveals Apolonia's discursive style, a direct and affirmative manner in which she expresses her refusal to be intimidated from stating her point of view and her refutation of Bonifacio's statement.

The elements identified as "bad customs" in the workshop are of great concern to women and reveal mechanisms of internal control that aim to demobilize them. They led to an intense discussion among the women, who were very interested in looking for alternatives. As a result, several of them suggested developing workshops on gossip and not only on women's rights. But they especially insisted on the need for public recognition of women who accompany other women, subsequently developing a proposal to have female justice promoters elected in every community who could support the local *comisario* when dealing with women's issues.

I will not examine here other problems analyzed during the workshop in Buenavista—women's participation and lack of access to justice; both confirmed the obstacles and gender exclusions faced by women in community assemblies and in their access to justice, because authorities tend to favor men when mediating disputes.[15] The problems discussed here underscore women's desire to stop being mistreated or slandered without questioning established gender roles. They reveal the central role played by women promoters, who despite the criticism dare to accompany their neighbors to the authorities, although they do demand recognition from the community's assembly to keep from being harassed. The men's participation in the workshops reflects male vigilance, but also a certain willingness to listen to women's complaints. As a Na'savi woman observed during the evaluation, "Men also want workshops, but it's not my fault there aren't any for them."[16]

One of the central aims of the workshops in both communities—Buenavista and Santa Cruz—was to discuss women's conceptions of rights.[17] Rather than definitions, we were interested in identifying their contextual meanings. It was surprising to observe how some women confused rights with what we perceived as duties, like one Na'savi woman from Buenavista who stated that her right was "to prepare the food for her children and her husband," while one of the men who were present said that "a woman's right is to go fetch her husband when he's drunk," a statement that was not too surprising for the women, although it did evoke some laughter. The need to work on the topic of women's rights became evident, emphasizing a holistic understanding in order to stress the fact that demanding rights does not imply neglecting duties, a distinction that the women promoters have deemed fundamental for their own workshops in communities.

For Rosa, a woman who participated in the workshop in Santa Cruz, the practice of rights is differentiated by gender: "We are afraid of participating, we have to have courage. We have to know our rights; nobody knows their rights because of ignorance or fear. How far will things go, even if they see us beaten because we have no rights? Women aren't allowed to go out, they don't have the right to, men do." The need to differentiate women's rights and duties as part of their domestic unit from their needs in terms of personal integrity also became evident. At the Santa Cruz workshop women stressed the importance of supporting their husbands' commitments to communal activities, revealing notions of complementary between gender roles as members of a domestic unit; such is the case, for example, with feeding detainees undergoing reeducation (a task related to the *comunitaria* justice system), accompanying their husbands in the rituals and ceremonies that are part of their responsibilities as authorities, providing food during community assemblies, and so on. The issue of single or abandoned women and their difficulties in complying with community commitments such as financial contributions was also discussed. Many other problems related to violence, abandonment, alcoholism, and debts motivated heated discussions.

The methodology we used to analyze the problems was very productive to motivate women to participate and proved central to generating trust and interest, eliciting qualitative information that would have otherwise been very difficult to obtain. The model was based on a tree diagram that provided a metaphor for analyzing problems by identifying the causes (the tree's roots) and the consequences (the branches) related to them (see Corzo, Cruz, and Sierra 2009). A fundamental achievement of the workshops was the production of local knowledge in a dialogical manner framed in the women's own language and cultural styles.

In short, the workshops conducted in the two communities generated highly valuable materials from an emic perspective that uncovered women's feelings regarding fundamental problems that affect their integrity. They also revealed that meanings are contextual and embedded in cultural models that define gender roles, as is the case with the notions of duties and rights distributed by sex. This also points to the multiple subordinations experienced by women, which determine the way they live, the grievances they identify, and the solutions they seek. Those grievances and solutions cannot be viewed from an a priori standpoint of gender subordination without taking into account the worldviews and structural marginalization that characterize the lives of indigenous women, intersecting issues of gender, class, and ethnicity. Undoubtedly, these contexts aggravate the exclusions and obstacles women face to gain access to justice and confront gender violence, thus revealing the severe insufficiencies of community justice. Nevertheless, for the women and men present in the workshops, talking about their problems, analyzing them, and identifying some alternatives to facilitate access to justice have had a liberating effect that has to be underlined. There is still much work to be done to ensure that women's rights become central to the communitarian system and that the progress made to integrate women into the regional body of justice and security is also reflected at community level. The experiences of women who have reached positions of authority at the CRAC in San Luis Acatlán illustrate the significance of this process and their stakes as justice promoters.

Rethinking Community Justice and Security from the Perspective of Indigenous Women

Women's participation in the administration of justice within the *comunitaria* is especially important because of their attempt to influence an institution that confronts state power and implements a counterhegemonic model of security and justice (Sierra 2013b), while questioning deeply rooted patriarchal power. Although women's organization in the *comunitaria* is still weak, the very fact that they are occupying positions of authority reveals the dynamic nature of indigenous law, something that has deep implications for discussions about gender justice within autonomous indigenous jurisdictions. By examining the testimonies of some of the women appointed to positions of authority within the CRAC, I am interested in highlighting the gender tensions they face as these collective spaces open up to their participation. I base my analysis on the testimonies of two women leaders whose experiences in the *comunitaria* have left a mark on the institution: Felicitas Martínez and Carmen Ramírez. Despite the differences in their trajectories, they reveal their courage in confronting the various faces of gender subordination, their commitment to the *comunitaria*, and a critical view of locally instituted sex/gender models. Their participation as justice promoters has allowed them to amplify their role in the institution, which is also one of the achievements of the collaborative project. Likewise, the participatory evaluation served to spark a personal and critical reflection on women's rights.

Felicitas Martínez: Betting on a Different Justice for Women

As emphasized above, women have participated in the *comunitaria* since its inception, as a women's commission working on various tasks: first in 1999, supporting the CRAC, and later in 2005, promoting women's organization.[18] However, it was not until February 2006 that they were finally included in the administration of justice and elected as CRAC coordinators in the Regional Assembly. According to Felicitas Martínez, the first woman appointed as coordinator of the Regional Security and Justice System,

> Only in February 2006 was a woman finally administering justice. Before that there were women companions in the comunitaria, but they were invisible to justice. . . . Yes, there were very experienced women leaders assisting with security, but they did not administer justice, because after

all the Assembly has to authorize it, . . . if the assembly doesn't elect you, you're not in the decision making, because decisions are made by the justice board, . . . but it isn't easy, you don't have the full support of your male colleagues, it's a minority, it's an everyday struggle between the women and their male colleagues. [Women's participation] makes a big difference because there's more trust with the women, there are closer relations because women value you more. We are there to listen to both versions . . . to see who is in error, not only to support women.[19]

Felicitas emphasized women's daily struggle to address issues that concern them in a space dominated by men, such as the CRAC. Their participation entails new ways of administering justice, which implies earning the trust of the women involved in complaints or offenses so they feel free to state their grievances, without however losing sight of errors they may have committed. In her testimony, Felicitas emphasizes that rather than tipping the scales of justice in favor of women, this is about exercising justice in a way that considers the versions of men and women.

Felicitas Martínez is a thirty-six-year-old Me'phaa woman from the community of Potrerillo Cuapinole, San Luis Acatlán, and currently the single mother of a five-year-old girl. She was able to study law at the University of Guerrero in Chilpancingo due to enormous personal efforts, making her an exceptional case in the context of the women in the *comunitaria*. Through the Guerrero Coordination of Indigenous Women—a regional organization of indigenous women—she has long participated in organizational processes related to the defense of indigenous rights in Guerrero, and of indigenous women's rights in particular.[20] Above all, Felicitas stands out for her eloquence and self-confidence when speaking to any audience, both within and outside her region. She has significant experience in regional, national, and international indigenous women's organizations, which has considerably broadened her perspectives and has given her access to knowledge about women's rights. For that reason, her interest in participating in local processes rooted in her own region and to promote women's involvement is particularly noteworthy. In her position as regional coordinator at the headquarters for San Luis Acatlán, she had to devote her efforts to the justice-related tasks of the CRAC, which implied an almost complete commitment in terms of her availability and time. Felicitas is the only woman to have been appointed coordinator for three different periods (one year in 2006, a few months in late 2010, and five months in 2012), which reflects both her commitment and her local legitimacy.

But what type of justice do women exercise, and to what extent does it reveal gender sensitivities that contribute to more adequate justice for women? Felicitas's following testimony offers some glimpses:

We had the case [at the CRAC] of a Mixteca woman from Tlacochistlahuaca, her husband always got home drunk, insulted her, beat her . . . , and the worst thing we saw was that she had a daughter that was hers, not her partner's, a two-year-old girl. I talked to her and she told me. The man admits that he did hit the girl, "I didn't hit her hard, I only slapped her in the face twice," the girl sat close to her mother and didn't look at him again. I told the woman, "the girl was fine with your mom, she gave her love and attention, why did you fetch her [to live with you] if you knew he wasn't going to love her as her father? Because fathers forgive everything, but he's not her father."[21]

This case highlights Felicitas's concern as a woman and mother in her attempt to understand not only the issue of the man's mistreatment of the woman, but also its effects on the child. Through these reflections, Felicitas reveals the everyday dramas experienced by women suffering domestic violence. These cases require the personal involvement of the coordinators, both men and women, in the face of difficult situations, which in this particular case implied trying to determine how to reeducate someone who is capable of hitting a two-year-old child.

Felicitas's experience as an authority figure implies an enormous emotional commitment that is not always easy to deal with. Both men and women in positions of authority are of course equally exposed to people's everyday dramas, but the ways they process them seem to be influenced by gender, in the sense that women tend to approach problems from a more holistic perspective (Arteaga 2013). This also explains the female coordinators' interest in caring for women detainees' health when they have been victims of violence, regardless of the crime committed. It is therefore common for the female coordinators to personally check on the women and, when necessary, take them to the health center to be cared for, as I was able to witness on several occasions. At the same time, the experience of administering justice and hearing people's testimonies, especially women's, strongly affects them. The emotional burden of having to listen to people's dramas and deliberate on them is not discussed within the spaces of community justice, but the women develop their own survival strategies.[22] In that respect, Felicitas says, "When I was in the CRAC I wanted to vent my feelings but I kept everything inside, I would go to the Internet but that didn't help unburden my mind."[23] In effect, for Felicitas, dealing with very complex situations every day is a great responsibility, and the impact is perhaps greater because many situations involve gender violence and are sometimes not very different from problems she herself has experienced.

The tendency to seek negotiated solutions has its limits in cases of rape, something that is very clear to Felicitas, but not so to the other coordinators (including some of the women): if the parties come to an agreement—usually the parents of the young couple involved—negotiated solutions that involve payment for the "damage" or the promise of marriage are often accepted.

Felicitas has been quite firm in questioning such arrangements in cases of rape, thus criticizing long-standing practices in community justice.

In spite of the personal costs for a woman participating in a male space such as the CRAC, because of the gossip involved and the implications for their spouses, the deep commitment of women like Felicitas to their position of authority is remarkable: "I am proud of my people for participating in the CRAC, but let me tell you it isn't easy being in this system as a woman. I would like to see more women participating. . . . [There have been] 16 years of the Community Police, there has been bloodshed, harassment, detentions . . . it hasn't been easy being an authority. My knowledge, what I've learned about justice, I owe it to the CRAC. . . . I still have a very big challenge, my dream of preparing new women leaders who are convinced of this project."[24] With these words, Felicitas synthesized the collective and personal dimensions that involve her in the *comunitaria* project, disputing her place as a woman, proud to be a member of the institution, and at the same time aware of what confronting the state has meant in political terms. She thus reveals the links that tie her to the collective process, stressing her personal growth in the administration of justice but above all her commitment to promote women's participation in the institution, which remains one of her main long-term projects.

Carmen Ramírez Aburto: The Strength of Commitment

Finally, I examine the testimony of Carmen Ramírez Aburto, perhaps the most emblematic woman in the *comunitaria*, whose presence has marked the institution since its inception. Although Carmen had little formal education—she completed only fourth grade of elementary school—she participated in different organizations such as the Rural Association of Collective Interest, but especially in the *comunitaria*, to which she devoted eight years of her life, sacrificing even her family, as she emphasized in several interviews and conversations. A Me'phaa woman born in Pueblo Hidalgo, Carmen has four daughters and one son and currently lives with her partner, after spending several years as a single mother. Not only was her participation in the *comunitaria* vital in the beginning when she was part of the women's commission to support the CRAC, conceiving ideas for reeducation; she has also participated in protection, detention, and security tasks without being assigned to a specific position to that end. Carmen's courage was tested on several occasions during operations to detain people together with community policemen.

> I know what it means to be in an operation, . . . no commander is going to deceive me telling me how an operation is done. . . . We arrived there . . . we went to look for the individual who had killed [the person], he was under some trash, there were banana leaves covering him, there he was and we had to surround him from a distance, each of us with our

weapons, and he came out, I think if we hadn't been ready he would have shot Commander Luis. He got up, came out of the trash, grabbed his M1 and shot in the commander's direction, and I jumped on him from behind. . . . I've been in a tough operation![25]

With courage and resolve, Carmen narrated her experience as part of the Community Police. She is in fact one of the few women who has participated in security tasks, which are usually performed exclusively by men, revealing both her audacity and her deep commitment to the institution. There are several accounts that demonstrate how she risked her own physical integrity, even successfully detaining a prisoner who had escaped. Even after the trauma she experienced when her two-year-old daughter died while she was performing her duties at the *comunitaria*, she continued participating. Carmen acknowledges that in those difficult moments she received considerable emotional and institutional support from her colleagues; because of that, she does not hesitate in praising the CRAC's solidarity and support, essential for her to overcome her pain. Later, Carmen was elected regional coordinator together with two other women—Catalina Rodríguez and Teófila García—in February 2007. I had the opportunity to share in and accompany the process of justice administration at the *comunitaria* during that period and especially to observe the women's work. Carmen in particular kept going to the Casa de Justicia every day and participating in the complex assignments they had to perform at the time, while simultaneously fulfilling her duties as a mother. She also paid close attention to kitchen and cleaning tasks at the CRAC's headquarters and made efforts to guarantee the security and health of women detainees during that period. She obtained monetary support from local market vendors to provide food for the community police and on several occasions even prepared it herself. In her role as coordinator, she participated in tours to follow up on the situation of detainees in reeducation to ensure that they were liberated when they completed their sentence and to address justice-related cases presented to the CRAC. I personally witnessed and accompanied all of this. For this reason, I was greatly surprised when, in a regional assembly in the community of Horcasitas, several CRAC authorities were dismissed, the women included. The accusations laid against them were never proven, and they had a severe effect on the women, more so than on the men. Similar cases of groundless accusations have occurred at various times within the CRAC without resulting in the authorities' dismissal. For the women this was a very tough blow, and it is yet another example of gender bias in the *comunitaria*, since women are more strictly controlled and punished than men. Beyond the fact of the injustice itself, I am interested in recording Carmen's testimony of what that experience meant for her:

Because of a mistake committed by the former coordinators, [the detainee] ended up with us, they didn't respect the agreement [between] the Public Prosecutor's Office [and the *comunitaria*] and they took on the case, which was already there [at the Public Prosecutor's Office]. The family put pressure on us. They had a big problem with me. On July 7 [2007], [the Assembly] said "we want the women out." . . . Women's participation [in the justice board] was dismantled, I don't know what happened to the councilors. Why does that happen? Because we're women! The comisarios, the policemen have made many mistakes and no one says anything. Oh, but with the women it's different: out with the women! I was really hurt. . . . At that moment I told myself that I would never return to the CRAC: I lost a child, I abandoned my daughters, all of it to support the people, and all of this happened.[26]

In the end, Carmen was a victim of conflicts between different factions within the CRAC, which in her case meant disregarding her commitment to the institution. Because of that, when I accompanied the female justice promoters to present the work we had been developing to the recently appointed CRAC authorities in April 2010, they were all deeply hurt when the new regional coordinators requested to see their justice promoter IDs: "We want to know who appointed you as justice promoters. Where are your credentials?" More than an understandable caution as authorities, this was an unfriendly gesture (to say the least) directed against all of us, myself included, resorting to unnecessary formalities in order to disqualify the women's work and emphasize the new power relations within the CRAC. Although the new coordinators later attempted to attenuate this unfortunate action, it left a deep mark and points to the offenses faced by women when trying to legitimize their work in the institution.[27]

In spite of everything, Carmen is still a very important figure for the *comunitaria*. Her experience has been central for elaborating alternative proposals for women, especially in the field of reeducation and community security.[28] In this respect, she made the following assessment of the role of female justice promoters:

Maybe we weren't able to make that much progress [as promoters] because there was a lot of gossip, and the gossip sometimes makes us believe that we're weak. There were several things that damaged us [including] slander and gossip. But that doesn't mean we're going to give up, on the contrary, we have to make an effort . . . as justice promoters. That's why it's so important for there to be more women [at the CRAC board of justice]. . . . Because we have to fight for a space where women can take care of women's cases. Yes, we need more women to look after the female detainees.[29]

In spite of the difficulties female justice promoters have had in consolidating themselves as a group, Carmen is very clear about the reasons why women's presence in the various tasks of the *comunitaria* is essential: "Our proposal is to have two female delegates from each community. Just like there are male policemen, there have to be female police officers, there have to be female commanders . . . because I have daughters, and I can't agree if a policeman disrespects a female detainee, as women it hurts us to see a female detainee abused. I think the proposal of appointing female delegates is important. . . . We have to go to the communities . . . there have to be female police officers, that's what's missing [in the CRAC]."[30] Carmen keenly expressed the importance of women's participation at all levels of the communal justice and security system. Her critical outlook derives from her own experience and has been fundamental in generating changes within the CRAC. The deeply rooted imaginary of community police officers as exclusively male has been decentered by the experience of women like Carmen. It is through practice that women are redefining the roles and tasks of the communitarian system from a gender perspective, even though this intervention is not yet legitimized.

In short, committed female leaders in the *comunitaria* have developed an internal critique, exposing the gender inequities that exclude them and yet continuing to defend the communal project against threats from the state. The female promoters do not have a solid mandate that allows them to consistently promote women's participation. And yet they continue making headway even with frequent setbacks, significantly enriching the *comunitaria*'s project. The gender identities they assert are therefore intimately related to the collective identities of their peoples, without which their struggle as women in the institution would be impossible.

Conclusions: Redefining Justice and Rights from the Perspective of Indigenous Women

This chapter has analyzed the results of a collaborative research project whose main objective was to support indigenous women in their demands for gender rights within the Community Police of Guerrero. This project provided a privileged vantage point for understanding the problems women face when seeking justice, revealing the intimate texture and everyday drama of their lives, but also their commitments to an institution that has afforded them dignity. I agree with Charles Hale (2008)[31] about the highly productive role of collaborative research and its implications for anthropological knowledge because it permits a deeper understanding of fundamental issues relevant to the social actors involved. I have been following the communal justice and security system in Guerrero for many years (Sierra 2009, 2010, 2013a, 2013b, 2013c), but my work with the female justice promoters has undoubtedly been the most significant space to which I have had access; it has allowed me to perceive the complexities involved in the *comunitaria*'s efforts to open venues for women's rights. But particularly I have had the privilege of getting to know incredible women who shared with me not only their lives but also their decisions to support other women who do not know that "they have rights," as Paula Silva stated. The idea of not having rights, together with the coupling of "rights and duties," was in fact a subtext that emerged in the discussions we had with the promoters of justice, the women involved in the research.

Gaining access to indigenous women's own notions of gender violence, rights, and justice constituted the main research challenge. In this respect the evaluation (*diagnóstico*) motivated women in the communities to participate in the workshops, sharing sensitive and complex issues that involved their personal lives. Instead of starting from abstract concepts regarding gender roles and legally established rights, we ensured that the women themselves named the problems that were relevant to them, taking into account their own contexts and worldviews. A wide range of issues was brought forward that revealed multiple subordinations: the marginalization and structural inequality of indigenous communities has a direct effect on the way women experience gender subordination. From an intersectional perspective gender violence cannot be understood in isolation from other social and cultural determinants that affect women's lives. In the face of problems such as mistreatment, abandonment by men, bad customs such as gossip and slander, and the fact that men can have other women, our analysis tried to identify the meaning of those grievances for women, reconstruct the ways in which they affected their dignity, and put into relief the actions women proposed to confront them. For example, rather than discussing forms of domestic violence, they emphasized the importance of having the support of other women when taking their complaints to the authorities, hence the importance of obtaining formal recognition as female justice promoters from the local community assembly. This type of concrete action, where the personal dimension is linked to collective action, can have a greater impact on reducing gender violence than appealing to abstract rights that are unattainable in the context of indigenous communities.

A cultural gender policy defined from the perspective of indigenous women necessarily will have to link the material and cultural dimensions of life (Hernández 2010; Mejía 2010) when speaking of rights. Indigenous women's expectations cannot be separated from social reproduction and access to resources that restrict them or the cultural models that define their worldviews. Notions of "good treatment" for women in the *comunitaria* include a critique of "bad customs"—gossip, violence, and abuse—and, most important, creating spaces for women's participation, without necessarily challenging male hegemony. Women's desires and aspirations develop in their cultural and social contexts. Mahmood's (2008) misgivings about judging women's expectations in the context of non-Western cultures are important references for the discussion of indigenous women's grievances and demands.[32] It is a matter not just of "vernacularizing" gender rights (Merry 2006) to translate them into local needs, but rather of identifying the conditions that hinder or make it possible to demand rights. If we are to contribute to reducing gender violence and promoting national and international laws for the protection of women against violence, we need to understand the significance of grievances in their local contexts before imposing external agendas that hinder the possibilities for social change. In the case of indigenous women in the *comunitaria*, this necessarily involves being part of a grassroots institution that has provided them with new horizons as indigenous peoples and the possibility to conceive their rights as women. This is what the justice promoters' life experience and testimonies show.

The research discussed in this chapter has revealed a number of key analytical elements. First, indigenous women's agency and their histories of participation in the CRAC point to the important role they have played throughout the history of the *comunitaria* and the ways in which they have enriched the justice and security model. In spite of the difficulties and obstacles they have encountered, women have been able to open spaces, albeit still marginal, in the CRAC's security and justice system, questioning in practice the gender ideologies that subordinate them. Second, like indigenous women in other contexts, the women of the *comunitaria* continuously faced the dilemma of subordinating their rights as women to defend the collective rights of an institution that is under constant attack by the state. The very dynamics of the system highlight women's role in addressing security and justice issues that men cannot resolve. In their role as members of the women's committee, coordinators, commanders, or justice promoters, women have earned their place in the CRAC, which also explains why their gender identities as women are intimately related to their collective identities. Third, women's participation in the *comunitaria* system has significantly enriched the indigenous justice model. Their mere presence does not guarantee access to justice with gender equity, but it has brought about important changes because of the fact that women are addressing other women's demands. Women authorities have also introduced a different style of dispensing justice and conducting reeducation. Their practices set in motion a holistic model of justice centered on the woman's body in both its physical and emotional dimensions. This also reveals the close relationship between justice, health, and violence as a necessary referent for discussing indigenous women's rights, an issue that was recurrent during the workshops. Without reflecting on the subject, women in the CRAC have put in practice an idea of healing, as other indigenous women have done in different contexts (Sieder and Macleod 2009). Fourth, the improvements achieved through the women's presence in the communitarian security and justice system, albeit limited, are especially relevant in the context of an emblematic institution for indigenous peoples of Mexico. Women's participation as authorities points to the emancipatory potential of indigenous justice regarding the efforts to respect both human and women's rights. Fifth, advances at the level of regional justice need to be more consistent in order to guarantee women's participation at the local level including community justice. There is still much to be done at this level to ensure women's access to adequate justice, as the women themselves expressed during the workshops. In both spaces (regional and communal), deeply rooted patriarchal customs, which tend to favor men, prevail in the exercise of authority. One of the biggest challenges faced by the female justice promoters is consolidating their place in the CRAC's regional system while creating spaces for women's participation in local power structures.

New obstacles have arisen due to the increase in violence and threats to the *comunitaria*'s territory from external factors, such as drug cartels, mining companies, and new forms of state control at the national and local levels. But the principal challenge is due to the internal conflicts that are fragmenting the system, as part of this cumulative process of violence and insecurity, which once again brings into relief the dilemma of women's place. It remains to be seen whether indigenous women's participation will be consolidated or diminished in the context of the new challenges faced by the indigenous peoples of Guerrero.

NOTES

1. The Community Police force was formally created on October 15, 1995, to combat the insecurity and violence that plagued the communities, while the state's inaction fostered impunity. Twenty-seven communities from three Na'savi, Me'phaa, and Mestizo municipalities from the Coastal-Mountain region of Guerrero joined forces to create security patrols. In February 1998, they decided to stop handing over detainees to the Public Prosecutor's Office, and to create their own institution for the administration of justice—the Regional Coordination of Communal Authorities (CRAC). Hence the Regional System of Community Security, Justice, and Reeducation was born (see Sierra 2013b).

2. The term *comunitaria* is used here to refer to the community security and justice system as a whole, in other words, both the Community Police (security forces) and the CRAC (administration of justice), known collectively by their Spanish acronym as "CRAC-PC."

3. For Santos, "ecology of knowledge" implies making visible and giving value to other knowledge unknown to hegemonic, Western knowledge; here I use the term to refer to the various forms of signifying rights and gender.

4. The project was called Indigenous Women and Access to Justice: The Women of the Community Police of Guerrero, sponsored at first by the Tides-Angélica Foundation (December 2008–December 2010) and later by the collective project that gave rise to this book.

5. See especially the General Law on Women's Access to a Life Free of Violence (2007). Available in English at http://www.summit-americas.org/brief/docs/Law_on_access_to_a_life_free_violence.pdf.

6. In total, eight women participated as justice promoters, several of whom had considerable organizational experience, including Felicitas Martínez, Catalina García,

Carmen Ramírez, Apolonia Plácido, Inés Porfirio, Paula Silva Florentino, and Enedina Galindo. I would like to thank them all for their commitment to the project's development. Úrsula Hernández also participated as a research assistant. At the time of writing (mid-2015), in a context of crisis experienced by the communal institution due to different internal and external factors, the group of justice promoters has ceased to function as such.

7. Some of the project's intermediary products are an informational brochure (Hernández and Sierra 2009), a video on women's participation (Sierra 2013a), and a book in progress on the collaborative research project with the women (see also Sierra 2009).

8. I would like to thank Imelda Cruz and Janette Corzo, from Jk'optik Association in Chiapas, whose contributions were central to facilitate and systematize the evaluation and the workshops.

9. Part of these dynamics can be seen in the video that resulted from the collaborative effort (Sierra 2013a).

10. The initial workshops took place from January to May 2009; based on the results, we later conducted a second phase of the collaborative research, which continued to May 2011.

11. *El Ejido* is a rural property for public use and includes a forest, land, and waters recognized by the Mexican agrarian law. The *Ejido* is a legal entity and in the case of Guerrero includes several communities united by the agrarian structure of the *Ejido* (https://es.wikipedia.org/wiki/Ejido).

12. Oportunidades is a federal program to support low-income female heads of household, who receive a certain amount of money according to the number of children they have enrolled in school.

13. A central aspect of the evaluation was to identify the main problems faced in the communities, which led to a reflection on the structural conditions of life and the environment. This revealed extreme material scarcities and severe deficiencies in the fields of health, education, and work (see Corzo, Cruz, and Sierra 2009).

14. CAMI was established in San Luis Acatlán in 2011 as part of the federal program led by the Commission for the Development of Indigenous Peoples (CDI) and the Secretariat of Health.

15. The dynamics generated in these spaces were recorded in the video mentioned above (Sierra 2013a).

16. Intervention translated from Tu'un Savi by Paula Silva.

17. During the workshop at Santa Cruz del Rincón, four topics were discussed: the lack of adequate justice for women, mistreatment, obstacles to exercising their rights, and gossip (see Corzo, Cruz, and Sierra 2009).

18. In 2005, the women's board was established for the first time, in a Regional Assembly held in Pueblo Hidalgo, San Luis Acatlán.

19. Interview by the author, June 10, 2011.

20. Felicitas Martínez's life story is narrated in Espinosa, Dircio, and Sánchez (2008).

21. Interview by the author during a meeting of promoters, June 10, 2011.

22. Ana Cecilia Arteaga also underscores the holistic vision that characterizes women's styles of administering justice in the CRAC, in particular the role of emotions and the alternative strategies applied when addressing cases (Arteaga 2013).

23. Interview by the author, June 10, 2011.

24. Ibid.

25. Interview by the author, April 18, 2008.

26. Interview by the author, July 21, 2011.

27. In the end the justice promoters received formal approval to continue with their activities in the Regional Assembly held in Jolotichán, San Luis Acatlán (September 10, 2010).

28. Reeducation is the last phase of the process of justice administration in the *comunitaria*: through social labor, detainees are expected to make up for the harm they caused.

29. Interview by the author, July 21, 2011.

30. Women's roundtable at the sixteenth anniversary of CRAC in Paraje Montero, October 15, 2011.

31. See also Leyva, Burguete, and Speed 2008.

32. Mahmood's (2008) research on Muslim women reveals that their notions of grievance, dignity, and autonomy differ radically from the liberal views of gender equality proposed by Western feminists, whose categories of emancipation and agency are questioned for their colonial gaze.

REFERENCES

Arteaga Böhrt, A. C. 2013. "'Todas somos la semilla.' Ser mujer en la policía comunitaria de Guerrero. Ideologías de género, participación política y seguridad." Master's thesis, CIESAS, Mexico City.

Canaval, B. 2008. "Mujeres de la Montaña de Guerrero. Nuevas actoras sociales." In Hernández, *Etnografías e historias de resistencia*, 361–414.

Corzo, J., I. Cruz, and M. T. Sierra. 2009. "Diagnóstico participativo con enfoque de género en dos comunidades de la policía comunitaria de Guerrero." Unpublished manuscript.

Crenshaw, K. 1991. "Mapping the Margins: Intersectionality, Identity Politics and Violence Against Women of Color." *Stanford Law Review* 43 (6): 1241–1299.

Espinosa, G., L. Dircio, and M. Sánchez, eds. 2008. *La Coordinadora Guerrerense de Mujeres Indígenas*. Mexico City: UAM-X.

Flores, J. 2007. *Reinventando la democracia. El sistema de Policía Comunitaria y las luchas indias en el estado de Guerrero*. Mexico City: Plaza y Valdés.

Foro Internacional de Mujeres Indígenas (FIMI). 2006. *Mairin Iwanka Raya: Mujeres Indígenas confrontan la violencia*. New York: FIMI.

Hale, C., ed. 2008. *Engaging Contradictions. Theory, Politics and Method of Activist Scholarship*. Berkeley: University of California Press.

Hernández, R. A., ed. 2008. *Etnografías e historias de resistencia*. Mexico City: PUEG-UNAM/CIESAS.

———. 2010. *Etnografías e Historias de resistencias. Mujeres indígenas, procesos organizativos y nuevas identidades políticas*. Mexico City: CIESAS.

Hernández, R. A., and A. Canessa, eds. 2012. *Género, complementariedades y exclusiones en Mesoamérica y los Andes*. Copenhagen: IWGIA.

Hernández, U., and M. T. Sierra. 2009. "Mirada desde las mujeres. Historia y participación de las mujeres en la Comunitaria." Brochure. http://www.policiacomunitaria.org.

Lang, Miriam, and Anna Kucia, eds. 2009. *Mujeres indígenas y justicia ancestral*. Quito: UNIFEM.

Leyva, X., A. Burguete, and S. Speed. 2008. *Gobernar en la diversidad. Experiencias indígenas desde América Latina. Hacia la investigación de co-labor*. Mexico City: CIESAS.

Macleod, M. 2011. *Nietas del fuego, creadoras del alba: Luchas político-culturales de mujeres mayas.* Guatemala: FLACSO.

Mahmood, S. 2008. "Teoría feminista y el agente social dócil. Algunas reflexiones sobre el renacimiento islámico en Egipto." In *Descolonizando el feminismo. Teoría y práctica desde los márgenes*, edited by L. Suárez-Navaz and R. Aída Hernández, 165–221. Valencia: Ediciones Cátedra.

Mejía, S. 2010. "Los derechos de las mujeres nahuas de Cuetzalan. La construcción de un feminismo indígena desde la necesidad." In Hernández, *Etnografías e historias de resistencia*, 453–502.

Merry, S. E. 2006. *Human Rights and Gender Violence: Translating International Law into Local Justice.* Chicago: University of Chicago Press.

Molyneux, M., and S. Razavi. 2002. *Gender Justice, Development and Rights.* Oxford: Oxford University Press.

Sánchez, E. 2012. *El proceso de construcción de la identidad política y la creación de la policía comunitaria en la Costa-Montaña de Guerrero.* Mexico City: UACM.

Santos, B. 2010. *La globalización del derecho. Los nuevos caminos de la regulación y la emancipación.* Bogotá: Universidad de Nacional de Colombia—ILSA.

Sieder, R., and M. Macleod. 2009. "Género, derecho y cosmovisión maya en Guatemala." *Rev. Desacatos* 31: 51–72.

Sieder, R., and J. McNeish, eds. 2012. *Gender Justice and Legal Pluralities. Latin American and African Perspectives.* New York: Routledge.

Sieder, R., and M. T. Sierra. 2010. *Indigenous Women's Access to Justice in Latin America.* CMI working paper. Bergen, Norway: Chr. Michelsen Institute.

Sierra, M. T. 2009. "Las mujeres indígenas ante la justicia comunitaria. Perspectivas desde la interculturalidad y los derechos." *Desacatos* 31: 73–88.

———. 2010. "Indigenous Justice Faces the State: The Community Police of Guerrero Mexico." *NACLA Report of the Americas*, September–October: 34–38.

———. 2013a. "Abriendo brecha. Las mujeres de la policía comunitaria de Guerrero." Video. Mexico City: CIESAS. http://www.youtube.com/watch?v=16c7iNPEgtM&list=UUFNNCZ fXgSALowd-BXZDHWQ.

———. 2013b. "Desafiando al Estado desde los márgenes. Justicia y seguridad en la experiencia de la policía comunitaria de Guerrero." In *Justicias indígenas y Estado. Violencias contemporáneas*, edited by M. T. Sierra, R. A. Hernández, and R. Sieder, 159–193. Mexico City: FLACSO-CIESAS.

———. 2013c. "Indigenous Women Fight for Justice. Gender Rights and Legal Pluralism in Mexico." In *Gender Justice and Legal Pluralities: Latin American and African Perspectives*, edited by Rachel Sieder and John McNeish, 56–81. New York: Routledge.

Speed, Sh., R. A. Hernández, and L. Stephen. 2006. *Dissident Women: Gender and Cultural Politics in Chiapas.* Austin: University of Texas.

5

Gender Inequality, Indigenous Justice, and the Intercultural State

The Case of Chimborazo, Ecuador

EMMA CERVONE AND CRISTINA CUCURÍ

By focusing on the case of Chimborazo, Ecuador, we highlight the challenges currently faced by indigenous women to ensure that their rights are incorporated in indigenous justice systems, and in the collective rights of indigenous peoples. In the past two decades, indigenous women in Ecuador have mobilized to promote their political demands of rights to gender equality vis-á-via the state, civil society, their own peoples, and the indigenous movement. This process is the result of the confluence of several factors, including the process of indigenous mobilization; the contribution of a gender equality agenda promoted by NGOs, which has provided grassroots training for women on topics of rights and gender equity; and a more recent process of participatory democracy that has created spaces for political participation for indigenous men and women at the national level. Our analysis outlines the progress made in the promotion of indigenous women's political agendas in Ecuador, using the case of the province of Chimborazo as a point of reference. We focus on the opportunities and limitations offered to women activists by the multicultural recognition of indigenous justice and the related territorialization of indigenous justice (that is, circumscribing it to the spaces recognized as "indigenous"). Such processes can create difficulties for indigenous women when new practices of community justice are not developed with the specific purpose of controlling and eliminating gender discrimination. Our anthropological study is based on Cristina Cucurí's long experience with political activism in the organization of indigenous women of Chimborazo, and on the results of several interviews, workshops, and focus groups that took place from April 2011 to December 2012. Our theoretical reflections on the various forms of discrimination that affect Kichwa women from Chimborazo contribute to understanding the challenges these women face in their efforts to ensure that their integrity and dignity as women become a shared concern in their communities, and to foster the development of mechanisms to control the violence they suffer.

The Sociality of Violence—Some Theoretical Reflections

Today because of my language or because I have not studied they don't pay attention to me, they ignore me.

—Men's focus group, Tixán, 2011

Our analysis of the various forms of gender violence internal to today's indigenous societies in Ecuador underscores the importance of historicizing gender violence and racism in the context of the relationships between indigenous peoples, civil society, and the state, and the ways these have been redefined in modernity (see Salgado n.d.). We draw on two debates: the first centers on the multiple ways in which the historical experience of colonialism has become a classifying pattern of exclusion and disavowal; the second focuses on feminist and critical race theories as developed mainly by women intellectuals of color.

Studies of colonial practices and legacies have shed light on postcolonial societies' hierarchies and forms of racial domination. Following these approaches we examine how those hierarchies of colonial roots got reformulated during modernity combining race, class, culture, place, and gender to maintain the privileges and the presumed superiority of "whites" and their global control over power and resources (see Quijano 2000; Mignolo 2000). The incorporation of a historical dimension in our analysis allows us to understand the processes whereby power relations, systems of representations, values, and racialized hierarchies have reproduced over time to relegate indigenous peoples (and peoples of African descent) to the limbo of the nonhuman. The colonial legacy in the testimonies we collected is also expressed by the internalization of dehumanizing notions and representations that historically undermined the subjectivity of colonized peoples, hindering their production of an alternative ontology of themselves (Fanon 1986, 2005). Following these perspectives, we problematize the violence present in indigenous societies, understanding it rather as a complex mesh of power relations that converges on the bodies of indigenous women, both symbolically and physically.[1] These complexities are embedded like atavistic sediments in the building blocks of everyday life interactions in the "dominant and dominated" binary.

The testimonies by Kichwa men and women collected in our research refer more specifically to the process of formation and consolidation of the modern Ecuadorian state and society, and to the position that the indigenous peoples of the highlands (*sierra*) have occupied in this process. Such memories and practices define political and social spaces that permit, and limit, indigenous emancipatory struggles in modernity. Our perspective seeks to recognize the continuities and discontinuities of exclusion rooted in colonial times, and the racist and patriarchal violence that surfaces in the memory, practices, and social interactions of indigenous men and women. We combine this historical perspective with Crenshaw's notion of intersectionality in order to analyze gender and racism. According to this, the predicaments of Kichwa women—violence and marginality—derive from the formation of their subjectivity as women and that of the ethnic, racial, and class group to which they belong; gender and race are therefore intimately interconnected (Crenshaw 1991; Lugones 2008). Violence against indigenous women in their communities is inseparable from the multiple forms of structural and individual violence that have been emblematic of certain racialized power structures at the local, national, and global levels in the process of development of modern Ecuadorian society (ECMIA-CHIRAPAQ 2013; FIMI 2006; Hill Collins 1990; Engle Merry 2011).

The voices we collected in Chimborazo suggest that social and historical memory is pivotal for consolidating political awareness and subjectivity. The testimonies point to three foundational moments in the definition and affirmation of the "indigenous woman" subjectivity and the violence that accompanies it. First, the power relations structuring the *hacienda* regime since the early twentieth century emerged as the historical referent from where the narration of submission begins. Accordingly, we treat the *hacienda* as a symbolic universe of power that transcends its historical referent to characterize a social imaginary that continues fostering submission and exclusion, in Ecuadorian society in general and in indigenous communities in particular. Such continuity is made possible by internalizing patterns of violence, where physical violence plays a central role in the definition of social hierarchies. We term this framework *the mentality of submission*, that is, the nexus between the historical processes of formation of power structures and social hierarchies, and the persistence of dehumanizing practices in everyday indigenous life. Corporal punishment, expressions of inferiority, rape, dispossession, and the whole set of racist and dehumanizing symbolic violence inflicted on the bodies of indigenous peons and their women at the hands of the *hacienda* owners and administrators have come to represent the set of practices of the mentality of submission that seeks to impose control and obedience (like *hacienda* owners did before) and maintain order. These practices and principles became legitimate mechanisms to establish social and family hierarchies in contemporary indigenous societies as they formed after the *hacienda* system was dismantled in Ecuador in the mid-twentieth century. Violence against women is, therefore, related not only to the systems of representations and values that allege male superiority, but also to the mechanisms of formation and reproduction of social and racial hierarchies and the mentality of submission. This approach helps demonstrate why power figures that reassert the patterns of domination from *hacienda* times are still endorsed today in indigenous contexts (Juncosa 2012: 171), as well as the complexity of the violence, mistreatment, and discrimination suffered by women in their communities.

A second pivotal moment in the reproduction of submission and exclusion that emerged in our research is the modernizing impulse that followed the reorganization and modernization of the agrarian society and its hierarchies in the sierra. The "indigenization of poverty" produced by the modernizing and assimilationist discourse of the Ecuadorian state since the 1960s defined a series of dichotomies (urban/rural, community/city, tradition/modernity) that had very negative impacts on the system of values attributed to indigenous women and men in their own communities (Cervone 2002).[2] Women found themselves trapped in a position of subalternity vis-à-vis indigenous men. Associated as they were with the realms of the community, tradition, culture, and domesticity, which in the modernizing discourse were considered the root of the economic and social backwardness of indigenous populations in general, women became both the cradle and the culprits of such traditions and backwardness. These practices and representations have resulted in very concrete and long-lasting obstacles that continue to hinder their process of development and political participation at all levels.[3]

The idea of backwardness as a racialized leitmotif that affects the indigenous world continued to be reproduced when the negative impacts of neoliberal political and economic policies aggravated the conditions of poverty and exclusion experienced by the country's indigenous population. In all of these conjunctures, the patriarchal system of colonial roots intertwined with other patriarchal forms of indigenous origin, exacerbating women's exclusion and hampering their struggle against violence and discrimination (see Paredes 2008; Salgado n.d.). However, the neoliberal period also bears the seeds of the process of consolidation of indigenous political awareness. The third foundational moment is therefore located in the 1990s, when the century-long process of indigenous mobilization against exclusion and discrimination reached its maturity. Indigenous organizations and leaders were able to create spaces for political participation in local government administrations, directly redefining Indian-state relationships on their own terms.[4] Despite the violence they suffered, indigenous women began a process of political mobilization with a gender equality focus, promoting new notions of rights, customs, and indigenous justice that challenged the existing violence in their communities and families. Their struggle has been very difficult and controversial. Speaking of domestic violence has been often interpreted as an act that delegitimizes and threatens the movement. Many of the movement's leaders have accused their female comrades of falling prey to the rhetoric of Western feminism elaborated by white, middle-class women, who understand women's rights as individual rights, hence contradicting indigenous people's collective rights.

Nonetheless, the official paradigm of multiculturalism has also fostered a process of political negotiation between indigenous peoples and the state, in which the official recognition of the validity and actuality of indigenous cultures has been key to define two areas of debate where indigenous women's demands could be acknowledged: the resignification/reconceptualization of customs and the recognition of legal pluralism. Regarding the resignification of customs and traditions—in other words, of autochthonous cultural elements and practices—women revisit, reconfigure, and reconstruct the Andean duality of *kari-warmi* (the equivalent of *chachawarmi* in Bolivia, as Ana Cecilia Arteaga Böhrt explains in chapter 6). This has been an important starting point for indigenous women to formulate their demands in their own communities and organizations, countering the accusations that portray them as victims of Western feminism. The *kari-warmi* pair, signifying equality and respect, represents the ideal of complementarity and horizontal duality without hierarchies between indigenous men and women, an example of gender parity and equality that must coexist in indigenous cultures and societies, in opposition to Western patriarchy.[5] This Andean element has allowed indigenous women activists to initiate a dialogue with their male comrades on gender equality, and on the most recent notion of Good Living introduced in the 2008 Constitution.[6]

The recognition of legal pluralism fostered in the country since the approval of the 2008 Constitution presented another opportunity to promote women's rights agendas. Beginning with Rafael Correa's election in 2006, the country entered a new political phase that has been defined as "post-neoliberal," as the president himself has declared. The new 2008 Constitution was proposed as an instrument for the recognition and inclusion of all forms of life under the protection of the Ecuadorian nation according to a principle defined as Good Living; in this case, good living promotes life with equality, respect, and harmony, both among humans and with nature (Walsh 2009). As detailed below, the indigenous women from Chimborazo successfully obtained constitutional recognition of their right to active participation in the life of their communities, and the inclusion of their gender demands as part of collective rights. This constitutional framework gave rise to a process of dialogue, negotiation, and elaboration of concrete intercultural forms and articulations to be implemented in many fields including justice. In what follows, we focus on the challenges organized indigenous women face to promote their rights agendas in both the ordinary and indigenous justice systems.[7] Their struggle for a more inclusive justice is an example of the "sociology of emergence" proposed by Rodríguez-Garavito and Santos (2005), in other words, a demand for justice that, as Cucurí (2012) observes based on her concrete experience of struggle, must be "invented." We believe that "invention" in this sense is a key element to analyze the process of negotiation that is taking place at the indigenous political level. It addresses the debates both around *kari-warmi* to critically invigorate customs and traditions (*usos y costumbres*), and around the new legal texts based on the 2008 Constitution that attempt to coordinate indigenous and ordinary justice. Any of these fields is subject to "invention." With the subordination of indigenous peoples rooted in colonialism, indigenous justice systems existing since pre-Colombian times became subaltern, meaning that they became subordinated to the state's ordinary justice and to the power of local, non-indigenous authorities (see García 2002; Cervone 2012; OACDH 2012). What is "invented," therefore, is not the practice of justice as such, but the institutionalization of indigenous justice practices as recognized systems. Article 20 of the 2009 Code of Judicial Function states that the resolutions and pronouncements made by indigenous authorities are unimpugnable and, therefore, must be respected by ordinary justice (see the discussion in Vintimilla 2012). These new legal articulations, defined in the 2008 Constitution in terms of cooperation and coordination of justice systems, imply the creation of new relations and legal practices identifying common principles on which both legal systems should agree. Debates on the principles guiding indigenous justice partake in the process of systematizing indigenous justice systems that went from being de facto to de jure systems (see García and Chávez 2004; OACDH 2012; Vintimilla 2012). Our analysis highlights the spaces and possibilities for indigenous women's demands to be addressed in the realm of the "invention" of new legal practices.

Methodology and Strategies

Our work followed a collaborative methodology whereby all stages of research, from fieldwork design to the actual writing of this chapter, were based on the knowledge contributed by and exchanged between the two authors. The testimonies collected come from interviews and focus groups with men, women, and council members in the parishes of Flores from the Riobamba district and Tixán from the Alausí district, and in the districts of Guamote and Colta in the province of Chimborazo, in June, July, and October 2011 and November 2012. A focus group was also held in Riobamba with leaders from women's organizations, and a two-day workshop with organized women was held at the provincial level in December 2012. All research was done in the Kichwa language, made possible by the collaborative efforts of the Provincial Network of Rural and Kichwa Women's Organizations of Chimborazo (REDMUJCH) and the Center for Development, Dissemination, and Social Research (CEDIS). For nine years, these two organizations have been supporting women's organizations from indigenous communities in the province of Chimborazo on topics related to production/food sovereignty, citizen/social participation, rights, and gender equality. The organizational process of indigenous women in Chimborazo began in the 1980s and 1990s with the support of NGOs and international cooperation focused on gender and rights. This process led to the formation of several women's grassroots organizations, which from 2002 to 2006 joined together, and created REDMUJCH. Since then, organizational, research, and training efforts have been made in the areas of gender and rights in several parishes and districts in the province.[8]

Our research was not quantitative, so we provide not statistical data but rather qualitative data on the forms of violence and the mechanisms of response available to women. We collected testimonies from indigenous women and men between the ages of twenty and fifty, male and female members of community councils, and leaders of women's organizations at the community and district levels. Testimonies and local newspaper articles were also collected on cases of femicides in indigenous communities, and on the application of indigenous justice in the communities of Chimborazo.

In the elaboration of our methodology, both authors agreed on the importance of incorporating men in our research and collecting their testimonies. We were interested in understanding how men explain the violence suffered by women and their opinions about it. As a result, the work with men became one of the main axes of our research, since it could directly contribute to understanding violence against women as a phenomenon that is inseparable from the racial violence and discrimination that affects indigenous peoples in general. Interviews with men were conducted by Arturo, an evangelical Kichwa comrade from Colta and Cristina's work colleague, who also helped prepare the questions for the focus groups. The questions for the focus groups with men and council members aimed at finding out what forms of violence they believed they suffered as men and, from there, to arrive at the forms of violence women suffer in their communities. To that end, we began with questions regarding the meaning of *sumak kawsay* (good living). Although the men seemed less willing to speak of those topics, the testimonies collected helped us significantly to explore the nexus between gender violence and racism in their everyday lives. Considering the sensitivity of the issues addressed, the names of all interviewees are pseudonyms.

Reconstructing the historical memory and the struggles of REDMUJCH was another important element of our research. A vital aspect of our methodology is the shared writing effort between an anthropologist scholar and an indigenous activist participating in women's organizations.[9] The writing phase was a critical moment of reflection in which we participated from our respective positions. Beyond the logistical challenges of writing different parts of the text in different places, the moment of writing was very different for the two of us.[10] For the anthropologist, it was an opportunity to share not only the data but also the elaboration of a theoretical framework that would enable the testimonies to make sense, not only within an interpretative framework, but also in regard to the activist's experience and knowledge, and the struggle she partakes in. For the activist, it was a moment of reflection on her own political practice and the practice of the organization to which she belongs. For her, the main challenge was related to the reconstruction of the political and historical memory of the struggle undertaken by her organization. Such a process meant contributing to the writing from within the struggle; it also entailed the responsibility of representing a collective voice capable of making visible all the contributions to knowledge and authorship made by the other comrades who participated in the actions discussed.

For both authors, sharing experiences of struggle and theories among all the other scholars and activists who worked in the collective research project that gave rise to this volume has been fundamental as a strategy to decolonize the production of academic knowledge and the research process. The various workshops of the project created the unique opportunity and the space for indigenous women to write, reflect, and share knowledge together with non-indigenous, scholarly friends and other sisters. In addition, writing about the indigenous women's struggles discussed in this volume, and of their contributions to knowledge, allows them to share their fight for their rights to a life with dignity as women with other indigenous women around the world, strengthening their process of empowerment. These two dimensions have given our work a very special meaning, since it was enriched, on the one hand, by the theoretical framework that continues to be produced in the academy and, on the other, by a political and experiential knowledge that goes beyond the ethnographic moment. Indigenous women's voices have functioned as an inexhaustible source of inspiration to which all the authors resorted whenever the data gathered, or the interpretative approaches used, seemed insufficient to reveal the richness and complexity of the lived experience.

The Tangle of Submission: Race, Gender, and Violence in Chimborazo

Analyzing the testimonies we collected challenged our interpretative methodologies, and suggested a transversal way of reading them that allowed us to perceive the connections between the various dimensions of violence and submission. These dimensions express themselves in a set of practices where past and present crystalize in the temporal dimension of the memories and experiences lived by the speakers. Our analysis aims at reproducing this crystalized image, where violence appears in different forms, and where racial, gender, and structural discrimination as well as their various temporalities intermingle, revealing the perniciousness of the mentality of submission. Among the threads of this mesh, the most noteworthy are the structural violence caused by poverty, the lack of resources, and the constant feeling of depreciation for being indigenous or for being a woman, all of which continue to be reproduced at all social levels: the community, the parish, and the country. The roots of these problems are both in the present and in the recent past, often with variations that depend on the age of the interviewees.

Before allowing the voices of the women and men with whom we worked in this study to help us understand the complex ramifications of violence in their lives, we present here some numbers that help contextualize the concrete impacts of gender discrimination in Chimborazo today. Executive Decree 620, enacted in 2007, declared the eradication of violence against children, adolescents, and women a national policy. As a result, the National Plan for the Eradication of Gender Violence was created. In this context, in 2011 the Ecuadorian state conducted the first national survey on family relations and gender violence against women. This survey demonstrated that, at the national level, eight out of ten women had experienced some sort of violence. There are twenty-four provinces in Ecuador, and gender violence affects more than 50 percent of women in all provinces, including Chimborazo. At all educational levels, gender violence affects more than 50 percent of all women; however, violence affects up to 70 percent of the women with low educational levels. More than 60 percent of the indigenous and Afro-Ecuadorian women included in the survey had experienced some sort of gender violence (INEC 2011).

Chimborazo is located in the central sierra of Ecuador, and, according to demographic data from the 2010 census, it is the province with the largest Kichwa indigenous population. Out of the 59 percent of the province's rural population, 58.3 percent are indigenous. Out of 450,581 inhabitants, 48 percent are men and 52 percent are women. According to sectional electoral data from 2009, out of a total of 315 popularly elected political positions, women hold 42 as members or presidents of rural parish boards, 14 as councilwomen, and 1 as vice prefect; there are no female mayors, nor female members of the provincial assembly, and women hold only 18 percent of political positions in the province. Out of all women aged fifteen or older, 8.35 percent are considered illiterate (from the perspective of formal/state education), compared to 4.67 percent of men.[11] Likewise, there are significant differences between different districts and between the three districts with the greatest indigenous population. Functional illiteracy is found in 35.5 percent of women, compared to 25.9 percent of men. In the three districts, women's educational level is slightly above second grade (2.2 in Colta, 2.2 in Guamote, 2.8 in Alausí). In all districts, men have at least one more year of schooling than women. With the exception of Riobamba, in the other districts fewer than 10 percent of women finished high school (2.4 percent in Guamote, 4.3 percent in Colta, and 4.9 percent in Alausí). According to the Farming Census, fewer than 1 percent of women in the province have received some sort of training (even though most of them live from agriculture).

In this province, discrimination, violence, and mistreatment in various public, private, and institutional spaces are still common for many women, adolescents, and children. Rape is a common practice at the beginning of young women's sexual life; according to one study, 43 percent of female adolescents/ youths younger than fifteen have been sexually abused in Ecuador. Among indigenous women, this number increases by 11 percentage points (CEPAR, CONAMU, UNIFEM, UNFPA 2006). In addition, according to local and national media, between 2009 and 2011 there were five cases of femicide perpetrated by former partners or spouses in indigenous communities in the districts of Guamote and Colta.

The Violence of "Nonbeing"

Our arrival at the communities and places where we held the focus groups and conducted the interviews seemed somewhat like a special event, something that interrupted the everyday routine. The meal provided was always an incentive to participate, as well as another opportunity to exchange questions and answers in a more relaxed setting accompanied by jokes and laughter, and different from the formality of the interviews. The first focus groups were held in Tixán, and the male voices collected came not only from the men's group, but also from the focus group with community council members, where most participants were men (a direct reflection of the numerical disparity between male and female council members).

In all of the focus groups with men, the younger ones (between twenty and fifty years old), many of whom had organizational or administrative political experience, tended to give the politically correct answer every time they were asked about good living and what they thought it meant, as this quotation exemplifies: "To live without mistreatment in the family, in the couple, and to live well with our children."[12] However, when asked to expand further on the difficulties and problems in their communities and families, the issue of violence was not the first to be discussed; rather the lack of resources, training, services, drinking water, agricultural materials, quality education for their children, poor roads, and so on were primary topics. Such reflections provided the starting point from which to begin discussing the issue of violence in its multiple forms.

The first level of violence identified by the men was strictly related to the structural context, that is, the lack of resources, which was directly related to the impotence they felt every time they had to navigate the institutional mazes—that highly hostile world of public offices, paperwork, demands, trips to the cities and markets. In the context of the modernizing transformations of Ecuadorian agriculture since the agrarian reform, indigenous peoples have had access to new economic relations, including access to land, the market economy, bank loans, state and nongovernmental policies for agricultural development, and formal education. This process has impacted indigenous social and political structures, leading to a process of development and consolidation of the "community" as the indigenous space par excellence. However, these transformations have not automatically led to a redefinition of the position of subordination and exclusion affecting the indigenous population. The men explain, "There is currently discrimination in the offices, there's manipulation, in those cases I would ask the national government to support us, to take indigenous peoples into account to have the good living, not just in the cities, but in the communities too" (Men's focus group, Colta, July 2011). "In high school, in school, in the offices, there is discrimination by the teachers and the employees; before, there used to be fights during festivities because of alcohol. Today they are because of language; or because I'm not taken into account because I have not studied; they ignore me" (Men's focus group, Tixán, June 2011). The topic of being ignored was brought up in several testimonies by men when speaking of their experiences in public offices. These spaces continue to reproduce the nonbeing, the invisibility in the eyes of public employees, who treat indigenous people as ignorant beings and pay no attention to their requests.

The loss of self-worth experienced in these spaces is one face of the mentality of submission that continues to affect the relationship between indigenous people, the state, and civil society. It also has direct consequences for community life. In the words of many men, the problems they suffer at the community level when they have to struggle against the lack of resources such as land, irrigation, and good schools, and their shared feeling of neglect and abandonment by the state, are directly related to domestic violence and internal divisions:

> For us to have *sumak kawsay* in the community we first have to have water for drinking and irrigation, we have to be organized in the community, to look for projects to strengthen the commune, we suffer without water. . . . If we have no water for our crops, how can we live well? . . . Not everything is good in the family, sadness always comes, difficulties, there's not enough money for agriculture, for food. We have many difficulties in the community, because of that we want to find a large agricultural project, water for our crops. I feel that in my community we're not in *sumak kawsay*, some here, some there, it's true that we all go out to work in the *mingas* [collective work], we also work as construction workers, as carpenters, some go to the coast or the sugar plantations, sometimes those of us who live in the communities only go out to the *mingas*. (Men's focus group, Colta, July 2011)

The lack of resources and the discrimination suffered in markets, where indigenous agricultural products are sold below the market price, have generated new intracommunity reciprocity relations that are asymmetric and unequal and have negative impacts.

> There are jealousies and fights within the family, they speak badly about us behind our backs, they say we can't do anything right. (Men's focus group, Tixán, June 2011)

> We do have problems in the community with the families that are part of it, we're not improving, instead we're going backwards, but if we were all united we could do anything. It's the same thing in the community; it would be so good if we were all united, to contribute with money, to carry out projects. This doesn't happen, but if there came a water project, they would show up saying, "I'm also a community member." (Men's focus group, Colta, July 2011)

In addition, the social criteria that define people's worth have been shaped by "modernizing" criteria, which have also redefined intergenerational relations. One elder complains that "some of us don't know how to read or write, some young people don't respect us in the communities, they don't take us into account" (Elder, focus group, Tixán, June 2011). It is interesting to note in this testimony that the same contempt suffered by young people in ethnically mixed public spaces, which they describe as "they don't take me into account" or "they ignore me," is reproduced within the communities against the elders and, as we shall see below, against women. While government employees treat indigenous people as ignorant, these same discriminated-against men reproduce this negative judgment on those who are perceived as even further away from being "modern," such as the elders and women in their community.

The oldest man in the men's focus group in Tixán made a connection between this attitude expressed by the younger men and the context of his own youth. His most vivid memory of violence was the *hacienda*: "If we go back a few years, the mestizo *hacienda* owners treated us as slaves because we didn't know anything; yes, I've been mistreated, especially by *hacienda* owners, and out of ignorance we drank alcohol and mistreated our children and spouses; it's terrible, you suffer, but today we don't pay attention to the *hacienda* owners, thank God the *haciendas* are gone" (Elder, focus group, Tixán, June 2011). The mistreatment and violence in the *haciendas* are renowned not only in Ecuador and the Andes, but in all of Latin America. In Ecuador, this land and labor exploitation regime lasted until the mid-1960s, when two agrarian reform laws completely redefined the country's entire agrarian structure. In addition to verbal abuse, *hacienda* landowners and their administrators often inflicted corporal punishment on their indigenous peons as a way to impose control and discourage insubordination. These practices, together with other mechanisms of control that tied indigenous workers to the *hacienda* system (debts, forced labor, local political control), contributed to turning *haciendas* into social microcosms that existed as universes apart from the rest of the country's political and social life. The landowner, the parish priest, and the local state authority—the parish civil officer—constituted the trilogy of power on which the indigenous population depended for their subsistence, with no other mechanism available to seek justice (Sylva 1986; Cervone 2012).

All of the testimonies point to different forms of violence that have undergone transformations in accordance with the social, political, and economic changes in the country's modernization process, and that continue to be expressed in the violence/submission binary. In spite of the positive changes identified by the men, including the agrarian reform, access to education, roads, and indigenous organizing, the physical and symbolic violence of racial discrimination and the mentality of submission continue to affect indigenous men and women in different ways. "We shouldn't place ourselves before the authorities as [if they were] the judges for all agreements, we should value ourselves as indigenous people, demonstrate our capacity to solve problems in our own communities" (Men's focus group, Colta, July 2011).

Sadness Has a Woman's Face

This affective dimension of contempt, common to the process of indigenous subject formation shared by men and women, is also present in the process of formation of the indigenous woman subject in the context of patriarchal, colonial, and racialized patterns that have been internalized by the "subjugated." The violence/submission binary reappeared in the words of the women interviewed every time they established a connection with the verbal aggression or the blows inflicted by fathers and husbands to ensure that their sons, daughters, and wives "obey." It is worth noting that many of the men interviewed said they were mistreated as children by their own fathers, although, according to them, this type of mistreatment is disappearing.

The testimony of Inés, a forty-four-year-old indigenous woman from Guamote and a leader of a local women's organization, establishes a line of continuity between *haciendas*, submission, and violence that reveals their legacy to this day. Inés narrated the various forms of violence and discrimination she suffered in her own family: from a very authoritarian father who used to beat and scream at his wife and children, to the way she was forced to defend her reputation in front of her brothers and other relatives by marrying a man just for speaking to him a few times. Once married she had to endure the violence that her husband would unleash on her every time she left the community to participate in the meetings of the women's organization to which she belongs. When we asked her about her grandparents, she told us that her paternal grandfather had been a *hausipunguero* (*hacienda* peon) and had married a much younger woman, whom he used to beat to make sure "she obeyed."

The feeling evoked by many of the women interviewed when speaking of violence is the same as that mentioned by men when speaking of the problems within the community: sadness (*llaqui*). While men tended not to elaborate much on this feeling and to distance themselves from it, attributing it to the overall situation, women connected it to their life and compared it with other situations of grief caused by the death of a loved one, the impossibility of fulfilling their desires, or feeling belittled by relatives. They lamented that the various forms of mistreatment, expressed in physical and verbal aggression by their spouses or relatives, derived from jealousy, mistrust, and the notion that women are good for nothing more than taking care of the house. They regretted not being allowed to leave the community other than for family affairs; a violation of this norm would gain them their husbands' insults and beatings. Some of them related these forms of violence to the violence they suffered in their childhood at the hands of their fathers and brothers, or to how they were denied an education or forced to marry against their own free will. "They say that women shouldn't go anywhere, some people put ideas in their heads telling them that we shouldn't be near anyone, that's what men's friends and even their relatives say, gossiping, chatting, and even our families go to them with comments and then our husbands beat us. They don't support us in our initiatives" (Focus group, Tixán, June 2011). One of the women in the Tixán workshop very clearly stated the effects of violence, which in the men's own words was referred to as falling ill:

> When he mistreated me, all I wanted to do was to go far away, to cry, but I never told anyone, not even my parents, I just went out to the hills with the animals. I would tell myself that I should let my parents know that I was living like that, but they would tell me that I should be with my husband, that I shouldn't leave. So I kept my mouth shut to avoid being more mistreated, and didn't tell anyone; after sending my children to school I would go out to the hills with the animals and cry, I didn't want my children to see me cry and even my mother-in-law was bad, to this day she's bad. (Women's focus group, Tixán, June 2011)

The connection between verbal aggressions, beatings, and domesticity stands out clearly. Women and children were and still are more directly related to the domestic sphere of the home and the community, which, as mentioned above, are considered by the modernizing discourse as backward and anti-modern spaces. Women have the least access to formal education and suffer their husbands' violence when "they do not obey," as stated by one man from the focus group in Tixán, or "because of bad thoughts they are mistreated and beaten" or "they are mistreated when the man has another woman, or because of alcohol, or if sober for some reason or gossip." All of these reasons that lead men to insult or beat their wives reveal a profound devaluation of the female sphere and of the concomitant notions of how women should behave. These forms of violence present today in indigenous families and communities are not always perceived or understood as "punishment"; rather, they are seen as "educational," directly related to the family and community hierarchies. They are expressed as strategies to establish control and impose respect for those hierarchies. Other studies at the Andean level conclude that domestic violence by husbands is a pattern in patrilocal arrangements after marriage that teaches the wife to respect her in-laws and her position within the family.[13] In another study on this topic in 1997, we found that in Chimborazo the women who suffered domestic violence would have the support of their family of origin only if the husband's family had a lower status in the community (Cervone 1998). The need to resort to verbal and physical aggression is an integral part of the mentality of submission that has endured since *hacienda* times as a legitimated way of imposing power and control, in this case over the bodies of women and children.

If physical violence as a mechanism for control had its origins in the *hacienda* regime, another notorious practice that belonged to that same logic of power and control was the systematic rape of indigenous women, especially younger ones, who served as domestic workers in the house of the master (Cervone 2012; Juncosa 2012). Raping women as a mechanism of control was redefined after the agrarian reform. In Tixán, for example, it became the method of choice for premarital sexual entertainment among the town's mestizo young men, to the detriment of young women who according to the post-*hacienda* redefinition of local social hierarchies were seen as inferior. After the demise of the omnipotent landlords, the mestizos—the town's "decent people"—recrafted the town's castes in a way that made *cholita* women—that is, the most indigenous and the poorest, who arrived from the countryside to serve as domestic workers in the town—the most deserving of being raped.[14] To this day, sexual aggression is another form of violence that affects the bodies and lives of indigenous women. It is difficult to obtain testimonies regarding this internalized form of violence, and the women with whom we spoke talked about it indirectly, not personally. Apparently, young single women are the most vulnerable to this type of aggression or sexual harassment by other family members (they mentioned fathers-in-law, cousins, uncles). These forms of violence are not understood as such at the community level unless they result in pregnancy, in which case they are classified as "teenage pregnancy." In such cases, the young women are often rejected by their own relatives because of the shame they bring upon the whole family. They often leave their communities and look for employment in nearby cities in order to survive. As demonstrated by one testimony, these cases can even lead to suicide: a young, single indigenous woman from Tixán became pregnant by a married indigenous man and finally ended her life with Furadan (a pesticide used in agriculture).

More recently, other cases of violence against indigenous women that could be classified as femicides occurred in Chimborazo. The murdering of women by their ex-husbands appeared to have been a way to avoid paying child support. Four cases were recorded in Guamote and Colta.[15] This phenomenon seems to us particularly relevant in the context of the approval of the 2003 Code of Childhood and Adolescence, which stipulates prison sentences for failure to pay support. Paradoxically, the disposition, which should in theory help women who become heads of households, appears to be having the opposite effect by putting their lives at risk.

The structural violence suffered by indigenous peoples under various political and social regimes, and the negative impacts derived from the combination of racial discrimination with agricultural modernization first and structural adjustments later, continue to give racism and gender discrimination in indigenous communities a woman's face. However, many women involved in organizational processes at the local and provincial levels are working against violence and discrimination by redefining the notions of what women "ought to be."[16] In the workshop in Riobamba with women from various organizations, most of the answers that outlined what it meant to be a woman mentioned being hardworking, a good mother and spouse, and a member of the community. Beside the hindrance of their heavy workload, the women agreed on many positive aspects of being a woman, highlighting their sensitivity, their sense of responsibility, and their capacities to foster change and to struggle for the well-being of their families and communities. One of the responses summarized it as follows: "[Being a woman] is the most marvelous and important thing on earth, it is a title that not everyone can have. It is doing things with sensitivity and reason" (Workshop, Riobamba, 2012).

Although the intertwining of violence, racism, and gender discrimination is inherent in many postcolonial societies, state policies, nongovernmental developmentalism, and even the indigenous movement tend not to include gender violence in the broader context of the eradication of the violence and discrimination that affect indigenous people in the country. In other words, gender violence is not incorporated as a transversal axis in antiracist struggles. However, organized indigenous women are pointing in that direction.

Building Networks among Indigenous Women in Chimborazo

The organizational process of rural indigenous women of Chimborazo began in the 1980s and 1990s with the contribution of local NGOs and international cooperation agencies with a focus on gender and women's rights that supported the creation and training of grassroots women's organizations to develop gender-related projects. "We began with the ALA Project, which helped by building Women's Homes, savings and micro credit associations, community stores, and especially training us on our rights" (Rosa, interview, 2012). These interventions were sometimes supported by community council members, men who—to gain access to funds for community projects—supported women's organization as their required gender component. "Some men gave us ideas, they would say, 'look, women, create an organization because there is help from the institutions for you'" (María, interview, 2012). This process goes hand in hand with the women's own internal process—motivated by their perceived need to unite as women against the violence, subordination, and discrimination they experienced in their family, community, and society in general. "My organization was created in order to learn how to speak out, because they didn't pay attention to us in the community, we couldn't give our opinion, much less make decisions, so we talked to each other and decided to create it to be able to express our needs, because we had lived too many years under the men's command" (Nieves, interview, 2012).

Some grassroots women's organizations are grouped in second-tier women's organizations at the district or parish level, while others act at the community level.[17] The first Inter-District Women's Coordination was created in 2002 during the Inter-District Encounter for the Economic Rights of Women, organized with the support of CEDIS, the Municipality of Alausí, and the government's National Women's Council (CONAMU) (today renamed the Commission for the Transition to Gender Equality and Women's Rights) with the participation of more than two hundred indigenous and rural women from organizations in districts of Chunchi, Alausí, Guamote, Colta, and Penipe. The Inter-District Women's Coordination linked actions that fostered women's economic and social development at their community, district, and provincial levels. In 2006 it was reconfigured as a third-tier organization called Provincial Network of REDMUJCH, conceived as a space for the convergence, articulation, and coordination of women's organizational, political, economic, and cultural efforts (based on their practical and strategic needs), with an emphasis on the struggle to overcome the discrimination, inequality, and inequity that affect women's bodies and lives.

REDMUJCH is composed of several second-tier organizations of San Luis Acatlán from the Riobamba district, and Tixán from the Alausí district. Its strategic objective is to position women's priorities and strategic interests and to elaborate concrete solutions, proposals, and actions to demand and exercise women's economic, political, social, cultural, and environmental rights, as well as the collective rights of indigenous peoples toward the construction of *Sumak Kawsay*, the plurinational and intercultural state, with participation and decision making by both women and men. REDMUJCH undertakes a number of actions: the creation of schools for women's political development, political interventions, organizational accompaniment, productive projects, and radio programs, among others.

The indigenous women interviewed recognize that organizing themselves, especially among women, has allowed them to reflect on the naturalization of the domestic roles assigned to them, and the violence and discrimination that affect their lives. In addition, they consider their organizational process as a mechanism for change in their lives, and to decolonize the mentality of submission. "Women's organization has allowed me to make decisions by myself without asking my husband's permission" (Rosa, interview, 2012). "We learned to speak out and to give our opinion in the organization; when I was a secretary, I learned to write official letters; with the training sessions, we stopped being afraid of speaking in public and it helped us to think of new things, and now we're valued by the community" (Rebecca, interview, 2012).

"So That Collective Rights Encompass the Other Half of the Indigenous Population": Narrating the Struggle of the Indigenous Women's Movement in Chimborazo

One of the issues for these organized women is life with dignity and free of violence and discrimination. This is because they are the ones who most feel the weight of racism, discrimination, violence, submission (colonial, patriarchal, racial, and capitalist patterns) on their bodies and everyday lives. The opportunity to elevate local indigenous women's demands to the national level came with the referendum that approved the 2008 Constitution. In mid-2007, the Constituent Assembly was established in a small coastal city of Ecuador— Montecristi. The Constituent Assembly went through a democratic and participatory process in its first phase under the presidency of Alberto Acosta, who called for broad sectors of Ecuador's society to contribute with their agendas and proposals in order to reach a new national agreement.[18]

At REDMUJCH we saw a window of opportunity for organized indigenous women to participate in political processes at a national level, including young women. We immediately began preparatory meetings to build the agenda of indigenous women of Chimborazo for the Constituent Assembly. We wanted to have the possibility to dream, to raise our voices, and to find solutions on the basis of our bodies and life experiences for a new national social contract and for the construction of good living with dignity and respect free of violence, exclusion, or discrimination. The objective was to gain political space in the community and in the indigenous movement, from which to promote women's demands for a life with dignity and without violence, with organization, participation, and access to natural resources such as water and land—the territory. At first, we all had doubts and even fears regarding the possibility of building an agenda; no one said it was easy, but neither did we believe it was impossible, and all the women supported the initiative. The challenge was how to move ahead in practice; in other words, how to develop a legal demand and implement strategies for political action. What most touched us—the indigenous women of REDMUJCH—in that process and inspired, encouraged, and motivated us were the actions, mobilization and process of struggle of the zapatista women in Mexico for their individual rights as women and the rights of indigenous peoples.

Reinventing Women's Rights

The period prior to the institution of the Constituent Assembly was central to developing political alliances. CONAMU organized an event in Riobamba to develop the Women's Agenda for the New Constitution of Ecuador—Us in the Constituent Assembly. REDMUJCH's board of directors, composed of twelve female indigenous leaders at the parish, district, and province levels, including Cristina Cucurí, prepared the agenda's document based on the proposals approved in several prior meetings. The document addressed a number of state policy issues: plurinationalism with a gender focus, official recognition of native languages among others, and solidarity economy. However, the core and most innovative aspect of the proposal was that of women's participation and full decision making in the system of indigenous justice: *"We asserted that violence, sexual harassment, femicide, discrimination, among other issues, severely affect women's bodies and lives, and we wanted our rights to a life free of those forms of violence to be guaranteed by all systems of indigenous justice."* More than two hundred leaders from the women's provincial organizations traveled by bus to the Andaluza Inn north of the Riobamba, the capital of the Chimborazo, where CONAMU was holding the Ecuadorian women's national convention with more than two hundred women from around the country. First, the buses were stopped at the San Andrés tollbooth (about twenty kilometers from the city) by the national police, who interrogated the women with many questions—*"Where are the 'cousins' going all together? Do you have permission to travel? Shouldn't you be at home with the animals? What is the purpose and destination of these buses full of indigenous women?"* Finally, they arrived at the inn's entrance, and the leader of REDMUJCH spoke with CONAMU director Miriam Alcivar to be admitted into the inn's auditorium. *"But the owner refused to allow us, indigenous women, to enter the building, arguing that we would stain the floors with our dirty and muddy shoes."* After a brief and heated debate with the hotel's administration and the director of CONAMU, the event's participants exited the building in order to welcome the collective of indigenous women and receive their constitutional proposals. After the ceremony/ritual to receive the document, they resumed the debates on the situation of Ecuadorian women and the constitutional proposals with the added presence of five REDMUJCH leaders.

The hardest blow was when the proposals by REDMUJCH—to incorporate women's rights in indigenous justice—were not included in the published proposal of the Ecuadorian women's movement Us in the Constituent. Indigenous women's demands were ignored because they were considered "too culturally specific." The agendas of the social and indigenous movements did not coincide with those of the indigenous women, which were repeatedly viewed as trivial and secondary. *"When we realized that our demands were considered less important, at the margins of the 'national political agenda,' we decided to take the matter into our own hands to influence the new constitutional framework."* With CEDIS's support, a prominent legal expert from the capital was hired, Dr. Ximena Endara O., who had ample experience in indigenous justice and collective rights issues:

We gave Dr. Endara the document with the constitutional demands of the indigenous women of Chimborazo, so she could translate our proposal into a legal language suitable for the constitutional level, with the following as the central axes: gender, women's individual rights, and the collective rights of indigenous peoples. REDMUJCH's proposal was disputed and questioned once again. Days later, when we spoke to the expert to hear of her progress, she told us that gender demands could not be integrated with those of indigenous peoples, since the former were conceived as individual rights and the latter as collective rights. She argued that the state could not impose gender conditions on collective rights because the latter are cultural rights, and doing so would imply a loss of autonomy and self-determination of indigenous peoples. Perplexed, we questioned her about this presumed legal incompatibility, and asked: "Where do rights come from? How do they emerge? Why can't gender and women's rights be combined with the collective rights of indigenous peoples?" To this, the specialist responded that rights are inventions, and that they are the result of long struggles, mobilizations, and many pressures from multiple social sectors to the state, until they succeed in transforming them into a normative framework (legislations, public policies, etc.) for positive coexistence. We, then, responded: "We too want to invent new rights to live with dignity and without discrimination or violence, for the good living of women and indigenous peoples, so that collective rights encompass the views, bodies, lives, and faces of the other half of the indigenous population." The legal expert maintained her position which forced us, together with some people who are very close to REDMUJCH and who trusted us and believed in our struggles, to transform the proposal we dreamed of into a document with a juridical language that could be incorporated in the new Ecuadorian Constitution.

Without the support of the women's movement or the experience of a lawyer, we looked for inspiration in the Bolivian Constitution approved in 2007 under the Evo Morales' administration. It contained proposals similar to those of Ecuador, but neither indigenous justice nor the collective rights of indigenous peoples [arts. 199, 200, 201] had a gender focus. We researched the part of the

Mexican Constitution that refers to the rights of indigenous peoples, and it gave us hints and ideas. We reviewed the document with the constitutional proposals by the indigenous movement, which contained international legal arguments. We, thus, transformed our proposals into a legal document, accompanied by strong and solid arguments and asserting the Constituent Assembly's duty to observe the UN Declaration on the Rights of Indigenous Peoples (2007), article 22 and article 44. Our arguments were based on gender issues, on what they implied for indigenous justice and the rights of indigenous peoples, on the consequences of recognizing cultural rights with a gender focus on the bodies and lives of women. Once completed, we sent letters, posters, and flyers with the proposed text to the Assembly members in Montecristi.

With CEDIS's support, one hundred twenty leaders traveled ten hours by bus from the highlands of Chimborazo to Montecristi. "*Despite our appointment, the police would not let us enter the Assembly at first and we finally entered thanks to the help of some friends. In the following months we made three interventions in the various specialized commissions of the Constituent Assembly, monitoring the entire process through the Internet, direct visits, and telephone conversations.*" Despite opposition by some non-indigenous leaders, REDMUJCH presented their demands (the agenda of the Kichwa women of Chimborazo and their constitutional proposals) to the president of the Assembly, Alberto Acosta.

Our dream [proposal] was finally positioned in the Assembly. The indigenous movement's leaders were caught by surprise, since they were, of course, unaware of our agenda. When we proposed a policy of participation and full decision-making by women in the access to indigenous justice, the strongest resistance came from indigenous assembly members like Vicente Masaquiza, representative of the government party Alianza País and a member of the justice commission. He and others accused us of trying to weaken and fragment the indigenous movement. Mónica Chuji, Amazonian Kichwa assembly member for Alianza País, and a member of the commission on natural resources, and other non-indigenous female assembly members linked to organizational processes and women's rights defenders were our strategic allies in the Assembly. Gina Godoy, also from Alianza País, and a member of the commission on access to justice, with experience working on issues of gender violence in the coastal region, immediately offered her full support to the indigenous women of Chimborazo. In the process of approval and voting, the president of the commission on access to justice, Fernando Vega, together with other assembly members allied to REDMUJCH, threatened to vote against the article on indigenous justice if a clause was not included asserting women's participation and full decision-making. These assembly members were key allies to ensure that the principle of equality between men and women was guaranteed in the text.

After the approval of what became numbers 10, 21, and 171 of article 57 of the Constitution of Ecuador, which explicitly recognize women's rights in conformity with the collective rights of indigenous peoples and nations, and indigenous women's participation and decision making in community justice, Lourdes Tibán, an indigenous lawyer and an expert on indigenous justice, gave televised interviews rejecting the approval of the text. Tibán maintained indigenous justice includes everyone (women, men, children, elders) and said the offending articles "must have been proposed by some feminist who doesn't know community life."[19] *"We, the indigenous women of Chimborazo, succeeded in reconfiguring the laws for our indigenous peoples in a way that was unprecedented in the region. Our struggle in REDMUJCH culminated in this phase of the process with the re-invention of new rights for the indigenous women of Ecuador."*

> *The mobilization process itself was transforming; indigenous women traveled to Montecristi to talk face to face with political actors. In rural communities, indigenous women are mostly illiterate or only have elementary schooling; it was their collaboration and desire to enjoy a different life that led to our legal and political victories. In spite of the obstacles encountered from cultural, patriarchal, colonial, racial, and capitalist models, we persisted in our struggle. Our comrades left their homes in the cold of the Andean highlands to travel to a foreign territory, far from their everyday lives, to participate in the Constitution's legal reform. Many of us traveled for the first time, in lengthy bus rides, to arrive at a small, hot, coastal town. After delivering our proposal, making cultural exhibitions, presenting mementos, and lobbying, one hundred and twenty representatives from the various organizations arrived at the beach. It was the first time many of them had seen the ocean, blue and immense. They raised their* anakos *above their knees and, for the first time, they walked in the water.*
>
> *Our organizational strength, our internal drive to live with dignity, and the motivation by other women from Abya Yala inspired us. We demonstrated that individual and collective rights can be interrelated, coordinated, and can cooperate with each other to establish and maintain balance and peace among women, men, living beings, nature, the cosmos, our ancestors. We are convinced that there is still much to be done, but the path has already been laid out: to build Good Living/Sumak Kawsay, the plurinational and intercultural state, against violence, (among other topics), from the perspective of the other half of the population, which is us.*

Women's Rights and Legal Pluralism

Since 2009, Rafael Correa's administration has created new legal frameworks for what has been defined as "intercultural justice" and "citizen participation," the latter understood as an inclusive practice in terms of Good Living that recognizes all existing social actors at the local level. Specifically, the 2009 Code of Judicial Function creates mechanisms to coordinate indigenous justice with the state's ordinary law (art. 286, title VIII, arts. 343, 344, 345, 346); for indigenous citizens their authorities and justice systems have jurisdiction over ordinary law, which remains the default system for those cases that indigenous justice cannot resolve. The 2009 Organic Law on Citizen Participation defines mechanisms for participation through local assemblies linked to plurinational assemblies for Good Living, and to sectorial and national citizen councils. The 2010 Organic Code for Territorial Planning, Autonomy and Decentralization attempts to articulate these processes with a territorial redefinition that incorporates (wherever there is citizen support) an ethnic component, thus delimiting territories as indigenous (indigenous territorial circumscription). Regarding women's rights, the definition of Good Living relates to the indigenous notion of harmony, including the right to gender equality and the eradication of gender violence. In addition, article 17 of the Organic Code of Judicial Function establishes a specific legal criterion to address cases of gender violence, which takes precedence over any other intercultural legal criterion when it asserts that "in cases of domestic violence, given its nature, mediation and arbitration shall not apply"—the latter criterion being very relevant in indigenous justice systems. More recently, the 2014 Integral Organic Penal Code (COIP) establishes the elimination of any privilege or exemption for people guilty of violence against women.[20] The changes implied by these legal frameworks are still in progress or in a "transition phase" in the provinces of Chimborazo. Debates within the indigenous movement contend the modalities to articulate indigenous justice systems with state law, and the validity of a territorial jurisdiction defined according to ethnic criteria. This is, therefore, an apparently favorable moment to promote indigenous women's rights and establish criteria for the eradication of gender violence in indigenous justice systems.

However, as the experience of REDMUJCH demonstrates, indigenous women still face many challenges in their everyday struggles against discrimination and violence. First, internal tensions and divisions within the movement have been aggravated by some recently approved laws. For example, in the 2014 COIP, social mobilization was criminalized by considering it a potential act of sabotage and terrorism.[21] These tensions have weakened the so-called second-tier grassroots indigenous organizations, which were pivotal in fostering political mobilization in the 1990s, including gender demands. The comrades from the focus group in Tixán, for example, observed that the weakening of the local second-tier Confederation of Organizations Inca Atahualpa badly affected their struggle as organized women. In the 1990s, when the Inca was at its peak (a common pattern among many second-tier organizations), the women who completed the training programs promoted by NGOs had found in that local organization an important ally to carry out their activities, even if they still had to struggle to be taken seriously by their male comrades. However, the training programs gradually ended and the organization lost its strength due to what women and men defined as *politiquería*, or party politics. Other debilitating factors also include the proliferation of evangelism (which discouraged women's political participation), the migration of increasing numbers of men, and young people's distancing from communal organization. Consequently, women felt alone and without a clear vision of how to advance.

A second challenge is inherent to the institutional articulation of ordinary justice with indigenous justice systems. In the recent legal frameworks formulated by the state, indigenous justice systems are the first priority for indigenous citizens who seek to resolve a conflict. Accordingly, cases of gender violence should be first addressed by indigenous justice. In theory indigenous women have access to both state and indigenous justice systems in Ecuador; in practice, the combination of racism and prejudice in public institutions and internal sexism in indigenous communities provides for very little protection, guarantees, and recognition of rights in either system in cases of domestic violence and rape. COIP 2014 eliminated the Commissariat for Women and the Family, which was the government body for immediate protection against domestic violence (created in 1994). Family Courts were created instead, with judicial units specializing in violence against women and the family. With the enactment of COIP, the Law 103 against Violence against Women and the Family (1995)—an initiative achieved thanks to the struggle of the women's movement in Ecuador—was also repealed. Despite these changes, indigenous women continue to distrust state institutions because of impunity and judicial inefficiency aggravated in those spaces by racism, sexism, classism, and language discrimination.[22] According to the women interviewed, in ordinary justice their demands are filed away, and they face codes, rules, and authorities who they don't know or understand; everything seems foreign, distant, and in another language. State laws that protect women's rights are still inaccessible to indigenous women. Some also expressed their concern regarding the annulment of Law 103; according to them, the immediate protection (*medida de amparo*) provided by that law has been lost in COIP, in spite of the introduction in the new code of transversal measures condemning violence against women.[23] Furthermore, they feel that the specificity of Law 103 worked as a potential means of dissuasion for indigenous men, compared to the dispersion resulting from the multiplicity of articles that regulate those crimes in COIP.

Despite the accessibility of indigenous/communal justice or *derecho propio*, it has shown signs of sexist, patriarchal, and colonialist bias, often failing to control domestic violence and rape (Cucurí 2007; Barrera 2016). According to all the testimonies collected in Chimborazo, there are apparently no mechanisms to support indigenous women in their search for community justice in cases of violence and mistreatment. First, they have to overcome their own fears, and the chance of being ostracized as inopportune—or, if they are leaders, even as traitors of the indigenous movement. If they decide to seek support from the indigenous authorities, they invariably find that cases of violence and mistreatment against women and children are considered family affairs. If a woman does not have the support of her family, or has to confront her own relatives, she has nowhere else to go. Many women said that communal authorities intervene only in cases of disputes related to custody or inheritance, in other words, when concrete economic resources are at play. Cases of spousal or parental problems are dealt with by relatives or godparents, who are in charge of counseling and potentially supporting the woman. Yet, in those few cases where there are women among the members of community councils, cases of domestic violence receive better attention. In the case of the femicide in Guamote, the council intervened out of solidarity with the orphaned children to find a solution to keep them from becoming destitute. The culprit was also arrested, punished, and delivered to ordinary justice to be imprisoned.

Evidently there are no established mechanisms in the systems of ordinary or indigenous justice to ensure that cases of gender violence are addressed by the elected community authorities. The different instances that intervene, beginning with the family, do not always provide support or find permanent solutions. As mentioned above, this seems to be an ideal moment to begin working on proposals to "invent" rules, norms, and mechanisms with the objective of eradicating discrimination and gender violence in indigenous justice systems. All these reflections also revealed another gray zone of ambiguity. According to article 20 of the Code of Judicial Function, which guarantees full autonomy to indigenous justice systems, the decisions made by indigenous authorities cannot be impugned by the ordinary state justice. Paradoxically, this clause can seriously affect women seeking justice against domestic violence, as demonstrated by the testimonies collected. When indigenous authorities do not consider domestic violence a field of their competence, or even rule against the affected women, the women feel trapped between indigenous and ordinary legal systems, and justice is not served.

Women's Perspectives on Transforming and Decolonizing Communities: A Difficult but Not Impossible Road

The struggle of the indigenous women of the REDMUJCH in Chimborazo continues with many challenges. The experiences described in this chapter highlight some: the lack of organizational support from the indigenous movement, the lack of institutional support from state authorities, and the influence of *politiquería*. The powerful process of mobilization described in this chapter has been insufficient to strengthen women's rights at the local level and to enforce local mechanisms to support women both within and beyond their communities.[24]

This suggests that, while it is essential to raise awareness of women's problems among themselves, mobilization alone is insufficient to transform their political demands into practices of equality—unless there is institutional support and a broader organizational network. The most compelling contribution of women's struggle is in the area of decolonizing practices: the REDMUJCH is attempting to counter resistance to women's demands by associating themselves with broader antiracist struggles. In a series of workshops in their affiliated cantons, the women in REDMUJCH proposed that communal organizations should not continue to reproduce and tolerate violent practices rooted in colonial times, the *haciendas*, racism, and patriarchy. Although many studies demonstrate the continuity of deeply rooted racist practices and structures, official gender equality agendas do not understand these two forms of violence as intersecting. Consequently, indigenous women's demands have been considered too "specific" to be prioritized vis-à-vis other demands formulated by the indigenous movement or the national women's movement. The incorporation of antigender violence into the antiracist agendas can foster the forging, or "invention," of a common platform of struggle in the indigenous movement, and can help revitalize the political role that grassroots organizations seem to have lost in their fight for the decolonization, emancipation, and political participation of indigenous peoples at all levels of the country's social and political life.

We believe that the interpretative framework presented in our study can connect to the political agendas of organized indigenous women. From her position as a REDMUJCH leader and researcher, Cristina Cucurí perceived the importance of diving deeper into the possible causes of gender violence in the communities. *"How can we work with our male colleagues if we do not understand why they beat and belittle their women?"* This line of questioning led us to work with men to bring to light the connections between gender violence and racism. As feminists of color in many racialized societies of the North and South have repeated once and again, nonwhite women are the most affected by discrimination, and yet political agendas often separate gender violence from racism. As demonstrated by Terven in chapter 2, this separation can be the result of a gender approach promoted by development agencies that leads to a limited understanding of the complexity of indigenous women's positions in their communities and organizations. The intersectionality approach, therefore, serves two purposes: to involve men in the processes of struggle and to redefine and broaden the political agendas of women's organizations. Based on their direct practice and experience, women are broadening the gender focus and creating avenues toward Good Living through decolonization. Their struggle has the potential to become an emancipatory struggle not only for women, but also for the communities and peoples to which they belong. As the women in REDMUJCH propose, they are the ones who must give a different face to communal living and, together with their men, develop proposals for a future of equality/equity in their families, communities, and country. We hope that our research can help Cristina and her comrades to enrich the processes of reflection in their own communities, not only on the issue of gender and violence, but also on racism and discrimination still affecting all indigenous peoples, so that men and women can work together toward their eradication. As Cristina said, the road is difficult, but not impossible.

NOTES

1. In this respect, we refer here to the definition of gender as an analytical category that functions as a "primary way of signifying relationships of power," as defined by Joan Scott (1986).

2. Ibarra 1992. The term "indianization of poverty" is meant to underscore the modernizing discourse of the Ecuadorian state and civil society, according to which indigenous peoples are poor because they are trapped in a backward and premodern culture.

3. For an analysis of this process in the Bolivian context, see Canessa 2012.

4. The three stages of suffrage in Ecuador occurred in 1861, when suffrage was extended to all literate men; 1929, when women were granted the right to vote; and 1978, when the right to vote was extended to illiterate people.

5. This ideal of complementarity is complex and subject to different interpretations: scholars and activists have debated whether it is used to obfuscate gender inequalities (see, e.g., Burman 2011; Cervone 2002; de la Cadena 1991; Harris 1986; Harvey 1994; Paredes 2008; Salgado n.d.) or is the ancestral antidote that needs to be emphasized to counter the negative image that the mestizo world projects onto the indigenous world (see the discussion in OACDH 2012). Burman argues that *chacha-warmi* is not an inherently silencing nor emancipatory concept, but a discourse that can be used either to render invisible or to combat discrimination against indigenous women, depending on the agendas and the identities of the actors who defend it (Burman 2011: 90). In order to avoid reifying discourses about violence and rights, we argue that analyses of the multiple meanings of these concepts must be complemented with an analysis of the practices that take place in indigenous communities, taking into account what indigenous women say and describe.

6. In this chapter, we capitalize Good Living when it refers specifically to the language used by the state in legal texts or in the Constitution. When referring to this concept more generally, we leave it lowercase.

7. See Barrera 2016.

8. CEDIS's support was very important to obtain resources from international cooperation to fund these efforts and strategic actions.

9. Although we had worked on collaborative efforts before, this was the first cowriting experience for both authors.

10. Different parts of this chapter were written by each of the authors, but after the initial writing we both discussed and edited the text. The first draft of this chapter was written in Quito, as we sat together at a cafe for days. The comments received in the project's workshops were essential to ensure that our arguments were well connected to the political struggle of which they speak. We thank all the other colleagues in the team for their important contributions and commentaries.

11. According to the 2011 census, the illiteracy rate at the national level was 6.8 percent, with women at 7.7 percent and men at 5.8 percent. This represents a significant decrease compared to 1990, when the total illiterate population was 9.9 percent, including 13.8 percent of women and 9.5 percent of men (INEC 2011).

12. The different focus groups with men and community councils in Tixán were held at the offices of the Confederation of Organizations Inca Atahualpa (Tixán), district of Alausí; the Sicalpa and Columbe focus groups were held at the offices of the Corporation of Indigenous and Peasant Women's Organizations of Colta (Cajabamba) in the Colta district; and the Flores groups were held at the offices of the Corporation of Indigenous Women from Flores (Flores) in the Riobamba district.

13. See, e.g., Harvey 1994, Harris 1986.

14. For a discussion on racism and servitude, see Cumes 2009.

15. For references, see the following newspaper articles: "Mataron a su madre y se llevaron a la bebé," *Diario La Prensa*, June 3, 2009; "El principal sospecho de este crimen es el exesposo, quien huyo en la madrugada sin dejar rastro," *Diario La Prensa*, December 23, 2009; "Comuna en Shock por un asesinato," *Diario El Comercio*, December 27, 2009; "El presidente de la Conaie Marlon Santi reconoció que hacen falta cambios pues solo en Guamote se lamentan cuatro muertes de mujeres a mano de sus cónyuges," *Diario Los Andes*, November 20, 2011.

16. This process is discussed in detail below.

17. According to the Law of Communes and Cooperatives, grassroots organizations registered as legal entities differently from communes are termed second-tier. Those that operate at the provincial level are termed third-tier.

18. This section contains the direct experience of Cristina Cucurí, who at the time was part of REDMUJCH's board of directors. It is therefore narrated in the first person plural to reflect the collective work carried out by Cristina and her colleagues. We have left her direct testimony in italics throughout.

19. Constitution of Ecuador 2008, art. 57, no. 10: "To create, develop, apply and practice their own legal system or common law, which cannot infringe constitutional rights, especially those of women, children and adolescents." Art. 57, no. 21, para. 3: "The State shall guarantee the enforcement of these collective rights without any discrimination, in conditions of equality and equity between men and women." Art. 171: "The authorities of the indigenous communities, peoples, and nations shall perform jurisdictional duties, on the basis of their ancestral traditions and their own system of law, within their own territories, with a guarantee for the participation of, and decision-making by, women."

20. See book 2, title I, chap. 1, art. 204, no. 11 of COIP 2014.

21. See book 1, chap. 6, single section, arts. 345 and 346 of COIP 2014.

22. This problem was also denounced by indigenous men in our focus groups.

23. It is still too early to determine the advancements and possible impacts of COIP 2014 in terms of specific legislations against gender violence. One advancement that is worth noting is that, for the first time, femicide is defined and condemned (see chap. 2, arts. 141–142).

24. There are other cases in the country of more successful experiences, such as the case of the indigenous women from Cotacachi in the province of Imbabura and of Sucumbíos in the Amazonia, where a process of reflection and analysis on gender violence and access to community and ordinary justice was begun with the support of

promoters of Good Living (Sieder and Sierra 2010). For reasons of space, however, our analysis does not cover those cases. It is worth mentioning that alliances with other local political actors were fundamental to supporting the women's process, and that when these actors left the political stage, the whole process weakened.

REFERENCES

Barrera, Anna. 2016. *Violence Against Women in Legally Plural Settings: Experiences and Lessons from the Andes*. New York: Routledge.

Burman, Anders. 2011. "*Chachawarmi*: Silence and Rival Voices on Decolonisation and Gender Politics in Andean Bolivia." *Journal of Latin American Studies* 43 (1): 65–91.

Canessa, Andrew. 2012. *Intimate Indigeneities: Race, Sex, and History in the Small Spaces of Andean Life*. Durham, NC: Duke University Press.

CEPAR, CONAMU, UNIFEM, UNFPA. 2006. *Endemain, Violencia contra la mujer*. Quito.

Cervone, Emma, ed. 1998. *Mujeres Contracorriente. Voces de líderes indígenas*. Ecuador: CEPLAES (Center for Social Studies and Planning), CEPLAES-FEG.

———. 2002. "Engendering Leadership: Indigenous Women Leaders in the Ecuadorian Andes." In *Gender's Place: Feminist Anthropologies of Latin America*, edited by Janice Hurtig, Charo Montoya, and Lessie Jo Frazier, 179–196. New York: Palgrave Macmillan.

———. 2012. *Long Live Atahualpa: Indigenous politics, Justice, and Democracy in the Northern Andes*. Durham, NC: Duke University Press.

Crenshaw, Kimberlé W. 1991. "Mapping the Margins: Intersectionality, Identity Politics, and Violence Against Women of Color." *Stanford Law Review* 43 (6): 1241–1299.

Cucurí, Cristina. 2007. "Documento de Horizonte Político de REDMUJCH." Unpublished manuscript, Riobamba, Ecuador.

———. 2012. "Re-inventando los derechos para el sumak kawsay de las mujeres indígenas en el Ecuador." http://conlaa.org.

Cumes, Aura. 2009. "'Sufrimos vergüenza': mujeres k'iche' frente a la justicia comunitaria en Guatemala." *Desacatos* 31: 99–114.

Cumes, Aura, and Santiago Bastos, eds. 2007. *Mayanización y vida cotidiana. La ideología multicultural en la sociedad guatemalteca*. Guatemala: FLACSO/CIRMA.

de la Cadena, Marisol. 1991. "Las mujeres son más indias. Etnicidad y género en una comunidad del Cusco." *Revista Andina* 9 (17): 7–29.

De la Torre Amaguaña, Luz María. 2010. "¿Qué significa ser mujer indígena en la contemporaneidad?" *Mester* 39 (1): 1–25.

De Oto, Alejandro, ed. 2011. *Tiempos de homenajes/tiempos descoloniales: Frantz Fanon*. Buenos Aires: Ediciones del Signo.

ECMIA-CHIRAPAQ. 2013. *Violencias y Mujeres Indígenas*. Mexico City: AECID, Ford Foundation.

Engle Merry, Sally. 2011. "Derechos Humanos, Género y Nuevos Movimientos Sociales: Debates Contemporáneos en Antropología Jurídica." In *Justicia y Diversidad en América Latina. Pueblos Indígenas ante la Globalización*, edited by Victoria Chenaut et al., 261–291. Mexico City: CIESAS/FLACSO.

Fanon, Frantz. 1986. *Black Skin, White Masks*. London: Pluto.

———. 2005. *The Wretched of the Earth*. New York: Grove Press.

FIMI-International Indigenous Women's Forum. 2006. *Mairin Iwanka Raya: Mujeres Indígenas Confrontan la Violencia*. New York: FIMI.

García, Fernando. 2002. *Formas indígenas de administrar justicia: Estudios de caso de la nacionalidad Quichua Ecuatoriana*. Quito: FLACSO.

García, Fernando, and Gina Chávez. 2004. *El derecho a ser: Diversidad, identidad y cambio: Etnografía jurídica indígena y afroecuatoriana*. Quito: FLACSO/Petroecuador.

Harris, Olivia. 1986. "Complementary and Conflict: An Andean View of Women and Men." In *Sex and Age as Principle of Social Differentiation*, edited by J. S. La Fontaine, 21–39. London: Routledge.

Harvey, Penelope. 1994. "Domestic Violence in the Peruvian Andes." In *Sex and Violence: Issues in Representation and Experience*, edited by Penelope Harvey and Peter Gow, 66–89. London: Routledge.

Hernández, R. A., S. Speed, and L. Stephen. 2006. *Dissident Women: Gender and Cultural Politics in Chiapas*. Austin: University of Texas Press.

Hill Collins, Patricia. 1990. *Black Feminist Thought: Knowledge, Consciousness and the Politics of Empowerment*. Boston: Unwin Hyman.

Ibarra, Hernán. 1992. *Indios y cholos: Orígenes de la clase trabajadora Ecuatoriana*. Quito: El Conejo.

INEC. 2011. *Encuesta Nacional de Relaciones Familiares y Violencia de Género contra las Mujeres*. Quito: Instituto Nacional de Estadística y Censos.

Juncosa, José. 2012. "'Una Raza Hiposexuada.' Raza, sexualidad y clasificación social en Los indígenas de altura del Ecuador." In *Miradas Alternativas desde la diferencia y subalternidad*, edited by Victor Hugo Torres Dávila, 143–178. Quito: ABYA YALA.

Lugones, Maria. 2008. "Colonialidad y género." *Tabula Rasa*, no. 9: 73–101.

Mignolo, Walter. 2000. *Local Histories/Global Designs: Coloniality, Subaltern Knowledges, and Border Thinking*. Princeton, NJ: Princeton University Press.

OACDH-Oficina de Alto Comisionado de Derechos Humanos. 2012. "Informe Anual." Quito: OACDH.

Paredes, Julieta. 2008. *Hilando Fino: Desde el Feminismo Comunitario*. Bolivia: CEDEC.

Quijano, Anibal. 2000. "Coloniality of Power, Eurocentrism and Latin America." *Nepantla* 1 (3): 533–580.

Rodríguez-Garavito, César, and Boaventura de Sousa Santos, eds. 2005. *Law and Globalization from Below: Towards a Cosmopolitan Legality*. Cambridge: Cambridge University Press.

Salgado, Alvarez, Judith. n.d. "Violencia contra las mujeres indígenas: entre las " justicias" y la desprotección. Posibilidades de interculturalidad en Ecuador." Unpublished manuscript.

Scott, Joan W. 1986. "Gender: A Useful Category of Historical Analysis." *American Historical Review* 91 (5): 1053–1075.

Sieder, Rachel, and Sierra Maria Teresa. 2010. *Indigenous Women's Access to Justice in Latin America*. CMI working paper. Bergen, Norway: Chr. Michelsen Institute.

Sylva, Paola. 1986. *Gamonalismo y lucha campesina*. Quito: Abya-Yala.

Vintimilla, Jaime. 2012. "Ley Orgánica de cooperación y coordinación entre la justicia indígena y la jurisdicción ordinaria ecuatoriana. ¿Un mandato constitucional necesario o una norma que limita a los sistemas de justicia indígenas?" Quito, Ecuador: Cevallos.

Walsh, Catherine. 2009. "Development as *Buen Vivir*. Institutional Arrangements and (De) colonial Entanglements." *Development* 53 (1): 15–21.

6

"Let Us Walk Together"

Chachawarmi Complementarity and Indigenous Autonomies in Bolivia

ANA CECILIA ARTEAGA BÖHRT

We now have our place, now we can . . . now we have the will to push for laws . . . we must continue resisting, we can't let ourselves be pushed around!

–Testimony by a female participant, Women's Event
in Totora Marka, August 12, 2011

Four women prepared to speak before the *tanta chawi* (regional assembly) in Totora Marka, a territory located in the Bolivian department of Oruro.[1] The president of the *estatuyentes*—the people in charge of drafting the statute— addressed the participants to announce that it was time for the *mamas* (women) to present their proposals for inclusion in the autonomy statute, the internal law of the territory. After greeting the *estatuyentes* and traditional authorities, Doña Sixta, one of the speakers, affirmed that the political Constitution of the state recognizes indigenous autonomies and indigenous women, and that it was for that reason that they had decided to participate in this process. After this introduction, she proceeded to read and explain the document with a firm voice and in Aymara. During the forty-five-minute presentation, some of the proposals generated murmurs, especially among the male participants.

Several male traditional authorities requested to speak. They agreed that machismo existed in their communities, but said that such attitudes and behavior could not be generalized across the entire territory; for example, the Mallku de Consejo (the highest authority in the Marka) said that the problem was national laws that divide and fragment the collectivity: "Now there are rights for women; there are no rights for men!" The participants smiled at this commentary and he continued, "That's the problem! They are dividing us. In

Andean thought there's no separation, everything is done communally, but that relationship no longer exists, now women tell men, 'I have my rights!,' and men can do nothing about it, that's why there are so many divorces nowadays." From the back of the room a voice intoned, "the mamas' proposals go against *chachawarmi*" (the Aymara principle that refers to complementarity between *chacha*, which is equivalent to man/male gender, and *warmi*, woman/ female gender). One of the authorities present said that the proposals clearly reflected the intervention of the outsiders who helped write the document. In response to the criticisms, the vice president of the *estatuyentes* said that the women's proposal was as valid as the men's: "Let's listen to the mamas. In Totora Marka every word counts." The various commentaries in favor of and against the women's proposals created a commotion, giving the impression that the meeting had gotten out of control and the vice president was forced to shout, "let's listen to the mamas!" in order to silence the assembly. At that moment, Doña Sixta got up and said firmly in Aymara, "I want to add that perhaps we women did not express ourselves well; beginning something is always difficult. Do you men always do things right? It was the same with you when you started to participate. We can move ahead to lead these laws in the right direction. We don't want you to humiliate us like this. . . . All of this is to make sure that our daughters get ahead and don't have to go through what we've experienced. Certainly, everything is *chachawarmi*, but we demand a few things. Forgive us for that!"

I begin this chapter with the description of a moment I observed during a year and a half of fieldwork in Totora Marka. Before I began the research, on December 6, 2009, a nationwide municipal referendum on whether or not to adopt indigenous autonomy, following the provisions set out in the new national Constitution, took place. In total II out of 339 municipalities voted in favor of conversion.[2] In Totora Marka, 74.5 percent voted in favor of indigenous autonomy. Six months later, on July 19, 2010, the Bolivian national assembly approved the Framework Law on Autonomies and Decentralization, which recognizes indigenous autonomies, understood as the expression of the right to self-government and self-determination of indigenous and peasant nations and peoples.[3]

The Council of Indigenous Authorities of Totora Marka—the main deliberative body charged with developing the statute—organized a process of revolving consultation (*muyu*) and socialization of this first draft throughout the territory, in order to develop a second, definitive version. In September 2015 Totora Marka's statute was the first in the country to be declared compatible with the Constitution by the Plurinational Constitutional Court.[4] Totora Marka and Charagua (Santa Cruz department) were the first territories on a national level to test their statutes through a referendum. In the case of Totora a no vote was declared by 70.04 percent of the population, so modifications to the text as well as a new referendum were still pending at the time this chapter was completed (April 2016).

I was fortunate to be able to accompany the first consultation for the statute; the indigenous authorities requested my collaboration in collecting and systematizing the proposals of the women who participated in the deliberative forums.[5] By participating in this process, I was able to analyze the limitations as well as the strategies developed by the women from Totora Marka to increase their participation in the document's elaboration.[6] A central element I focused on was *chachawarmi* complementarity; therefore, in this chapter I also analyze debates on this principle and proposals that emerged to resignify it, in an attempt to put discourses on equality and equity into practice on the basis of the cultural referents and frameworks of the men and women from Totora Marka. I address the following questions: To what extent do cultural constructions and gender ideologies related to *chachawarmi* complementarity affect women's participation in Totora Marka? What alternatives do women propose for increasing their participation in processes such as the elaboration of the autonomy statute? To what extent did the language of rights allow them to express their problems, and what effect did state discourses have on that language?

To answer these questions, I first analyze government discourses on depatriarchalization and decolonization in Bolivia, and consider the ways these incorporate indigenous discourses on complementarity. I then examine the meanings and representations of the principle of *chachawarmi* complementarity in Totora Marka, before analyzing how this principle is developed in practice, describing women's perceptions of the spaces where *chachawarmi* is respected, where it is violated, and why. Finally, I consider the impact of human rights discourses on the women's proposals to resignify complementarity.

Between Laws and Discourses: Legislative Changes in Bolivia

Structural transformations in Bolivia cannot be understood without briefly analyzing the social movements that partly drive them, and underscoring the importance of indigenous women's participation in these. The March for Territory and Dignity in 1990 was the first time that women gained significant national spaces for participation and leadership, especially in the lowlands (McNeish and Arteaga 2012).[7] The Bolivian Gas War in 2003, in which the Bartolina Sisa National Federation of Bolivian Peasant Women and the Guaraya Indigenous Women's Central actively participated, had similar repercussions (Costa 2004).[8] According to Arnold and Spedding (2005), through these social movements women attempted to recover political spaces from which they had been excluded because of their gender, including neighborhood assemblies, school assemblies, and *ayllu* (a group of various communities), all in the context of a democracy that is still more delegative than participatory.

These movements and others deeply questioned the government and prevailing forms of democracy, particularly criticizing the privatization policies implemented since 1985 and demanding the creation of a Constituent Assembly (Chaplin 2010). In the context of these mobilizations, Evo Morales won the presidential election in December 2005 with 54 percent of the vote, becoming the first indigenous president elected in Bolivia. In 2006, just months after his election, the Constituent Assembly was established. As a result of the implementation of the Special Law Calling for a Constituent Assembly,[9] eighty-eight female members joined the assembly, reaching a historic 34 percent representation by women (Coordinadora de la Mujer 2011). The participation of indigenous women in the assembly was significant, symbolized by the appointment of Silvia Lazarte, a Quechua woman, as the assembly's president.

Political participation by indigenous and non-indigenous women subsequently increased. According to data from the Gender Observatory of the Women's Coordination, in 2010 some 50 percent of ministerial positions were held by women, a number of them from low-income sectors (INSTRAW 2006). However, in 2012 only seven of the twenty ministerial positions were held by women, and only one of them was indigenous.[10]

Although indigenous women in Bolivia have gone from being almost entirely invisible and disqualified to becoming participants and protagonists in politics and decision making in recent years, resistance has been considerable. Acts of racist and sexist violence have increased, and were particularly egregious against indigenous women throughout the development of the Constituent Assembly (Paz 2007). Calla (in Hernández and Canessa 2012) observes that the presence of indigenous women in the assembly challenged both the monopoly of the Spanish language and the monopoly of legal knowledge, in other words, of lawmaking by experts.

The new Constitution was approved by a referendum in January 2009, broadening the scope of fundamental rights to include practically all human rights recognized in various international declarations and agreements (Rojas 2010). Gender equity is transversalized throughout the entire constitutional text and particularly in the catalogue of human rights, which denounces different forms of discrimination, in particular gender discrimination, establishing that "everyone, *in particular women*, has the right not to suffer physical, sexual or psychological violence, in the family as well as in society."[11]

In order to guarantee equity and combat gender discrimination, the Vice Ministry of Decolonization was created in 2009. Idón Chivi (the first vice minister) and Amalia Mamani have argued that decolonization is the main instrument to confront coloniality (*colonialidad*) and therefore colonialism, a weapon to combat injustice and inequality, and the key element in the government's process of change (Mamani and Chivi 2010). Chivi (2011) proposes decolonizing the state from within, directly confronting its colonial structure and logic. The concept of decolonization is thus the focus of state efforts to combat racism and patriarchy, both identified as the foundation of *colonialidad* (Mamani and Chivi 2010).

A "Depatriarchalization Unit" was created in August 2010 as part of the Vice Ministry. Its objectives were to identify and destabilize the social relations underpinning the patriarchal order, and transform them in order to build a fair and harmonious society. According to Mamani and Chivi (2010), twenty-five articles of the new Constitution underpin depatriarchalization: some of these officialize normative models that transgress the established patriarchal order (for example, by recognizing indigenous autonomies), and others refer to institutional innovations that aim to challenge gender discrimination.

The link between depatriarchalization and gender complementarity is established by the Plan for Equal Opportunity: Building the New Bolivia for Good Living (2008), which begins by observing that the patriarchal nature of power structures existed prior to the Conquest, in other words, that patriarchy is not a colonial heritage, but also existed in pre-Columbian cultures. The plan aims to "decolonize and de-neoliberalize gender" and to incorporate feminist demands to dismantle patriarchy, recognizing the historic connections between precolonial and Western forms of patriarchy. It also invokes complex Andean relations of complementarity and reciprocity between male and female, or *chachawarmi*.

Meanings and Representations of the *Chachawarmi* Principle of Complementarity in Totora Marka

In Totora Marka, complementarity is regarded as one of the central tenets of the community's worldview. In this respect, Choque and Mendizábal (2010: 93) believe that duality does not imply antagonism, "but opposites that complement each other, founded on a profound philosophy of the peoples, such as: life and death, day and night, bad and good, up and down, left and right, man and woman, reflected in the division of the territorial space, communities or *ayllus* that belong to the realm above, and communities that belong to the territory below."

In Bolivia, it is common to define complementarity as *chachawarmi* (*kariwarmi* in the case of Ecuador, as Cervone and Cucurí explain in chapter 5), a category today more commonly applied to the conjugal bond and strongly related to an idea of equality and duality between both sexes. Mamani (1989: 313) observes that "in *chachawarmi*, the wife has the same position and category as the husband. She is not subordinated to the husband, or the husband to the wife: both have equal positions, the same status, and complement each other."

When women from Totora explain *chachawarmi*, they mainly refer to the system of community authorities. Totora Marka is characterized by ancestral forms of organization based on the *ayllu-marka-suyu*.[12] Returning to *chachawarmi*, the women explained that the married couples constitute the system of authorities, so that at the *marka* level the highest authorities are the *Mallku* and the *T'alla de Consejo*, and the *Mallku* and the *T'alla de Marka*. At both the *ayllu* and the communal levels, the highest authorities are the *Tamani* and the *Mama Tamani*. Positions are held according to *sara-thaki*; in other words, they rotate according to the plots of land being cultivated (*sayañas*), which means that all members of the community must exercise a position of authority at some point in their lives.

Positions of communal authority are held only by married men and women, since, according to the interviewees, it is through marriage that one becomes a full person. As Albó and Mamani signaled (1976, in Choque 2009), people become *jaqi-persona-chachawarmi* only when they marry and acquire their own plot of land. Before that, they have no say in community affairs. The *jaqi/chachawarmi* category entails the right to citizenship—dual and diarchic—expressed in terms of economic, social, and political rights, as well as duties involving participation as authorities (Choque 2009). For women in Totora Marka, *chachawarmi* is exercised not just through the system of traditional authorities; it is a condition that transcends all conjugal relations. In the case of traditional authorities the women say it refers to "walking together," while for regular community members it has to do with "mutual help."

The Practices of *Chachawarmi*: Compliance and Noncompliance with the Principle of Complementarity

The previous section described discourses explaining the principle of complementarity as one that determines the world and establishes man and woman as opposite yet complementary elements, whose immediate reference in Totora Marka is *chachawarmi*. *Chachawarmi* manifests itself in the exercise of authority and in conjugal relations among community members, demonstrating why it is considered essential in the territory. In the paragraphs that follow I analyze how this principle develops in practice, describing the spaces where women perceive that *chachawarmi* is respected, and those where it is violated, and the causes they attribute to this noncompliance.

Spaces of Compliance with Chachawarmi

When I asked the women where the principle of complementarity is respected in practice, many of them mentioned that the presence of both men and women is essential in rituals, and several of them pointed out that in recent years, due to migration of men from the countryside to the cities, women are now in charge of performing certain rituals, especially those related to sowing. Ritual observance is one of the most important functions of the Marka's authorities. Besides rituals, the women stated that observing the principle of complementarity is mandatory in meetings of the Marka's traditional authorities: "All Mallkus must be with their *Mama Tamanis*, otherwise they are fined." This was verified through observation at assemblies of Marka, attended equally by men and women. These assemblies are important spaces to address disputes due to the high level of female participation, which allows women to challenge gender ideologies and pose their claims in a language of rights.

Spaces of Noncompliance with Chachawarmi

The women of Totora Marka believe that there are occasions where complementarity is not observed, such as meetings where ordinary community members participate—"only men go!"—and workshops or short courses held in the *ayllus*. In both spaces, women are in charge of preparing food, further limiting their chances of actively participating. Women also believed *chachawarmi* was not fully observed in the elaboration of the autonomic statute. I summarize this process below, focusing on women's participation and the strategies they used to ensure that their proposals were included.

After Totora Marka's population voted in favor of indigenous autonomy, the Council of Indigenous Authorities of Totora Marka was established, composed of *estatuyentes* who were elected in assemblies in each of the *ayllus*. In contrast to other positions in the territory, the *estatuyentes* were not structured according to the principle of complementarity. This was strongly criticized by the women, who stressed the importance of ensuring that the system of authorities, including those in charge of elaborating the statute, was exercised by couples. During the time I accompanied the process (during the first consultation), no woman was elected as *estatuyente*. Community members explained it was best to choose men because women's domestic responsibilities hindered their participation in meetings and prevented them from making the various journeys required. The relation between women's work and the impossibility of complying with *chachawarmi* is analyzed below.

As mentioned, the Council of Indigenous Authorities elaborated the statute's first draft and subsequently planned the first revolving consultation in order to elaborate the second version. Before the consultation began, the indigenous authorities, especially the men, expressed their interest in developing methodologies capable of gathering the women's proposals, acknowledging that at times their participation was minimal. Together with the authorities, the women and I made efforts to create a group composed exclusively of women. Even though there is an interest in opening inclusive spaces for women, since the first forum the men's platform opposed the formation of a women-only group, arguing that it would go against the notion of complementarity. Women formed the group despite this resistance, but the tension was visible again when they set out their proposals at the plenary session. Nonetheless, it is important to point out that the lack of openness by men was not widespread.

After the events in the Wara Wara *ayllu*, the *estatuyentes* decided that participants would no longer be divided in groups, but that each of the statute's articles would be read aloud in order to generate suggestions collectively. While women did participate in several forums organized in this fashion (for example, in the Lerco *ayllu*, around 55 percent of the participants were women), few of them spoke or put forward proposals. Because of this, the authorities asked me to collaborate with them by conducting interviews alongside the deliberative forums.

The first consultation was carried out through nine deliberative forums held in the Marka's nine *ayllus*, with 684 participants. A meeting was subsequently held to evaluate, plan, and analyze the proposals to be included in the second draft of the autonomy statute; in preparation for this meeting, the initial idea was for the female authorities of the territory to present the systematization, but no woman was summoned. According to the male authorities, this was because the meeting took place in the city of La Paz, which meant that the women would have had to leave their homes and neglect their domestic duties in order to attend. However, the authorities and *estatuyentes* expressed their interest in including the female proposals in the autonomy statute: "Everything that the women request is right, autonomy is not just for men."

Weeks later, a *tanta chawi* of the entire *marka* was held to conclude the analysis and incorporate the proposals of the first consultation. A number of conflicts arose as a result of a reconfiguration of the *estatuyente* council and the withdrawal of several organizations that supported the process, and the women's proposals were abandoned for several months.[13] Thanks to pressure exerted by the highest level indigenous authorities, new *estatuyentes* were appointed and the elaboration of the document resumed.

The visit that authorities from the municipalities of Chaquí and Vitichi (in the department of Potosí) made to Jesús de Machaca and San Pedro de Totora in order to learn from the experiences of both territories in their conversion from municipalities to indigenous autonomy contributed to a resumption of the work.[14] At this meeting the authorities presented the incomplete second draft of the statute. Following the encounter four commissions were created, respecting the proposed structure of the autonomy statute. Only four or five women participated regularly in the work of the commissions, and they were present more as listeners than active participants. When asked about this they said that the overly legalistic language of the ministry's experts and the authorities made it difficult for them to frame an opinion on the articles analyzed: "We from Tawantisuyo haven't studied law, the authorities don't explain well, in the community some of us know laws, others don't."

Given this meager participation, in one of the planning meetings the four or five women requested that a women's meeting be held to collate their contributions and thus incorporate the work they had done in the first consultation.

Despite the apparent reluctance of indigenous authorities, several female leaders, collaborators, and I were able to secure their agreement for a Women's
Event of Totora Marka. Representatives from the nine *ayllus* participated,
including female authorities and community members. The meeting was facilitated by Lucila Choque, a trainer on Indigenous and Peasant Autonomies and
Gender from the Ministry of Autonomies, and myself. In response to a sugges-
tion by the Ministry of Autonomies and particularly the requests of the women
present, the proposals were elaborated as articles ready to be included in the
statute, in a legalistic language similar to that used in the draft autonomy
statute. Several of the participants saw this as the only way to ensure their
proposals would be included: "that way they'll go straight to the statute." All
the proposals were presented in a plenary session at the deliberative council of
estatuyentes and delivered, signed, in writing.

Similar to when the women's proposals were presented at the plenary session of the *marka*'s assembly, heated arguments ensued among male authorities, *estatuyentes*, and community members. Most of the comments revolved
around the view that the women's proposals ran counter to the principle of
complementarity. However, some male authorities also argued in favor of the
women's demands.

Despite the lack of openness to the women's proposals, many of the articles
proposed in the Women's Event were inserted in the next draft of the statute,
which was socialized through a second consultation that took place once again
through deliberative forums along the territory's nine *ayllus*. Around 915 people
participated. As a result of the first and second consultations, on December
18, 2011, the Council of Indigenous Authorities of Totora Marka approved
the final version of the autonomy statute, presented in February 2012 to the
Plurinational Constitutional Court for approval and submission to a referendum. As mentioned in the introduction, in September 2013 the Plurinational
Constitutional Court declared the autonomy statute of Totora Marka compatible with the national Constitution.

The process described here demonstrates that although complementarity was invoked and the male authorities themselves sought women's input,
their participation in many of the spaces working to develop the statute was
minimal. The creation of the Indigenous Authorities Council of Totora Marka
without including *chachawarmi* in the exercise of the *estatuyentes*, the men's
opposition to the women creating a group or organizing a meeting, the debates
that ensued every time the women presented their proposals in plenary sessions, the fact that the women were neither summoned to nor participated in
events that took place outside the territory, and women's meager participation
in the work of the commissions and more generally demonstrated the difficulties women faced in articulating their demands. Political conflicts and the use
of an overly legalistic language in the statute, and hence in the accompanying

debates, hindered women's active participation. The women's proposals were often interpreted as defying the principle of complementarity, even though it was in fact the governing principle of each and every one of the demands they presented. Finally, the process described here suggests that in some spaces we see echoes of what Cervone and Cucurí observe in chapter 5 in relation to the notion of complementarity, namely that it is not synonymous with equality; relationships between indigenous men and women can be complementary yet asymmetrical.

Despite all these obstacles, women from Totora successfully developed a series of strategies to make themselves heard, such as the Women's Event in Totora and the request to their collaborators to help them elaborate their proposals in the same legalistic language that had hindered their participation in previous activities. It is also worth noting that men's closed-mindedness was not all-inclusive; several of them publicly supported the women's proposals, and a number of authorities expressed their commitment to incorporate their demands, recognizing that they contributed to the exercise of *chachawarmi*.

Reasons Why Chachawarmi Is Violated

When I asked the women why *chachawarmi* is not observed in some contexts, they identified several reasons, but three were mentioned most often. The first is the distribution of gender roles. Women commonly have multiple responsibilities and activities related to domestic chores, cultivating the land, feeding and herding animals, spinning and weaving clothing, and especially taking care of children: "If men gave birth to children and we only raised them, it would be so good! But we give birth, we carry them in our womb and continue carrying them on our backs. After giving birth to so many children, I keep doing chores the day after childbirth, there's no one to help us and we have to do it. In addition, we're always spinning and weaving. We never just do nothing. Women have so many chores!" (Testimony by a female participant, Women's Event in Totora Marka, August 12, 2011). Most women said that few men take care of their children: "Men go around with their hands free, carrying a backpack." Some women said that women themselves do not allow the men to take care of children because it contravenes gender ideologies. The social control exerted by the community is also a factor, since many people criticize men who assume roles attributed to the female gender and criticize women for participating in meetings. The relation between sharing the responsibility for raising children and complying with the principle of complementarity is evident when women confirm they are able to participate in communal matters only because their husbands are also responsible for the care of their children.

The second reason is that men have more cultural capital, facilitating their participation. Certain forms of knowledge and education effectively place them at higher levels in communal decision making. The women from Totora attribute these differences to the fact that education is usually prioritized for male children. In the deliberative forums women frequently commented that they studied up to the third grade of elementary school, while several men had finished high school. Women remember that parents prefer girls not to study, because when they grow up they will abandon their community to go and live with their husband. *Patrivirilocal* postmarital residence, which establishes that newlywed couples must go to live at the husband's paternal home, is related to indigenous women's position as *mayt'ata* ("borrowed person"), as analyzed by Choque and Mendizábal (2010). Choque (2009: 10) explains that "in the domestic space, women constitute beings that are not one's own, that do not belong to the family . . . therefore, the investment made to raise them must be minimal." This condition persists when the woman leaves her family of origin and arrives at her husband's home.

According to the women I interviewed, the fact that men receive more formal education means that they master both Spanish and Aymara, while women mainly speak Aymara. This fact is not taken into account by some male authorities, who conduct meetings exclusively in Spanish, hindering women's participation: "Those of us who don't understand [Spanish] are not informed [of the meetings], that's what happens." This difference in formal education also contributes to the fact that men tend to better understand legal matters. This became evident during the elaboration of the autonomy statute; for example, in the interviews I conducted in parallel to the forums, the women constantly said they were afraid to participate and be criticized by the men. Others said that the fear of participating applied to all community meetings and not only to the process linked to conversion to indigenous autonomy, which means that these limitations are associated not only with the use of a complex, legal language, but also more broadly with discrimination and women's exclusion.[15]

According to the women, a third reason, closely related to gender ideologies, is the fact that compliance with *chachawarmi* is required more of women than of men. This came to light when we inquired about the community's perception of "single women" (a notion that interviewees related to "single mothers"). Both men and women told me that single women are respected but that it depends on whether "they behave well," which implies respecting men who have a partner. In some cases, their own families of origin are opposed to these women inheriting land, believing that doing so would violate patrivirilocal postmarital residence.

When I inquired about cases of single women or widows who had held positions of authority, all of them responded, "You can hold a position alone, but together with someone." They gave as examples several women between 2010 and 2011 who were accompanied by close relatives who were authorities. The ideal is for single women to hold positions of authority accompanied by a male relative, to comply with the principle of complementarity, even though in recent years there has been more flexibility in this respect, with cases of women accompanying the exercise of another woman's position.

One fact that is dramatically changing perceptions toward single women, and hence the exercise of *chachawarmi*, is migration, a phenomenon that means men leave their communities of origin for several months a year and women are left entirely in charge of the home as well as in positions of communal authority. The women constantly referred to these and other elements that transform the representations and practices of *chachawarmi*.

The causes for noncompliance with *chachawarmi* analyzed here are closely related to gender ideologies, that is, to the position assigned to women by the sex/gender system, which implies a number of cultural notions of what is female and male (De Lauretis 2000). In the case of Totora Marka, women are charged with multiple responsibilities, among them raising children—seen as essential to their compliance with *chachawarmi*. Male children are prioritized in terms of schooling; men are also able to hold positions of authority unaccompanied, while "single women" suffer multiple forms of discrimination. All of these elements contribute to lower levels of female participation and cultural capital, hindering their influence on communal decision making. However, the issues the women identified also reflect their analysis of elements that can be transformed in order to fully respect the complementarity they so eagerly demand.

"We Must Be *Chachawarmi–Warmichacha*": Resignifying the Principle of Complementarity in Totora Marka

Up to now this chapter has focused on the multiple meanings attributed to *chachawarmi* and the practices whereby, according to the women from Totora Marka, this principle is either observed or violated. This final section analyzes to what extent the language of rights allowed them to express their problems and what effect state discourses had on that language.

Among the various reforms and states discourses, I was mainly interested in those related to depatriarchalization and gender decolonization. Through interviews, I enquired what men and women from Totora Marka understood by these concepts. I also documented whether they used these terms during the elaboration of the autonomy statute. During the first consultation, the structure of the statute itself was considered a decolonizing element. As early as the first draft, it was elaborated around the four elements of the *jach'a qhana* (Andean cross):[16] *ajayu* (spiritual energy), which referred to the articles relating to indigenous autonomy of Totora Marka; *yatiña* (knowledge), which encompassed the articles on human development, education, health, and other topics; *luraña* (doing), which included everything related to the economy and the territory; and *atiña* (power), which referred to the political and legal structure and organization of Totora Marka's autonomy. Historic leaders of the territory believed that this symbolism belonged to Totora Marka because it was part of the pre-Incan Tiwanacota culture and synthesized the principles and values of the Andean worldview, especially the principle of complementarity. In interviews all these leaders argued that decolonization was a means to establish fundamental norms based on Andean worldviews, without contravening national laws.

The term "depatriarchalization" was used less often than "decolonization" during the elaboration of the statute. Some women who participated in events organized by the central government believe that the meaning of "depatriarchalization" is "recuperating respect between tatas and mamas" and "discussing their daughters' future." Finally, they said that it was a term they did not understand, but that they hoped that the statute would ensure that *chachawarmi* would be observed. Expectations among women were high; they claimed that once the statute was approved, men would have to "obey" their proposals, since indigenous women are recognized by the national Constitution. Claims by Totoreña women in the context of the Statute are similar to the proposals in the Women's Revolutionary Law (1994) by the Zapatista National Liberation Army (Mexico), which, as Speed, Hernández Castillo, and Stephen (2006) point out, was the first written text in which Mayan women expressed specific gender demands. Debate around the Revolutionary Law centered on "the presumed contradiction between indigenous communities' collective rights to maintain their culture and the rights of individual community members, in particular, women, that might be violated by those cultural norms and practices" (Speed, Hernández Castillo, and Stephen 2006: 203).

In general, women in Totora know little about the Constitution and the concepts of decolonization and depatriarchalization. However, elaborating the statute was an important process enabling discussion of the principles underpinning the plurinational state. Sally Merry's (2009) concept of vernacularization signals an intersubjective process of deconstruction and reappropriation of state or international discourses. Although people cannot easily define decolonization and depatriarchalization, in practice these concepts are used as strategies to promote indigenous autonomy. This was the case with decolonization, incorporated into the structure of the autonomy statute in the form of the *jach'a qhana* (Andean cross), and the relationship that Andean women saw between depatriarchalization and their participation in the elaboration of the statute. These debates demonstrate what Moore (1973) proposes regarding the semiautonomous social field, in the sense that it is society that controls the law. In other words, paraphrasing Moore, the community generates rules, customs, and symbols, but at the same time is vulnerable to the external legal system that surrounds it without, however, always dominating it, thus leaving space for resistance and autonomy (Moore 1978; Merry 1988; Sieder 1997; Sierra and Chenaut 2002), in this case to use those concepts in defense of self-government.

Chachawarmi and the Struggle for Collective Rights and Indigenous Women's Rights

All of the women's proposals revolved around revaluing and restructuring the principle of complementarity, proposing *chachawarmi–warmichacha* instead of *chachawarmi*. This transformation is linked to discourses invoking the rights of indigenous peoples and indigenous women. Several women mentioned that they heard the word "rights" for the first time in the social movements of the early 2000s, especially in the Gas War of 2003 in which many of them participated: "There we said that indigenous communities had rights." At the same time, they associated the rights of the mamas with the presence of indigenous women as Ministers, Congresswomen, and Assembly members in national decision-making: "In Parliament no women wore *polleras*, but now we're there. . . . Those women wearing *polleras* in the Constituent Assembly spoke, they did things for the country."

Importantly, when women refer to *mamas'* rights they consistently mean the rights of the rest of the community's members as well: in their proposals they developed the rights that *tatas* (men), *yocallwawas* and *imillwawas* (boys and girls), *jaju* and *majta* (youths), *awichas* and *achachilas* (elders), and people with disabilities should have. Recovering this holistic view of communal discourses, the National Plan for Equal Opportunities (2008) affirms that no community member can be perceived as an individual, since the collective takes precedence and gives meaning to all forms of identity.

The inability to split rights as indigenous women from the rights of the rest of the community members confirms the position of Foro Internacional de Mujeres Indígenas (2007) that rights need to be approached from the intersection of the rights of indigenous peoples, human rights, and women's human rights, which is why the dichotomy between individual and collective rights must be overcome. In this book, Hernández, Sierra, Lozano, and De Marinis make visible the fact that women's struggles fall within wider struggles for collective rights, contributing importantly to set up an emancipatory vision of justice and indigenous rights in their organizations and territories.

The women's proposal of restructuring *chachawarmi* as *chachawarmi–warmichacha* relates to five fundamental rights that the autonomous territory must strive to guarantee in order to comply with the principle of complementarity. The first is the participation of both *mamas* and *tatas*: the women argued that all positions of authority at every level of the community should be exercised according to the principle of complementarity, and they criticized the fact that the second draft of the autonomy statute did not establish *chachawarmi* for the exercise of several positions, such as members of the communal territorial representation and the indigenous legislative council, executive bodies, and secretariats. They argued that if the principle of complementarity was not incorporated in the statute, then the document should establish that half of the positions must be held by women (parity).

One proposal to promote women's participation was the creation of an Organization of Women from Totora Marka to support the indigenous government according to the principle of complementarity. Two goals were identified for the organization: (1) productive projects to generate economic resources for families, but especially for women and children, and (2) support in the administration of justice, mainly in cases of domestic violence, for which they proposed creating a women's committee in charge of ensuring the well-being of the whole population of Totora Marka. They argued that changes were needed not only at the territorial level, but also in the home.

In order to ensure more women's participation in community meetings and workshops, they proposed that men and women equally share the tasks of child care. Once *mamas* decide to participate, changes occur in gender relations within families, which can influence the distribution of domestic responsibilities and lead to the exercise of *chachawarmi* demanded by women. This echoes Paredes's (2008) observation that recognizing alterity should have an effect on the redistribution of domestic work. Along these lines, the women claimed that their future autonomous government should administer funds to create *wawa-utas* (children's homes) to provide child care while women participate in meetings: "Now I tell him, 'serve your own breakfast, I'm no longer here to serve you, now you have to serve me the same way.' This is what we have to say now: 'Why should I be the only one to have children? Now you have your place to raise the children just like I do. You have your place to wash the children's clothes like I do. Everything you do I do too, that way we'll work together'" (Testimony by a female participant, Women's Event in Totora Marka, August 12, 2011).

The second right invoked is that both men and women should decide how many children they want to have. They recalled that years earlier the goal was to have many children, to have more family members tilling the land. At that time, it was common for men to decide when to have sexual relations and the number of children they would have: "My grandma used to tell me that my grandpa would come home drunk and she would be pregnant; he didn't even ask her if she wanted to." Currently, with ever greater divisions of land into smaller and smaller plots, having many children is no longer advantageous. Women's participation in this decision is important because they know which months are good for giving birth and how much time to wait before having the next child, making sure their health is not compromised.

The third right was that "we all have the right to study." To this end, they proposed that once the autonomous territory was established, funds should be managed to facilitate larger and better educational institutions to keep young people from migrating from the countryside to the cities. One demand related to the dispositions of the statute was that the requirements to hold positions of authority be modified, since the second draft established that all people in executive positions in the autonomous government should have completed secondary school. The women claimed that this requirement established educational levels that most of them, as well as many men, could not attain. In addition, they argued that higher educational levels were not necessarily synonymous with great aptitudes to properly manage and lead the territory.

A fourth proposal had to do with rights to land. Because of postmarital, patrivirilocal residence (the newlywed couple lives in the husband's family home), women do not inherit land from their fathers, and if they do, it is significantly less than what men receive. Brothers often pressure their parents to bequeath more land to them. Women perceive that when they resort to indigenous justice, the authorities tend to support the men. To end these inequalities, they argued that with *chachawarmi–warmichacha* women must inherit the same amount of land as men, and that widows should inherit their husband's land.

A fifth element analyzed, one of the issues most frequently discussed in the forums and the women's event, was access to more gender equitable forms of community justice. Many women believed that cases of extreme violence existed in part because of the lack of an autonomy statute. Domestic violence is usually first solved by the couple—"we first speak among ourselves"—but if the man repeats the offense, the woman usually resorts to her godparents. If the man assaults her again, the woman rarely denounces him to the indigenous authorities: "we're ashamed of saying those things." The women complained that communal authorities usually minimize domestic violence complaints— "they tell us that we have to solve it among ourselves"—or transfer the cases to the state justice system, where they also remain unresolved. In chapter 2 Terven indicates how women have to constantly confront gender- and sex-based models and how their claims tend to go unsupported, because they are considered guilty of provoking the actions against them. In Totora Marka the participants proposed that for all cases of domestic violence, the authorities elaborate good behavior agreements, and that all violent acts against anyone in the community be punished, especially those committed against women. Nonetheless, women expressed awareness that even if the Autonomous Statute includes a plan to prevent and sanction gender violence, practices are unlikely to change rapidly. In chapter 3 Sieder shows that although in 2010 the first Municipal Gender Policy was enacted in Guatemala, structural inequalities mean it is extremely difficult for victims of gender violence to make a formal charge against their perpetrators, with the consequence that cases of domestic violence unreported and sexual violence is hardly ever formally charged.

The document that was broadly approved on December 18, 2011, and subsequently presented to the Plurinational Constitutional Court, includes several of the women's proposals summarized above. In its articles 6 and 29 the document decrees that *chachawarmi* is the foundation of Totora Marka's autonomous government, and that this principle will therefore determine its policies once it is established. Article 18 (regarding the family) establishes equality of rights, duties, obligations, and opportunities for men and women, which implies an education based on complementarity (article 21), integral health (article 31), recognizing, respecting, and promoting the right to safe maternity, and resorting to ancestral or Western practices, which implies sexual/reproductive educational programs and orientation.

Several of the women's proposals regarding political participation were also included. Article 80 of the statute establishes *chachawarmi* complementarity as the principle governing most of the positions that will be instituted once conversion to indigenous autonomy concludes. In this regard, it establishes that the election of authorities for the Jiliri Uñanchayiri Legislative Body (composed of seven elected representatives), for the Jiliri Irpiri Executive Body (a representative from each Aransaya and Urinsaya *parcialidad*),[17] and the Jiliri Arkiri Major Officer (chosen among the seven representatives of the legislative body) must be done on a rotating basis and guarantee gender equity. It states that the representatives of the Legislative Body, which has deliberative, legislative, and overseeing faculties, must be elected "with equity expressed in the form of gender parity and alternation," and that "the position of the highest executive authority is based on the principles of dual government, where the exercise of authority is *chachawarmi*." The women's proposal regarding the eligibility criteria for authorities was also incorporated; the educational level requirement was eliminated, replaced by a stipulation that authorities of the autonomous territory should have prior experience in leadership and service.

Regarding greater access to gender justice, article 19, on the protection of persons, establishes that the autonomous government shall contribute to eliminate "domestic violence, providing protection to women, fostering policies of family reflection, motivating families to recover the ancestral principles and values of Suma Quamaña in coordination with the central government. All forms of violence against women are forbidden."

Some of the women's proposals, such as the creation of an Organization of Women from Totora Marka to support the autonomous indigenous government in accordance with the complementarity principle, were not included. Measures to promote women's participation and to restructure gender relations, such as shared child care and an analysis of the redistribution of responsibilities, were also rejected. Likewise, the issue of women's right to land ownership and inheritance was ignored. Yet despite the fact that not all of their demands were incorporated into the statute, the women's discourse on rights, as Merry (2010) observes, generated alternative, less individualistic views of social justice, more focused on the communities' needs. In this case, a rights discourse based on a collective worldview was used by the women to formulate and legitimize their proposals. Lozano notes something similar in chapter 7 in her analysis of women's strategies in the Cauca Regional Indigenous Council (Colombia). In order to position their agenda and strengthen their movement, women made use of the organization's narratives of "integrality" and "communality" to build on their proposals. Such approaches did not mean they avoid questioning power systems or cultural practices that violate their rights within their organizations.

Conclusions

Processes of legal reform in Bolivia are creating new options for indigenous women from Totora Marka to defend and demand their rights based on a resignification of the principle of complementarity, culturally reframing discourses of equality and equity in a way that aims to eliminate the existing differences between meanings and/or concepts and practices of *chachawarmi*. For the women of Totora Marka, the principle of complementarity creates spaces to negotiate relations between men and women. This process, whereby complementarity, duality, and equilibrium are resemanticized and given new meaning, turns culture into a space or location for resistance and liberation (Hernández and Sierra 2005; Macleod 2007, 2011). In other words, culture is a dynamic and shifting terrain where the meanings of symbols, principles, and norms are constantly negotiated (Merry 2003). The proposals to resignify *chachawarmi* and the transformations in its practices and representations discussed in this chapter demonstrate that complementarity is a complex and flexible principle, subject to change.

In the process described in this chapter, two different positions emerged regarding the enforceability of gender rights. One was based on the opinion of some—mainly male—authorities who interpreted the women's demands as an affront to the principle of complementarity, even though complementarity was the guiding principle that oriented their proposals. As Sanabria, Nostas, and Román (2006) observe, some men use the principle of complementarity as an essentialist and static concept in order to deny women's specific demands. In response to the men's closed-mindedness, the women developed a number of strategies to make themselves heard, demonstrating their agency and their abilities to produce knowledge, visions, and policies capable of revealing new horizons of meaning (Burman 2011). Ultimately, the language of rights allowed them to express and legitimize their demands. Toward this end, they invoked both their rights as indigenous women and the collective rights of the future autonomous government of Totora Marka, as interdependent demands.

Another position regarding the enforceability of gender rights was the support received by several male authorities and ordinary men, indicating that not all men reject greater women's participation. Their support was vital for the inclusion of the women's demands in the autonomy statute. The women's central focus on revaluing and resignifying *chachawarmi* meant many men felt included in their proposals. As Hernández (2001) and Macleod (2011) have observed, the complementarity demanded by women invites men to put in practice the principles and values they claim.

Regarding the vernacularization of rights through the discourses and practices of depatriarchalization and gender decolonization, this chapter has shown that both concepts have yet to be translated into clear policies and actions aimed at securing greater gender equity. Nonetheless, the elaboration of the autonomy statute created important spaces for reflection on gender relations and on the new constitutional order more generally. The vernacularization, deconstruction, and reappropriation of state discourses demonstrate that although a number of concepts central to the plurinational state are not well known, they are used in practice as a means to defend and demand self-government. Paraphrasing Chávez et al. (2010), the proposals of the women from Totora Marka can be understood as a strategy for depatriarchalization and decolonization from their position as women and from their concrete individual and collective struggles.

NOTES

1. Totora Marka corresponds to the province of San Pedro de Totora in the department of Oruro, located in the northwestern corner of the department.

2. The municipalities included Huacaya, Tarabuco, and Mojocoya (department of Chuquisaca); Charazani and Jesús de Machaca (La Paz); Pampa Aullagas, San Pedro de Totora, Chipaya, and Salinas de Garci Mendoza (Oruro); Chayanta (Potosí); and Charagua (Santa Cruz).

3. The Framework Law on Autonomies recognizes three types of autonomies in addition to indigenous autonomies: (1) departmental autonomies, (2) regional autonomies (constituted by municipalities or provinces), and (3) municipal autonomies.

4. In September 2013, the court declared constitutional 90 percent of the statute. Only 10 out of 102 articles were found incompatible with the Constitution.

5. As part of the collaborative methodology, in addition to systematizing the women's proposals, the proposals and contributions of the new forums held in the context of the first *muyu* were also systematized; based on this, the second draft of the statute was reworked. Upon request of the authorities and community residents, a video documentary of the entire process was made.

6. During the fieldwork, the support of the Construir Foundation, which developed the Dialogue and Agreement for the Conversion to Indigenous Autonomy of Totora Marka project, was essential. This institution facilitated contact with the organization and with the people with whom we jointly developed most of the activities. Teresa Arteaga's literature review of research on depatriarchalization and complementarity was vital for the writing of this chapter.

7. The purpose of the march was to pressure the government of then President Jaime Paz Zamora to institute three presidential decrees recognizing indigenous territories in eastern Bolivia.

8. This conflict was the result of the attempt of then President Sánchez de Lozada to sell some of the country's natural gas to the United States. This movement led to the demands to nationalize fossil fuels and to call for a constituent assembly to draft a new Constitution.

9. Article 15 of this law established gender equity and alternation in the election of the 255 *estatuyentes* of the Assembly.

10. Nemesia Achacollo, Minister of Rural Development and Land, who was Executive Secretary of the National Federation of Peasant Women of Bolivia.

11. Art. 15.II. in chap. 2 on Fundamental Rights.

12. The *ayllu* is the basic unit composed of several communities and families (*sayañas*), a group of several *ayllus* constitutes a *marka*, and a group of several *markas* composes a *suyu*. Totora encompasses thirty-two communities grouped into nine *ayllus* (each of them with two to five communities), which make up Totora Marka, which is in turn part of the *Jach'a Karangas Suyu*, which is part of the National Council of Ayllus and Markas of Qullasuyu (CONAMAQ).

13. During the *tanta chawi*, allies of the municipal government, which had an important number of members of the Movement for Socialism (MAS), questioned the president of the *estatuyentes* elected in 2009, who was municipal candidate for an opposing party. The conflict between the Estatuyentes Council and the municipal government had been apparent since the beginning of the first *muyu*, where several of the *estatuyentes* noted that there was little collaboration from the mayor and that he even opposed the autonomy of Totora Marka, because conversion to indigenous authority would effectively reduce his administration to three years. During the same *tanta chawi*, some NGOs were questioned and charged with manipulating the wording of the statute. At the same time as the *tanta chawi* was held, the change in communal authorities that occurs at the beginning of every year took place, so new authorities who were unaware of the process developed during the first consultation came in. All of these facts paralyzed the statute for around two months.

14. Encounter organized by the Tierra Foundation and the ACLO Foundation.

15. Arnold (1997) warns that we should not overestimate the importance of public rhetoric and interpret silence in communal assemblies as an unequivocal proof of discrimination. Harris (1980) and Arnold (1997) argue that, while it is true that men have privileged access to the language of power (that is, the language used in public discourse), women have access to discursive power through other means, such as weaving and singing, which allows them to influence their sociopolitical context and effect change, moving "beyond silence," countering male oral discourse with different yet complementary discursive powers.

16. *Jach'a qhana*, which means "four ladders" (*tawa jach'a qhana*) in Quechua, has the form of a square and graded cross with twelve tips. It is a symbol that developed in the Andean cultures and later in the territories of the Inca Empire of Tawantinsuyo (Lozano 1990).

17. The *marka* is subdivided into two *parcialidades* according to the dual logic of *Aransaya* (*parcialidad* on the southern side of Totora) and *Urinsaya* (*parcialidad* on the north of Totora).

REFERENCES

Arnold, Denise. 1997. *Más allá del silencio: las fronteras de género en los Andes*. La Paz: CIASE/ILCA.

Arnold, Denise, and Alison Spedding. 2005. *Mujeres en los movimientos sociales en Bolivia 2000–2003*. La Paz: CIDEM-ILCA.

Burman, Anders. 2011. "Chachawarmi: Silence and Rival Voices on Decolonisation and Gender Politics in Andean Bolivia." *Journal of Latin American Studies* 43 (1): 65–91.

Calla, Pamela. 2012. "Luchas legales y política de las calles en torno al racismo: descentrando la patriarcalidad del Estado Plurinacional de Bolivia." In *Género, complementariedad y exclusiones en Mesoamérica y los Andes*, edited by Aída Hernández and Andrew Canessa, 43–60. Quito: Abya Yala.

Chaplin, Ann. 2010. *Movimientos Sociales en Bolivia: De la fuerza al poder*. Oxford: Oxford University Press.

Chávez, Patricia, Mokrani Dunia, Radhuber Isabella, and Quiróz Tania. 2010. "¿A prueba las mujeres o el proceso de cambio?" *Revista Herramienta*, no. 45. Buenos Aires.

Chivi, Idón. 2011. "Descolonización y despatriarcalización en las políticas públicas." In *Políticas Públicas, Descolonización y Despatriarcalización en Bolivia, Estado Plurinacional*, 77–103. La Paz: Ministerio de Cultura, Viceministerio de Descolonización.

Choque, María Eugenia. 2009. *Chacha warmi. Imaginarios y vivencias en El Alto*. La Paz: Centro de Promoción de la Mujer Gregoria Apaza.

Choque, María Eugenia, and Mónica Mendizábal. 2010. "Descolonizando el género a través de la profundización de la condición sullka y mayt'ata." *T'inkazos*, no. 28: 81–97.

Coordinadora de la Mujer. 2011. "Paso a paso. Así lo hicimos. Avances y Desafíos en la Participación Política de las Mujeres." Unpublished document.

Costa, Jimena. 2004. "La 'Guerra del Gas.' Representaciones sobre neoliberalismo y y defensa de los recursos naturales en la crisis política de octubre de 2003 en Bolivia." Colección Monografías, no. 14. Caracas: Programa Globalización, Cultura y Transformaciones Sociales, CIPOST, FaCES, Universidad Central de Venezuela.

De Lauretis, Teresa. 2000. "Tecnologías del Género." In De Lauretis, *Diferencias, Etapas de un camino a través del feminismo.*, 111–146. Madrid: Horas y Horas, cuadernos inacabados.

Estatuto Autonómico Originario de Totora Marka. 2011. "Approved Broadly and in Detail by the Deliberative Body of Totora Marka." Unpublished document.

Foro Internacional de Mujeres Indígenas. 2007. "Mairin Iwanka Raya, Mujeres Indígenas confrontan la violencia." Companion report to the Study on Violence against Indigenous Women by the UN Secretary General.

Harris, Olivia. 1980. "The Power of Signs: Gender, Culture and the Wild in the Bolivian Andes." In *Nature, Culture and Gender*, edited by Carol MacCormack and Marilyn Strathern, 70–94. New York: Cambridge University Press.

Hernández, Aída. 2001. "Entre el etnocentrismo feminista y el esencialismo étnico. Las mujeres indígenas y sus demandas de género." *Debate Feminista* 24: 1–24.

Hernández, Aída, and Andrew Canessa. 2012. *Género, complementariedad y exclusiones en Mesoamérica y los Andes*. Perú: Abya Yala.

Hernández, Aída, and Teresa Sierra. 2005. "Repensar los derechos colectivos desde el género. Aportes de las mujeres indígenas al debate de la autonomía." In M. Sanchez, ed., *La doble mirada. Voces e historias de mujeres indígenas*, 105–120. Mexico City: UNIFEM—ILSB.

INSTRAW (Internacional de Investigaciones y Capacitación de las Naciones Unidas para la Promoción de la Mujer). 2006. *Gobernabilidad, género y participación política de las mujeres en el ámbito local, Participar es llegar*. Santo Domingo.

Lozano, Alfredo. 1990. *Cusco-Cosqo Modelo simbólico de la cosmología andina*. Quito: Coedición FAPUCE.

Macleod, Morna. 2007. "Género, cosmovisión y movimiento maya en Guatemala. Deshilando los debates." In *Política, etnicidad e inclusión digital en los albores del milenio*, edited by S. Robinson and L. Valladares, 295–324. Mexico City: UAM-Izt. and Porrúa Eds.

———. 2011. *Nietas del fuego, creadoras del alba: Lucha político-culturales de mujeres mayas.* Guatemala: FLACSO.

Mamani, Amalia, and Idón Chivi. 2010. "Descolonización y Despatriarcalización en la Nueva Constitución Política Horizontes Emancipatorios del Constitucionalismo Plurinacional." Ciudad de El Alto: Centro de Promoción de la Mujer Gregoria Apaza.

Mamani, Manuel. 1989. "Structure of the Livestock Marking Ritual in the Chilean Andes." Master's thesis, University of Florida, Gainesville.

Manual de Funciones de las Unidades del Viceministerio de Descolonización. 2010. Unpublished document.

McNeish, John, and Ana Cecilia Arteaga. 2012. "An Accumulated Rage: Legal Pluralism and Gender Justice in Bolivia." In *Gender Justice and Legal Pluralities: Latin American and African Perspectives*, edited by R. Sieder and J. McNeish, 263–291. New York: Routledge.

Merry, Sally. 1988. "'Legal Pluralism' and Franz Von Benda Beckmann, 'Comments on Merry.'" *Law & Society* 22 (5): 869–901.

———. 2003. "Rights Talk and the Experience of Law: Implementing Women's Human Rights to Protection from Violence." *Human Rights Quarterly* 25 (2): 343–381.

———. 2009. "Vernacularization on the Ground: Local Uses of Global Women's Rights in Peru, China, India and the United States." *Global Networks* 9: 441–461.

———. 2010. "Introducción. Cultura y Transnacionalismo." In *Derechos humanos y violencia de género: El derecho internacional en el mundo de la justicia local*, 21–77. Colombia: Siglo del Hombre/Universidad de los Andes Colombia: Siglo del Hombre/Universidad de los Andes.

Ministerio de Culturas, Viceministerio de Descolonización. 2012. "Caminos de la Despatriarcalización. Boletín informativo." Unpublished document.

Molina, Ramiro, and Ana Cecilia Arteaga. 1998. *¿Dos racionalidades y una lógica jurídica?: La justicia comunitaria en el altiplano boliviano*. La Paz, Bolivia: Compañeros de las Américas and Fundación Diálogo.

Moore, Sally Falk. 1973. "Law and Social Change: The Semi-autonomous Social Field as an Appropriate Subject of Study." *Law & Society Review* 7: 719–746.

———. 1978. *Law as Process: An Anthropological Approach*. New York: Routledge.

Paredes, Julieta. 2008. *Hilando fino, desde el feminismo comunitario*. La Paz: Mujeres Creando.

Paz, Eduardo. 2007. "Anulando al antagonista político en las comisiones de la Asamblea Constituyente." In *Observando el racismo: Racismo y regionalismo en el proceso constituyente*, 99–113. La Paz: Defensor del Pueblo y Universidad la Cordillera.

Plan Nacional para la Igualdad de Oportunidades. 2008. "Mujeres construyendo la nueva Bolivia para vivir bien." Unpublished document.

Rojas, Farit. 2010. "Análisis y comentario de la Primera Parte de la CPE." In *Miradas: Nuevo Texto constitucional, Instituto Internacional para la Democracia y la Asistencia Electoral (IDEA Internacional)*, ed. Instituto Internacional de Integración del Convenio Andrés Bello, 283–295. La Paz: Vice Presidency of the Plurinational State of Bolivia, Universidad Mayor de San Andrés.

Román, Olivia. 2008. *Participación política y liderazgo de las mujeres indígenas en América Latina*. Case study. Bolivia: PNUD.

Sanabria, Carmen, Mercedes Nostas, and María Jenny Román. 2006. *Bolivia. Nudos, tensiones y esperanzas, en Boletín Cotidiano Mujer, No. 42*. La Paz. http://www.cotidianomujer.org.uy/2006/42p13.htm.

Sieder, Rachel. 1997. *Derecho consuetudinario y transición democrática en Guatemala.* Guatemala: FLACSO.

Sierra, Teresa. 2010. "Mujeres indígenas, derecho y costumbre: Las ideologías de género en las prácticas de la justicia." In *Los códigos del género: Prácticas del derecho en el México contemporáneo,* edited by Helga Baitenmann, Victoria Chenaut, and Ann Varley, 177–200. Mexico City: UNAM-United Nations Development Fund for Women.

Sierra, Teresa, and Victoria Chenaut. 2002. "Los debates recientes y actuales en la antropología jurídica: las corrientes anglosajonas." In *Antropología jurídica: perspectivas socioculturales en el estudio del derecho,* edited by E. Krotz, 27–58. Barcelona: Anthropos/ Universidad Autónoma Metropolitana-Iztapala.

Speed, Shannon, R. Aída Hernández Castillo, and Lynn M. Stephen, eds. 2006. *Dissident Women: Gender and Cultural Politics in Chiapas.* Austin: University of Texas Press.

7

Participate, Make Visible, Propose

The Wager of Indigenous Women in the Organizational Process of the Regional Indigenous Council of Cauca (CRIC)

LEONOR LOZANO SUÁREZ

More than forty years of organization and resistance by the indigenous movement of Cauca have placed the Regional Indigenous Council of Cauca (CRIC) at the forefront of indigenous struggles not only in Colombia, but throughout Latin America. In addition to its success in recovering ancestral territories, the CRIC has gained respect for its own system of authorities and development pathways, consolidating health and educational systems and positioning itself as an important social and political force in the country. From its inception, the CRIC prioritized education in order to form community leaders. Schools were conceived as spaces to strengthen identity, native languages, and indigenous people's history and worldviews. These have been the pillars of an autochthonous education system that gradually became a space to build autonomy and critically reflect on Colombian state policies. The work of the CRIC's Intercultural Bilingual Education Program (PEBI) has involved constant evaluation of the communities' needs, to develop not only curricula but also policies that guide the CRIC's efforts in almost every field. In 2003 this extended to higher education with the creation of the Autonomous Intercultural Indigenous University (UAIIN).

In this chapter I examine two initiatives undertaken by the UAIIN and CRIC's Women's Program in response to the domestic problems and inequality suffered by women within their communities, problems made more acute by the armed conflict affecting their territories. One of the initiatives was a diploma on "The Indigenous Family, Participation, and Gender Equity" launched in 2008 by PEBI (through UAIIN) and the Women's Program to develop concepts and research with a view to creating a permanent program for education and research on gender and the family. The other process analyzed is a participatory evaluation (*diagnóstico*) in which I participated, initiated by the women participants in the diploma, that analyzed problems affecting families and women with the aim of developing the CRIC's policies to strengthen the family and address the situations experienced by women. My interest here is to explore how the women gradually modified the focus and purpose of the diploma, using strategies and methodologies developed in CRIC's educational processes, such as intercultural dialogue, historical memory, or the use of their own worldviews to generate new spaces of reflection. Drawing on their own experiences and worldviews, they were able to reconceptualize and cotheorize gender concepts that were undervalued or rejected by the organization's leaders. In what follows I analyze how women developed new languages to reflect on the problems they suffer due to the internal armed conflict and those that occur within contexts they identify as intimately interrelated: family, community, organization, and nature. This was achieved through innovative epistemological and method-ological proposals, developing arguments and narratives grounded in their political and organizational environment, such as the importance of the family, unity, harmony, and "communitarianism."[1]

The issues that emerged during the diploma workshops led to a partici-patory evaluation in the various zones of the Cauca. In subsequent sections I explain in detail how the process developed, signaling the problems most frequently discussed in the community workshops. I also consider how women developed a more political agenda on the basis of these inputs, such as propos-als for gender and family inclusion in CRIC's regional and zonal development pathways or Life Plans (planes de vida).[2] In the medium term, the women pro-posed a permanent school on gender and the family as a space to socialize and research those issues and orient parents, teachers, and cabildo members. They know that indigenous education has been an important strategy and argued that a gender school could contribute to combating inequality, physical and psychological intrafamilial violence, obstacles to women's participation in deci-sion making, and the invisibility of their role in organizational struggles.

But where did the women's strategies and methodologies come from? Since its inception in the 1970s the CRIC has privileged community education as a means to build autonomy and strengthen indigenous identities, and develop strategies to advance and defend its political project. Education is a field that has created spaces for women's participation and constitutes a privileged scenario to renegotiate gender relations. In the following section I signal how women in the CRIC demand recognition of their historic and current contribu-tions; this is intimately linked to their efforts to secure greater gender justice in the present.

Women in the History of the CRIC

The department of Cauca, located in the Colombian southwest, is one of those most affected by the war waged in the country over the past fifty years. With a population of over a million inhabitants, it is the department with the second largest indigenous population in the country, with a quarter million people belonging to various ethnic groups: Nasa or Paez, Yanakuna, Guambiano, Kokonuco, Totoró, Ambalueño, Inga, and Eperara Siapidara from the Pacific region (CRIC 2008). These came together in the Regional Indigenous Council of Cauca, created in 1971. The CRIC has a decentralized structure made up of ten zonal cabildo associations (Asociaciones Zonales de Cabildos), which group the 115 *cabildos* in the region according to specific geographic areas. *Cabildos* are the basic unit of indigenous government of each of the *resguardos* and are recognized by the communities and the state as their traditional authorities.[3] The Consejería Mayor, composed of one delegate from each zone, is the body responsible for CRIC's overall direction.

Indigenous resistance in the Cauca dates from the colonial period, when caciques persuaded the Crown to recognize their *resguardos* through Royal Titles, which remain one of the principal legal instruments to defend their territories (Cortes 1984; Rappaport 2000; Vasco Uribe 2002). The *resguardo* system weakened after Independence, and although Law 89 of 1890 provided some stability,[4] many lands had already fallen into the hands of large landowners, who employed indigenous labor through the *terraje* system (Cortes 1984; Vasco Uribe 2002).[5] In the first years of the twentieth century a regional movement arose called "the Quintinada," led by Manuel Quintín Lame, a Nasa laborer, and Gonzalo Sánchez, a native of Totoró (Romero 2006; Lemaitre 2009). These indigenous leaders tried to defend ancestral territories through recourse to state law, demanding rights for indigenous people and an end to *terraje*. Women actively participated in the Lamista project, and some accompanied Quintín Lame on his travels (Romero 2006). In 1927 "The Rights of Indigenous Women in Colombia" was published; through this document, signed by fourteen thousand Lamista women from several departments, women demanded their rights over the lands they tilled alongside men and denounced injustices, rapes, the theft of their lands, and their abandonment by the national justice system.

> Today women, with our courage and energy, demand protection and justice as we have always done. We have lost our petitions and our rights, but not our faith. This faith assists poor women laborers like us who, in sun and rain, facing hunger and thirst, help indigenous men as wives, sisters, daughters, and mothers, to cultivate our lands, which the bourgeoisie have stolen without giving us one cent because the [state] authorities, violating their duties, violated rights and the interests of justice.[6]

In the late 1940s and part of the 1950s, Colombia suffered brutal partisan violence between liberals and conservatives, a period known as La Violencia.

Indigenous and peasant communities aligned with one side or another weakening the *cabildos* and many *resguardos* were dismantled, once again facilitating land grabbing by large landowners. The government tried to promote an agrarian reform, but this was never implemented, generating constant agrarian struggles and the birth of guerrilla groups that have persisted to this day, such as the Popular Liberation Army (EPL) and the Revolutionary Armed Forces of Colombia (FARC). In 1971, indigenous *terrajeros* from the north and east of Cauca, who were the most seriously affected by dispossession of their lands and subjection to *terraje*, gathered in an assembly with more than two thousand participants to create the CRIC. From its inception, CRIC supported and organized land takeovers or "recoveries," *terraje* was eradicated, and many community enterprises were created. In exercises that aim to recover historical memory, women elders have described their participation in land recoveries. An emblematic case is the recovery of the Cobaló *hacienda*, which was in the hands of the Archbishop of Popayán. Here women confronted the police and were mistreated and imprisoned. Some female teachers were murdered because they promoted land recoveries through the schools.

As the CRIC recovered a significant part of its territory, it gradually modified its scope of action; priorities extended beyond the right to land to include the exercise of autonomy in their territories, defining their own vision of development through the Life Plans, and consolidating their own educational and health systems, together with national representation and political participation. The armed conflict has become one of the greatest threats to its autonomy, its security, and the development of its Life Plans. Indigenous authorities have repeatedly expressed their rejection of the war waged in their territories, for example through actions such as the Minga of Social and Communal Resistance organized in 2008, in which more than ten thousand people marched from Cali to Bogotá to protest the militarization of their territories. Women participated in these actions and proposed new forms of protest and repudiation of the war in their territories, such as the monthly Minga for the Defense of Life, a women's protest that arose after the death of six children and the murder of the elder Lisandro Tenorio. Women demand that their children not be recruited or killed, and that they (the women) are not used as war booty.

Education: A Field That Has Created Possibilities for Women

CRIC's PEBI is the backbone of the organization's cultural and autonomy project promoting research about indigenous worldviews together with the elders and the *thë'wala*.[7] This local knowledge is mobilized in an ongoing intercultural dialogue between indigenous intellectuals, external collaborators, and teachers. The importance of indigenous worldviews and their strategic use became clear when indigenous linguists and leaders and a team of external collaborators began translating the 1991 Constitution. Their methodology was to build new epistemologies in order to make intelligible foreign concepts that did not exist in Nasa Yuwe, the language of the Nasa (CRIC 2004). They did this by critically appropriating external ideas and assuming control of theorization "from the inside" through intercultural dialogue.[8] Such negotiation has strengthened other fields requiring similar control over theorization, such as indigenous law, health, and economy. Women linked to the PEBI's training and professionalization have found it to be a very important space for developing an awareness of gender identity. Many currently work as teachers or continue with their education; others occupy various positions at the zonal level as part of the PEBI team, or contribute to other CRIC programs. The women have followed the PEBI's methodology of generating new epistemologies "from the inside" in order to (re)theorize gender. This echoes other initiatives explored in the chapters on Puebla (Terven, chapter 2), Guatemala (Sieder, chapter 3), and Bolivia (Arteaga Böhrt, chapter 6), where indigenous women have sought to pair indigenous gendered concepts with external political and legal terms, or have used indigenous concepts to elaborate new understandings (such as *chacha-warmi*, discussed by Arteaga Böhrt in chapter 6).

However, the appropriation of new discourses and roles has generated internal tensions and contradictions for female indigenous intellectuals, locating them as borderline indigenous people (Rappaport 2004, 2008): people who move "inside," that is, in the community's everyday life, and "outside," in the intercultural experience where they have become cultural activists. Men also experience these tensions, but they tend to be more dramatic for women because representations of the feminine are such important symbols for indigenous people—according to the CRIC's narratives, women are bearers of life, weavers of culture, guardians of tradition and language, and protectors like the mother Earth. Therefore activists, in their condition as borderline women, are judged as transgressors of tradition (Piñacué 2004).

In addition, working in the organization demands a great deal of time and considerable mobility to attend regional, zonal, and even international meetings. Few women enjoy their husband's support, so their children are left unattended, the women cannot participate in everyday community life, and their relationship with their partner often breaks down as a result. Things are different for male intellectuals and leaders; they invariably have the support of their wife, who takes care of everything, not only the home and children, but also the family's crops. Her husband can come back whenever he wants, or not come back at all, which often happens—revealing the leaders' double standards, struggling as they do to defend the autonomy of indigenous peoples but often at the expense of their family life. Personally, women experience deep and painful contradictions in what Rappaport (2004), borrowing the concept from Du Bois ([1903] 1989), calls "double consciousness." Alicia Chocué defines it as follows: "Double consciousness is the confrontation of two characters that act in all of us; for example, I, an indigenous Nasa, am confronted with two worlds—the Nasa world and the European or white world. For that reason, two types of characters act within me: one of them is always discussing her own world, while the other one seeks to know that different world. . . . These two people are constantly arguing; sometimes they reach an agreement" (Chocué 2000: 14). Nonetheless, this double consciousness has been a fundamental tool for women, allowing them to analyze and question the conditions of inequality they experience in the family, the community, and the CRIC, creating possibilities for dialogue with other organizations of indigenous and non-indigenous women, and prompting them to seek their own ways to participate in the struggle for collective rights.

In the context of the growing problems of domestic violence, abandonment, forced recruitment of young men by armed groups, rapes, and early pregnancies, a group of women supported by young people and elders were able to get the assembly of the CRIC's 2005 Twelfth Congress to approve the inclusion of a tenth point in the organization's manifesto: "To work toward strengthening the family as the nucleus of indigenous organization." With this "mandate" of the congress, the Women's Program (approved in 1993, but never implemented) requested a part of the budget originating in state transfers to the *cabildos* in order to subsidize their coordinators' travel expenses and support their regional assemblies and programs. This has occurred in some (though not all) of the ten zones, as is the case with the Women's Program of the Association of Indigenous Cabildos of the North (ACIN),[9] which was able to consolidate a structure in teams to develop specific projects and support local women's committees in the zone.

Obstacles to Positioning a Women's Agenda

CRIC leaders and even community members are resistant to the topic of gender, considering it an "outside" import of Western feminism or disagreeing with an exclusive focus on gender oppression. Berrío Palomo (2010) argues that the highly vocal and combative nature of organization in the Cauca—which has successfully recovered land and denounced human rights violations in the territories—makes it appear as if women participate under equal conditions in political and decision-making spaces, postponing the need to develop an agenda that addresses women's problems and gender inequity, obscuring the reality of patriarchy in their communities, and, in the words of Renya Ramírez (2009: 40), "silencing women's political activism."

From a different standpoint, CRIC leaders argue that indigenous thought is holistic, which means they must speak of the family and not only of women, since that runs counter to the unity of indigenous organization. It is interesting to note that women are aware of what can be disputed and in which contexts; as I discuss below, they use the same terms as the organization, such as holistic approaches (*integralidad*) and communitarianism (*comunitariedad*), to develop their proposals. Yet speaking of gender and concretely of gender violence implies confronting power within organizations, as well as cultural practices related to sexuality, marriage, the family, and child care. Many women who took part in the diploma spoke of their husbands' or partners' objections to their participation in spaces outside the home, alleging that this implied leaving the children and the home unattended and even risking situations of potential infidelity. In the one workshop held in Chimán as part of the diploma, one female authority said:

> The lack of support from husbands creates problems in the couple. . . . We often don't have the support of the family either, and we have to take our children everywhere with us. But there is also selfishness amongst other women and in the community, which leads to gossip. . . . We are fearful and lack confidence. The many responsibilities and meetings positions of authority require make us neglect our children. The lack of funds, especially for those of us who work in the Women's Program, and the scant value given to us by the men in the *cabildo* and their mistrust of our abilities also hinder our initiatives.[10]

The women emphasized that most men in the CRIC did not accompany the internal women's movement; on the contrary, they appeared to fear losing power not only in the organization, but in the community and at home: "Women are seen as a danger if we organize ourselves . . . so we in the Women's Program have tried to incorporate men so they see that the work should be done together, so they don't think that we're walking on our own. . . . That doesn't mean they will make decisions for us. What's important is that they see the work we're doing to make sure it doesn't divide the community, because we're all part of the same organization."[11] However, some men do support the women's work, especially those close to the activities of the Women's Program, as demonstrated by a comment made by one of the men who attended the UAIIN's course on gender and the family: "The *cabildos* don't pay any attention to the Women's Program. Once I told the authorities in my territory that we needed to take the proposals of the Women's Program on board and the governor and the other men laughed at me. . . . The work of the women is not being valued."[12]

The Course on "The Indigenous Family, Participation, and Gender Equity"

As part of their efforts to develop autochthonous education at all levels, the PEBI educational program created the UAIIN in 2003, with programs on Community

Pedagogy, Indigenous Administration and Management, and Indigenous Law. These respond to ongoing evaluations by the communities in the context of their Life Projects or development plans, which determine the training needs of leaders. The diplomas or degree programs offered by UAIIN are in the form of mixed-mode instruction, aimed at preventing the detachment of students from their communities and facilitating research carried out in each student's immediate context.

In order to analyze the multiple problems affecting families and women reported but not resolved in the *cabildos*, UAIIN and the Women's Program of the CRIC organized a course titled "The Indigenous Family, Participation, and Gender Equity," which was held twice with eight-day on-site workshops at the university campus at La Colina attended by a total of one hundred cabildo delegates. In late 2010, I joined the workshops on the second round of the course with the aim of presenting to UAIIN and the Women's Program a proposal for collaborative research involving a team with some of the course students. We proposed to analyze how cases relating to domestic violence and violence against women due to the armed conflict are dealt with by the *cabildos* and the CRIC's legal teams.[13] My relationship with the CRIC goes back several years, first in the Educational Program, and later with UAIIN and the School of Indigenous Law; this facilitated relations with the course coordinators and with UAIIN's directors. Although the topic was deemed relevant, the UAIIN directors suggested I join the process to carry out a collaborative systematization of the course (whose on-site workshops were about to conclude), and support the implementation and systematization of the evaluation in the ten zones that would be carried out as a second phase of the process.

The needs of the Women's Program and the course coordinators were much more political. They wanted the systematization not simply for the purpose of elaborating a report for the cooperation agency that financed the project, but rather to collect the reflections and theoretical and methodological constructs developed therein in order to foster reflection on the topic of gender in the communities. The longer-term aim was to gradually develop the CRIC's policy on the topics of family and gender equity and institute a permanent school to these ends. This desire was expressed in the course as follows:

> This is a dream we have had since our first reflections in the course, because we see that training, research, interrelations, and constant work with the communities are the only way to change the inequalities between men and women in every aspect of our relations. It is a commitment that we, the course students, developed. . . . The idea of a permanent school has nothing to do with the idea of a physical space, it is an effort whereby we learn together in interaction with the communities. . . . We must work in all spaces possible; for example, when we attend

congresses, assemblies, *cabildo* and program meetings. We must seek opportunities in schools to sensitize teachers and students on this topic, to propose research projects with the students on the issue.[14]

The fact that intercultural collaborative work in the CRIC has a long history facilitated the development of conceptual and methodological tools in an exercise of retheorization and reconceptualization (Rappaport 2008; Ramos and Rappaport 2005), or of construction of what Vasco Uribe (2002, 2010) calls "concept-things."[15] This usually occurs through workshops, assemblies, program team meetings, and especially the Education Program, but also in the exercise of joint writing and in the discussion of texts that are systematized. Systematization is also an opportunity for collaborative work and, in my opinion, a very fruitful one (I have personally participated in systematizations of several CRIC projects in the context of indigenous education and with the project on indigenous law).[16] The resulting products are usually not official reports or documents for an academic audience, but joint constructions with the people we work with to develop texts, primers, or other materials designed for work with the communities.

We began systematizing the course in July 2011 and finished in February 2012 with the team from the Woman's Program, composed of Margarita Hilamo, a Nasa from the northern zone, Roseli Finscue, a Nasa from Tierradentro, Enriqueta Anacona, a Yanacona from the southern zone who participated in the course, and Graciela Bolaños, the course coordinator, a very committed collaborator who has accompanied CRIC's entire process since the beginning. As agreed, our purpose was to elaborate a pedagogical document in simple language, with questions for reflection and including the participants' voices. The idea was that the course students could use it as an aid for their work with the local teams of the Women's Program, and also present it to the *cabildo* authorities, thus contributing to a better understanding of the realities faced by women and families in their localities.

Concepts Developed and Systematized in the Course

The text first discusses the cotheorization and reconceptualization of the concepts of gender, gender relations, and gender equity, which were discussed in the course from the perspective of indigenous worldviews. Some indigenous researchers in CRIC are developing analyses similar to those described by Macleod (2010) and Sieder and Macleod (2009) by Mayan women from Guatemala, who, based on their worldviews, their myths of origin, and the concepts of complementarity, reciprocity, duality, and equilibrium, are struggling to recover women's value in their culture and to achieve fairer relations between men and women in their communities and organizations. In order to reconceptualize the concept of gender equity, the women drew on texts by

Joaquín Viluche, a Nasa researcher of indigenous worldviews. Viluche argues that male and female forces developed in parallel since the beginning of the universe and that, according to the Nasa worldview, the creator parents (Uma and Tay) have the same authority and their knowledge and powers complement each other. All human beings are born in couples, women are accompanied by a male Ksxa'w, and men's Ksxa'w is female.[17] The women apply these principles to everyday life to assert that men and women are capable of performing all tasks and that neither is more powerful than the other, that if both Uma and Tay have a *chonta* (staff of authority), and if history says that Gaitana and other female caciques were authorities in colonial times,[18] then they have demonstrated that they too can be authorities. Such framings echo the efforts of Aymara women in San Pedro Totora described by Arteaga Böhrt in chapter 6 to emphasize gender complementarity, parity, and indivisibility as constitutive of indigenous authorities. In Cauca the women also resort to historical memory to frame their struggles, and hope that indigenous worldviews can be the basis of a strategy to transform inequalities in their everyday lives.

After analyzing the traditional family or the "hearth" family,[19] participants in the course reflected on changes in the family, covering topics such as how people fall in love and marry, important rituals, stages of children's growth, and the role gathering around the hearth plays in transmitting the meanings of territory, language, values, and respect for authority and for parents' advice as a means for correction. According to indigenous law the family is the foremost authority—as Guambianos put it, "law is born in the kitchen" (Vasco Uribe 2002: 320): "We learned from our mothers how to be women around the hearth; we learned to weave, to spin, to cook, and to care for our siblings, since they told us that these were women's tasks. Very few of us could go to school because schooling was for men. During our menstruation we couldn't leave the house because we were seen as impure. . . . But we have been struggling to change things, and today women hold different positions in the community and the *cabildos*."[20] Through this analysis participants identified a broader conception of the family that goes beyond the hearth. They proposed that the community, the organization, and nature be understood in a broader political sense as the CRIC family. This concept of the CRIC family in its four dimensions (hearth, community, organization, and nature) is a theoretical-methodological proposal that articulates the CRIC's core principles of holistic organization (*integralidad*) and communitarianism (*comunitariedad*), and allows for the development of strategies to articulate the relationship between the home, the community, the organization, and nature. In this way women sought to facilitate the exploration of problems specific to women in each of these dimensions and develop concrete proposals to help solve them. This understanding of the CRIC family and the relationship between its various dimensions was represented in one of the workshops as a drawing of a tree that was explained as follows:

> The roots represent the values of the home family because it is there we learn culture and develop our identity. . . . If the roots are strong, the trunk will grow healthy and strong and it will have many branches and bear many fruits. The trunk represents the community family that is constantly growing and [acquiring] knowledge. . . . Its strength expresses resistance to situations that harm our territory, identity, and culture. The branches symbolize the organization family; branches represent the different peoples that make up the organization. The leaves and fruits are the result, the harvest of the struggles that has been made possible thanks to the strength of the roots and the trunk. The tree can live because it is connected to the territory, which is like a large home that shelters us all.[21]

Although the broad concept of the CRIC family refers to holistic integration (*integralidad*) as a principle of indigenous thought—a principle defended by leaders as an argument to determine actions "for the family," thus silencing the inequality existing between men and women—it also reveals the particularities and problematics of each of its members, as demonstrated by women, young people, and elders, who often feel discriminated by the organization's dynamics. This model favored the strengthening of alliances with the youth program, including the Indigenous Guard,[22] and the elders.

One of the purposes of establishing the Women's Program was to make visible women's contributions throughout the entire organizational process. The women's communiqués and publications very often begin with or include a paragraph alluding to the historical memory of female *caciques*, especially Gaitana, and the role of women who have given their life in the organization's struggles.

Another important contribution of women is in the field of health. The 1991 Constitution recognized indigenous people's autonomy to define not only their own form of education, but also to value and promote ancestral health and justice systems.[23] In the Caldono *resguardo*, health projects are under way to cultivate and research medicinal plants and to revitalize ancestral knowledge, such as that of midwives, *sobanderas* (traditional massage therapists), and *pulseadoras* (who read movements of the blood). Women propose forms of inclusion such as the creation of a council of female elders to accompany the *Consejería* at the regional level, and the presence of a woman in the legal teams of the *cabildos*, especially when addressing complaints related to women or families. In 2000, ACIN's Women's Program organized a leadership training project for indigenous women. Coordinator Margarita Hilamo said, "The school focused on overcoming fear and enabling women's political development. I was very afraid to speak in public about the topic of women, but I wanted to overcome my fear. Like me, there were many women who said: 'I want to be a leader, I want to know, but I am afraid.'"

Women complain that although their presence is increasing in all areas of organizational work and community events, few of them are in decision-making or leadership positions. The reasons they identified were several. On one hand, their abilities are undervalued, with the belief that their place is at home and taking care of children. Even where their contribution has been recognized, such as in education, teachers complain they are rarely appointed to leadership positions in the schools. Other factors are the lack of support from partners or families, which means that they have to assume the double responsibility of taking care of the family and the many tasks required by the organization. This often results in separation from their spouses and neglect of their children. They also have to face gossip and envy from other women and men who believe that women's place is at home. On the other hand, the armed conflict in Cauca puts both male and female indigenous leaders at risk. According to one of the female leaders who participated in the course, "Being a leader means you run the risk of being criminalized, stigmatized, or killed. . . . They have called us terrorists, which is a way to create fear and keep us from expressing what we are and defending our rights."[24]

Despite these threats, women leaders have continued to demand security and justice. Aida Quilcué, an indigenous leader who has faced significant internal opposition as well as threats from paramilitaries and the army because of her activism, has been an example for many. In the 2008 Minga of Social and Communal Resistance she was the official spokesperson for the indigenous movement in the public debate that took place with then President Uribe Vélez, questioning government policies of democratic security and the criminalization of protests. In December of that same year, her husband Edwin Legarda was murdered. Despite this Aida continues to work with the movement, and currently coordinates the CRIC's Human Rights group. Another example is Lisinia Collazos, a leader who survived the Naya massacre in April 2001 and led a legal action to obtain a farm for the survivors in Timbío, where they live today, rebuilding their lives.[25]

> There was no timely response by any government body, we could not return to the territory, especially since we were a military target. We therefore filed a legal action and in less than two months we got the Timbío farm where we live today. We organized a *cabildo*, built the indigenous school, and today we have houses, but very small and without running water. . . . The little we have obtained has been through our struggle and strength. In 2005 we met with the President of the Republic

[Uribe Vélez]. He apologized for the massacre . . . but declared human rights organizations were terrorists simply because they were helping the communities learn the truth and demand justice. On the other hand, the guerrillas put pressure on us to avenge my husband's death, but I absolutely rejected this position, which led to serious confrontations. I returned three years later and met again with the commanders, who could no longer keep on intimidating us. As a woman, it is good to lead a community, but you have to be smart and not overestimate your importance. As compensation for my work, the community helps me work the farm. . . . I will never forget those events.

Lisinia became governor of the new Kite Kiwe *resguardo*, obtained through her efforts and the community's support. They refused to remain in the condition of "displaced victims," acting instead as subjects with collective rights to truth, to justice, to a new territory to rebuild their personal and communal lives, and to their own form of government, education, and health.

As the armed conflict has intensified, women have denounced an increase in rape by all armed groups operating in their territories, especially after the start of Uribe Vélez's Policy on Democratic Security, which established permanent police units in the municipalities.[26] This not only exposes a defenseless population to attacks and confrontations between the various armed groups, but also alters the life of indigenous communities. Young women end up engaged to members of the armed groups, who later abuse them or use them as domestic servants. These women are subject to surveillance by all parties to the conflict, who see them as informers, thus exposing them to the risk of being murdered. On the other hand, many young men and women from indigenous communities are tempted to join the guerrillas or the paramilitaries, or are forcibly recruited, and no one ever hears from them again. Cases of rape and forced recruitment are not addressed by the *cabildo* authorities because they fear reprisals from the armed groups involved or because they argue that "the women ask for it."[27] As a result, many cases are not denounced because the women are ashamed and afraid of being rejected and stigmatized in their community. On the other hand, some cases of rape and abuse by community members are also silenced.

Figure 7.1, taken from the report presented by the National Indigenous Organization of Colombia (ONIC) to the United Nations Special Rapporteur on the Rights of Indigenous Peoples in July 2009, indicates an increase in violent acts against indigenous women in the periods 1998 to 2002 and 2002 to 2009 (ONIC 2009:7).[28]

The "Humanas Colombia" corporation, which works on international humanitarian law, organized symbolic trials on sexual violence in the context of the armed conflict and in September 2011 ACIN's Women's Program

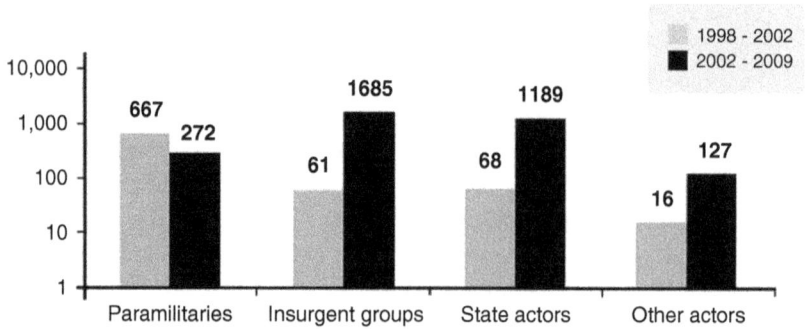

FIGURE 7.1 Violent acts against indigenous women by perpetrator, 1998–2009.
Source: ONIC 2009.

participated in the first symbolic trial, presenting the case of a young woman from the Huellas *resguardo*, municipality of Toribío, who was kidnapped by the FARC, raped, and murdered. On this issue ACIN's Women's Program is undertaking other actions in coordination with the ACIN's Justice and Harmony program (*tejido de justicia y armonía*).[29] The team travels to the *resguardos* for an integral accompaniment that addresses both the material and the spiritual through traditional medicine; the *Thë'wala* harmonizes the family, the community, and the territory to reestablish equilibrium. They speak with the communities and the *cabildo*'s authorities to coordinate accompaniment for women and child victims of the armed conflict. Thanks to this initiative, more women have made denunciations, but "much still needs to be done to ensure that crimes are punished; both indigenous and state authorities often ignore these victims because they are women and indigenous. On the other hand, not all *cabildos* are prepared to address these issues; avenues need to be created to improve access to indigenous justice" (Programa Mujer de la Asociación de cabildos indígenas del norte 2012: 3).

The Participatory Evaluation: Results and Proposals

CRIC evaluates communities in order to develop policies emanating from their programs. The need to perform an evaluation (*diagnóstico*) of the problems faced by women and the family surfaced in the course's workshops. Participants concluded that communities should hear ordinary women's voices about the problems they experience in their everyday lives in their family, the community, and their relations with *cabildo* authorities. They also wanted to know what cultural and organizational resources were available to devise policy proposals for the organization on the topic of gender and the family. The evaluation consisted of two stages. First was a preliminary evaluation to be used as a roadmap during the second phase.[30] This consisted of discussion sessions with four focus groups: teachers, women who had held positions of authority, young people and members of the Indigenous Guard, and coordinators of the Women's Program at zonal and local levels. In the sessions in which I participated, we considered the most relevant problems for women and the family in the hearth family, the community family, the organizational family, and nature. These discussions identified issues for deeper analysis in the communities, focusing on causes, consequences, and proposed solutions.

The more extensive evaluation was undertaken in nine of the CRIC's ten zonal associations. In each zone, two workshops lasting two days were held, each in a different *resguardo*, with the participation of women, men, young people, elders, and some of the *cabildo*'s authorities. For this phase we created a team with three members of the Women's Program who traveled to the zones. I participated in those workshops that the women colleagues from the program decided I could attend, taking into account security conditions and their judgment about the impact of my presence. Working with community members is entirely different from working with leaders or intellectuals who move inside and outside. It is much slower; in some *resguardos* Spanish is not often used and women are shy to speak when the issues affect them directly and men are present. The harmonization ritual before the beginning of a workshop is very important, since it opens the way to obtain good results. On the other hand, *cabildo* authorities tend to take advantage of workshops to make announcements or delegate tasks, reducing the time for analysis. The topics community members most wanted to discuss were related to domestic violence, the armed conflict, youth migration to the cities, or poor communication in the family. The work was carried out in small groups to facilitate discussion; these reflections were presented in a plenary session through playacting, flip charts, or oral presentations, and conclusions were then drafted.

We periodically organized encounters with the team to discuss the results of these workshops in order to fine-tune methodologies and evaluate progress; for example, we realized we needed to separately interview elders or women who had held positions of authority in the *cabildos*. Another strategy was to ask the zone or local coordinators of the Women's Program who participated in the course to continue working in their communities, addressing other issues. Some of them sent us reports, others did not.

We began the process of systematization with information from the memoirs of the initial evaluation, the workshops with the communities of the nine zones, interviews, reports of local and zone coordinators, and reflections of the research group. This time the goal was to elaborate a report for the authorities and the university that presented detailed information zone by zone, as well as a summary of all the issues identified and proposals made by the communities, with sufficient elements to work with the authorities to develop policies on gender and the family. The team decided the first part would be organized by zone, with brief descriptions of the zone, its organizational structure, and the Women's Program in order to determine what human, organizational, and economic resources were available to support the implementation of policies at the local level. We created a table for each of the four dimensions of the family. The columns signal problems identified, causes, consequences, and proposed actions or solutions (see Table 7.1).

It is impossible to enumerate here all reflections expressed in the evaluation in each of the four dimensions of the CRIC family, but I highlight the problems repeatedly identified in the community workshops, such as discrimination and domestic violence against women in all stages of their life cycle, lack of alimony payments, and men's abandonment of the home. These are the problems that women claim are not solved by the traditional authorities. They are transferred either to courts or to other state institutions. The women in the evaluation workshops as well as the female participants in the course requested training programs for authorities on indigenous law, and unified criteria to address women's complaints. They also requested representation by women in the *cabildos* or in the legal teams. Women also denounced the consequences of the armed conflict: not only rape, forced displacement, and the use of young people as informants, but also the recruitment of minors and youth. The women proposed that the organization support and prioritize youth programs, promoting economic projects to give them opportunities and strengthening the Indigenous Guard as an option.

This methodology of examining women's problems in the context of their day-to-day lives allowed for a detailed mapping, helping to unveil and denaturalize the violence, inequality, lack of opportunities, and discrimination they face at the various stages of their lives and in different contexts. This map also reflects a holistic view so strongly demanded by indigenous thought, which not only provides women with robust arguments to position their gender agenda as something more than "women's things," but frames it as essential for strengthening the organization, requiring the incorporation of policies and actions in the Life Plans. It also demonstrates how women appropriate strategies of resistance developed in the indigenous movement and adapt them to their own objectives.

Conclusions

In this chapter I have outlined women's long history of participation in the indigenous movement in Cauca, their contributions, struggles, and new strategies, such as introducing and reconceptualizing languages of their own developed on the basis of indigenous worldviews and CRIC's political and organizational contexts in order to speak of gender, inequality, and opportunities. Their objective is to develop policies for the organization and, in the long

TABLE 7.1
Axis: Home Family

Problem	Causes	Consequences	Actions
1. Loss of spaces for dialogue in the families and loss of important cultural norms	TV/computer use takes time away from family dialogue, including for giving advice to control behaviors. Parents are away because of work. Domestic chores are not shared. The umbilical cord is not buried ("planted"), care is not taken in raising children. The *Thë'wala* is not consulted.	Loss of language, values, affection, traditions, and a space to advise and correct. Children grow without traditional values, without connection to the culture. Identity is weakened. Parents' authority is diminished or lost.	Seek spaces/time to share as a family daily. Return to advice as a way to control children. Use the native language. Foster equity among children assigning equal tasks. Return to cultural practices and traditional rituals. consult the *Thë'wala*. Recover women's value on the basis of indigenous worldviews and foster balanced relations in the couple.
2. Leaders offer a bad example by behaving poorly in front of their own families	Long absences due to positions in the organization that make them neglect their children. Alcoholism. They prefer the city. Many cases of infidelity.	Work overload for women in all respects. Dissolution of the family, children migrate to the city. Loss of authority before children and the community.	Leaders should acknowledge mistakes and change their attitudes toward the family to recover moral authority. Leaders who offer a bad example should be punished and prevented from holding positions of authority.
3. Women have no opportunities to manage economic resources, and the *cabildos* discriminate against them in access to land	People believe that only male heads of household have rights, and that female heads of household do not. When land is inherited by a woman, it is transferred to her husband. *Cabildos* do not support handicraft or production projects for women.	Economic dependence and women's submission without access to economic resources. Husbands control women's actions and lives.	Review the *cabildos'* decisions on this issue. The *cabildos* should undertake a census of families to find out who has land, how it is administered in the family, and how it is used. Give land to female heads of household. *Cabildos* should promote production projects and support commercializing handicrafts.

term, to establish a permanent school on gender and the family. Indigenous women in Cauca believe that these new languages open the way for negotiating relations of equilibrium and complementarity between men and women, and can be incorporated in the organization's narratives without being disqualified as "feminisms from the outside." I also underscored the women's proposal to understand the family in a broader sense as the CRIC family in four dimensions, and to position analysis of gender issues in an organizational and political context in harmony with broader indigenous principles of holistic and communitarian culture. Women know that incorporating the policies as part of the CRIC's Life Plans has both a symbolic and practical function, symbolic because it is a means of legitimizing their program before the authorities and the community, recognizing that they have made and continue to make important contributions to the good living of the families and the communities (the central purpose of the Life Plans); practical because if the policies are based on an evaluation and proposals are developed within the communities, they stand a chance of being implemented. Is it utopic to think that policies on gender and the family can change a situation of deeply rooted inequality and power relations in the indigenous communities of Cauca, in a society as patriarchal as Colombia and in the context of the armed conflict? As Rappaport has observed, "For the native activists of Cauca utopias are not impossible dreams, but objectives to fight for, sometimes over the long term" (2008: 26).

NOTES

1. In Spanish, *comunitariedad* is a term very often used by CRIC leaders, alluding to the sense of collectivity that has been promoted with the active participation of the communities in schools and other programs. It also refers to the relations that should exist between the local, zonal, and regional levels of the organization.

2. The Life Plan is a long-term proposal elaborated "from the inside" for the integral development of the *resguardos* (officially recognized indigenous territories), which considers every aspect of life in the communities. It is a counterproposal to the government's development plans (Gow 1998, 2004).

3. Decree 2164 of 1995 defines traditional authorities as "the members of an indigenous community who exercise powers of organization, government, administration, or social control according to the structures of their respective culture." The *cabildos* are the traditional authorities of indigenous peoples and are recognized by the same decree as a special public entity.

4. This law protected *resguardos* by declaring them immune from seizure, inalienable, and imprescriptible.

5. *Terraje* was a system whereby indigenous people were forced to work on large haciendas without remuneration, in exchange for the right to live on a small plot within the *hacienda*.

6. This document appeared on May 18, 1927, as the first publication of the Indigenous Women's Movement, and is included in a compilation of some of Manuel Quintín Lame's writings organized by the Committee for the Defense of Indians (1973: 20–36).

7. The *thë'wala* or traditional healer is a spiritual and political guide, with a profound knowledge of Nasa worldviews. He plays a very important role in the communities, both to reestablish harmony and equilibrium in cases of illness, and to "clear the way" for many of the CRIC's political or organizational activities.

8. Cultural insides and outsides are indicators or metaphors used by Nasa intellectuals—in the words of Rappaport—"to conceptualize politicized notions of culture that are in the process of being created" (2008: 24). As such, they do not refer to concrete places, essences of culture, or anything observable; they form a relational concept that serves as a useful methodological resource to characterize intercultural dialogues between researchers and collaborators and indigenous intellectuals. On the other hand, Rappaport (2004, 2008) argues that this dialogue, in which all forms of knowledge have the same value, locates indigenous people and their collaborators in a border zone. It is a mobile concept, for example, when it refers to those who speak Nasa Yuwe, who are further "inside" than those who do not, or to indigenous people who live in the cities and feel more "outside" of the culture than those who live in rural areas. Even the position of collaborators committed to the indigenous cause is perceived (by the collaborators themselves as well) as being more "inside" than that of scholars or representatives from NGOs or the state.

9. The Association of Indigenous Cabildos of the North (ACIN) is one of CRIC's zonal associations that gathers fifteen *cabildos* from the northern zone.

10. Course workshop held in Chimán, *resguardo* of Guambia, February 2011.

11. Final report, "Evaluation for a Gender and Indigenous Family Policy in the Regional Indigenous Council of Cauca," elaborated by the coordinating team with the aid of Luz María Londoño, 2011.

12. Memoir of the first workshop of the course "The Indigenous Family, Participation, and Gender Equity," 2010.

13. With the 1991 Constitution's recognition of the special indigenous jurisdiction, CRIC saw the need to strengthen indigenous law and restructure the functions of *cabildos* so they could perform legal tasks. In some areas, especially in the northern zone, Zonal Legal Committees, which coordinate local teams to support the *cabildos* in conflict resolution, gathering information, researching cases, and defining the application of the remedy (crime is considered an illness), were created. In order to strengthen indigenous law, a training process was initiated through the Cristóbal Sécue School of Indigenous Law, under the direction of ACIN and UAIIN.

14. UAIIN, CRIC's Women's Program. Document systematizing the course "The Indigenous Family, Participation, and Gender Equity," 62–63.

15. This term was coined by Vasco Uribe (2002) in his work with Guambianos to designate material objects that express knowledge or have conceptual contents. For example, the snail's spiral form represents history and the way knowledge is developed, from the center to the outside and back to the center. It is a way to "gather concepts in life."

16. After the murder of Cristóbal Sécue and Aldemar Pinzón, Nasa leaders who had coordinated the Legal Committee of the northern zone of the Cauca, the Association of Indigenous Cabildos of the North (ACIN) created a space for Education in Indigenous Law, as a strategy to strengthen the exercise of their government by recuperating and revitalizing ancestral legal systems and generate better relations with the national legal systems and state institutions. This educational experience began in 2004 with one hundred representatives from seventeen *cabildos* of the Cauca and concluded in 2008.

17. There is ample literature for internal consumption on the topic of worldviews, such as the *Cxayu'ce* magazine published periodically by the Educational Program, ACIN's publications from the diploma in indigenous law, the publication by the Juan Tama Association of Cabildos, and the research developed by students of schools and the university.

18. During the European invasion, the female *cacique* Gaitana fiercely opposed the conqueror Pedro de Añasco. In retaliation, he ordered her son to be burned alive. Gaitana finally defeated the conqueror and avenged her son's death. She and other colonial *caciques* such as Juan Tama are ancestral heroes of the Nasa people.

19. The hearth or woodstove was—and in some places still is—a part of the house with great cultural significance. It is the place where the umbilical cord of newborns is buried to "root them in the earth," where the family gathers in the evening to share the day's work experiences and plan the next day, where the stories of the ancestors are told, where children are disciplined, and where rituals to maintain harmony and equilibrium in the family are performed. This space has been losing significance because television has taken the place of family conversations and because families tend not to gather around modern electric or gas stoves. Nonetheless, it remains a symbolic place, and in workshops people metaphorically spoke of "returning to the hearth," in the sense of transmitting culture and sharing as a family.

20. Memoir of the second on-site workshop of the course, April 2008.

21. Memoir of the second round of the course "The Indigenous Family, Participation, and Gender Equity," UAIIN campus, La Colina, July 28, 2010, to February 13, 2011.

22. The Indigenous Guard is a collective composed of community members, especially young people. It is a strategy of civil resistance to defend territory, autonomy, and life in the communities, keeping guard over and warning its members of actions by armed groups. The Indigenous Guard accompanies authorities and helps organize events such as congresses and marches. It has become an alternative to keep young men from leaving their communities or enlisting in the various armed groups.

23. The CRIC currently has its own health system, instituted through the indigenous health care organization (EPSI). It has 60 community health agents, 142 health promoters, and 66 trained indigenous nursing assistants, in coordination with the Cauca Department Health Direction. See http://www.cric-colombia.org/portal/proyecto-cultural/programa-de-salud/.

24. Extracted from the memoir of the third on-site workshop of the first diploma "The Indigenous Family, Participation, and Gender Equity," July 2008.

25. The region bordering the Naya River, located at the border between the Valle and Cauca departments, was controlled by the FARC and the ELN until 1999, when the paramilitary Calima and Pacífico blocks of the United Self-Defense Forces of Colombia (AUC) took control of this drug-trafficking route to the Pacific. In the Naya massacre, or what was called the "race of death" that occurred in April 2001, more than three hundred members of the AUC, in complicity with soldiers from the Third Brigade of the Pichincha Battalion of Cali, tortured and brutally murdered indigenous people and peasants of the region, arguing that they had collaborated with guerrilla groups. Many women were raped. The exact number of people killed over the three days is unknown, but it is estimated that more than two hundred were massacred and at least three thousand were forcibly displaced. See http://www.verdadabierta.com.

26. According to a study by a group of NGOs publicized by Intermon Oxfam, "In the period from 2001 to 2009, in the 407 municipalities where public security forces,

guerrillas, and paramilitaries are present, 17.58% of the women—in other words, a total of 489,687 women—were direct victims of sexual violence." In addition, 82.15 percent of the women who have suffered some type of abuse do not denounce the events. "In this regard, 73.93% of the victims claim they [do not denounce sexual violence] because of the presence of armed groups." The study underscored that "the abuses suffered by these women range from rape to forced prostitution, forced pregnancy, forced abortion, forced sterilization, sexual harassment, forced domestic service, and regulation of their social life." Almost all of these actions remain unpunished. See http://www.observatorioviolencia.org.

27. Memoir of the second on-site workshop of the diploma "The Indigenous Family, Participation, and Gender Equity," 2008.

28. "Violent actions" refers to sexual and physical violence, forced displacement, servitude, murder, disappearance, forced abortion, and "many more nuances and effects of the war."

29. In 2004, the indigenous authorities of the north of Cauca restructured the ACIN as a result of an evaluation of their organizational process in order to strengthen solidarity and reciprocity between the various *cabildos* and the social processes they promote, giving it the structure of a web through five *tejidos* (literally "weavings") or programs: the Defense of Life *tejido*, the Economic and Environmental *tejido*, the Peoples and Culture *tejido*, the Communications and Foreign Relations *tejido*, and the Justice and Harmony *tejido*.

30. The first phase of the evaluation was accompanied by Luz María Londoño, a researcher from the University of Antioquia.

REFERENCES

Berrío Palomo, Lina Rosa. 2010. "Sembrando sueños, creando utopías: Liderazgos femeninos indígenas en Colombia y México." In *Etnografías e historias de resistencia. Mujeres indígenas, procesos organizativos y nuevas identidades políticas*, edited by Rosalva Aída Hernández, 81–216. Mexico City: Publicaciones de La Casa Chata, CIESAS, and Programa Universitario de Estudios de Género (PUEG), UNAM.

Chocué, Alicia. 2000. "Nuestra doble conciencia." In *Revista Cxayu'ce*, no. 4, 14–15. Popayán: CRIC, PEBI, Editorial Fuego Azul.

Comité de Defensa del Indio, La Rosca de Investigación y Acción Social. 1973. "1927 El derecho de la mujer Indígena en Colombia." In *Las luchas del indio que bajo de la montaña al valle de la civilización*, 20–36. Bogotá: Editextos.

Consejo Regional Indígena del Cauca (CRIC). 2004. "¿Qué pasaría si la escuela? . . . 30 años de construcción de una educación *propia*." Bogotá: Editorial El Fuego Azul.

———. 2008. *Lineamientos del Plan de vida regional de los Pueblos indígenas del Cauca*. Popayán.

———. 2012. "Familia, participación y equidad de género en los pueblos indígenas de Cauca." Popayán.

Cortes, Pedro. 1984. "Desarrollo de una organización indígena, El Consejo Regional Indígena del Cauca, CRIC." Popayán: Banco de la República.

Du Bois, W. E. B. [1903] 1989. *The Souls of Black Folk*. New York: Bantam.

Gow, David. 1998. "¿Pueden los subalternos planificar? Etnicidad y desarrollo en el Cauca, Colombia." In *Modernidad, identidad y desarrollo*, edited by María Lucía Sotomayor, 143–172. Botogá: Instituto Colombiano de Antropología, Colciencias.

———. 2004. "Desde afuera y desde adentro: La planificación indígena como contra-desarrollo." In *Retornando la mirada: una investigación colaborativa interétnica sobre el*

Cauca a la entrada del milenio, edited by Joanne Rappaport, 65–96. Popayán: Editorial Universidad del Cauca.

Lame, Manuel Quintín. 1927. "El derecho de la raza indígena en Colombia ante todo. El misterio de la naturaleza educa al salvaje indígena del desierto." In *Manuel Quintín Lame Chantre. El indígena ilustrado, el pensador indigenista*, edited by Romero Loaiza Fernando, 468–476. Pereira: Editorial Papiro.

———. 1973. "Las luchas del indio que bajo de las montañas al valle de la civilización." Bogotá: Comité de defensa del Indio, Editextos Ltda.

Lemaitre Ripoll, Julieta. 2009. *El derecho como conjuro. Fetichismo legal, violencia y movimientos sociales*. Bogotá: Siglo del Hombre Editores, Universidad de los Andes.

Macleod, Morna. 2010. "Voces diversas, opresiones y resistencias múltiples: las luchas de las mujeres mayas en Guatemala." In *Etnografías e historias de resistencia. Mujeres indígenas, procesos organizativos, y nuevas identidades políticas*, edited by Rosalva Aída Hernández, 127–179. Mexico City: Centro de Investigaciones y Estudios Sociales; Universidad Autónoma de México, programa Universitario de Estudios de Género.

Organización Nacional Indígena de Colombia (ONIC), Área Mujer, Familia y Generación. 2009. "Derechos humanos de las mujeres indígenas." In *Mesa de Trabajo "Mujer y Conflicto Armado." IX INFORME sobre violencia sociopolítica contra mujeres, jóvenes y niñas en Colombia*, 109–125. Bogotá: Ediciones Antropos. http://www.observatoriogenero. org/ddv/informes/20MUJER%20web.pdf.

Piñacué, Susana. 2004. "Liderazgo y Poder: una cultura de la mujer nasa." In *Retornando la Mirada: Una investigación Colaborativa Interétnica sobre el Cauca a la entrada del milenio*, edited by Joanne Rappaport, 55–64. Popayán: Universidad del Cauca.

Programa Mujer de la Asociación de cabildos indígenas del norte (ACIN). 2012. "El camino de Resistencia de las Mujeres Nasa: Creando y Luchando por la Dignidad." http:// www.nasaacin.org.

Quintero, Julio Cesar. 1988. "¿Qué pasó con la tierra prometida?" Bogotá: CINEP.

Ramírez, Renya. 2009. "Nacionalismo tribal y sexismo. Reflexiones desde las mujeres nativo-americanas de Estados Unidos." In *Reivindicaciones étnicas, género y justicia. Desacatos* 31: 35–50.

Ramos, Abelardo, and Joanne Rappaport. 2005. "Una historia colaborativa, retos para un diálogo indígena-académico." *Historia Crítica*, no. 29: 39–62. http://historiacritica. uniandes.edu.co/view.php.

Rappaport, Joanne. 2000. "La política de la memoria. Interpretación indígena de la historia en los Andes colombianos." Popayán: Editorial Universidad del Cauca.

———. 2004. "Retornando la mirada: una investigación colaborativa interétnica sobre el Cauca a la entrada del milenio." Popayán: Editorial Universidad del Cauca.

———. 2008. "Utopías interculturales. Intelectuales públicos, experimentos con la cultura y pluralismo étnico en Colombia." Bogotá: Universidad Colegio Mayor de Nuestra Señora del Rosario, Escuela de Ciencias Humanas.

Romero, Fernando. 2006. "Manuel Quintín Lame Chantre. El indígena ilustrado, el pensador indigenista." Pereira: Editorial Papiro.

Sieder, Rachel, and Morna Macleod. 2009. "Género, derecho y cosmovisión maya en Guatemala." In *Reivindicaciones étnicas, género y justicia. Desacatos* 31: 51–72.

Vasco Uribe, Luis Guillermo. 2002. "Entre selva y páramo: viviendo y pensando la lucha indígena." Bogotá: Instituto Colombiano de Antropología e Historia.

———. 2010. "Recoger los conceptos en la vida: una metodología de investigación solidaria." Working paper, seminar workshop Pensamiento Propio, Universidad y Región, Ethnoliterature Master Instituto Andino de Artes Populares Universidad de Nariño, Pasto. http//www.luguiva.net/artículos.

PART THREE

Women's Alternatives in the Face of Racism and Dispossession

8

Voices within Silences

Indigenous Women, Security, and Rights in the Mountain Region of Guerrero

MARIANA MORA

They grabbed six kids. . . . We made them turn on the lights of their police truck. . . . I said that they were all my nephews. They weren't, but you have to defend the town's youths as if they were your own. . . . The police arrived wearing ski masks. . . . We're Indians, but even though we're poor, we still have rights. . . . They act just like hitmen, with their faces covered, pointing their weapons. They don't identify themselves and grab anyone they find on their way. . . . They took them away. . . . So we had to take one of them in exchange for the kids. . . . We threw rocks at them. . . . We've reached our limit. We're desperate. . . . The only thing left for us is to pick up rocks to throw at them.

A small group of women in Atlixcala, a Nahua community in the municipality of Tlapa de Comonfort, in the Mountain region of the state of Guerrero, Mexico, describe the violence they experience in their communities, the role of state institutions, and community responses.[1] They are participating in a focus group organized by the human rights project, the Civilian Police Monitor (Mocipol by its Spanish acronym), based in the city of Tlapa, the region's political and administrative center. In 2013, together with the head of the municipal government's Office of Indigenous Matters (DAI, by its Spanish acronym), the Mocipol assessed conditions of violence and insecurity in the region as experienced by local indigenous communities. Those testimonies in Atlixcala centered on police violence.

As the epigraph illustrates, the women's defiant tone impels and even oversteps a testimonial sequence that linearly describes their efforts to rescue the youths detained by the municipal police. As the coordinator of the focus group, I try to follow their description, but I realize that, more than a strict narration of facts, it is the conveyance of affective tones, which vacillate from nervousness to a rebellious pride, that shape their collective testimony. While I attempt to distinguish the content of the voices speaking simultaneously, the community *comisionado*, a middle-age male authority, who had been listening in a corner of the building, rises from his seat, looks directly at us, and, with a firm voice, interrupts, "All right, I'm going to explain what happened. It was on February 24th of this year. The municipal police entered our community. They went through town looking for a young man, but since no one told them where he was, they grabbed any youth they found walking on the street. The people organized. They stopped the pickup truck at the entrance of town. We detained one of the policemen in exchange for the young men. They did release them, but I won't lie to you, we damaged their truck with all the rocks we threw." The *comisionado* emphasizes the "I" at the beginning of the sentence, together with the precise date of the event, in order to provide a coherent structure to the women's apparently disorderly testimony. His intervention is that of one male authority addressing another, in this case the head of the DAI, with a narrative that attempts to order and legitimize women's voices from his village.

This chapter focuses on small acts such as these that filter and displace the voices of Nahua women from the Mountain region, along with their experiences of violence and claims for justice. Through these acts of displacement, gendered theorizations of violence are silenced, theorizations emerging not only from dramatic events such as those narrated by the women from Atlixcala, but from a dense intertwining of acts of dispossession together with an increase in acts of physical violence, which reveal, as Feldman, Geisler, and Menon argue, an accumulation of insecurities in everyday life (2011). This accumulation, whether through violence inflicted against their bodies, the extraction of productive vital and work force, or the destruction of the natural resources of indigenous territories, organizes life through alienation. It is a form of gendered alienation surfacing after thirty years of neoliberal development policies in Mexico, whose impacts, in conjunction with today's security policies, are experienced as a profound crisis of the social reproduction capacity of rural populations, particularly indigenous populations in states like Guerrero. From this vantage point, police and criminal violence, rather than the principal expression of violence, form part of a continuum of insecurities experienced through the precariousness of everyday life, the devastation of the environment, and dispossession of a collective capacity to live with dignity.

The actions of two types of local actors oftentimes marginalize such female interpretations of violence: the first being male community actions, as the *comisario*'s intervention illustrates, the second human rights actors, whose need to adhere to juridical frameworks runs the risk of reproducing dominant narratives of who is considered a victim and what type of violent actions substantiate grievances. In differing ways, both these actors filter and displace the indigenous women's interpreted experiences of insecurity. In doing so, they run the risk of reproducing current hegemonic narratives centered on highlighting dramatic acts of physical violence, largely in public spheres. Since the administration of President Felipe Calderón (2006–2012), mass media and social networks in Mexico have focused on spectacular scenes of violence and death, along with a constant display of body counts. Images circulate widely of hypermasculinized actors, including the armed forces and the federal police, presumed members of organized crime, and even community police, disputing sovereign power through territorial control.[2]

In contrast, I demonstrate that an intersectional gender analysis unsettles and dislodges dominant representations of insecurity, thus allowing the voices and experiences of indigenous Nahua women to surface. I focus on everyday events, on matters that some consider minor or secondary, such as police harassment, arbitrary detentions, extortions, or the destruction of collective property; events that often go unnoticed, except for the individuals who experience them. And yet such critical events (Das 1985) for victims represent moments that unsettle and inject new meanings to their life conditions as well as affect understandings of their social geography.

The content of this chapter is based on both everyday life and events peripheral to collectively organized experiences. While in the Mountain region indigenous actors, such as the Community Police-CRAC and OPIM, discussed in chapter 4 by Teresa Sierra and in chapter 1 by Aída Hernández, have embarked on important long-term social struggles that modify the local sociopolitical landscape, the subregion where I conducted research had, until the time I completed research in 2013, a high degree of social fragmentation, with resistance largely limited to community actions and collective memories that remain in hidden transcripts (Scott 1990). In the municipality of Tlapa, the most visible political actors in the past two decades have been the Tlachinollan Human Rights Center, the dissident teacher's union and bilingual teachers, citizen police, and the self-protection forces.[3] In this context, human rights work becomes a central terrain of political struggle, as it boosts local actors' ability to name acts of violence. For that reason my research focuses on the various human rights activities of local organizations.

The chapter is divided into four sections. The first examines the regional context in which human rights work develops. The second section analyzes the processes whereby cases of human rights violations are recorded and documented, in particular the distinction between direct and indirect victim and the ways this distinction renders invisible the grievances of a considerable number of indigenous women involved in cases of police violence. The third section focuses on the different constructions of (in)security in communities that belong to the municipality of Tlapa. Finally, I examine several conversations with a Nahua woman who, by detailing the emblematic case of her brother-in-law, offers a proposal of what might be called an "inverse rearrangement," that is, an analytic framing that permits listening to how women in the Mountain region conceive of grievances and hence notions of security and justice.

Human Rights Work and Trajectories of Violence

> Mexican soul, I represent the Mountain
> car tire strap *huaraches*
> that's what they say about me
> my back is wet from not speaking like them
> My culture is trampled in Tlapa
> those who think they have Spanish blood call me Indian
> But I'm proud to be Mexican and to speak Nahua . . .

Indigenous Me'phaa, Nahua, and Na Savi youths rap as part of the hip-hop project *Indigenarte*. Their words provide glimpses of the acts of racism and dispossession that form part of this arid region, a region that inherited an ecological system ill-suited for agriculture, but where indigenous peoples obstinately defend their territory and languages. For better or for worse, the state is notorious for being a *guerrero bronco*, a wild warrior, where inhabitants defend by all means what is theirs and who, for the same reason, suffer diverse acts of state repression (Bartra 2000). In recent decades, state violence has taken the form of counterinsurgency operations against indigenous and peasant organizations, hence linking current security policies to the military's combat of guerrilla groups in the 1960s and 1970s (Montemayor 1991). At the end of that period known as the "dirty war," the region was baptized "the Red Mountain," in recognition of the mobilizations organized by leftist groups to position the teacher Othon Salazár as the first mayor of the Communist Party in the municipality of Alcozauca (Ibáñez Martínez and Cabañas Ramírez 2012).

In the 1980s, a decade that holds the inglorious distinction of initiating neoliberal policies in Mexico, the region transitioned from wearing a revolutionary-colored label to boasting the image of the poppy flower. The Mountain region is currently the largest producer of the plant—the raw material for heroin—according to recent data from the Secretariat of National Defense, which in turn justifies the permanent presence of military forces and militarized forms of police action (CNN 2011). According to local media, during the past two decades, several drug cartels have disputed territorial control over the Mountain region, primarily those headed by drug lords from the state of Sinaloa (González Benicio 2010). Such violent clashes transformed Guerrero into the state with the third highest homicide rates during the Calderón administration.[4] In its

2013 annual report *Digna Rebeldía: Guerrero*, the Tlachinollan Human Rights Center reported an increase in human rights violations registered in the Costa Chica and Mountain regions of the state.[5] During the same period, the National Commission on Human Rights received 1,662 complaints of torture, although no state official was tried for this crime.[6] As in previous decades, state security institutions justify their actions through default states of exception, directed not only against those classified as "enemies of the state," but first and foremost against the poor, mostly indigenous population, what I have described as the criminalization of racialized poverty (Mora 2013).

In recent years, the Nahua, Me'phaa, and Na Savi communities of the Mountain region have responded to increasing acts of violence through varying initiatives designed to protect their families, communities, and territory, including collective self-defense strategies and strengthening local traditional systems of authority. Communities asked to join the CRAC or other intercommunity organizations such as the Union of Peoples and Organizations of the State of Guerrero (UPOEG). In extreme circumstances they detain government employees, throw rocks at police forces that enter their communities, or violently expel them, as the woman in Atlixcala explained in the epigraph to this chapter.

Such conditions of insecurity operate in gray zones (Auyero 2007) blending legality with illegality that creates a hazy border separating state and parastate agents, where historic agrarian or interfamily conflicts combine with new power struggles over resources. At the same time, current expressions of insecurity link to the dispossession of resources, to what Emma Cervone refers to as the indianization of poverty (2012), that result from thirty years of neoliberal development policies. Migration flows clearly illustrate such phenomena. Since the 1980s, the expulsion of cheap labor has increased in the Mountain region, first as migrant labor in the coffee plantations of the Costa Grande region, later in the agricultural fields of the states of Michoacán and Morelos, and eventually in the tomato plantations of Sinaloa. In fact, Guerrero is the state of origin of most of the country's internal migrants. From 2006 to 2013, Tlachinollan documented the expulsion of more than 32,000 agricultural laborers from more than 350 indigenous communities in the Mountain region (Centro de Derechos Humanos Tlachinollan 2011). Since the 1990s, migratory flows have expanded across the border, into New York's restaurants and businesses. The term "TlapaYork" is how many now name their place in the world.

The past three decades have also witnessed a density of grassroots organizational processes, beginning with the 500 Years of Indigenous, Black, and Popular Resistance movement of Guerrero, in the early 1990s (Espinosa, Libni, and Sánchez 2010). Since 1995, the Community Police (CRAC) has operated in the region, as Teresa Sierra describes in chapter 4. And despite current political divisions, the presence of bilingual teachers and the actions of youth undoubtedly reflect the seeds of complex genealogies of rebellion (García 2010). In this context, the Tlachinollan Human Rights Center emerged in 1994, in the midst of intense mobilizations for indigenous autonomy and self-determination in the country. Tlachinollan has formed part of the rise of networks of human rights organizations that offer a juridical discursive frame that establishes the terrain through which individuals and collectives denounce acts of state violence and appeal to the terms of justice and reparation (Goodale 2008).

I highlight a specific point here: while human rights efforts during the past twenty years in the states with the largest indigenous populations in Mexico—such as Chiapas, Oaxaca, and Guerrero—have prioritized the defense of social, economic, and collective rights, the physical violence that erupted during the Calderón administration led human rights organizations to focus largely on civil and political rights, including the defense of rights in the context of an alarming increase in arbitrary detentions, torture, and forced disappearance.[7] It was precisely during the shift toward prioritizing fundamental rights that the Mocipol was founded in 2007 to register and defend victims of human rights violations committed by public security institutions. The objective was to identify concrete patterns of police violence and elaborate recommendations for reform.

From 2009 to 2013, I accompanied the Mocipol in its classification of cases and analysis of patterns of police violence. I decided to both participate and analyze the project based on a political reading of the national context. In the abysmal gap created in a few years between the struggle for recognition of indigenous autonomy and the death machinery of the war against organized crime, I perceive an urgent task for political and legal anthropology in indigenous regions: to identify, delimit, and analyze the effects of the new expressions of state formation and the counterhegemonic use of rights regimes. From the perspective of committed and positioned anthropology, ethnography helps us understand the current expressions of violence as part of the necessary steps toward the construction of alternative actions.

(In)security, Gender, and Constructing the Data

The human rights activities that provide sustenance to those questions guiding this research were the site of productive interdisciplinary tensions between anthropology and law. Although at the beginning of the research work I agreed with Sally Merry, who argues that though human rights and anthropology collect similar data, their interpretations and analysis are oftentimes substantially different (Merry 2005), this research led me to reconsider that statement. Not only are the data collected different, but oftentimes the very notion of what is considered data is one of the main sources of disciplinary tension. In fact the research process was marked by constant, no doubt productive minor differences, regarding what are valid and useful data to document the human rights cases and the sources of information illustrative for ethnographic work. The most complex issue undoubtedly entailed my insistence that the Mocipol analyze current violence from a gendered perspective. However, of the 413 cases of police violence documented by Mocipol between late 2007 and mid-2011, only 12 percent affected women directly. At first glance it appeared that there was not much to say on the matter (Monitor Civil de la Policía 2011: 70).[8]

However, as recent research on violence and gender illustrates, dominant narratives are generally founded on masculinized conceptions, which tend to render invisible the effects of violence on women (Yagenova 2013). Public security policies tend to disregard gendered components, specifically women's needs and conditions of vulnerability. By focusing almost exclusively on the public arena, these policies fail to consider domestic violence as part of public matters that take place in the so-called private spheres. Similarly, the separation between the public and private tends to prioritize issues in the former sphere, and secondary issues in the latter; central "security" problems are the crimes committed by criminal groups or human rights violations perpetrated by the police, while issues such as domestic violence are deemed less relevant. This is in turn reflected in the lack of official data from a gendered perspective as well as how oftentimes human rights work can be limited by the same juridical definitions and frameworks.

It was in response to this dilemma that I offered, as part of collaborative research efforts, anthropological tools that observe beyond quantitative data and strict juridical definitions of the category of victim found in the Mocipol's database. In fact a central discovery resulting from disciplinary tensions was how the distinction between direct and indirect victim in the Mocipol's case records largely erased women's experiences. The distinction begins when recording the initial testimonies of those seeking the legal support of the Mocipol. Although in the majority of cases the wives, mothers, and daughters of the detainees seek assistance, their names are not recorded in the database; rather, only the victim's name is listed, in this case that of the man who suffers the arbitrary detention. The data recorded serve to verify events suffered by the person whose rights have been violated, together with the necessary information to eventually file a complaint, to enable the lawyers to intervene to liberate them and to seek reparations. All other information is deemed secondary, including the role of the detainee's female relative, and the possible impacts of the detention on the family's life.

Yet as part of interdisciplinary engagement in this project, the human rights lawyers and myself eventually reconstructed certain cases and interviewed victims after the fact. What emerged was a much more complicated conceptualization of the grievance itself, which revealed the impacts on the family, not as a secondary issue, but as a direct impact of the arbitrary detention, with collective emotional, mental, and economic costs. While few women were direct victims, they were by and large the ones who negotiated with the police, dealt with threats and harassment, and figured out how to gather money to pay the oftentimes exorbitant extortions (up to fifty thousand pesos, about four thousand dollars) or how to make do in the house until a case underwent legal defense for the liberation of an innocent husband illegally detained. Yet in a formal sense, the family is considered at best an indirect victim; there is little legal space to recognize the collective impacts of an act committed against an individual, much less so in cultural contexts distinct from Western definitions of rights. By distinguishing between direct and indirect victims, the legal framework in Mexico, primarily the General Victim's Law,[9] individualizes acts of violence, removes the subject from his or her collective surroundings, and renders invisible the impacts of police violence on the family nucleus, particularly on women in the household.

The analysis we were able to extract from the records and documentation of the cases lacked, however, information that allowed us to register individual perceptions of insecurity and violence from people's everyday lives, or to delve into the different perceptions of concepts such as security, violence, and justice by indigenous men and women. For that reason, we decided to conduct a participatory assessment in six Nahua communities of the municipality of Tlapa, the municipality where Mocipol recorded the largest number of cases of police violence. We conducted the study between March and September 2013 in coordination with the DAI of the Tlapa municipal government, which selected those communities most affected by conflict and violence in recent years. In the following section, I focus on the findings from this latter phase of fieldwork.

The Social Geography of the Mountain:
Between Police Violence and Accumulated Insecurities

It is the dry season. A layer of dust covers the roads that connect the communities of the municipality of Tlapa to the city bearing the same name. The landscape consists of yellowish hills devoid of vegetation, severed stalks, the remnants of the last corn harvest, piled in geometric shapes on the soil exposed to the smoldering sun. Maty and Jesús, the lawyers from Mocipol, the municipality's DAI team, and I travel to Zatlicalco, a Nahua community one hour away from the city of Tlapa. On the way we encounter a number of security checkpoints; the armed presence in the state suggests a sovereign region in apparent dispute. When we pass the preventative state police checkpoint, Jesús explains, "They've only been here a month, the police established themselves at the entrance to town because the UPOEG set up their own checkpoint."[10] He refers to a recently created self-defense group that formed its own community police forces: "Since the government doesn't want self-defense forces to exist, the preventive police arrived and substituted them," he continues.[11]

As we pass the intersection, we see an army checkpoint that was established more than a year ago to supposedly control the traffic of illegal merchandise. Men we later interviewed explained that its presence solves nothing; it only displaces the "problem" to other routes, and now the "criminals" who traffic drugs and other illegal products go through the dirt roads that lead to their communities. When we reach the stretch of road that leads to Zatlicalco, I notice a number of crosses aligned at the side of the road, and further ahead, a yellow tape encircling an area on the ground. We later learned that the previous day a drug cartel assassinated an individual at the spot, the second in a month. And the crosses commemorate a group of the communities' men murdered while they dug a trench at the side of the road.

This type of visual map that I automatically elaborate to identify my surroundings served as the methodological basis for the focus group. More than forty community residents arrived to reflect on what generates fear, anguish, and senses of vulnerability in their everyday lives—that which in its entirety can be encapsulated under the term "insecurities." The Mocipol and the DAI were interested in documenting the perceptions of the local population regarding current expressions of violence, identifying the role of public security institutions, and recording the potential alternatives or solutions proposed by communities' members. To meet these objectives, we invited the participants to draw a community map, including the most significant elements—the homes, the commissioner's office, the church, the school, the cornfields, the water wells, the roads to Tlapa.

Although the dynamics varied in each community, men generally located specific sites of violent events in their everyday geography, such as roads where the ministerial police detain and extort individuals, places where "criminals" attack their victims, territorial limits in dispute with neighboring villages, traces left by presumed members of organized crime in their nightly travels, areas where youth gangs engage in territorial disputes with their rivals. In general the men participating in these focus groups would then locate these "problems" on the map. These were later classified under the broad category of "Insecurities," what one Nahua interviewed described as *Ti mo koalinia onka millek tlahuel*, which translates as "there are many problems in the *pueblo*," understanding *pueblo* not in its literal meaning in Spanish as town, but as the set of social and affective relations that are interconnected to a specific territory.

After conducting this exercise in the six communities, we realized that the direct confrontation the women held with police officers in Atlixcala was not the norm. In fact, the vast majority of women stated in the focus groups that they had never experienced a direct confrontation with security forces. As Gloria, from Zatlicalco, explained, "We can't say much about those things [experiences with the police]. We stay in our homes, we rarely leave our houses. And we don't have a car to travel to Tlapa or elsewhere." However, such affirmations, rather than representing a lack of relevant information, pointed to the need to expand the restricted map drawn by the men.

In addition to the issues described above, the participating Nahua women drew a map that pointed to alternative definitions and meanings of insecurity. They highlighted the importance of the forest in their daily lives and stated that illegal woodcutters are destroying what little remains. The entire region has suffered severe deforestation, hence increasing the already arid climate of the Mountain and reducing water resources. In terms of daily life, the women explained that the wells are drying out; women in their communities compete with each other over buckets of the vital liquid. They also pointed to the high electricity rates charged by the Federal Electricity Commission. They live in very humble homes, with a few light bulbs and meager household appliances, and yet their bimonthly bills range from eight hundred to two thousand pesos (seventy to one hundred eighty dollars), an exorbitant amount if one considers that the average daily wage in the region is thirty-five pesos (less than three dollars). Such household costs not only generate sentiments of anguish and anxiety, but directly impact their domestic chores. "They cut off our electricity and we have to grind the corn by hand instead of the electric mill; it makes preparing tortillas take a long, long time." While the women associate the increase in cost of living as a form of theft by those in power, they were quick to locate other more explicit examples. The police, especially the *judicial* (Ministerial Police), show up in their towns or on the roads and also "squeeze [money out of] us."

As a whole, the women in these communities chose to highlight those conditions of insecurity that affect and fragment their capacity for social reproduction. By social reproduction I refer to survival strategies of families and communities, based on social and political relations and economic strategies that foster their capacity for action (Canabal Cristiani 2001). This definition allows us to underscore how the women interviewed refer to environmental destruction of the resources that sustain them and grants particular meanings to their lands. At the same time, the lack of access to basic services hinders the reproduction of an already extremely precarious life of subsistence. This includes high electricity rates resulting from neoliberal state-promoted slashes in those subsidies previously directed at the poorest regions of the country.

Such levels of marginalization are reflected in the statistics of the National Council for the Evaluation of Social Development Policy (Coneval). In contrast to the national average, which identifies 46 percent of Mexico's population living under poverty conditions, 251 out of the 257 municipalities with the largest indigenous population have a poverty rate greater than 70 percent. While 9 percent of the total population lives in conditions of extreme poverty, almost 45 percent of the indigenous population lives under these same conditions. And the states with the greatest indigenous populations have average rural incomes that are much lower than the national average of around fourteen hundred pesos (one hundred dollars) (Coneval 2013). Such figures point to the close entanglement between class and ethnicity or race, since it is evident that conditions of poverty are concentrated in the country's indigenous communities and regions. This type of indianization of poverty (Cervone 2012) requires a gendered analysis, in particular, how it tends to be accompanied by what researchers refer to as the feminization of poverty (Pearce 1978).

I am suggesting not that the women participating in the focus groups failed to address experiences of physical violence, but rather that these descriptions form part of an accumulation of insecurities experienced in their everyday lives. This accumulation includes aspects of structural violence such as the extreme poverty rates concentrated in indigenous communities and regions. During the focus group in Zatlicalco, the women exemplified experiences of structural violence through their lack of access to health care. They explained their community lacks a medical center, which in turn sparks a chain of other forms of violence: "The clinic is very far away. But they force us to go almost every week to have our children weighed. It's part of the Oportunidades program. We have to take several children. But since we're poor, we don't have money for transportation, so we have to walk. But the road is very unsafe, women have been raped there."[12]

The fear of sexual violence was a main concern communicated by women as part of what they defined as experiences of insecurity. Although they located acts of sexual violence at the center of a series of accumulated factors, this was not *the* grievance injecting meaning to everything else. This is not to say that the threat of sexual violence did not figure centrally; such acts were addressed at length when the women reiterated that the "criminals" and "muggers" have the power and ability to rape them. Recently a female nurse from Tlapa was raped and murdered on that same road connecting Zatlicalco to the nearest health clinic. What I am suggesting is that instead of displacing other forms of insecurity to then focus primarily on acts of sexual violence, these women highlighted that the multiple expressions of insecurity, including those associated with poverty and racism, accumulate, and hence intensify, the conditions of physical violence. Although no case of extreme violence is a minor affair, limiting meanings of current expressions of violence to acts of physical violence risks neglecting other important dimensions and densities, such as forms of structural violence and the feminization of racialized poverty.

However, the men participating in the focus groups tended to render invisible such viewpoints of the women through subtle (and not so subtle) gestures that silenced their opinions, not without our involuntary complicity as human rights coordinators of the discussions. In the community of Xipietlapa, for example, we began the focus group with a small number of women who sat in a semicircle. Unfortunately, the room proved too limited in size, so the community's men, who arrived late, sat outside to then observe and participate from a distance. The human rights defender who facilitated the session noticed that this failed to foster their active participation, so she suggested we take the chairs outside. Of course, the new spatial redistribution displaced women to the margin of the group, their chairs now positioned behind the men's. The same happened with their voices. The women ceded their participation to their husbands, neighbors, and fathers, who described the issues concerning their community, including the current death threats against the teachers, extortions by the ministerial police, and the risks associated with walking the streets at night.

After noticing how as facilitators we had displaced women's participation, I took advantage of a pause in the conversation to ask those women present what insecurity meant to them, what problems and fears they wanted to add to the discussion. They remained thoughtful, looking at each other, creating the space of silence necessary to formulate responses. Fabricio, sitting beside the women, took advantage of the pause to offer his opinion: "The thing is that the women don't know, they're always locked up in their houses, they're very submissive and don't talk."

Aurelia and Hortencia turned to look at me, with a certain level of laughter in their eyes. Hortensia had been following the discussion very attentively and opted to interrupt him by explaining, "The problem is that we're always at home, we don't have a car and we almost never go out, we don't know much about those things. About the police we don't know much."

Fabricio interrupted her again: "They're submissive, they don't know anything, what they need is guidance. They don't defend themselves. If they mistreat them, they don't say anything, someone has to explain it to them. They don't know their rights." A chain of interruptions resulted between the two, a form of veiled struggle between the power of silence and its enunciation. Hortensia defined the final round by providing the last words and by opting to not confront the men from her community. She acknowledged the problems of domestic violence, discrimination, and revictimization in her village, but she decided to not highlight those issues, as that would spark internal conflicts with the men in the community. She opted instead to focus on external agents: "Well we don't denounce because if we go to Tlapa it costs a lot, it's expensive, and the institutions themselves mistreat us as if we were the problem. They discriminate us and silence us again. They discriminate us for being poor indigenous women and it's worse."

During the remaining focus groups, other Nahua women added that although they do not interact with state police, they do interact with traditional authorities. In these communities, the communal security commission, the *comisionado*, and the *principales* act as those responsible to engage in conflict resolution, as administrators of justice, including cases of domestic violence. In Zatlicalco, we divided the focus group into two subgroups, one of men and one of women. Once they were by themselves, the women ventured to speak of these issues of domestic violence. Florentina stated, "If the woman complains, she's worse off than if she didn't say anything. Sometimes they put her in jail together with her husband for them to resolve their problems." Other women explained that they do not like to denounce cases of domestic violence because if they go to the authorities, often the men pay a fine of several thousand pesos. "But that only harms us, because we have to figure out where to get the money and how to feed our children, it puts more pressure on the family."

For the purpose of this chapter, I focus my attention on two aspects expressed by the women in these Nahua communities. First, insecurity and violence transcend public spaces to also form part of the so-called private spheres. The division between the public and the private locates real problems as public issues and personal matters as private matters. From this perspective, the main issues are the public actions committed by actors such as "criminals," "cattle robbers," and the Ministerial Police, while issues such as domestic violence are considered "minor" or delegated as secondary problems. In the communities we visited, all conflicts, including acts of domestic violence, are resolved using public problems as a referent—the men are fined or jailed for a certain period of time. The authorities who eventually punish men who commit acts of violence do not contribute to transform gender relations or to modify the conditions that make domestic violence permissible. Prevailing definitions of insecurity, and therefore justice, set the stage to resolve other issues considered marginal.

Second, since few women have direct experiences with the police or with the armed forces (which is not the case of Ayutla or other parts of the Mountain and Costa Chica regions of Guerrero, as María Teresa Sierra and Aída Hernández explain in chapters 4 and 1, respectively), they tend to emphasize broader sets of issues as those which reflect conditions of insecurity, particularly the entangled relationship between structural and physical violence. Such linkages generate an accumulation of insecurities and the fragmentation of social reproduction capacities of families and communities in the region, a phenomenon described by Beatriz Canabal Cristiani in *Los caminos de la Montaña* (Canabal Cristiani 2001). Canabal points to the ways in which the neoliberal development model resulted, over the past thirty years, in a significant loss of agricultural land, ecological destruction, and the use of inappropriate technology, all of which directly affect community survival strategies and their ability to create economic and social alternatives.

At the same time, dispossession associated with the capacities for social reproduction suggests the presence of current logics of capital. David Harvey argues that under neoliberalism the mechanisms of alienation inherent in capitalism are exacerbated and express themselves in its form, magnitude, and administration. The processes of capital accumulation alienate entire populations, which are seen no longer as potential citizen reserves, but as superfluous or even as threats to material and political order (2004). Accumulation through dispossession, argues Harvey, destroys entire communities and deprives them of their possibilities for social reproduction, as a requirement for capital to ensure its own reproduction.

The women who participated in the focus groups in Tlapa offer a perspective of insecurities articulated by these acts of dispossession. Expressions of structural violence are not the backdrop where violent acts occur; rather, those acts of physical violence form part of a violent continuum. In this respect, the Nahua women interviewed indicate that the accumulation of insecurities is lived through the interrelated effects of development and security politics. Precarious conditions and the extraction of their vital and productive forces exist in relation to the creation of a police state and the militarization of everyday life, which is simultaneously the object of and an action in the defense of the sovereign entity (Buur, Steffen, and Stepputat 2007). In the book *Accumulating Insecurity: Violence and Dispossession in the Making of Everyday Life*, the authors express their concern that, in a context where the responsibilities of the state are redirected to its armed withdrawal, it is necessary to look beyond "security as weapons, to inquire into experiences of insecurities in the realm of social reproduction and everyday life" (Feldman, Geisler, and Menon, 2011). Likewise, the women interviewed explicitly invited us to direct our attention to the current violent conditions of social reproduction and to unveil how the uncertainties of current political and material conditions emerge from everyday life.

Considering the set of processes described above, we now face the task of resorting to the testimonies of women victims in order to map how they construct grievances and potentially seek to transform their current conditions through the use of legal frameworks. We turn to that task by analyzing the testimonies of Doña Verónica and her husband.

Rearrangement from Testimonies: Between the Law's Promises

On March 20, 2012, in the auditorium of the Miguel Agustín Pro Human Rights Center in Mexico City, lawyers held a press conference on the case of Bonfilio Rubio Villegas, a Nahua indigenous man extrajudicially murdered by the Mexican army at a military checkpoint in the town of Huamuxtitlán, Guerrero. In June 2009, the twenty-nine-year-old man, a native of the Mountain region, traveled in a passenger bus on the way to Mexico City, the first stop of a long trip to the other side of the border. The vehicle stopped at an army checkpoint and the soldiers searched the passengers' belongings. Shortly after the bus resumed its voyage, the soldiers opened fire for no apparent reason. The bullets pierced Mr. Rubio's body, killing him almost instantly.

In the context of the so-called war against organized crime, in which the armed forces head the operations to "reestablish the nation's internal security," complaints of human rights violations by the army increased by 250 percent in five years.[13] The human rights organizations that convened the press conference that day have made great efforts in recent years to include cases such as Bonfilio's in a series of legal and political strategies that push reforms considered indispensable to decrease the level of impunity of the armed forces. Human rights lawyers begin the conference by stressing this point through technical explanations and legal arguments. The lawyers then turn the microphone over to Rubio's family members—his brother and his sister-in-law, Don José and Doña Verónica. Don José thanks the presence of the media and representatives of civil society organizations. He describes the tragic events that ended his brother's life. The volume of his voice increases as he questions the army's unilateral actions, emphasizing, "We come here to condemn everything the army has done. There are more than fifty thousand families whose relatives have been deprived of their lives by Calderón. We demand to be treated like citizens. Because we speak a native tongue—we speak Nahua—they treat us as citizens who are not worthy of participating."

By chance, an intense tremor shakes the city in the middle of the press conference. There are no major consequences, but it takes some time for us to recover from the scare. For that reason, I sit with Don José and Doña Vero in a corner of the auditorium. We talk about the interventions in the press conference; I am particularly interested in hearing more about why they believe they are treated as noncitizens. Don José resumes the direction of his intervention on stage and says, "We, as indigenous peoples, are third-class citizens. The soldiers are the first-class. Rights are made for them [the armed forces], to protect them and their interests. The laws are not made for us citizens, and less so for those of us who are indigenous, who speak another language, who live in poor regions. But here we are, struggling for justice."

Here, I reflect on the apparent contradiction of his words. Both he and his wife state that they are determined to struggle for justice through the state legal apparatus, but at the same time they emphasize that the laws are not made for "citizens" and much less for those whom Don Antonio categorizes as "third-class citizens," those who live processes of racialization and gender construction that inferiorize them in a hierarchical scale of social and life values. He says that his experience with the legal system has made him understand that laws ensure the permanence of the sovereign entity, beginning by protecting the institutions whose function it is to defend it. They are not designed to protect the population. Why do victims of violence and their relatives, such as Don José and Doña Vero, who hold such strong distrust of the law and of the ability of government bodies to effectively respond to injustice, decide to risk their physical integrity, endure threats and harassment by military personnel, and undergo a process of years of struggle for justice? Why do they resort to the law?

These questions are relevant regarding the issues discussed in the previous section, since human rights activities currently form part of the central disputed terrain in Mexico, a terrain that both regulates and renders invisible certain complexities of social reality (as I described in the analysis of how Mocipol initially recorded the cases), as well as potentially reverts hegemonic processes, by creating counternarratives that name reality so as to propel its transformation. To continue with the analytical framework developed throughout this chapter, I seek tentative answers to these questions not at the center of legal cases or in public spaces such as the press conference at the Pro's facilities, but in fields of knowledge and actions located at the margins, such as the conversation that the tremor made possible the day of the press conference. I head to the house of Doña Vero and Don José, located in the outskirts of the city of Tlapa.

I arrive at this first meeting with a list of carefully structured questions divided into thematic groups that I agreed to pose to victims of cases managed by Mocipol. However, I modify the methodology and decide on informal conversations as soon as I realize that the narrative structure of Doña Vera's testimony contains an analytical wealth. I fear that, if I lead her narration according to my questions, I would be regulating her interpretations just like the male authorities did with the disorderly testimonies of the women from Atlixcala described at the beginning of this chapter.

We begin the conversation with the topic I had proposed—her experiences throughout the legal process. As soon as I mention the issue and without inviting her to reflect upon a particular question, Doña Vero starts to describe what justice means to her. She begins with the immediate objective of the case—justice understood as punishment for those who took the life of her brother-in-law. However, she lingers there just a moment before moving on to broader aspirations for indigenous people. She says, "It's time for us indigenous people to raise our voices. We've always been stepped on as indigenous people by the military. We don't want people to be mistreated. Now it was a twenty-nine-year-old man, but later it can be someone else. They think that by giving us ten or twelve thousand pesos, we'll be content. But that's not what we want." She explains that racism and discrimination are evident not only in their attempts to "buy" justice with an informal offer of compensation, but also in the corrupt actions of private lawyers and the threatening, violent actions of the army against indigenous people. "The army terrorizes us, they scare us because we don't speak Spanish. People are afraid that the army will take a young man, or steal children, or rape women. They are the first ones to mistreat people."

From the beginning of the interview, I notice that the meaning of justice is broadened as she speaks of the impact of the army's presence in the region—an almost permanent presence that began with counterinsurgent tactics during the so-called dirty war of the 1960s and 1970s, but that since the 1980s has been justified by the operations to eradicate drugs. Doña Vero guides the direction of the conversation: the role of the army in the region, the fear she feels on her way to work or when she is teaching her students, or her fear that something might happen to a relative. In the sequence of her reflections, she returns to the acts of racism they suffer at the hands of the army: "We're neither animals nor objects, but they treat us as if we were." She grounds her convictions in a series of concrete memories, beginning with the army's actions that regulate the local population through fear:

> In 1996 I worked in a town near Metlatonoc, they're all indigenous people, they can't even say "yes" in Spanish. I saw how the army arrived and knocked on the door. I saw how they hid in a corner at the back of the house. They were very scared. As teachers we had to tell the army to leave them alone, that they're poor and have no money and no food. But they said: "What are we going to do if the *guachos* [soldiers] come back?" I think that, if they're afraid, it's not for nothing, something must have happened to them or to acquaintances, no one is afraid just like that, especially if they've never done anything.

She then jumps to another memory, this time of her childhood, of the *guachos*, the soldiers in the region. When she was a child, she believed that something she had experienced had been a dream, but when she heard Inés Fernández publicly denounce the rape she suffered at the hands of the army, she realized that the dream had been true.[14] She says that a girl she knew came home running one day, with her pants stained with blood. She couldn't speak. She only made gestures meaning that she had been in the field harvesting corn. She raised her arms to show that it was a tall, armed man, and she pointed to her legs. She wept. Her mother asked her if it was the *guachos*. Doña Vero explains that the girl nodded her head. They raped her in the cornfield. Doña Vera sighs as she tells the story. "It remained unpunished, like many other cases," she says, and she remains silent. Then she adds: "I pray for all the people who have been trampled on by the soldiers. You don't forget a case of rape so easily. It must be hard for Inés's husband to live with the anguish of thinking that they can do something to his wife again. I pray and I say, my God, don't let this happen again to other indigenous women. Sometimes my son sees me praying and he probably thinks I'm crazy. But those memories, you don't forget those memories so easily." The weight of these memories ends the session. I don't want to stir the pain—hers or ours—brought to life when listening to the stories. Before leaving, we speak of other things, I acknowledge her and her husband's courage to continue struggling, and I tell her how important her struggle is for other people in the region.

We resume the interview the next day with the same dynamic. Doña Vero mixes details of the legal process with memories of regional events. She recalls another act of sexual violence, this time against a young woman who traveled in a passenger bus. She then goes back to Rubio's case, to how she understands human rights work and the efforts by human rights defenders, who are "lawyers who defend the poor, not like the other ones, who take advantage of the fact that we're indigenous people." She then shares experiences and what she believes reflect omissions by the state that foster conditions of insecurity for people: "Security doesn't improve at all, nor does education or health, the government is not concerned about services, they turn a blind eye. Like in Inés's community, they simply don't exist. . . . The government gives things to those who have the most, or gives away food to the poor, but nothing changes. . . . In the villages there's nothing, no road, no electricity. The government doesn't want those people educated, because if they are, they open their eyes and can rebel." After speaking for some time on the conditions of poverty experienced by indigenous people in the Mountain region, Doña Vera returns to the sense of justice that leads her to continue struggling for her brother-in-law's case: "We sought justice because we don't want them to continue being mistreated. We are victims like so many people. We want respect for the community as indigenous people, and also economic respect."

I describe the interviews in detail and emphasize the sequence of Doña Vero's narration because it is important to highlight that when asked about the various stages of the legal strategies in those three years, she responds resorting to memories of her past. For that reason, I analyze her testimony in the sense proposed by several scholars, who identify its relevance as part of processes of naming and pointing out injustices in order to heal collective wounds (Pérez 1999; Saldaña Portillo 2003; Tuhiwai Smith 1999). I revisit John Beverly's proposal of understanding testimony as action, since "if the point of *testimonio* were simply to represent the subaltern as subaltern, victims as victims, then . . . it would be little more than a kind of postmodernist *costumbrismo*. . . . *Testimonio* aspires not only to interpret the world, but also to change it" (Beverly 2004: xvi). In this sense, in this marginalized domestic sphere, Doña Vero chooses to emphasize what does not fit in legal strategies, yet is present in the political, social, and affective meanings mobilized through the struggle for rights.

Doña Vero's testimonial action is divided into two interrelated axes: the construction of the grievance she attributes to her brother-in-law's extrajudicial killing and the significance she posits to justice by resorting to the use of the law, despite her deep misgivings. Regarding the former, it should be noted that, during the interviews, Doña Vera does not reduce the case to its investigation and to punishment of those responsible for her relative's death, not even to an act of justice for the family, but rather stresses an accumulation of injustices centered on the nearly permanent presence of the armed forces in the region and the dispossession of lives in indigenous territories. Her testimony acts by naming the local reality based on memories that denounce how the army treats the residents through "preventive" measures, classifying the local population de facto as a threat to national security. The sum of military actions reinforces constructions of inferiority of the indigenous population, together with a perpetual devaluation of their lives, including through acts that result in death. Her testimonies echo the arguments of other studies in Mexico. In her research in Ciudad Juárez, undertaken during the same period in which the present study was done, Melissa Wright argues that the violence unleashed in the context of the combat against organized crime, instead of reflecting a failure of the state, is used by it discursively to demonstrate its reinscription of power (Wright 2011).

In the case of indigenous regions, exercising or boasting the state's capacity to end life reflect acts of territorial reconquest by the sovereign power through its armed forces. Doña Vero observes that part of this territorial control takes the form of acts of sexual violence, as a means to control the bodies of indigenous women. In her narration, memories of sexual violence provide coherence to her testimony. She is not the only one to observe this; both Inés Fernández and Valentina Rosendo also locate their rape at the hands of the armed forces as part of what constitutes the state in Guerrero. Their observations are related to those of indigenous scholars in the United States who assert these acts to be genocide because, alongside other expressions of territorial control, rape controls the possibility of future indigenous generations. "Native people become marked as inherently violable through a process of sexual colonization. By extension, their lands and territories have become marked as violable as well" (Smith 2005: 55).

Those who are responsible for protecting sovereign power act against indigenous people because of their conditions of poverty, and since they live in such conditions, indigenous people are deemed to be located at the margins of the political community. State security forces are therefore more likely to act against them. But as she argues in her testimony, the permanence of indigenous people in this state of marginalization is an effect of the state's own policies, given that sovereign power administers the margins of the state rather than establish forms of incorporation. It would not be to their advantage, says Doña Vero, if we left our conditions of exclusion, because then we would truly represent a collective dissident force.

Through an explanation that resembles those of women in the focus groups, Doña Vero locates the repressive acts by security institutions as part of a continuum. In this respect, she points to acts of violence intertwined with accumulated acts of dispossession and to the anguish generated by a crisis of their capacity to guarantee minimum conditions of survival. Structural violence is not the background for the acts of violence suffered; those acts of physical violence are a part of the whole. They are not the context in which the grievance takes place, but the grievance itself. Doña Vero's testimony, like those of other women who participated in the focus groups, suggests that their precarious conditions and the extraction of their vital and productive forces are related to the creation of a police state and the militarization of everyday life.

Regarding the significance Doña Vero attributes to the law, she emphasizes that to struggle through state rights regimes reflects not only a legal dispute, but a dispute over meanings in a profoundly unjust social field. In her book *El derecho como conjuro*, Julieta Lemaitre Ripoll invites us to understand the law as a symbolic resistance against the networks of meanings proposed by violence, against progress and development, against the construction of entire populations as expendable (Lemaitre Ripoll 2009). The author argues that the law is like an incantation as it allows us to name the world, it summons solidarity, it execrates enemies and turns them into taboo. The law is "the excess of its real possibilities of application. It is an emotion related not to concrete benefits, but to the political and cultural significances invoked by the law" (2009: 386). The excess of its possibilities refers not to what is excessive, but to what exceeds pragmatic and strategic calculations, what goes beyond the limits of the content of meanings, generating alternative significances and appealing to them as that which overflows the use of the law, even though it is inevitably related to it. Thus, Doña Vero resorts to the language of human rights to name a social life not only through meanings but also through concrete activities such as four years of active participation in her brother-in-law's case.

Conclusions

I conclude this chapter through Doña Vero's voice, in order to reflect on the relationship between representations of the current violence and mobilizations of counternarratives and countersenses based on the use of the law. Throughout this chapter I have described how indigenous community and human rights spheres become disputed fields over the construction of social meanings marked by violence. In both realms, the possibility of resorting to the law "from below," as part of actions that dismantle hegemonic constructions of the current violence, relies on the capacity of various actors to listen to interpretations by indigenous women in their local context. A central point of these interpretations is the various ways they identify a profound crisis in the capacities for social reproduction of their families and communities, as an accumulated effect of dispossession and of repressive acts exercised on the biological and social body of the population. Therefore, their voices act as an anchor point in the elaboration of other social meanings that relate alternative notions of security to territorial control, defense of the body itself, and the conditions of a dignified life safe from progressive devaluations. Between the silences, the voices of women victims such as Doña Vero seek a transformational praxis in the collective field of action enunciated in these broader notions of the law. It is the responsibility of the various actors involved in human rights work, including scholars, to position themselves through innovative analytical frames that allow them not only to listen, but to act at their side.

ACKNOWLEDGMENTS

The author would like to thank Matilde Pérez and Jesús Peralta, lawyers from Mocipol, for their commentaries and accompaniment; Fundar, Tlachinollan, and Insyde organizations, which coordinated the project; Lisbeth Rasch for her support as assistant during part of the fieldwork; and the team of the Women and Law in Latin America: Justice, Security and Legal Pluralism project for their valuable feedback throughout fieldwork.

NOTES

1. All the names of the communities and the people interviewed are fictitious, except for those of the Mocipol lawyers and the relatives of Bonfilio Rubio Villegas.

2. As María Teresa Sierra states in her chapter, the CRAC, as a community police organization, was founded in 1995. For many years, it was the only organization in Guerrero that administered justice. In early 2013, the Union of Peoples and Organizations of the State of Guerrero (UPOEG) was founded, with a presence mainly in the Costa Chica region. At the end of that year, other self-protection organizations that call themselves Citizen and Popular Police Forces also emerged in the Mountain region.

3. Since January 2013, different indigenous and peasant self-protection groups have emerged, particularly in the states of Guerrero and Michoacán. In spite of their diversity, they have been homogeneously categorized as self-defense groups, which has sparked public debates about their legitimacy and their role in the possible reproduction or containment of the actions of criminal networks and unpunished actions of state authorities.

4. According to data from INEGI, a total of 11,070 cases were registered in Guerrero. See *La Jornada*, July 13, 2013.

5. See Centro de Derechos Humanos de la Montaña, Tlachinollan (2013).

6. See Comisión Nacional de Derechos Humanos (2013).

7. According to the National Human Rights Commission (CNDH), during the Calderón administration more than eleven thousand complaints were filed against the Secretariats of National Defense (SEDENA), the Navy, Public Security, and the Attorney General's Office, most of them for cruel treatment, arbitrary detentions, and irregularities during searches. At the same time, the CNDH reported almost seventeen thousand cases of forced disappearance from the beginning of the administration to November 2011.

8. The established patterns of police and military violence in the nineteen municipalities that make up the Mountain region were published in December 2011 in the report *Desde la mirada ciudadana* (Monitor Civil de la Policía 2011).

9. See the General Victims' Law in Mexico, specifically article 4 of chapter II that defines direct and indirect victims as follows: "Direct victims are natural persons who have

suffered some economic, physical, mental, or emotional harm, or in general any risk or injury to their juridical goods or rights as a consequence of the commission of a crime or a violation of their human rights recognized in the Constitution and in International Treaties signed by the Mexican state. . . . Indirect victims are the relatives or natural persons in charge of the direct victim who are immediately related to them."

10. See Cervantes Gómez 2013.

11. See Redacción 2013.

12. Oportunidades (2000–2012) was a program to combat extreme poverty intended to develop the capacities of families in conditions of extreme poverty through economic transfers in exchange for changes in habits and the culture of the target population. In 2012, its name was changed to Prospera. For a critical analysis of the program, see Mora (2013).

13. See *El Universal*, December 23, 2011.

14. She is referring to the case of Inés Fernández, a Me'phaa woman raped by Mexican soldiers in 2002, whose case was presented to the Inter-American Court of Human Rights, which ruled against the Mexican state in August 2010 (see chapter 1, by Rosalva Aída Hernández Castillo).

REFERENCES

Auyero, Javier. 2007. *La zona gris. Violencia colectiva y política partidaria en la Argentina contemporánea* . Buenos Aires: Siglo XXI.

Bartra, Armando. 2000. *Guerrero bronco: campesinos, ciudadanos y guerrilleros en la Costa Grande*. Mexico City: Era.

Beverly, John. 2004. *Testimonio: On the Politics of Truth*. Minneapolis: University of Minnesota Press.

Buur, Lars, Jensen Steffen, and Finn Stepputat. 2007. *The Security-Development Nexus: Expressions of Sovereignty and Securitization in Southern Africa*. Cape Town: HSRC Press.

Canabal Cristiani, Beatriz. 2001. *Los caminos de la Montaña, Formas de reproducción social en la Montaña de Guerrero*. Mexico City: CIESAS.

Centro de Derechos Humanos de la Montaña, Tlachinollan. 2013. "Dignidad Rebelde Informe Anual." http://www.tlachinollan.org/informe-digna-rebeldia-guerrero-el-epicentro-de-las-luchas-de-resistencia/.

Centro de Derechos Humanos Tlachinollan. 2011. *Migrantes somos y en el camino andamos*. Especial, Tlapa: Tlachinollan.

Cervantes Gómez, Juan. 2013. "UPOEG demanda legalización de autodefensas." *El Universal*, April 15. http://www.eluniversal.com.mx/notas/916906.html.

Cervone, Emma. 2012. *Long Live Atahualpa: Inidgenous Politics, Justice and Democracy in the Northern Andes*. Durham, NC: Duke University Press.

CNN. 2011. "Guerrero, donde la pobreza 'fertiliza' el cultivo de amapola." November 7. http://expansion.mx/nacional/2011/11/07/guerrero-donde-la-pobreza-fertiliza-el-cultivo-de-amapola.

Comisión Nacional de Derechos Humanos. 2013. *Informe Anual*. http://www.cndh.org.mx/sites/all/fuentes/documentos/informes/anuales/2013_I.pdf.

Consejo Nacional de Evaluación de la Política de Desarrollo Social (Coneval). 2013. *Medición de la Pobreza. Estados Unidos Mexicanos, 2012*. México: Coneval.

Das, Veena. 1985. *Critical Events: An Anthropological Perspective on Contemporary India*. New Delhi: Oxford University Press.

Espinosa, Gisela, Iracema Dircio Libni, and Martha Sánchez, eds. 2010. *La Coordinadora Guerrerense de Mujeres Indígenas*. Mexico City: UAM.

Feldman, Shelley, Charles Geisler, and Gayatri A. Menon. 2011. *Accumulating Insecurity: Violence and Dispossession in the Making of Everyday Life*. Athens: University of Georgia Press.

García, Jaime. 2010 "Indígenas, disidencia y lucha social en la Montaña de Guerrero, México: 1950–2000." PhD thesis, Universidad Autónoma de Barcelona.

González Benicio, Carmen. 2010. "Confusión en Tlapa por el encarcelamiento de dos funcionarios del cártel de los Beltrán." *El Sur Guerrero*, June 15.

Goodale, Mark. 2008. *Surrendering to Utopia: An Anthropology of Human Rights*. Stanford, CA: Stanford University Press.

Harvey, David. 2004. *The New Imperialism*. Oxford: Oxford University Press.

Ibáñez Martínez, Noé, and Catalina Isabel Cabañas Ramírez. 2012. *Othón Salazar Ramírez, una vida de lucha*. Chilpancingo: Fundación Académica Guerrerense.

Lemaitre Ripoll, Julieta. 2009. *El derecho como conjuro: Fetichismo legal, violencia y movimientos sociales*. Bogotá: Siglo del Hombre Editores.

Merry, Sally. 2005. "Anthropology and Activism: Researching Human Rights across Porous Boundaries." *Political and Legal Anthropology Review* 28: 240–257.

Miranda, Juan Carlos. 2013. *La Jornada*, July 31. http://www.jornada.unam.mx/2013/07/31/politica/005n1pol.

Monitor Civil de la Policía. 2011. *Desde la mirada ciudadana: Informe de la policía y de las fuerzas de seguridad en la Montaña de Guerrero*. Mexico City: Mocipol, Fundar, INSYDE, Tlachinollan.

Montemayor, Carlos. 1991. *Guerra en el Paraíso*. Mexico City: Diana.

Mora, Mariana. 2013. "La criminalización de la pobreza y los efectos estatales de la seguridad neoliberal. Reflexiones desde la Montaña, Guerrero." *Revista de Estudos e Pesquisas sobre as Américas* 7: 174–208.

Pearce, Diana. 1978. "The Feminization of Poverty: Women, Work, and Welfare." *Urban and Social Change Review* 11: 28–36.

Pérez, Emma. 1999. *The Decolonial Imaginary: Writing Chicanas into History*. Bloomington: Indiana University Press.

Redacción. 2013. *Reporteros*, January 27. http://reporteroscom.blogspot.mx/2013/01/ahora-en-chiepetepec-tlapa-en-guerrero.html.

Saldaña Portillo, Josefina. 2003. *The Revolutionary Imagination in the Americas and the Age of Development*. Durham, NC: Duke University Press.

Scott, James. 1990. *Domination and the Arts of Resistance: Hidden Transcripts*. New Haven, CT: Yale University Press.

Smith, Andrea. 2005. *Conquest: Sexual Violence and American Indian Genocide*. Cambridge: Southend Press.

Tuhiwai Smith, Linda. 1999. *Decolonizing Methodologies: Research and Indigenous Peoples*. Berkeley: Zed Books.

Wright, Melissa. 2011. "National Security versus Public Safety: Feminicide, Drug Wars and the Mexican State." In *Accumulating Insecurity: Violence and Dispossession in the Making of Everyday Life*, edited by Shelley Feldman, Charles Geisler, and Gayatri Menon, 285–297. Athens: University of Georgia Press.

Yagenova, Simona V. 2013. *La violencia contra las mujeres como problema de seguridad ciudadana y las políticas de seguridad. El caso de Guatemala, El Salvador, Honduras y Nicaragua*. Guatemala: Unión Europea, Diakonia, FLACSO–sede Guatemala, Red Regional por la Seguridad de las Mujeres: Alianza Política Sector de Mujeres, Red Feminista Frente a la Violencia Contra las Mujeres, Foro de Mujeres por la Vida, Red de Mujeres Contra la Violencia.

9

Grievances and Crevices of Resistance

Maya Women Defy Goldcorp

MORNA MACLEOD

Hundreds of people overflow the large hall of El Calvario in San Miguel Ixtahuacán. Most are indigenous peasants from San Miguel and neighboring Sipacapa. There are also delegations from Valle de Siria, Honduras, and Carrizalillo, from Guerrero, Mexico, as well as Maya groups from other regions of Guatemala and international networks. At the front sit the ethical tribunal expert witnesses and judges—activists, doctors, scholars, and environmentalists from Canada, Chile, Guatemala, El Salvador, and Mexico.[1] At center stage, there is a Maya offering in the form of a circle marked with the cardinal points, decorated with fruits, flowers, pine leaves, *pom* (incense), and candles.

The last notes of the marimba vanish, voices hush, and the multitude looks expectantly as Sister Maudilia, microphone in hand, opens the Peoples International Health Tribunal.[2] She delivers a longue durée narrative of grievances. The Peoples Tribunal, she says, is a space where villagers' voices can finally be heard:

> The purpose of this event is to express our feelings, to express everything that hurts us as indigenous people, as women who suffer so much done to us throughout history. We know the story of the Spanish arrival, deceiving us with little mirrors. And later they seized our lands, leaving us in spots they considered useless. . . . Then came the war, many, many people were killed: children, women, indigenous people. How much blood was spilled in those times! After that, according to . . . the powerful, we're told that there's now freedom. Freedom for them, for the rich, for the powerful. . . . But for us, the war continues. . . .
>
> They're no longer killing us with weapons, but they are killing us with ideas. Now they've realized that our lands and the ravines they left us, they've realized that there is wealth underneath those lands. So they want to take them from us again. This is completely unjust. . . . None of

our governments throughout history has had the will to defend us as peoples, as persons, as the human beings we are. What they want is to get rich, to ensure their own interests, but they forget ours.

This denunciation of government and powerful elites' continuous dispossession and historic neglect of communities sets the tone of the event. The Peoples Tribunal (July 15 and 16, 2012) symbolically "brought to trial" the Canadian Goldcorp corporation and governments that allow large-scale mining to operate in territories without consulting the people who inhabit them. Three open-pit gold mines were the focus of the event: Marlin in Guatemala, San Martín in Honduras, and Los Filos in Guerrero, Mexico. After two days of denunciations, testimonies, expert witness accounts, questions, and internal debate among the judges, the jury disclosed their verdict, condemning the governments of Canada, Mexico, Guatemala, and Honduras, and in particular Goldcorp, for flagrant human rights violations. The jury carefully included people's testimonies in their verdict. The effect for many was feeling that they had finally been listened to and believed, that "authorized" voices acknowledged their suffering: "I thought it was great, it really motivated me that there were so many people . . . disbelievers realized it was true. . . . And others came, for example from San José del Golfo, so now I see that it's not only us, there are others as well, and the more people there are, the more strength there is. That motivated me a lot" (Doña Crisanta Pérez Bámaca, interview, July 17, 2012). Ethical tribunals are thus a way of juridifying social conflicts and fostering the agency of those affected.

Goldcorp's Marlin mine in San Miguel Ixtahuacán and Sipacapa, San Marcos, is the first open-pit gold mine in Guatemala and the second largest in Latin America.[3] Since operations began in 2005, there has been extensive local, regional, national, and international protest against the mine. Where are the Maya-Mam women of San Miguel in the polyphony of actions in support and in opposition to the mine? Their voices resound at specific moments and in particular texts, especially in some videos.[4] But more often they are lost, decontextualized, or rendered invisible. The preferential arenas of dispute around mining activities, including highly specialized, technical knowledge in legal, environmental, and medical fields, exclude Mam women and men from San Miguel. Their knowledge is disqualified by Goldcorp, their community and life trajectories are disdained. The judicialization and juridification of politics tend to exclude Mam women's voices and feelings, while their acts of resistance are criminalized.[5] Centering on Mam women who resist the mine, I ask the following: How do Mam women resist, name grievances, and denounce impacts the mine is having on their personal and collective lives?[6] What are their notions of security and "quality of life"? How do they navigate—or not—the multiple expressions of judicialization of social protest?

I aim to capture the feeling, thinking, and doing (Harding 2010) of Maya-Mam women in a context of social protest, judicialization, and state criminalization of resistance, by exploring the women's views of justice and security and their understandings of the mine as a cataclysm in their personal and community lives. I examine the notions of grievance and violence, the indigenous epistemologies shaping their views, discursive strategies, and acts of resistance. I also document their critiques of neoliberal development and highlight their understandings of *tb'anil qanq'ib'il* or "quality of life." By using an ethnographic and hermeneutic approach (Theidon 2004) I seek to capture the texture of the Mam women's views and experience of the mine as part of a continuum of violence, in a longue durée context of suffering and grievances.

The chapter centers on the testimony and dialogue with various Maya-Mam women who resist the goldmine. The best known are eight women from the community of Ágel, led by Doña Crisanta Gregoria Pérez Bámaca. The women received arrest warrants in 2008 for their rebellious acts against the mining corporation's impositions. Other women include the elderly Doña Diodora Antonia Hernández Cinto, from San José Esperanza, shot point-blank in the head in July 2010 by two men who left her for dead. Doña Diodora miraculously survived, though lost one eye and her hearing in one ear. Doña Diodora's unflinching refusal to sell her lands—located in the heart of the mining zone—has had a high emotional cost for her and her family, facing harassment by the mining company in local courts, and hostility from her community: "My God, the worst is my community! My community no longer wants to set eyes on me" (Interview, October 17, 2012). The parish also constitutes a source of organization and resistance. Sister Maudilia López, a Maya-Mam woman from Comitancillo, has lived among and accompanied the people from San Miguel Ixtahuacán for twenty years, backed by Flemish Belgian Father Eric Gruloos, San Miguel's parish priest for more than thirty years. Father Eric, a Maya speaker, is strongly committed to the values of Mam culture and language in the face of rampant racism, a remnant of the *hacienda* culture that still prevails in the region (González-Izás 2010). Both Sister Maudilia and Father Eric devote their lives to the well-being, spirituality, and self-esteem of their Mam parishioners, paying special attention to women, and to analyzing the mine's impacts. (Another) Crisanta Pérez, from the parish, is in charge of the women's pastoral, and sub-coordinator of Kolol Qnan Tx'otx' (Defense of Mother Earth), the environmental pastoral, composed mostly of women. Many also participate in the San Miguel Ixtahuacán Defense Front (FREDEMI), which brings together several local organizations. I also carried out long conversations and interviews with immigrants, who keep close contact with San Miguel. It is through their different testimonies that I examine Mam women's views, opinions, and analyses on the impact of the mine on their lives, their views of justice, and their forms of resistance.

I went to San Miguel Ixtahuacán accompanying the Indigenous Women's Movement Tz'ununija' and their work with the Catholic Church's Women's Pastoral and with women from Ágel.[7] Over time, my collaboration included different kinds of support to Tz'ununija,' as well as facilitating the participation of several Miguelense women in events in Mexico and Ecuador. I systematized Doña Crisanta Pérez Bámaca's life history and struggle (Macleod and Pérez Bámaca 2013), and, with the support of our collective research team, organized Doña Crisanta's campaign visit to Mexico in October 2013.

San Miguel Ixtahuacán, 314 kilometers from Guatemala City, is a municipality in San Marcos, bordering southern Mexico. According to the Presidency's Planning and Programming Secretariat (SEGEPLAN), San Miguel covers 180 square kilometers and has 35,276 inhabitants: 97.9 percent are Maya-Mam (National Statistics Institute, 2002 census, cited in SEGEPLAN 2010: 12). The majority speak Mam, with different levels of proficiency in Spanish. In all, 91.4 percent of the population lives in rural areas, 86.39 percent of the population is poor, and 32.84 percent lives in conditions of extreme poverty. Unemployment has led to extremely high levels of migration: an estimated 60 percent of the population migrates in search of work (SEGEPLAN 2010: 15); most seek seasonal labor on the coffee plantations on Guatemala's southern coast and in the Soconusco, Chiapas, Mexico. There is also considerable migration to the United States. In 2010, Goldcorp, through its Guatemalan subsidiary Montana Exploradora, employed 2,030 people, including foreign professionals and workers from other regions of Guatemala.

Extractivism, Judicialization, and Grievance

The Marlin mine in San Miguel Ixtahuacán is an example of late capitalism extractive industries, or what Harvey (2004) calls "accumulation by dispossession," accompanied by the premise of *Terra nullius* or "empty land," both central to the imperial project (Shiva 2009). These legitimize the occupation of "idle" lands and justify the colonial enterprise (Kayman 2006: 239). Dispossession was also justified—and still is—by the racial/ethnic classification of the world's population (Quijano 2000). Previously, colonial powers claimed to bring "civilization" to the "primitive and barbarous" New World; today, extractive companies claim to bring "development" to poor rural communities and to "backward" indigenous people. In countries like Guatemala, the extractive industry finds cheap labor, favorable conditions negotiated between governments and companies, connivance, and lax state oversight. The dispossession, mercantilization, and appropriation of communal lands in San Miguel (Sandt 2009: 25) cleared the way for open-pit mining.[8] To extract relatively small amounts of gold, entire hills are leveled, devastating ecosystems that do not regenerate through simple reforestation.[9] Immense craters and artificial lagoons containing contaminated water remain. Open-pit mining also requires large amounts of water. "Montana's ESIA [Environmental and Social Impact Assessment] (2003) states that the mine uses 250,000 liters per hour. Critics of the project have calculated that the amount of water used by the mine in a single hour amounts to what a typical family in the area uses in 22 years" (Sandt 2009: 34).

The extractivist model is accompanied by a neoliberal "governance paradigm" (Rodríguez-Garavito 2011: 277), a political matrix of neoliberal globalization to exercise hegemony. This includes market priority, state decentralization, transferring the responsibility for social provision to civil society, in particular to businesses and NGOs, and the judicialization and criminalization of social protest. The paradigm displaces the political to the technical, popular participation to expert knowledge, public to private (Santos 2005: 34). It creates a "common" ground for dialogue and negotiation, naturalizing and dismissing power inequalities between the parts in conflict. The awareness of social conflict is replaced with notions of "social cohesion" and "stability." In terms of judicialization, it prioritizes procedures (Rodríguez-Garavito 2011: 276), leaving aside the substantive issues at stake (Coumans 2011). There is a "fetishism of the law," whereby the central role of politics is displaced to the courts (Comaroff and Comaroff 2009: 41), criminalizing social protest.

There are gaps, however, in this context of neoliberal judicialization, used by organizations and social movements to promote their claims for justice. Despite the uneven playing field, possibilities for communities can be significant. The multiple strategies undertaken to stop mining operations in San Miguel Ixtahuacán and Sipacapa have been widely studied (see, e.g., Yagenova, Donis, and Castillo 2012; Sandt 2009; Seider 2010).[10] Strategic litigation has been undertaken within the inter-American system of human rights;[11] the Pastoral Commission for Peace and Ecology has drawn up technical reports; Goldcorp's stockholders have been lobbied at their annual meetings by Canadian solidarity movements and Guatemalan delegates. The Marlin mine case was presented before the nongovernmental organizations of the Latin American Water Tribunal and the 2010 Permanent Peoples' Tribunal in Madrid on transnational corporations.

A complex web of judicialization and juridification surrounds the Marlin mine in San Miguel and Sipacapa, signaling the ways in which social and political relations have been pushed into legal and quasi-legal arenas. Formal channels include legal actions taken by the company and the state against the people who resist the mine, such as issuing arrest warrants and initiating lawsuits against local inhabitants. Judicialization also encompasses defensive measures adopted by organizations to support local residents—for example, the legal defense provided by Tz'ununija' to eight Mam women from Ágel to annul their arrest warrants. Strategic litigation in the Inter-American human rights system is an example of counterhegemonic and proactive use of international law, but the case also demonstrates the difficulties this can entail.[12]

It is in the quasi-legal field of juridification where the mining company legitimizes itself and disqualifies or neutralizes protests and complaints against the mine. This is effected through technical reports drawn up by experts (regarding water quality, human rights, damage to houses, etc.), activities presented as "consultations," and the company's preferential use of the discursive field to underscore its respect for human rights and its actions in favor of the "development" of the local population. It also encompasses quasi-legal and counterhegemonic actions against the mine, such as community consultations and ethical tribunals on health, water, and transnational companies. Judicialization and juridification take on specific characteristics when indigenous peoples are involved. Drawing on the Comaroffs' concept of "Ethnicity Inc.," Rodríguez-Garavito (2011) calls this process "ethnicity.gov." It includes laws and international instruments on collective rights and "socially responsible" enterprises, and reflects the juridification of indigenous struggles (Rodríguez-Garavito 2011). Free, prior, and informed consent (FPIC) is part of counterhegemonic juridification when used by indigenous communities. By mid-2012, fifty-nine community consultations had taken place in Guatemala (Sieder 2010; Yagenova, Donis, and Castillo 2012).[13] These were clearly counterhegemonic, as the state neither approved of them nor respected their outcomes. FPIC becomes part of neoliberal governance when the state and corporations are successful in imposing their rules of the game.

Judicialization of social demands runs the risk of leaving local indigenous women—and men—voiceless. Much depends on the way they are included and provided accessible information to understand and appropriate such complex processes. Antimining struggles bring together lawyers, environmentalists, doctors, scholars, international aid practitioners, and regional and national indigenous leaders who intercede in arenas unreachable to local indigenous communities. The challenge lies in including them in significant ways, avoiding the risk of displacing local resistance or fomenting nominal participation, as mere victims of human rights violations (Ross 2010: 76).

Therefore, "technical/scientific arguments can strengthen the movement's position, but they can also erase problems experienced by people" (Risdell 2011: 70). By prioritizing the technical field, frequent in socioenvironmental struggles, Risdell warns that key social, economic, political, and cultural grievances risk being pushed back, and those affected reduced to mere spectators. Thus, important exceptions apart, judicialization can obscure rather than emancipate (Fulmer, Godoy, and Neff 2008: 97), emptying social demands of their deeper meanings. Pseudo-"consultations" of those in favor, organized by the company or government, constitute another risk.

Faced with such an uneven playing field, women who oppose the mine prioritize two strategies to further their demands. The first is direct action, mobilizing their bodies and voices to condemn the mine. These traditional forms of protest, including marches, occupations, roadblocks, and even sabotage and setting vehicles on fire, are criminalized by the state. The second strategy is discursive, framing moral indignation (Tarrow 1998), where Maya-Mam women find a space to speak and name their claims, critiques, and grievances, revealing other ways of naming and being in the world. This discursive field is nurtured by their history and "collective memory of grievances" (Leyva 2001), characterized by a moral grammar based on outrage and indignation. Mining has trampled on community customs and social rapport, increasing the sense of moral grievance and social injustice (Moore 1989: 18). The discursive frames of Mam women in resistance, as we shall see below, are suffused with deep emotions and feelings of grievance as well as illuminated by indigenous epistemologies. There is a richness of expression, cadence, and metaphor when the women speak in Mam, which is often lost when speaking Spanish. Capturing indigenous epistemologies also provides another entrance, as well as a rights framework, to understand indigenous women's viewpoints, interests, and demands (see Arteaga Böhrt's chapter 6 and Lozano Suárez's chapter 7). Arteaga Böhrt (in process) explores the ways in which indigenous epistemologies—both locally and nationally—are having an impact on constructing Bolivia's plurinational state, in sharp contrast to the scarce impact local and indigenous movement epistemologies are having on influencing the Guatemalan state.

While the notion of moral grievance defines the injustice experienced by women—and men—in resistance to the mine, "living well," *tb'anil qanq'ib'il* in Mam, a concept that is still being formulated and sometimes remains somewhat fuzzy, refers to the parameters of quality of life valued, in this case, by the Maya-Mam women in San Miguel, analyzed below.[14] The notion of quality of life is intimately related to cultural relations between humans and nature. Walsh (2010) warns us of the co-opted and trivialized appropriations of the concept, and underscores social, economic, and epistemic aspects, the interrelation between human beings, knowledges, and nature. Here nature is understood as "the constitutive—sociocultural, territorial, spiritual, ancestral, ethical, epistemic, and aesthetic—conditions and practices of life itself" (Walsh 2010: 18). Eduardo Gudynas emphasizes the dimension of nature's rights (Gudynas 2009: 41) and land as responsibly managed inherited patrimony. This dense understanding of nature and its interconnection with other living beings is illustrated by several women later in this chapter.

Mam Women in Resistance against the Marlin Mine

Most of the women in resistance against the Marlin mine had no previous organizational experience beyond communal participation and attending church. The mine's arrival has awakened new capacities, such as Doña Crisanta Pérez from Ágel and Sister Maudilia's innate leadership skills, as well as their consciousness and ability to act quickly and resolutely against perceived injustice.

Many of the Mam women in resistance have participated in judicialization and juridification strategies, giving testimony, presenting denunciations, taking part in activities. These include the above-mentioned strategic litigation in the inter-American system; the organization of a Goldcorp stockholder tour in 2008 to assess the situation of human rights, water, and royalties; and petitions presented to the United Nations. These actions are led by experts, groups, and organizations with social capital, know-how, and access to funds. In some, though not all, Maya-Mam women have participated significantly. This is the case when regional and international social movements and even aid agencies have provided information, accompaniment, and training to women, facilitating the exchange of experiences and including the women in their actions. These include marches in Guatemala City, national and international events in Guatemala, and trips to events in other countries. In these spaces, Maya-Mam women have been able to exercise their *agency*, strengthen their levels of training, organization, and ability to speak in public, and broaden their horizons. Thus Doña Crisanta Pérez introduces herself in the following terms: "I am the coordinator of Women in Resistance here in my community, and I am also president of Women Struggling for a New Dawn. We chose that name as we didn't know our rights before. Other women have also learned their rights like us" (Interview, July 17, 2012).

Women were the first to protest against the mine at local level. However, with time and more formal organization, they were pushed aside by some of the male leadership. Women and men in Ágel, where a considerable part of the mine is located, have been particularly combative. Arrest warrants were issued against Doña Crisanta Pérez and seven other women from Ágel in June 2008. According to her testimony, Doña Crisanta had given permission for the company to install high-voltage cables over her property, and was made to sign a blank piece of paper. However, the company installed an unauthorized electricity pole on her land in May 2005: "When I realized it, the pole and anchors were already planted. I got so angry. How was that possible? For us in the community, what is said is what is done. If there's no agreement it cannot be done" (Interview, July 17, 2012).[15] Doña Crisanta started visiting the various companies involved in the mining project to complain, but they always avoided her: "About a month or twenty days later, I went to the IASA office, where they said they had already settled accounts with Montana so they couldn't fix it. I went back to Montana's offices and the same thing happened."[16] She finally had enough: "I made the decision to remove the anchors. I pulled them out. Another neighbor did the same thing, she pulled out the anchors. And we left it like that." The company's legal representative visited Doña Crisanta's house; then the company summoned her on three occasions, but they were unable to reach an agreement. Finally, the company installed the anchors again.

Tensions rose in January 2007 when some residents from San Miguel who had sold their land to the mine learned of the company's earnings and the high prices they offered people like Doña Diodora Hernández, who had refused to sell their land. The neighbors felt cheated for having sold their lands so cheaply,[17] and they blocked the road for thirteen days, demanding additional payments for their lands. Among them were mine workers, who were later fired. Other neighbors joined the struggle, including Doña Crisanta:

> We had seen the problem of the cracked houses, and the drying up of water springs where the company drilled. So we decided to denounce the problems of cracked houses, water, and human rights violations. [Previously] I didn't know about San Miguel inhabitants' territorial rights. I didn't know, and that's how I learned how it had happened, who signed, who sold the town of San Miguel, that's how I found out. And we started to raise awareness with people from other communities who are now with us. We went from one community to another to speak of the problems the company was creating here, and to tell the people about the violations of the territory of San Miguel. So thank God there are people who are aware of all those problems and are now part of the struggle.

In this narrative we can see how, through protest and the exchange of information, Doña Crisanta begins to gain a deeper understanding of the issues at stake and appropriates discourses on the collective rights of indigenous peoples. Her knowledge of human rights grew in 2008 when she went to the Human Rights Ombudsman's Office (PDH) in San Marcos's main city, and to the Public Prosecutor's Office, to file a complaint. She appealed to international human rights organizations, "where they further oriented me, saying that a private company has no right to install light posts or mark the land without permission. That's how I gained courage to continue denouncing this violated right."

They also filed a complaint at the indigenous mayoralty or *alcaldía indígena*.[18] Revitalized by the resistance to the mine movement, this coordination of Mayan community authorities later gave in to municipal government and mining company pressure. During those first months, however, "the people from the *alcaldía indígena* supported us, issued an order, and that order was delivered to the company obliging them to remove the electricity posts. So the company's manager no longer went to speak directly with us, but with the *alcaldía indígena*, to tell them that they would remove the pole in three months." When they did not comply with their word, Doña Crisanta once again cut the energy in May, with her colleagues' and neighbors' support.

> And thank God my colleagues supported me when I went to cut the energy again. Then in June 2008, almost a month later, I cut the electric energy again, I cut it in May, then in June, and we no longer left them in

peace. We no longer let electricity pass through, so they issued an arrest warrant against eight of us. But thank God they couldn't arrest us that year. Since "human rights" [the governmental human rights ombudsman] issued communiqués, and we were also organized, the company was afraid, because they saw that there were many organizations looking out for us. . . . First they issued an arrest warrant, then they tried to convince us, but we said no, the struggle is not about money, it's about defense of territory, water, Mother Nature, land, and health. So they could do nothing more and they no longer sent the police to arrest us.

At one point, about one hundred policemen were sent to accompany the mine's workers to fix the anchors again, but the women did not let them: "We chained ourselves together and didn't let them pass." Another critical moment was when the company set up machinery near a well by the water spring, in Sacmuj village in June 2009. "We were angry then. We were even angrier because they don't understand us." On this occasion, police officers and even soldiers came:

We weren't afraid of them, I even told the policemen that they are the sons of indigenous people, I also told the soldiers that they don't have to defend the company, because they are also sons of indigenous people, that the company also affects them. And they're going to be affected because it's not only in San Miguel that there are mining concessions, they are all over the country. They didn't harm us, the police did nothing to us. We talked peacefully with the police, with the army, with everyone. Our anger was against the mine, against the company manager.

Doña Crisanta's perception is interesting, seeing policemen and soldiers as "sons of indigenous people" and understanding that those responsible are the top hierarchies of the mining company, though the Guatemalan and Canadian governments' responsibility is less apparent to her. On this occasion, the conflict intensified after the manager signed an agreement committing to remove the machinery, which he then did not respect.[19] This lack of compliance angered locals, and in response, on June 12, 2009, they burned the machinery and a car owned by the mine.

Doña Crisanta's colleagues insisted that she had to hide far away. She was away from her house for six months, and returned to give birth in late December 2009. She was captured soon afterward, in February 2010: "I was not afraid, what I felt was anger against the Canadian company that's harming us in our municipality. We're indigenous people, we're owners of our land, and they did this to us." When she was arrested, "several women came to defend me, to tell the police that what they were doing wasn't fair. A cousin of my husband who lives in San Miguel saw what was happening and she confronted the police. She told them that what they were doing wasn't fair," but they didn't listen to the women. They put Doña Crisanta in a car with her baby in her arms: "But thank God when I got there, to Las Escobas, some brothers [companions] were celebrating activities in the church. They stopped the car and didn't let it pass. . . . So I was freed." Doña Crisanta was forced to stay another week in Las Escobas village, but she refused to leave San Miguel again. Later in this chapter we will see how the Tz'ununija' was able to invalidate the arrest warrants through accompaniment and a meticulous legal defense.

In 2012, two new organizations were formed. One of them was Women Struggling for a New Dawn, with twenty-three women from Ágel headed by Doña Crisanta. Its vice president, Crisanta Hernández, and spokesperson, Doña Patrocinia Mejía, also had arrest warrants out against them. About the same time, the parish Women's Pastoral, having gained strength in 2010 and 2011, decided to join the newly formed Kolol O'nan Tx'otx' ("Defending our Mother Earth" in Mam) environmental group. Kolol O'nan Tx'otx' was one of the main forces behind the Health Tribunal; it has a weekly program on the parish's radio station and works in the communities through its promoters.

Organization in San Miguel is not robust; local dynamics have their own pace and their ups and downs. In the following section I analyze the narratives of resistance, moral grammar and principles of *tb'anil qanq'ib'il*, or "living well," and views of (in)security and (in)justice expressed by women in resistance.

Women in Resistance's Views of (In)security and (In)justice

Maya-Mam women's semantics of justice and security are both collective and relational with their surroundings. Their categories of malaise traverse the "disorders in social relations and spiritual and moral confusion that characterizes a post-war society" (Theidon 2004: 58), increasing with the mine. This "spiritual and moral confusion" weighs heavily on women in resistance as they witness abrupt changes taking place locally with the mine and influx of money. Obviously San Miguel had not been a "closed corporate community," given seasonal agricultural migration, women's domestic work in cities, recent migration to the United States, and radio, television, and growing connectivity, but in terms of Guatemala, San Miguel was "remote."

Understanding the impact of the mine on community life in San Miguel Ixtahuacán is key to understanding Maya-mam women's semantics of (in)security. The sudden increase in monetary flows has gone into building burgeoning businesses: hotels, coffeehouses, and restaurants, and bars. According to Father Eric, there was only one bar before the mine, but by 2011 there were over fifty, accompanied by escalating domestic violence, prostitution, and previously unknown cases of HIV/AIDS (Maudilia López, interview, July 16, 2012).

Family and community are now fraught with divisions, with those in favor and those against the mine. Patriarchal bias regarding land ownership, usually registered in the men's names, has increased women's vulnerability: "The women are the most affected . . . most of the men sold their lands without even consulting them" (Ixina Ajsac, Tz'ununija,' interview, June 13, 2012). Before the mine, despite material poverty, there was a quality of life with close relations to land and nature, and Maya-Mam families' intimate space was secure. Doña Crisanta from Ágel says,

> When I was small, my mother and I used to take the animals to graze. When I was older I used to go with my little brothers. It was lovely seeing those places, we would herd the animals and the air was pure. It was delightful, we met cousins, friends, and we played. While we were out, the sun set and we returned to our homes, happy, without a worry. It was really beautiful. But now when I look at the place where they're extracting gold, it makes me cry. It hurts so much. The company destroyed the forests. There are no more places for pasture, there's only noise from the company's machinery. It's very sad. (Interview, May 29, 2011)

Rather than interpreting her testimony as "nostalgia," I suggest that it captures the women's feeling of loss of *tb'anil qanq'ib'il* or "living well." Although poverty drove San Miguel's inhabitants to work on the coffee plantations, "you go work for a month but you come back, you have your patrimony" (Luz, interview, June 8, 2012). And the patrimony of land has a connection and continuity over time, by being inherited from one generation to the next. This is precisely one source of anguish that emerged time and again among the women: "Our ancestors, our parents bequeathed us a marvelous memory and a legacy: the land. They left land to us as they passed through this world. They thought wisely, they knew how to interpret the future of their children and their grandchildren. But now, what will we leave as a memory to our family? We will leave them in slavery and poverty" (Workshop, Women's Pastoral, May 30, 2011, translated from Mam). This suggests that an intergenerational, communal, and ethical code has been transgressed by selling the land and failing to provide for future generations.

When asked about insecurity, some women mentioned *susto*, or fright. Most constantly spoke of *tristeza*, or sadness. A member of the Women's Pastoral, having gone on an exchange visit to the San Martín mine in Valle de Siria, Honduras, said,

> What's happening here happened in Honduras. . . . It fills me with sorrow. I was so sad coming back thinking: How can I interpret all that is happening? How can I really understand? When will we women rise up? This is most important to us as women; we value the land, as we bring up our children. What will we be able to give our children and our grandchildren after them? What will they drink? Where will they live? Where will they get their firewood? In Honduras, I saw that there is no longer

water or vegetation, nothing. (Workshop, Women's Pastoral, May 30, 2012, translated from Mam)

This narrative highlights that the mine has been cataclysmic in women's lives. It is hard to apprehend its magnitude, to "interpret everything that's happening." The company's invasion of their ancestral lands triggers a deep uncertainty, a bewilderment before a fearful future of being left as a people without land and food.

The woman who most spoke of her sadness was Doña Diodora Hernández. Harassed by the company, despised by her neighbors for not selling her land, and later a victim of assault and attempted murder in which she lost an eye and part of her hearing, she cries when giving her testimony. In her broken Spanish she says, "I am sad, things were calm before. Such a pity, I was working in peace and now I am sad. . . . [The mine has brought] so many problems to my life. Look how I am, almost blind, God made me normal, but look at me now, just look at me!" (Interview, July 17, 2012). The mine brought a turning point in Doña Diodora's life—before she was "calm," but now she is overcome with sadness.

Luz expresses profound sadness caused by the mine:

Now we're seeing what the mine brings. . . . It's polluting all the water springs. And where is the water going? Of course, it's affecting families and animals: cows and all kinds of animals, as we all depend on water. This is something we ask ourselves: what is happening? The people who are doing this, do they really feel it or do they only care about getting the gold no matter what happens? It is really sad. . . . [This sadness] damages your inner being; it damages families and their feelings. The elders are very sad about what's going on; nothing like this has ever happened here before. (Interview, June 8, 2012)

The mine's arrival is perceived as a calamity in the lives of women in resistance. It has unsettled their lifestyle, their intimacy, their security. The idea of access to security is remote as the women's narratives reflect a loss of security, dispossession, and a lack of well-being. This produces in Luz's words a "cooling" of the heart:[20] "feelings, values live in the heart, and what in Mam we call q'ixkojalel: empathy, putting oneself in the other's shoes. This is what's being lost, we no longer care about others, cold creeps in, that's the terrible thing that's happening" (Interview, November 19, 2012). She thus describes the community's disintegration, ripping apart former social cohesion.

Indigenous Women's Relationship with Nature

Maya-Mam women's narratives suggest a very special relationship with nature and a heartfelt defense of land and territory. A common explanation is that rural women defend territory given their close contact and dependence on natural resources as producers and reproducers (Merchant 1992: 197). This explanation illuminates indigenous women's everyday practices, culture, and specialized knowledge. From a Mayan worldview or hermeneutical perspective, energies intertwine with life-giving women. Miriam Pixtun, from Tz'ununija', says,

> Women are more steadfast in their decisions. The explanation given to us by the *ajq'ij* [spiritual guide] is that this has to do with women's energetic view of and relation to earth and water. But also, women are much more visionary because they look out for their second generation, they think of their children, while men usually only think about what to eat today, not tomorrow. And usually women tend to stay firmer in their decisions than men. . . . And we see it almost everywhere, we see it in Barillas, in Quiché, even in San José del Golfo, how women always react quickly and there they are. It's like an instinct, they know. And it's not necessarily that the men place them in the frontline [when the police arrive]; they put themselves there. (Interview, July 13, 2012)

That women position themselves on the front lines when faced with police repression is mentioned by social and environmental activists from other countries. We need to scrutinize Maya-Mam women's intimate relationship to nature. In her famous article "Is Female to Male as Nature Is to Culture?" Sherry Ortner (1974) questions the tendency to "minimize" women by relating them to nature and to exalt men by placing them in the sphere of culture. Ortner's Eurocentric assumption, however, is that nature is inferior. Among indigenous peoples, women have a special relation to "mother Earth," but men also relate to nature. In Maya-Mam culture, male energies relate to rain and lightning, sun and sky (Ovidio Jerónimo, interview, San Miguel, May 30, 2011). A central finding of this study was Maya-Mam women's close relationship with nature and its importance in their everyday lives and notions of living well.

(In)justice

Breakdown in social cohesion and a lack of *q'ixkojalel*, or empathy, have contributed to a climate of injustice: "Nowadays we're doing a lot of evil, often in the community we hate each other. We're divided, there's division between committees. . . . The mayor no longer listens to those of us who oppose the [mining] companies" (Workshop, Women's Pastoral, May 10, 2011, translated from Mam). This is one of the most insidious aspects of the impact of the mine in San Miguel Ixtahuacán. The mining corporation speaks with and "consults" only adepts, and local authorities follow suit, as do pro-mine villagers. Rather than listen, they disqualify and symbolically cast out antimining women and men from the community. "Divide and rule" appears to be a deliberate mining company strategy. To counter these divisions, the parish excludes local mining workers from their critique:

> One very damaging effect of the company is the [upsurge] of social conflict. The company pits us against each other, it's made us fight with one another. And while we fight, the company profits. We always explicitly say in our declarations that we're not against the local mine workers, that's always been our line. And we accompany mine workers, we defend their labor rights. But the company has tried to brainwash their workers and resentment begins, as they think that we're fighting with them. . . . There's conflict between parents who don't see eye-to-eye with their children, siblings who don't speak to each other, who can't even sit down together for a meal or get together, as one works for or is in favor of the company, or has received a small project and another opposes the mine. (Maudilia López, interview, July 16, 2012)

One of the mine's most tragic consequences is social conflict, revealing the breach between Maya-Mam collective and traditional values, and capitalist individualistic "progress."

Maya-Mam women's narratives emphasize respect of oral agreements and respecting "one's word." They act according to this code, but the mining company does not respect agreements, illustrated by company actions regarding the electricity post on Doña Crisanta Pérez' land. Maya-Mam principles in San Miguel include fair treatment, respect and being taken into account as people and as part of the community. Disrespect of these principles causes pain and indignation: "We're human beings. We have feelings. Why do they treat us like this? . . . It wasn't like this before," says Luz (December 26, 2012). Gossip constitutes another strategy to discredit antimining men and especially women. Reyna Jerónimo, in her testimony to the Health Tribunal, denounced that during protests in Siete Platos in February 2011, company employees falsely spread the word that women had been raped, thus staining their honor.

Perceptions run high that government and law favor the company. Sister Maudilia says, "People from the communities have been complaining for a long time, denouncing corporation injustice and atrocities in San Miguel, but state institutions ignore them. All lawsuits filed have been resolved in favor of the company" (Maudilia López, interview, July 16, 2012). This lack of access to justice and the feeling that the law favors the mine are shared by Doña Diodora: "That's my doubt, there's no law for me. I have to go when the law summons me and tell them what I'm doing" (Interview, July 17, 2012). Doña Diodora points to the courts' double standard, as they did nothing when she denounced the attempt on her life, but she is always being summoned for refusing to sell her lands to the mining company: "They summoned me two or three times to appear before judges in San Miguel. The assistant came with a note from the judge summoning me. What does San Miguel's judge want with me? I went to testify when they tried to blow my head off and the judge did nothing for me. . . . When I went to him, there was no justice" (Doña Diodora Hernández, interview, July 17, 2012). It is clear to Doña Diodora that "justice" is not on her side. The judges and courts are yet another obstacle she has to face; they leave her no peace. The company also has double standards: defending private property yet accusing Doña Crisanta of "aggravated usurpation" of her own land, and harassing her for refusing to sell up.

The topics of justice and fairness came up over and over in the women's narratives, however, only Crisanta Pérez from Ágel, the priest, Sister Maudilia, and Tz'ununija' leaders spoke specifically of rights. One of most deeply felt grievances was not being listened to, not being taken into account: "They don't listen. They hear, but they don't listen. . . . And what we're saying is true, [it] comes from our deepest feelings" (Luz, interview December 26, 2010).

Not being taken into account is both a personal and a collective, community grievance. "Development," they said, was bringing death to the Maya-Mam people of San Miguel: "The company is killing us ideologically, spiritually, culturally, it's exterminating us, it's wiping us out" (Maudilia López, interview, July 16, 2012). The women in resistance have tried to warn community and authorities of this calamity, but they have not been heeded.

Finally, the issue of injustice extends to nature, eloquently expressed by Luz: "Birds come to drink the water from that well [referring to the tailings pond] . . . what happens to the birds? They turn up dead by the lake, as the lake is polluted. . . . The birds die that go there to drink. We don't understand, they say there's no problem, that it's harmless. Who's going to speak up for the animals that die? We're witnessing nature and birds dying. Who's going to speak for those animals? Who's going to protect them?" (Interview, December 26, 2010). These Maya-Mam women speak up for the lives of human beings, animals, and nature, but their words often go unheard.

Small Victories

There have been small but significant victories. One of them is that international bodies like the United Nations have expressed their concern over water, pollution, and social conflict created by the mining company's presence. Especially forceful was the report by then UN Special Rapporteur on the Rights of Indigenous Peoples, James Anaya, after his visit to San Miguel Ixtahuacán in March 2011. An important but ephemeral victory was the Inter-American Commission on Human Rights' (IACHR) precautionary measures, and the possibility of the case proceeding to the Inter-American Court of Human Rights (IACtHR). Lawyer Carlos Loarca's strategic litigation in representation of petitioners from Sipacapa and San Miguel Ixtahuacán, obtained a historic resolution in May 2010. The IACHR demanded precautionary measures to establish the levels of water pollution, address health problems, and guarantee the life and physical integrity of the residents of eighteen communities from San Miguel and Sipacapa, and even suspension of mining operations until the levels and harmfulness of mining pollution was established. The victory turned sour, after a series of reports presented by the mining company and what appears to have been a deal between the company and the mayor of Sipacapa, previously one of the most outspoken opponents of the mine and a key player in Sipacapa's community consultation.[21] San Miguel and Sipacapa Mayors and an NGO were included, leaving lawyer Loarca as a fourth and not sole representative of miguelense civil society. In December 2011, the IACHR modified the precautionary measures, withdrawing its call for suspension of mining operations and diminishing its recommendations to simply ensuring that "members of the 18 beneficiary Maya communities have access to drinking water apt for human consumption, domestic use, and safe for irrigation." Under such conditions, the case was unable to reach the IACtHR. This led to a public complaint in February 2012, signed by 233 European, North American, and Latin American social organizations.[22] Montana, San Miguel, and Sipacapa mayors and the Municipal Development Institute signed an agreement to provide the eighteen communities with water, "which is currently lacking in most of the towns of San Miguel Ixtahuacán and Sipacapa" (agreement 28/12/2012: 4),[23] scarcity of water did not exist prior to mining operations. Doña Crisanta Pérez is in charge of the community drinking water projects.

Arrest Warrants Revoked

Tz'ununija' started to accompany and provide legal support to eight women from Ágel facing arrest warrants in 2011. The lawyers they contracted worked closely with the women, explaining the available options, so that the women themselves could appropriate this complex process and make informed decisions. Under Tz'ununija's guidance, cultural, psychosocial, socioeconomic, and technical expert reports were submitted to the court. Tz'ununija' also provided training and healing activities for the women.

The lawyers considered the case straightforward in legal terms, but a burning issue politically. Tz'ununija' demonstrated its skills at political maneuvering: the case was handled discretely. Goldcorp's subsidiary Montana Exploradora's plaintiff lawyers only found out when they were summoned to the hearing. Tz'ununija' also sought the support of feminist organizations. After painstaking legal and political work, the eight women's arrest warrants were successfully repealed in May 2012. The company was obliged to remove the electricity pole from Doña Crisanta's land. Days later, thanks mainly to the cultural expert report presented during the trial, a piece of land was also restored to

Doña Crisanta. Success was possible given the expertise and the large amounts of time, money, and technical support the women from Ágel received.

Conclusions

In this chapter I have highlighted that judicialization of social struggles tends to exclude Maya-Mam women, and that their participation in direct actions—or simply their refusal to comply with mining company requirements—is criminalized. Some Maya-Mam women, such as Doña Crisanta Pérez, have been able to participate significantly in juridification processes including activities involving Goldcorp's stockholders and the Health Tribunal.

But spaces of resistance are limited. Located at the epicenter of globalized capitalism and the extractive industry's increasingly conflictive scenarios, local Maya-Mam women have few opportunities. Visions of justice, security, and development reveal the incommensurability between the mining corporation and Maya-Mam women in resistance. While the former focuses on money, profit, and individual "progress," women who oppose the mine are concerned about collective well-being—which encompasses their ancestors and future generations—nature and fauna, family and community. However, the views of the Maya-Mam women are rendered nonexistent, transformed by the mining company into the "active production of the non-existent" (Santos 2006). Their semantics around justice, security, well being, and relationship with nature can even, at times, be rendered invisible by social organizations.

Filling the void, making space for Maya-Mam women's "feeling, thinking, and doing," uncovers another kind of narrative, where the cataclysmic mine is part of a long history of grievances, repression, land dispossession, poverty, and humiliation. In these long-term narratives of grievance, both state and law are absent or favor the powerful. But there is a significant difference today: proximity. In the past there was suffering on the coffee *fincas*, or working as maids in cities; but then one could return to the intimacy of home and refuge of territory. That safe and intimate space no longer exists. Even the armed conflict had less of an impact on family and community relations. Thus, a common thread runs through the Maya-Mam women's narratives: in the words of an elderly woman, "We don't want the mine. I feel sorry for my grandchildren, I feel sorry for my children and their suffering" (Interview, December 26, 2012). In their experience, there is no room for negotiation, only the feeling of grievance and the wish for "the mine to go away."

The mine has also awakened a fierce defense of life, nature, and community. There is a new awareness—stronger in some than in others—of the wealth of Maya-Mam values and principles, handed down from one generation to the next, guiding their lives and relations with nature. There is a new awareness of *tb'anil qanq'ib'il*, or living well, previously taken for granted. It encompasses multiple dimensions of life: nature, water, forests and hills, birds and all animals, indigenous culture, humanity, community, and spiritual life. The fight for life of Maya-Mam women and other antimining opponents takes place in an extremely uneven playing field. As Father Eric says, "the monster is so big, little ones can rarely win. David only once won against Goliath" (Interview, May 29, 2011). Many of the women in resistance know that it will not be easy, but they're "putting their life" into the struggle. Crisanta Pérez from Kolol Onan Tx'otx' sums this up: "It is like breaking ground for others to follow. And if one starts, others follow, it's like a chain." Given the very real threat, in Sister Maudilia's words, "of killing us little by little as a people," the only option is to fight.

NOTES

1. Among the judges invited to take part in the Tribunal were Rachel Sieder and myself.

2. Guatemalan/Canadian student Susana Caxaj finished her doctoral fieldwork in nursing in San Miguel in 2011; she wanted some form of symbolic retribution for those she had worked with. After much discussion, they opted for a Health Tribunal.

3. For Sipacapa, see Yagenova and García (2009) and Gramajo Bauer (2009).

4. See *El negocio del oro en Guatemala. Crónica de un conflicto anunciado*, directed by Grégory Lasalle and Marcos Pérez (Collectif Guatemala, 2008), available at http://www.youtube.com/watch?v=8dDnkljjYuk&feature=watch-vrec and http://www.youtube.com/watch?v=itlzp3DGLWY, among others.

5. I understand "judicialization" in its broader sense, as politics transferred to the legal field and, specifically, to the preferential use of courts to resolve conflicts. Juridification in turn refers specifically to the judicialization of social relations outside the formal system of justice (O'Donnell 2005). Going beyond national and international judiciaries, juridification comes to encompass nonjudicial negotiating and decision making, through quasi-judicial (legalistic) procedures and rules (Tate and Vallinder, cited in Sieder, Schjolden, and Angell 2005: 5).

6. Many men from San Miguel also oppose the mine and share many of the women's views and grievances. In the resistance movement, some male leaders—not all— exclude women.

7. Tz'ununija', formed in late 2007, is a national movement that coordinates the struggles, demands, and proposals for indigenous women's individual and collective rights, including the use of national and international legal instruments.

8. The external human rights assessment commissioned by Goldcorp and developed by On Common Ground (2010) indicates that the companies contracted by the Canadian mining company carried out individual negotiations to purchase land, ignoring the fact that it is communal property.

9. In 2011, the Marlin mine produced a record 382,000 ounces of gold (see http://www.goldcorp.com/files/april-24-2012/operational-highlights.html). This amount dropped by 46 percent in 2012 (see www.goldcorp.com/files/doc_financial/Goldcorp_AR12_FINAL.pdf).

10. See also plurijur.blogspot.com.

11. On February 1, 2008, lawyer Carlos Loarca and residents of eighteen communities of Sipacapa and San Miguel Ixtahuacán presented a request to the Interamerican

Commission for Human Rights (IACHR) for precautionary measures. These were granted on May 20, 2010. The government ordered a suspension of activities for twenty days to investigate water pollution and health impacts on the residents, but the company continued operating.

12. See the "Small Victories" section.

13. The first took place in Sipacapa in 2005; villagers categorically voted no to the mine (Yagenova and García 2009). Given divisions and mining operations in San Miguel Ixtahuacán, only some communities have carried out consultations, but not at the municipal level.

14. Plenitude, living well, or quality of life—*sumak kawsay* in Ecuador or *suma qamaña* in Bolivia—coined by indigenous intellectuals and movements, has gained momentum in recent years as a critique of modern "development" (which emphasizes economic growth and dominating nature). These notions have gained leverage and have been enshrined in the 2008 Ecuadorian and 2009 Bolivian Constitutions. In Guatemala, movements in defense of life, territory, and natural resources have adopted and contributed to this discourse.

15. The following citations are part of the same interview recorded with Doña Crisanta Pérez in Ágel on July 17, 2012. To facilitate the reading, I do not repeat this each time, and mention only the dates of other interviews.

16. The IASA contractor is mentioned in a Goldcorp report without specifying its full name. Montana is Goldcorp's local subsidiary company.

17. Q.400 per cuerda or US$11,537 per hectare (Sandt 2009: 27).

18. There was until the mid-twentieth century an indigenous mayoralty (*alcaldía indígena*)—in addition to the municipal mayor's office—in San Miguel Ixtahuacán. In 2007, after the ill-fated protests in January, the mine's opponents decided to recuperate and revitalize the indigenous mayoralty as a counterweight to the municipal corporation (Sandt 2009: 54–57). The *alcaldía indígena* still exists, though not with the clout the resistance movement had sought.

19. See http://acoguate.blogspot.mx/2009/08/nueva-alza-de-tension-entorno-la.html.

20. As with the Quechuas of Ayacucho, for the Mam in San Miguel the heart is central; it is "the most important organ for health and malaise, and also plays a central role in the processes of repentance and reconciliation" (Theidon 2004: 68).

21. According to Yagenova, "on June 18, 2010, the mayor had announced the decision to receive eight million quetzales from Montana Exploradora for royalty back payments since 2005" (2012: 241).

22. See http://latinamericasocialforum.blogspot.com.es/2012/02/carta-la-cidh-con-el-apoyo-de-233.html.

23. Umbrella agreement for interinstitutional cooperation and strategic alliance, signed by Montana Exploradora de Guatemala, the Institute for Municipal Development, and San Miguel Ixtahuacán and Sipacapa municipalities, department of San Marcos, November 28, 2012 (five pages).

REFERENCES

Arteaga Böhrt, Ana Cecilia. In process. "Entre la despatriarcalización y la complementariedad: Discursos y prácticas de descolonización del género en Bolivia." PhD diss., CIESAS, Mexico CDMX.

Comaroff, Jean, and John I. Comaroff. 2009. *Violencia y ley en la poscolonia: una reflexión sobre las complicidades Norte-Sur*. Buenos Aires: Katz Editores.

Coumans, Catherine. 2011. "Occupying Spaces Created by Conflict: Anthropologists, Development NGOs, Responsible Investment, and Mining." *Current Anthropology* 52 (3): 29–43.

Fulmer, Amanda, Angelina Snodgrass Godoy, and Philip Neff. 2008. "Indigenous Rights, Resistance, and the Law: Lessons from a Guatemalan Mine." *Latin American Politics and Society* 50 (4): 91–121.

González-Izás, Matilde. 2010. "Guatemala : modernisation capitaliste et racisme dans les circuits du café." *Alternatives Sud* 17: 119–133.

Gramajo Bauer, Lizbeth. 2009. "Construcción de poder 'desde abajo' y apropiación del territorio: la experiencia organizativa en Sipacapa, San Marcos (2003–2010)." Bachelor's thesis, Universidad de San Carlos de Guatemala.

Gudynas, Eduardo. 2009. "Seis puntos clave en ambiente y desarrollo." In *El Buen Vivir. Una vía para el desarrollo*, 39–49. Ecuador: Abya-Yala/UPS Publicaciones.

Harding, Sandra. 2010. "¿Una filosofía de la ciencia socialmente relevante? Argumentos en torno a la controversia sobre el Punto de vista feminista." In *Investigación feminista. Epistemología, metodología y representaciones sociales*, edited by Norma Blazquez Graf, Fátima Flores Palacios, and Maribel Ríos Everardo, 39–65. Mexico City: Universidad Nacional Autónoma de México (UNAM), CEIICH, CRIM and Facultad de Psicología.

Harvey, David. 2004. "El 'nuevo' imperialismo: acumulación por desposesión." Translated by Ruth Felder. *Socialist Register* 40: 99–129.

Kayman, Martin A. 2006. "'America Again?' Locating 'Global Culture.'" In *Estudos Em Homenagem a Margarida Losa*, edited by Ana Luísa Amaral and Gualter Cunha. Oporto: Faculdade de Letras da Universidade do Porto. http://ler.letras.up.pt/uploads/ficheiros/4238.pdf.

Leyva, Xochitl. 2001. "Neo-Zapatismo: Networks of Power and War." PhD diss., University of Manchester.

López Mejía, Lorena. 2000. "Participación de la mujer en el movimiento revolucionario guatemalteco y su reinserción social en el contexto actual del país." Master's thesis, Universidad Autónoma de Madrid, Quetzaltenango.

Macleod, Morna, and Crisanta Pérez Bámaca. 2013. *Tu'n Tklet Qnan Tx'otx,' Q'ixkojalel, b'ix Tb'anil Qanq'ib'il, En defensa de la Madre Tierra, sentir lo que siente el otro, y el buen vivir. La lucha de Doña Crisanta contra Goldcorp*. Mexico City: CeAcatl.

Merchant, Carolyn. 1992. *Radical Ecology: The Search for a Livable World*. New York: Routledge.

Moore, Barrington. 1989. *La injusticia: bases sociales de la obediencia y la rebelión*. Mexico City: Instituto de Investigaciones Sociales de la Universidad Nacional Autónoma de Mexico City: IIS-UNAM.

O'Donnell, Guillermo. 2005. "Afterword." In *The Judicialization of Politics in Latin America*, edited by Rachel Sieder, Line Schjolden, and Alan Angell, 293–298. New York: Palgrave Macmillan.

On Common Ground Consultants. 2010. *Evaluación de los Derechos Humanos de la Mina Marlin de Goldcorp*. Assessment commissioned by the Management Committee for the Assessment of Human Rights Impact of the Marlin Mine, in representation of Goldcorp.

Ortner, Sherry. 1974. "Is Female to Male as Nature Is to Culture?" In *Woman, Culture and Society*, edited by Michelle Zimbalist Rosaldo and Louise Lamphere, 68–87. Stanford, CA: Stanford University Press.

Quijano, Anibal. 2000. "Colonialidad del Poder y Clasificación Social." *Journal of World-Systems Research* 6 (2): 342–386.

Risdell, Nicholas Matthew. 2011. *Construyendo la justicia ambiental; agravios y diversidad en el movimiento ambientalista en Morelos.* Mexico City: CONACYT, ENAH, CONACULTA.

Rodríguez-Garavito, César. 2011. "Ethnicity.gov: Global Governance, Indigenous Peoples, and the Right to Prior Consultation in Social Minefields." *Indiana Journal of Global Legal Studies* 18 (1): 263–305.

Ross, Fiona C. 2010. "An Acknowledged Failure: Women, Voice, Violence and the South African Truth and Reconciliation Commission." In *Localizing Transitional Justice: Interventions and Priorities after Mass Violence,* edited by Rosalind Shaw and Lars Waldorf, with Pierre Hazan, 69–91. Stanford, CA: Stanford University Press.

Sandt, Joris Van De. 2009. *Mining Conflicts and Indigenous Peoples in Guatemala.* The Hague: CORDAID. https://www.cordaid.org/media/publications/Mining_Conflicts_and_Indigenous_Peoples_in_Guatemala.pdf.

Santos, Boaventura De Sousa. 2005. "Beyond Neoliberal Governance: The World Social Forum as Subaltern Cosmopolitan Politics and Legality." In *Law and Globalization from Below: Towards a Cosmopolitan Legality,* edited by Boaventura de Sousa Santos and César Rodríguez-Garavito, 29–63. Cambridge: Cambridge University Press.

———. 2006. *Renovar la teoría crítica y reinventar la emancipación social (encuentros en Buenos Aires).* Buenos Aires: CLACSO.

SEGEPLAN. 2010. Consejo Municipal de Desarrollo del Municipio de San Miguel Ixtahuacán, San Marcos, y Secretaria de Planificación y Programación de la Presidencia. Dirección de Planificación Territorial. Plan de Desarrollo San Miguel Ixtahuacán, San Marcos. Guatemala: SEGEPLAN/DPT.

Shiva, Vandana. 2009. "La civilización de la selva." In *Derechos de la Naturaleza. El futuro es ahora,* edited by Alberto Acosta and Esperanza Martínez, 139–171. Quito, Ecuador: Ediciones Abya-Yala.

Sieder, Rachel. 2010. "Legal Cultures in the (Un)Rule of Law: Indigenous Rights and Juridification in Guatemala." In *Cultures of Legality: Judicialization and Political Activism in Latin America,* edited by Javier A. Couso, Alexandra Huneeus, and Rachel Sieder, 161–181. Cambridge and New York: Cambridge University Press.

Sieder, Rachel, Line Schjolden, and Alan Angell, eds. 2005. *The Judicialization of Politics in Latin America.* New York: Palgrave Macmillan.

Tarrow, Sidney. 1998. *Power in Movement: Social Movements and Contentious Politics.* New York: Cambridge University Press.

Theidon, Kimberly. 2004. *Entre prójimos. El conflicto armado interno y la política de la reconciliación en el Perú.* Lima: IEP.

Walsh, Catherine. 2010. "Development as Buen Vivir: Institutional Arrangements and (De) colonial Entanglements." *Development* 53 (1): 15–21.

Yagenova, Simona Violetta, Claudia Donis, and Patricia Castillo. 2012. *La industria extractiva en Guatemala: Políticas públicas, derechos humanos y procesos de resistencia popular en el período 2003–2011.* Guatemala City: FLACSO-Guatemala.

Yagenova, Simona, and Rocío García. 2009. "Guatemala: el pueblo de Sipakapa versus la empresa minera Goldcorp." In *OSAL,* CLACSO, year X, no. 25, 65–77. Buenos Aires.

10

Intersectional Violence

Triqui Women Confront Racism, the State, and Male Leadership

NATALIA DE MARINIS

This chapter analyzes an experience of testimonial and memory work with Triqui women belonging to the movement for autonomy of San Juan Copala, located in the state of Oaxaca, in the southeast of Mexico.[1] It focuses on their reflections on the multiple forms of violence they face and the type of male power, leadership, and protection present in the region. Research was carried out between 2010 and 2012 in two different but related spaces: within the organizational dynamics promoted by displaced women from San Juan Copala in the city of Oaxaca, and in rural Triqui communities that are part of the movement for autonomy. I analyze the reflections of women who have been historically marginalized and silenced, focusing on what their testimonies reveal about the racism they suffer as indigenous people, as well as processes of state construction, and the male leaderships in the region who provided protection and security. I focus on how this reflection on the nature of male leadership allowed women to make analytical connections about the intersectionality of violences they face. Such perspectives decentered unilateral views of violence as something exercised primarily by the state, allowing them to locate themselves within multiple and decentered forms of harm (*agravio*). These ranged from counterinsurgent practices against their movement and historic racism, to intracommunal and domestic violence legitimized by a certain type of male leadership.

The movement for autonomy was a wager for peace in a context of armed political violence suffered by Triqui women and men since the 1970s, when the formation of state and party institutions first linked political dynamics in the communities of the lower Triqui region (Triqui Baja) to state-level electoral disputes. This subsequently led to the creation of different groups that competed for territorial and political control—those linked to the ruling Revolutionary Institutional Party (PRI), and an independent movement with links to leftist and peasant mobilizations in Oaxaca and nationally.[2] Many years of armed confrontation exacted a heavy toll: the murder of over a thousand people, the exile, imprisonment, and assassination of leaders from the independent movement, as well as forced displacements that resulted in over half the population today living outside the region.[3] In the 1990s the nature of the violence changed, with the murder of women and children and the targeted rape of women. These transformations signaled the increasingly fragile and contested mechanisms of political domination in the Triqui region. Political ruptures and realignments occurred in a context of indigenous mobilizations throughout the country, especially with the appearance of the Zapatista Army of National Liberation (EZLN) in Chiapas in 1994, which encouraged several dissident communities to create the movement for autonomy. In 2007 San Juan Copala was declared an "autonomous municipality" not aligned with political parties, after local activists had participated in the Popular Assembly of the Peoples of Oaxaca (APPO) the previous year.[4]

Even though Triqui women were always the visible face of political movements and constitute a powerful visual representation of what is "Triqui," they were largely invisible during the armed conflict. Through their subsequent reflection on their incorporation into these lethal political dynamics, women identified the murders of women and children as part of a historic continuum of violence and exercise of power centered on forms of male leadership that were both protective and violent. As has been widely documented in other cases, demanding collective rights as indigenous peoples implied greater women's participation and differentiated the autonomy movement from the leftist organizations created in the 1980s.

Three years after the autonomous municipality was declared and as other communities began to align with the movement, the two Triqui political organizations that had historically dominated the region blocked the only access road to San Juan Copala and laid siege to the town. Over the subsequent months they murdered more than thirty people, including women and one child, forcibly displacing about 150 families—80 percent of the town's population. The siege lasted over nine months, during which dozens of women were wounded with firearms and raped. In August 2010 displaced families from the lower Triqui region organized a sit-in at the entrance of the state government building in the city of Oaxaca to demand justice, security, and safe return to their town. It was at this time that I began the work described in this chapter, collecting testimonies and elaborating written and audiovisual materials to be used in the presentation of a case before the Inter-American Commission on Human Rights and Mexico's National Human Rights Commission.[5] As I detail in this chapter, I worked together with women from this community, interviewing people and elaborating audiovisual materials on Triqui myths of origin. In the wake of the initial urgency to denounce the violations, this process generated spaces where

Triqui participants could come to see themselves as a people and as women confronting racism and systemic lack of access to justice and security.

The Female Body at the Intersection of Violences

Triqui women are situated at the crossroads of political and structural violence. They suffer gender violence, counterinsurgent violence, and the historic stigmatization of the Triqui people due to the continuous armed conflict between the communities. They also suffer the poverty and economic and educational marginality affecting men and especially women in the entire Triqui-Mixteca region.[6] I use the concept of intersectionality to explore the ways in which Triqui women spoke of their experiences of different kinds of violence permeated by gender, ethnic, and class identities (FIMI 2006; Sieder and Sierra 2010). Intersectionality, a concept developed by Crenshaw (1991), allows for the analysis of intersubjective categories of identity where women locate themselves and are, in turn, located by others. It also reveals how this intersection of categories is shaped by broader political structures of patriarchal violence (1991: 1241). I explore the interrelations that women made visible as a result of their participation in spaces opened up during the autonomy project, as well as during their forced displacement in 2010.

Luz was the spokesperson of the sit-in established by people displaced from San Juan Copala in August 2010. Around thirty women together with their children camped at the entrance of the state government building, while most of their relatives remained back in the town. They demanded a safe return, security for their families, and justice for the more than thirty murders, rapes, and firearm wounds committed since the siege began. Luz became the sit-in's leader around two months after it was established, and was in charge of attending the meetings they were able to arrange with the state's legal representatives. Following the murder of a man in San Juan Copala, the women at the sit-in requested a meeting with the state's attorney general to demand her intervention to allow for removal of the body, which had lain untouched for three days in the street because of the threat of snipers in the surrounding hills. They also demanded she ensure safe passage for everyone who was still alive in the town and wanted to leave. Months later, Luz shared the attorney general's response with me: "I argued with the attorney general. At first, she told us nothing could be done because it came from the Triquis' blood, the custom of seeking revenge among themselves. I told her we're not doing anything. . . . The ones who are doing the killing now are the paramilitaries, the dead are on our side, not theirs, but the attorney general said [that wasn't true]. . . . She kept saying that this came from the people's blood, that it was like a legacy."[7] During the first months of the siege in 2010, declarations by government officials were imbued with the same prejudice, identifying the Triquis' "bellicose and belligerent nature" as the cause of the violence and referring to the conflict as an "intraethnic problem" dating back to the 1970s. The attorney general who had refused to intervene to protect those under armed siege in San Juan Copala made a public statement in similar terms: "These people are recalcitrant, stubborn with their traditions and customs, bellicose and belligerent."[8]

This declaration echoes those of other government officials at the time that aimed to create the appearance of a sort of "absence of the state" in the lower Triqui region. These views about the Triquis were similar to others I had heard since starting to work in the region in May 2008. During years of fieldwork, I had gathered opinions from Mixteco and mestizo neighbors, Triquis from other communities, and scholars and government officials that maintained that violence was a cultural expression of the Triqui, a heritage related to blood feuds and logics of revenge. From the 1940s to the 1970s, a number of anthropologists related the effects and/or causes of violence to the "miserable semblance" of this indigenous group, defining San Juan Copala as "a town adrift" (Benítez 1997). Views that rendered Triquis as "barbarous and uncivilized" are somewhat older, dating back to their rebellions against the land usurpations that took place after Mexico's independence.

During the 1970s state institutions linked to the dominant PRI party increased their presence in the region, and those movements that attempted to break with *cacique* domination over their lands and coffee production were met with repression.[9] In regions that constitute "the margins of the state," legal and illegal practices of power and security are not mutually exclusive dichotomies but rather an integral part of state formation (Das and Poole 2004; Sieder 2011). Networks of *caciques* throughout this primarily coffee-producing region, and the establishment of a military battalion in San Juan Copala in 1960 (before the creation of "development" institutions such as school and health services) suggest that the Triquis not only have been the object of violent security interventions, but were also marginalized from postrevolutionary Mexican state policies for the integration of indigenous peoples.

The first independent group in the region that denounced state domination and violence was the MULT (Movement for Triqui Unity and Struggle). Created in 1981, the MULT's history is marked by persecution, illegal detentions, and the murder and exile of many of its leaders. By the late 1990s levels of insecurity in the Triqui region, fostered by counterinsurgent policies against the independent movement, meant that community forms of self-regulation became increasingly centered on violent masculinities in order to guarantee security and protection. Insecurity also concentrated power in the hands of leaders who provided land, resources, and security and controlled the communities under their command.

Over time the MULT suffered a significant loss of its leadership and abandoned its earlier insistence on political nonalignment and autonomy. As it moved increasingly close to the PRI (which continued to govern the state of Oaxaca, despite its historic loss of the national presidency in 2000), the MULT became a political party in 2003 under the name of Popular Unity Party. Triqui communities in the region and leaders exiled in Mexico City subsequently began to denounce misappropriation of resources and abuses of power.[10] They also denounced the fact that the accepted codes of conduct of disputes for political control had changed, evidenced by the increasingly frequent murder of women and children.[11] These emergent dissident factions within the Triqui communities opposed both the supposedly "independent" organizations and those openly linked to the PRI. All this occurred within a context of increasing violence aggravated by the militarization and paramilitarization of many indigenous regions in Mexico and the neoliberal policies implemented since the 1990s.[12] Dissident groups incorporated discourses on collective rights that had circulated since the EZLN's uprising in 1994 and within the political mobilizations in Oaxaca that led to the creation of the APPO in 2006.

The participation of several Triqui communities in the APPO, which lent them its political support, led them to declare San Juan Copala an "autonomous municipality" in 2007. This was intended to sever relations with political parties (identified as the main sources of intracommunal conflict) and drive police and military forces out of the town in order to establish their own security system in charge of community protection. Triqui women had a significant presence in the APPO mobilization and the emergent movement for autonomy, bringing new perspectives to the ongoing political conflict.

The community radio station the Voice That Breaks the Silence, inaugurated as one of the autonomous municipality's main projects, allowed women's voices and opinions to circulate publicly both in the region and beyond. However, women workers at the radio station soon became targets of the repression: Teresa Bautista and Felicita Martínez, two broadcasters working in the radio station in defense of autonomy and indigenous and women's rights, were murdered in April 2008 in an ambush on the car they were traveling in back to town. These murders sent out shock waves in Mexico and abroad, demonstrating the risks women faced in this context of permanent harassment and extreme violence. Triqui women's most visible struggle was during the forced displacement in 2010, when they denounced the armed men laying siege to the town as paramilitary soldiers who had links to the state and municipal governments. In contrast to previous processes of displacement in the region, armed attacks now targeted women because of their vital role in the town's resistance, going out as they did into the mountains and walking for hours in search of food for their families. Many women were attacked during these excursions and subsequently fled to the city of Oaxaca in search of external protection. With the help of organizations that had previously participated in the APPO, they established the sit-in in August 2010.

When women broke their silence through organizing together, they also began to denounce other practices of legitimized violence in the communities, including forced marriage and corporal punishment against women in the name of "community justice." However, I argue here that control over female sexuality, which relies on patriarchal hierarchies and forms of collective shaming as a way of exercising justice based on violent leaderships, cannot be understood without considering the overall structural and historical context.[13] Triqui women were attacked not only as men's "property," but also as key elements of the resistance during the siege. The female body became the part of the terrain for counterinsurgent practices that aimed to control and silence the movement. As Luz explained, attacks against them worsened as they gained voice and political strength: "Since we set up this sit-in women have been attacked. If they didn't attack us before it's because they thought we were useless, that we couldn't do anything, so why waste their time with us? When we raised our voices and started to speak, to defend [ourselves], they started to attack other women, even though they weren't part of the sit-in. More than anything else they fear women; it's dangerous for them that women are doing what they never expected they would do."[14] According to Luz, the women's visibility and their denunciations, especially of rape, exposed them to more attacks. In contrast to armed exchanges in the 1990s, where women were "innocent victims," they were now being silenced for their political participation. In addition, the way rapes were experienced—no longer as an individual act resulting from a woman's relationship to the man the attacking group was targeting, but rather as an attack against the entire group itself—implied a transformation in the women's perception of violence.

Miriam, a forty-two-year-old woman, was first attacked together with her daughter and daughter-in-law. A group of armed men intercepted them on the road and stole their food. They threatened them, telling them to leave the town, but they were able to escape and return to their homes. That afternoon, their house was shot at by the same group of men. In spite of the constant aggressions, they remained in San Juan Copala together with the eleven children under their care. Miriam's husband had been murdered many years before, and her oldest son was in the United States.

Miriam went to the sit-in for a few days. There she gave interviews on the aggressions she had suffered together with her daughter-in-law. After these denunciations she returned to San Juan Copala to take care of her family and defend her home and belongings, traveling together with five other women and two girls. On September 3, she and another woman, Teresa, went out in search of food and were intercepted on their way back by a group of armed men. In this ambush, Miriam was beaten with weapons and raped by several of the men. Teresa was shot and wounded in the back as she attempted to flee. The men cut Miriam's long hair with a machete and stripped her of her clothes. She arrived at her home naked.

Women spoke of the attack as a collective harm against all the women in the sit-in. One of the things that most caught my attention at the time was their emphasis on the fact that the men cut Miriam's hair, an offence against her "being a woman," even more so than being raped. What I understood much later is that rape can be concealed, but cutting one's hair cannot. The humiliation was thus made visible and public, in contrast to denunciations of rape, which shielded the victims' names, especially when they were young, unmarried women. This emphasis on preserving "female honor" and Miriam's public shaming revealed the ways in which the conflict was played out through women's bodies. Rape continues to be silenced because of the subsequent exposure and humiliation women face. Since going public can make things worse for the victim, they constitute a form of future protection through silence. But silence is broken when humiliation is made visible and is intended to silence a collective: the attack against Miriam was interpreted as an attack against Triqui women's mobilization and public denunciation as a means to demonstrate their strength in the face of the attempt to break their resistance through Miriam's body.

The women's testimonies told a different story about violence in the region: for the first time they related the structural and racist violence originating in the stigmatizing views of the Triquis to the violence they experienced directly. The verbal aggression they experienced from other organizations present in the main square in Oaxaca City also revealed deep mistrust of the women's motives: "They told us that we just want money for our comrades and relatives who died, that they bought us off with six sacks of corn."[15]

For women in the communities, political violence linked to the parties was historically materialized in violent masculinities based on a certain type of leadership that tacitly sanctioned domestic violence and rape by failing to intervene when such matters occurred. Their defense of the more peaceful forms of male leadership that emerged during the period of the municipal autonomy, and their descriptions of the ways this male leadership took them into account, offered a different perspective on autonomy. While the men who dominated the movement described autonomy as a break with political parties, women observed that these ruptures had an impact on micro-political dynamics: the party links that prevented political freedom in their communities also cultivated forms of local leadership that inhibited their freedom as women and as a collective.

Women's testimonies framed male leadership as the microcosm of patriarchal power, enabling the materialization of processes of state construction within the intimate spaces of their communities and homes. Their testimonies can be read as a narrative interweaving the various levels of gendered violence and discrimination they suffer. As they made these connections visible, offering alternative perspectives to predominant readings of the conflict, they also located their actions in defense of autonomy as a way of building alternative masculinities.

The Effects of Displacement on
the Political Struggle of Triqui Women

Numerous studies of forced displacement have shown how terror is a form of control that imposes new geographies and imaginaries, whereby gender relations are also unsettled (Oslender 2008; Malkii 1995). For Luz, fear of speaking had rendered women invisible for the many years of the conflict. It was through forced displacement that women began to give their testimonies and understand that their participation was crucial for the defense of their people's autonomy. In common with other experiences across Latin America, the emergence of discourses on women's rights in the Triqui region took place in conjunction with indigenous movements' demands for collective rights.

At the same time, in common with the experiences of other indigenous movements, the Triqui movement for autonomy opened opportunities to renegotiate gender relations and women's participation, challenging "customs" that prejudice women. Triqui women denounced state violence, impunity, and the networks supporting those who sought to put a violent end to their movement. But they also discussed the effects of so many years of conflict on forms of community leadership, resulting in the exercise of specific forms of power and security through highly violent masculinities.

During their displacement, Triqui women were confronted with new possibilities for participation, responsibilities, and political roles: "As women, it was more difficult for us to come to the sit-in. But when we got here we realized that we had to do what we had never thought of doing, or what we didn't know how to do. We had never participated, at least in political matters, like we do now. It was the men who participated and we didn't even know how to speak, or how to speak in front of many people, least of all of political issues."[16] As Luz says, at the start of the sit-in the women thought they did not know what to say, and when the press arrived they were afraid to speak. The fear of being murdered like those who had dared to speak out was also a constant concern. As other analysts of violence and gender violence have observed, silence became a mechanism for protection in the face of so much impunity (Ross 2010; Crosby and Lykes 2011). Yet their initial silence was also related to their inability to express themselves in certain discursive terms. Over time they realized that rather than worrying about how they were speaking, they needed to express what they felt in order to try to save their lives and those of their relatives who remained in San Juan Copala. They therefore began giving their testimonies

by framing their own personal trauma—which many of them had formerly
silenced—as a collective grievance.

Despite all these initial difficulties and men's initial mistrust of them as
politically inexperienced, Triqui women not only became the "visible face" of
the conflict and important political actors in the struggle for security and justice, but also the main economic providers for their families, since the sit-in
on the main square in the city of Oaxaca also offered a space to sell and resell
handicrafts: "We no longer needed someone to tell us 'participate' or 'do something.' We had to do it. We made many decisions on our own and fortunately
they never rejected them because they had nothing to do with personal things;
we understood the problem and were able to defend what belongs to us all."[17]
Thus women began the struggle for greater security for their people through
visibility and testimony, as well as the support they sought in other political
organizations and national and international bodies of justice,[18] actions fundamental to guaranteeing their protection. We gathered about fifteen individual
and collective women's testimonies at the sit-in, in addition to those of five
other displaced women in Aguas Azules. Many of the women translated from
Triqui to Spanish and actively participated in the interviews, reading the transcriptions, and editing the audiovisual materials.[19] These were subsequently
projected in Oaxaca City's main square and circulated in the sit-in and at meetings with other organizations. The testimonies denounced state political violence as well as that experienced at the hands of leaders of the different Triqui
political organizations.

Women insisted that their displacement was not just a response to violence against them and their families—an immediate response to the fear
caused by the terror imposed—but also to how they foresaw their future in San
Juan Copala under the control of the leaders they referred to as "paramilitaries":

> Their custom is to force women to marry older men or themselves; girls
> are not free to choose their fiancés. When they see a couple, they punish
> them, they punish the girl; they make them marry an older man or a man
> who is already married. That's what I don't like and that's what the lead-
> ers are doing there, they have three or four women, and they force the
> girls at the age of twelve or fourteen. The parents are afraid because
> they're assassins; they're scared something will happen to them, they
> threaten them. You can't be free, they are the ones in command; you
> have to do what they tell you. . . . There are several leaders, not because
> the people choose them, they're just murderers and the people are afraid
> and that's how they become leaders. They fine people they don't like;
> they charge twenty or thirty thousand pesos. Women have the right to be
> free and they don't let them, they think that people are ignorant. . . .
> They can defend themselves but because of the threats they're

afraid. . . . They remain silent. . . . If you do something they don't like, they fine you. If you have no money, they put you in jail, they lock you up for days and make your family go look for the money somewhere, and they have to do it because otherwise they punish you.[20]

In their testimonies, many of the women underscored the freedom they experienced during the period of municipal autonomy. When they stated that they wanted to be "free" or that they felt "free" with autonomy, they referred to a collective freedom not only from domination by political parties, but also as women in the context of communal power relations. This freedom expressed itself in the way male leadership was exercised, treating women as more equal and as subjects with rights—in contrast to their previous treatment during the years of the armed conflict.

Displacement therefore implied not only greater visibility and participation for Triqui women, but also a space to rethink gender relations and the meanings of autonomy. As the women mobilized to denounce what they understood as state violence, they also reflected on its effects on masculinities. The "attacker" was not only external to the communities, but also personified in the types of leaderships present. As noted in other contexts, insecurity justifies the emergence of violent security technologies and hierarchies of unequal gender relations (Alonso 2005; Burke 2007). The importance that armed male protection acquired in the Triqui region increased violent practices against women—both directly in the form of attacks against their bodies and by creating power and protection dependencies that disrespected their rights. As Alonso (2005) proposes, "bare life" under states of exception is not only identified with violence, but also control over sexuality and reproduction. Images and experiences of insecurity strengthen patterns of dependence and submission to patriarchal structures of protection.

Testimonies and Memories of Triqui Women

"Truth-telling," reconstructing the act of terror, is not a neutral act; it is necessarily a gendered, political, and cultural construction (Crosby and Lykes 2011; see also the introduction to this book). For triqui women, it was a strategy in the face of the silencing and impunity implied by terror but also a way to get protection in the absence of measures by the official institution of justice. The construction of collective memory through testimony had the effect of broadening the scope of women's possibilities to include their voices, as observed by Stephen (2013) in women's testimonies of the APPO. The importance that collecting testimonies acquired among displaced triqui women was soon echoed in the communities of the lower Triqui region aligned in the struggle for autonomy, and it was because of their interest when they saw the video testimonies of the displaced women that we proposed a second phase of work to the community authorities.

In January 2011 we began a project with five women from Aguas Azules. At first their interest, together with those of the community's authorities, centered on reconstructing the region's history and underscoring Aguas Azules' importance as the birthplace of the independent and autonomy movements. A few days before the authorities and the women were due to begin, news started to circulate in the community about the project. In one of the celebrations to which I was invited, people narrated Triqui stories and legends. *Cuento'a* (male/female story) was the word commonly used to refer to the project. Gradually, those who were curious but also excited about sharing their knowledge of the history—and especially the myths and legends—of their town started to come forward.

The five women developed a historic timeline marked by the community's different leaders. This was an important way in which time was remembered and constituted the main references for many elders. Each leader thus represented a moment of history where different processes had taken place: displacements, confrontations, pacification of the region, the presence of soldiers, or the construction of homes or roads. Rather than years or dates, these moments were associated with leaders who had exercised power at a certain time.

Women and men of different ages came forward to share their testimonies about the historic violence they had experienced in the community. They also talked about Triqui marriages and how these had changed, about different leaders and their characteristics, the construction of roads and public institutions, and Triqui myths and legends. There was no temporal linearity in the narrations; everything was part of the same story that stretched from the origins of the sun and the moon through to the militarization of the region, the role of women in the face of military incursions, and the power differentials between leaders. The richness of the narratives revealed the importance afforded to history and to leaders in charge of security and the administration of justice in the community.

As we translated and organized the materials, women's references to Timoteo stood out. The first leader to speak of the importance of the participation of women and young people, he had helped many women obtain land and build their homes and invited others to participate in the APPO's sit-ins in the city of Oaxaca in 2006. The women recalled how Timoteo had spoken to them, advised and protected them, and how many of them had been able to study outside of the community thanks to his help and intervention with their families. In these sessions it was clear to us that if they and I were sharing knowledge it was because of all the changes Timoteo had brought about in the region. His influence was not limited to Aguas Azules, but also extended to other communities where he met with leaders to tell them how important it was for young people to continue studying. Many people referred to Timoteo as the "leader of leaders" in the region, and "the leader for peace."

The work sessions with the women did not have the fixed format of workshops, but often developed spontaneously in meetings among themselves, and with other leaders of the movement and communal authorities. The women brought other people to the encounters to narrate their experiences and memories; at times they came to fetch the filming equipment to interview elders who lived in the hills. They later reviewed the materials and translated them, and sometimes brought along testimonies they had recorded with their own families. Together with her family, a young woman from the community wrote down the last words Timoteo addressed to the community, shortly before his murder:

> Before, with military and police surveillance and the work of the government's representatives, many Triqui comrades were the object of repression and murder. Today we have the community police, which is in charge of security for the whole community. This police force never harasses people. . . . We think it's the best way to achieve peace and progress for our people. . . . It's up to us to achieve it, because often we go to the authorities of Juxtlahuaca or Oaxaca City to solve our problems, but we don't need them here. . . . Because they don't solve anything. We can organize the [thirty-two] neighborhoods . . . to create a single front and force the mestizo authorities of Juxtlahuaca and Oaxaca to respect us and recognize our president, to keep them from continuing to con us (*engañarnos*). Because if each group walks on its own, we don't achieve anything, but it's the mestizo authorities not us Triquis who are at fault. Right now we're facing very difficult times because we want peace, but they want the conflicts to continue.

Timoteo was born in 1966 in Aguas Azules. He was orphaned at an early age when his father was murdered. When he was in elementary school in San Juan Copala he started to organize the children in the school boarding house because he disagreed with how the older children treated the younger ones. Back in Aguas Azules, he started to earn respect and renown when he was in charge of the school boarding house. He was named to the municipal office of police agent then finally became the community's leader, starting to earn the sympathy of other communities.[21] He worked together with other leaders, some of whom were exiled in Mexico City, and in the mid-1990s they created the organization MAIZ (Movement of Indigenous Zapatista Artisans). In 2005 his eighteen-year-old son was assassinated following Timoteo's rejection of attempts by the president of Juxtlahuaca to buy him off. Timoteo was convinced the bullets had been meant for him, and in 2008 he told me that sooner or later he would become one more victim of the conflict. In May 2010, while he slept in his house with his wife Tleriberta and their three-year-old daughter, two men who had been frequenting his store for over six months to sell corn and beer entered and opened fire with a gun with a silencer, killing both adults.

"Timoteo spoke well to all men and women"; "He always gave credence to our problems as women"; "I didn't do anything without consulting him because he was a great counselor"; "He used to tell us that we should never harm anyone"; "*tin comani* (calm-peace) *chaani'a* (people)." These were some of the commentaries that arose in our sessions with the women, which somehow contributed to two interconnected processes: to think of themselves as a collective, but also as women. In this way spaces for reflection were generated that ran counter to the stigmatizing views of Triqui culture described at the beginning of this chapter.

In May 2012 communal authorities attended a meeting where young women presented the rough cut of a video about the origin myths of the Triqui region, illustrated throughout by drawings the children had produced in workshops organized by the women. The *cuento'a* discussed the power imbalance that at some point had generated conflict "among brothers," the narrator Amalia stating that this had been caused by men who wanted to be "more important than others."

The women told the authorities why they had decided to narrate the story from the leaders' perspective. They said Timoteo had been a very important leader for them, and related moments when they had consulted him about their doubts, problems, and decisions they had to make, explaining how he listened and advised them. For the first time, a leader had told them that they had the same rights as the men. The authorities at the gathering listened attentively to the women. At one moment, a man said he had always laughed at that aspect of Timoteo, disparagingly calling him a woman because of his sensitivity to "women's" problems. The laughter with which the man narrated this recollection started to fade before the gaze of the women present. With tears in his eyes he concluded, "I never paid attention to that side of Timoteo. Now he's gone. I always focused on Timoteo's political discourse, not on this human side. We have to rescue that human side."

At that moment I interpreted the "human side" as referring to the cultural dimensions of Triqui leadership, often denied by the leaders themselves. But that "human side" also signaled a gender and generational perspective Timoteo had that set him apart from previous leaders. I realized that the importance assigned to Triqui leadership by the women, and particularly to Timoteo's distinct style of leadership, had not been an object of reflection during the struggle for autonomy in San Juan Copala. It seemed that "the political" and "autonomy" were somehow distant from their own exercise of politics, something constituted by discourses external to their communities. The women had recovered an aspect of Triqui leadership that was not taken into account by either their authorities or the movement's leaders. This was due in part to the fact that the men failed to perceive the more micropolitical changes that had brought about great transformations for women in the communities.

Both "good" and "bad" leaders provide some form of protection, ensuring a degree of legitimation among women: "because when he [the leader who attacked the town during the forced displacement] was there . . . [he would tell] anyone who went near 'we're going to kill him,' 'we're going to capture him.' Because when you're united nothing happens, but when you're divided: 'that's your enemy.' He has no heart. I don't know what kind of person he is. . . . I don't know how to tell you about him, because he's a very evil person who doesn't respect women, he doesn't respect people."[22] Leadership is a central source of security and justice in Triqui communities, and it is perhaps one of the most defining characteristics of this particular indigenous group. Male warriors and/or peacemakers appear as central to the exercise of power in people's historical narratives. Leadership styles play a vital role in communities' self-regulation, but also in gender relations. Here I focus on Triqui women's perceptions of their different historic leaders and the effects they had on them. I am also interested in the extent to which broader national and international discourses about indigenous rights opened up the possibility of developing a different type of leadership. As Victoria stated,

> Timoteo's idea was to respect elders, he didn't believe he was superior, he used to say that we are all equal, that we should do things right; if someone did wrong he would say we shouldn't do those things because they would stop us from getting ahead. . . . That's what we liked about Timoteo, he didn't believe he was superior, he believed he was like us. He solved things right, we were uniting, no one was fighting. . . . He was respectful, that's why young people also followed him. . . . He didn't feel like a leader, he got along with everyone, kids, women, men, they talked, not like a great person, he didn't feel like a leader, he didn't boast, that's why people loved him. He got together and talked with everyone, brought people together, everyone with their own ideas solving problems together. . . . And young people too, when there were problems they called a meeting with the people and talked to them to stop us from looking for trouble, to [let us] live in peace.[23]

It has been proposed that the Triqui leader represents the *principal* in the system of traditional authorities or cargo system common throughout Mesoamerica.[24] Other works distinguish Triqui leaders from *principales*, seeing them instead as "war chiefs" constructed in the context of the armed conflict (García Alcaráz 1997; Parra and Hernández Díaz 1994). Everyone refers to their community's leader as the *Xinga mu xi'a*, the "father" of all, the "chief," and the "natural leader" (which means that his ancestors are from the community).

This includes leaders who sought war, those who fostered peace, and those who attempted to stay out of the political conflict in the region. They all structured the community's protection and determined its political direction.

In many cases Triqui leaders had not been traditional authorities before becoming leaders; in fact, a considerable number were young people from their communities. The temporality of different types of leadership in the region was defined according to various external political alliances and needs in terms of protection. Timoteo, the leader for autonomy, had emerged from alliances with exiles from the region who built ties with indigenous movements in other parts of the country. In addition, by the early 2000s the unprecedented murders of women and children in intracommunal conflicts meant that his peaceful leadership was also the expression of a collective desire in the face of the unpredictability of the attacks.

For the Triquis the power exercised by the leader is not delegated, but rather constitutes a shared power in equilibrium with the kinship and alliance network that defines the group. In contrast to the municipal authorities (police agency, municipal agency, and municipality), the leader is not visible. Rather, his is a concealed form of power understood as something that emanates and is exercised from the collective. A leader's emergence is not public; his election is a lengthy process that can last up to two years whereby people evaluate how the leader speaks to them and his skills in mediating conflicts and administering justice: "It is he who resolves everything, a problem, any problem: conflicts between families, problems in the family, between couples, everything, everything goes to him, the [municipal] authority . . . intervenes in simple problems . . . in communal works. . . . But difficult problems don't involve the [municipal] agent, they go directly to the leader, he's the one who resolves everything, and with the authorities from other towns when there are problems, they all get together, discuss how it was, what happened, all of that."[25]

The *cuento'a* also narrated stories of warrior leaders, "brave men" (*hombres valientes*, synonymous with murderers) who sought power through war between the communities. The accumulation of power and resources through party alliances generated a despotic form of power that differed from the qualities characterizing a good leader as a peacemaker. Our analysis demonstrated how the context of violence (whether due to militarization, domination by political parties, or disputes over state resources and territorial control) led to the formation of a centralized and hierarchical type of leadership based on a protective and violent masculinity that was very harmful to women in many respects. One woman remembered a historic leader in the community who failed to intervene in cases of rape, and indeed perpetrated rapes himself, as well as marrying off young women to elderly men: "Since he was the leader, no one could say anything." Although this leader had abused and marginalized women, she nonetheless concluded that he greatly protected the community. Disconcerted,

I wondered what protection meant and what "security" had implied during the years of the armed conflict.

Many of the testimonies narrated how families that lived dispersed in the hills around the communities settled together for security, in a context where dispersion implied exposure, facilitating attacks by opposing groups. The possibility of creating these communities relied on the capital of leaders capable of guaranteeing families' protection either through securing economic resources to acquire weapons or collaboration with the state's security forces. Larger organizations in the region effectively became umbrellas for protection that not only provided safe passage between the different communities, but also secured economic resources because either of their direct connection to the governing party or the political pressure they exerted through mobilizations. This dichotomy between independent leaders and those aligned with political parties, examined in several studies on the Triquis, became more diffuse over time. The murder of independent leaders (many of them native to the community of Aguas Azules) meant the MULT was eventually taken over by people external to the Triqui region linked to party political dynamics in Oaxaca City, who promoted violent forms of leadership within the communities of the Triqui Baja.

The project for autonomy emerged through denunciations against the political organizations and local leaders that highlighted their connections with party politics, and their abuses and concentration of resources and power. These demands for autonomy questioned the limited legal acknowledgment of indigenous rights expressed in the multicultural reforms of the Oaxacan state Constitution in 1998. For Triqui communities, autonomy implied a change in perceptions of the state, party politics, and themselves as a collective. They fought against both their stigmatization and historic racism, and prevailing hierarchies of power and gender relations. The context of acute violence limited the transformative power of this movement, but it is precisely those limits which led me to understand Timoteo's peaceful leadership and the women's participation as a transformation from within, involving "freedom" not only from domination by political parties, but also as women, listened to and respected for the first time.

Conclusions

Indigenous women face multiple forms of violence. Racism, discrimination, and economic marginalization are constants in their lives, as well as domestic and community violence based on patriarchal systems of family, justice, and security. If we add to this territorial dispossession, armed conflicts, militarization, and repression, their situation becomes even worse. Not only do their bodies become battlefields and violence against them increases, but greater power dependencies on men are generated for the armed protection of life. However, although the outlook is extremely negative for indigenous women in contexts of war, in this chapter I have tried to show how violence not only generates death and destruction, but also unsettles and restructures gender relations, allowing women to encounter spaces (albeit limited) to denounce their situation and render it visible. The voices of Triqui women emerged from fissures in the conflict itself and gave rise to new understandings of violence in the region, as well as of their condition as indigenous people in the legality and illegality of the margins of the state.

My focus here on Triqui women's perceptions of male leadership shows how their reflections on the type of masculinity and the exercise of power in the region allow them to make analytical links between the intersectional violences they experience. Their perceptions of the exercise of power in the communities through protective masculinities point to racism, processes of state construction, counterinsurgent practices directed against their bodies, and community violence based on a type of violent leadership constituted throughout the armed conflict. Triqui women denounced the violent construction of the state in their communities, countering the stigmatizing and racist views that link Triqui culture to violence.

The collaborative, collective work described here was a means to imagine "themselves" as women and as a people, away from dominant constructions that establish Triqui culture as something "bad" for women. Instead they came to understand that the violent exercise of power in the communities is linked to mechanisms of state formation in the region. In the peaceful exercise of leadership power in the movement for autonomy, the women found a means to disassociate violence from their own political organization and a path to justice. By naming state power in their testimonies and narrating Triqui myths about the causes and consequences of intracommunal imbalances and conflicts, women analyzed their own culture from a place removed from the stigmatizing labels historically attached to the Triqui people. Spaces for testimonial reconstruction and historical memory fostered this reflection and introduced new perspectives by including women's voices.

Even as victims of violence, Triqui women were rendered invisible during decades of armed conflict, a situation that came to an end with their participation in the project for autonomy. Their testimonies reclaimed narratives of the conflict and offered new perspectives: first, because women are in a marginal position within security and protection structures in the community; second, because their discourse was based on "feeling" and not on recognizable discursive structures; and third, because they are victims not only of state counterinsurgent violence, but also of violence within their communities. Through testimony Triqui women were able to link the intersectionality of violences they suffer as indigenous women in a context of war.

NOTES

1. The Triqui live in the northeast of the state of Oaxaca, in the region known as the Mixteca. It is divided into the "upper" Triqui region, whose center is Chicahuaxtla, the "middle" Triqui region, whose center is Itunyoso, and the "lower" Triqui region, whose center is San Juan Copala, together comprising a population of around fifteen thousand people.

2. During the early 1980s the MULT (Movement for Triqui Unity and Struggle), a movement formed by exiled Triqui leaders, developed links with the leftist Worker and Student Coalition of the Istmo (COCEI), formed in 1974, and other independent campesino movements.

3. According to 2005 census data, out of the 23,846 Triquis living in Mexico territory, only 18,000 lived in the state of Oaxaca, approximately 15,000 in the Triqui region and the rest in other cities. An analysis of Triqui migration carried out by Paris Pombo (2011) revealed that over half of the Triqui population lived outside its historical territories, mainly because of the violence.

4. The Popular Assembly of the Peoples of Oaxaca (APPO) emerged in the city of Oaxaca in June 2006, after repression against the annual sit-in organized by the teacher's union. Solidarity from social organizations, students, unions, and people who participated politically for the first time led to the creation of the APPO, which used sit-ins, radio broadcasts, and barricades as a means to contain police attacks. The APPO extended beyond Oaxaca, even to immigrant communities in the United States. See Salcida Olivares 2011; Stephen 2013.

5. The written testimonies were collected in the book *A solas contra el enemigo*, published in 2011 by the Autonomous Municipality of San Juan Copala (Municipio Autónomo de San Juan Copala 2011).

6. The most recent census data (2010) for the district of Juxtlahuaca, where a part of the lower Triqui region is located, indicate that illiteracy among indigenous women is more than double that of men—74.7 percent are illiterate, compared to 25.3 percent of men. The number of women who are monolingual (65.3 percent) is also greater. Lack of access to education combined with a "very high" level of marginality, as characterized in the census, is a feature shared by many indigenous women throughout Latin America (Sieder and Sierra 2010; FIMI–Indigenous Women's Forum 2006).

7. Interview, Luz, April 22, 2011.

8. "Ulises Ruiz se desentiende de caravana que viaja a Copala," *Revista Proceso*, June 7, 2011, http://hemeroteca.proceso.com.mx/?p=104749.

9. Parra and Hernández Díaz 1994; López Bárcenas 2009; De Marinis 2009, 2013; Daria 2013.

10. In the 1990s, many MULT leaders in exile created the organization Movement of Indigenous Zapatista Artisans (MAIZ) in Mexico City. The PRI-aligned organization called UBISORT was created in 1994.

11. According to the media, between August 2005 and November 2009 there were thirty murders in the San Juan Copala region, nine of which were of children and teenagers. Five of the thirty deaths were of women older than twenty. The kidnapping of two girls was also denounced in the media, but never solved.

12. The massacre of Acteal in 1997, when forty-five indigenous people were murdered, including many women, demonstrated the presence of paramilitaries in the state

of Chiapas (Hernández Castillo 2006; Castro Apreza 2004). In Oaxaca the forced displacement in Loxicha dating to 1996 was provoked by police and military attacks and resulted in 150 community members being arrested and many being forcefully displaced (Stephen 1999: 828–829). The relatives of the detainees maintained a sit-in for over four years outside the seat of government in Oaxaca City, to no avail.

13. See Cumes (2009) on Guatemala, Hernández Castillo (2010) on Chiapas.

14. Public testimony, Luz, Oaxaca City.

15. Interview, Ana, December 2010.

16. Interview, Luz, Oaxaca City, April 2011.

17. Ibid.

18. Part of the responses they obtained to complaints presented to national and international human rights institutions was the follow-up of the case by the Inter-American Commission on Human Rights, as well as a document with recommendations to various government bodies by Mexico's National Commission on Human Rights, published in May 2011. Available at http://www.cndh.org.mx/sites/all/fuentes/documentos/Recomendaciones/2011/REC_2011_026.pdf.

19. The testimonies were collected with the collaboration of human rights activist Marisa Villareal and the women at the sit-in, who collaborated in the editing of a documentary video together with Meztli Rodríguez and myself.

20. Public testimony, Victoria, Oaxaca City.

21. Police agencies are part of the municipal structures that administer the localities, tied to municipal agencies and municipalities. In order to be categorized as a police agency, a town must have at least five thousand inhabitants. Both structures depend administratively on the municipality and receive the corresponding financing.

22. Public testimony, Victoria, Oaxaca City.

23. Ibid.

24. Many studies analyze indigenous power based on the system of traditional authorities and categories of representation that articulate civilian positions (*presidente*, *principal*, *síndico*, etc.) and religious positions (*mayordomía*). The *principal* is appointed as an authority only after having held various civilian and religious positions; he holds the highest moral authority within his community (Velázquez 2000).

25. Interview, Horacio, Oaxaca City, July 2010.

REFERENCES

Alonso, Ana. 2005. "Sovereignty, the Spatial Politics of Security and Gender: Looking North and South from the US-Mexico Border." In *State Formation: Anthropological Perspectives*, edited by Krohn-Hansen, C. and Knut Nustad, 27–52. London: Pluto Press.

Benítez, Fernando. 1997. *Los indios de México. Antología.* Mexico City: Era.

Burke, Antony. 2007. *Beyond Security, Ethics and Violence: War Against the Other.* New York: Routledge.

Castro Apreza, Inés. 2004. "San Pedro Chenalhó: La cúspide de la violencia en tiempos de guerra." In *Tejiendo historias: Tierra, género y poder en Chiapas*, edited by M. Peréz Ruíz, 321–354. Mexico City: Escuela Nacional de Antropología e Historia.

Crenshaw, Kimberlé. 1991. "Mapping the Margins: Intersectionality, Identity Politics and Violence against Women of Color." *Stanford Law Review* 43 (6): 1241–1299.

Crosby, Alison, and Brinton Lykes. 2011. "Mayan Women Survivors Speak: The Gendered Relations of Truth Telling in Post-war Guatemala." *International Journal of Transitional Justice* 5: 456–476.

Cumes, Aura. 2009. "Sufrimos verguenza: Mujeres K'iché frente a la justicia comunitaria." *Desacatos* 31: 99–114.

Daria, James. 2013. "Writing in Blood and Ink: Agrarian Reform, Intercommunity Conflict and the Struggle for Communal Lands of San Juan Copala, Oaxaca." Master's thesis, University of Oregon.

Das, Veena, and Deborah Poole. 2004. "State and Its Margins: Comparative Ethnographies." In *Anthropology in the Margins of the State*, edited by V. Das and D. Poole, 3–33. Santa Fe: SAR Press.

De Marinis, Natalia. 2009. "Entre la guerra y la paz: La intervención política partidaria, el conflicto armado y la autonomía como paz entre los triquis de San Juan Copala, Oaxaca." Master's thesis, CIESAS, Mexico City.

———. 2013. "Indigenous Rights and Violent State Construction: The Struggle of Triqui Women in Oaxaca." In *Gender Justice and Legal Pluralities: Latin American and African Perspectives*, edited by R. Sieder and J. McNeish, 156–179. New York: Routledge.

FIMI–Indigenous Women's Forum. 2006. *Mairin Iwanka Raya: Mujeres indígenas confrontan la violencia*. www.indigenouswomensforum.org.

García Alcaráz, Agustín. 1997. *Tinujei: Los triquis de Copala*. Mexico City: CIESAS.

Hernández Castillo, Aída. 2006. "Fraticidal War or Ethnocidal Strategy? Women's Experiences with Political Violence in Chiapas." In *Engaged Observer: Anthropology, Advocacy and Activism*, edited by Sanford Victoria and Asale Angel-Ajali, 149–159. New Brunswick, NJ: Rutgers University Press.

———. 2010. "Violencia de Estado y violencia de género: Las paradojas en torno a los derechos humanos de las mujeres en México." *TRACE* 57: 86–98.

López Bárcenas, Francisco. 2009. *San Juan Copala: Dominación Política y Resistencia Popular, De las rebeliones de Hilarión a la formación del Municipio Autónomo*. Mexico City: UAM Xochimilco.

Malkii, Liisa. 1995. *Purity and Exile*. Chicago: University of Chicago Press.

Municipio Autónomo de San Juan Copala. 2011. *A solas contra el enemigo*. Mexico City: Editorial Huapasingo Tierra Roja.

Oslender, Ulrich. 2008. "Another History of Violence: The Production of 'Geographies of Terror' in Colombia's Pacific Coast Region." *Latin American Perspectives* 35 (5): 77–102.

Paris Pombo, María Dolores. 2011. *Intervención Institucional y Migración en la Región Triqui Baja*. Mexican Rural Development Research Report 20. Washington, DC: Wilson Center.

Parra Mora, León, and Jorge Hernández Díaz. 1994. *Violencia y Cambio Social en la Región Triqui*. Mexico City: UABJO.

Ross, Fiona. 2010. "An Acknowledged Failure: Women, Voice, Violence and the South African Truth and Reconciliation Commission." In *Localizing Transitional Justice*, edited by R. Shaw and L. Waldorf, 69–91. Stanford, CA: Stanford University Press.

Salcida Olivares, Juan Manuel. 2011. "La(s) APPO(s): Prácticas políticas y juegos del lenguaje en movimiento." PhD diss., CIESAS, Mexico City.

Sieder, Rachel. 2011. "Building Mayan Authority and Autonomy: The Recovery of Indigenous Law in Post-peace Guatemala." *Studies in Law, Politics and Society* 55: 43–75.

Sieder, Rachel, and María Teresa Sierra. 2010. *Indigenous Women's Access to Justice in Latin America*. CMI working paper. Bergen, Norway: Chr. Michelsen Institute. http://www.

cmi.no/publications/publication/?3880=indigenous-womens-access-to-justice-in-latin.

Stephen, Lynn. 1999. "The Construction of Indigenous Suspects: Militarization and the Gendered and Ethnic Dynamics of Human Rights Abuses in Southern Mexico." *American Ethnologist* 26 (4): 822–842.

———. 2013. *We Are the Face of Oaxaca: Testimony and Social Movements.* Durham, NC: Duke University Press.

Velázquez, María Cristina. 2000. *El nombramiento: Las elecciones por usos y costumbres de Oaxaca.* Oaxaca: Instituto Estatal Electoral de Oaxaca.

PART FOUR

Methodological Perspectives

11

Methodological Routes

Toward a Critical and Collaborative Legal Anthropology

ROSALVA AÍDA HERNÁNDEZ CASTILLO AND
ADRIANA TERVEN SALINAS

In this final chapter we reflect on the challenges of coproduction of knowledge and the methodological routes we adopted to reach the results shared in this volume.[1] As a research team we were confronted with the epistemological and political tension of always maintaining a critical stance toward positive law, as a practice and a discourse, and toward human rights as universalizing and globalizing discourses, while at the same time supporting national and international political struggles for recognition of indigenous people's rights. Some authors have argued that these are conflicting options: either undertake a critical analysis of the law and the judicialization of political struggles, or support legal activism thereby consolidating hegemonic perspectives on law and rights (Brown and Halley 2002). Such a binary would seem to suggest that struggles for the recognition of cultural rights tend to reify hegemonic definitions of culture and indigenous people, and end up limiting political imaginaries on justice. In the current era, "so saturated by legalism is contemporary political life, that it is often difficult to imagine alternative ways of deliberating about and pursuing justice" (Brown and Halley 2002: 19).

Disagreeing with such perspectives, we believe that it is possible to maintain a sustained and critical reflection on law and rights and simultaneously to support struggles for justice by indigenous peoples and organizations, which in turn appropriate and resignify national and international legislation and norms. Stances that disqualify legal activism end up once again silencing subaltern groups by failing to recognize the counterhegemonic legal discourses and practices they have been developing in the "Global South." In this volume we have tried to account for what Cesar Rodríguez Garavito and Boaventura de Sousa Santos (2007) term "subaltern cosmopolitan legalities," in other words, the counterhegemonic uses of law by marginalized populations to confront various forms of domination in the new global world order. As a research team we were inspired by at least two theoretical and methodological traditions:

on one hand, critical legal anthropology, which in Latin America has a long tradition of ethnographic analysis of interlegal spaces and power relations in the legal arena; on the other, action research or collaborative research, which since the 1960s has been committed to developing research in dialogue with the social actors with whom we work.[2] Several of the team members also resorted to the contributions of feminist anthropology in an effort to develop a culturally situated gender perspective in our studies of spaces of justice (see Hernández Castillo 2002, 2003, 2016; Hernández Castillo and Sierra 2005; Mora 2008; Sieder and McNeish 2012b; Sieder 2012; Macleod 2011; Arteaga 2013; De Marinis 2011, 2013).

In the past decade, so-called *activist anthropology* in the United States (see Naples 2003; Hale 2008; Speed 2008) and the modernity/coloniality group (Castro-Gómez 1998, 2000; Castro-Gómez and Mendieta 1998) have called for the decolonization of the social sciences, questioning extractivist methodologies and confronting positivist outlooks that end up reifying the status quo in the name of "scientific neutrality." Along the same lines, androcentric science has been questioned by feminist scholars in various parts of the world. For feminist anthropology, the link between knowledge production and political commitment to social transformation has been a central axis for its theoretical and methodological proposals (see Moore 1996). Feminists have made important contributions to the critique of power networks that legitimize and reproduce scientistic positivism—contributions that have not always been recognized by contemporary critical anthropology or postmodern theoreticians.[3]

For our research team, collaboration with indigenous organizations took place through various forms of exchange based on different dialogues and political alliances. The possibilities for greater or lesser collaboration were determined by several factors, including our own political genealogies, our prior relations with indigenous organizations, the political context, and the conditions of security or insecurity in the various regions where the studies were carried out.

Reflections on the Coproduction of Knowledge

One of the goals of our collective project was the creation of networks for the coproduction of knowledge. This implied a number of challenges, discussed in this section. As a starting point, we decided to undertake a joint methodological reflection in an international workshop organized by the project on November 29 and 30, 2012, where we reflected on the challenges of writing from a collaborative perspective and maintaining a critical stance toward local authorities and state violence. We thus hoped to respond to what Boaventura de Sousa Santos (2010) calls the phantasmagoric relationship between theory and practice, approaching it from the tension between power and knowledge

(Foucault 1980) in regard to the academy versus activism. This perspective conceives the construction of knowledge as inseparable from social relations of power and structural inequalities present in specific contexts, and asserts that social groups can either be approached as objects of study or recognized as coproducers of knowledge (Hernández Castillo 2016). Knowledge can therefore be seen in its capacity to (re)produce and reinforce inequalities, but also in its emancipatory potential. How can we render intelligible the context-specific tensions between power and knowledge that develop during research? María Teresa Sierra pointed to a constant disqualification of the work of female promoters by the Community Police and CRAC commissioners; Natalia De Marinis spoke of how Triqui women's participation was discredited through gossip and rumors; Aída Hernández mentioned the death threats against the women in OPIM and against Inés Fernández by paramilitaries, hindering the creation of a rights center for Me'phaa men and women; Ana Cecilia Arteaga referred to the narrow-mindedness of some male authorities and community members when incorporating the women's proposals in the autonomy statute (Exercise of Reflection, workshop, November 29–30, 2012, CIESAS, Mexico). All these examples reveal how women's organizational work is undervalued by the authorities and how contexts of violence limit their actions, hindering the development of initiatives and proposals or the creation of epistemic communities—in other words, anything related to the production of knowledge by indigenous women. Recognizing the position of the academy, but also of other power structures such as local authorities and state violence, posed several challenges for theory and practice: How do we establish collaborative work relations from different realities and expressions of power? To what extent does the coproduction of knowledge contribute to defend the rights of indigenous peoples and, more specifically, the rights of women?

As Toledo (2011) signals, these challenges demand that we clearly identify the dynamics between the various social actors generated during our research as well as the specific focus for the research encounter: in our case indigenous women's concepts of security and justice.[4] This requires close attention to social relations and dynamics, and to the tensions related to power differentials between state actors, local authorities, and scholars in different scenarios of struggle and study. María Teresa Sierra observed that it was necessary to earn legitimacy in the eyes of the CRAC and the comisionados in the different communities in order to carry out the workshops; at certain moments, the indigenous women that participate in the workshops were questioned, "Who appointed you as justice promoters?," which made it difficult for them to do research in the CRAC's archives. Leonor Lozano commented that many CRIC leaders did not believe it was important to address violence against women as a topic separate from family issues; Rachel Sieder spoke of deep-rooted male ideologies of domination that are reflected in scant willingness on the part of community authorities to address the issue of domestic violence; Morna Macleod observed how women were often rendered invisible by men in the localities she worked in (Exercise of Reflection, workshop, November 29–30, 2012, CIESAS, Mexico).

Regarding the implications of state violence, Aída Hernández observed that militarization hindered mobility in the Costa-Mountain region both for the members of the OPIM with whom she worked and for herself. Leonor Lozano noted that "the context of the armed conflict often forces activities to be delayed or shifts the focus of the communities' attention to more urgent matters." Natalia De Marinis said that "many of them [Triqui women] commented that if they become involved in certain 'political' issues they are later obliged to assume positions of authority in the community that pose a risk to their lives" (Exercise of Reflection, workshop, November 29–30, 2012, CIESAS, Mexico).

Regarding the position of the academy, Adriana Terven commented on the difficulty of carrying out joint research with the same person whose work and life history are being analyzed; Oligaria often felt it was she who was being evaluated and therefore often preferred to keep a distance. Mariana Mora observed that

> In the case of human rights work in contexts of police violence, the data with the greatest weight is quantitative; numbers that allow an understanding of the phenomenon and translate reality into a type of scientific knowledge that actors related to the government can recognize as legitimate. This gave a greater emphasis to the work of examining case records in databases, analyzing these data together with other variables, and searching for information through requests to the Federal Institute for Access to Public Information. It was only towards the end of the project that priorities changed, making room for a more qualitative and anthropological analysis, specifically the perceptions and experiences of violence and insecurity lived by indigenous women and men in the region. (Exercise of Reflection, workshop, November 29–30, 2012, CIESAS, Mexico)

These comments point to how dialogues in contexts of high levels of marginality and insecurity, expressed in gender, ethnic, and class inequalities, often begin with mistrust, imposition, or resistance. We believe that no one has an "objective" or neutral position, and rather that the production of knowledge is political and ethically situated (Haraway 1988). Our research was therefore designed according to the specific context, where social relations of power between the various sectors defined to a large extent the type of participation that was possible. Although it might at first seem that these situations limit the scope of collaborative work, analyzing these tensions was in fact fundamental to understanding how power struggles are reconfigured in processes to defend indigenous people's rights and, in particular, indigenous women's rights.

The recording and analyzing of this type of situation was usually combined with actions of intervention, through discussion in workshops, procedures with authorities, or accompaniment in various scenarios. It was here that the border between academic work and activism became more diffuse in our networks of collaboration, which themselves had an effect on social dynamics in our research locations. The research processes therefore contributed in various ways to the defense of indigenous women's rights and to the transformation of cultural and gender identities.

Methodological Routes

Workshops as Spaces for Intercultural Dialogue

One of the methodologies used in the different case studies were workshops for collective reflection. This methodology, together with the systematization of collective discussions, is an inheritance from popular education and the pedagogical and political proposal of Paulo Freire. Since the 1960s, Freire's theoretical and methodological proposals have inspired a whole generation of social scientists who developed a series of research strategies to generate knowledge with low-income sectors, promote processes of political awareness, and, through these, achieve social transformation. Many people consider action research or coparticipatory research one of Latin America's main contributions to social sciences around the world. The Participatory Research Network was created by Orlando Fals Borda, Francisco Vio Grossi, and Carlos Rodrigues Brandão as an academic and political space to promote activist research in alliance with social movements. Although, as mentioned above, "raising political awareness" was not one of our project's objectives, we did resort to the methodologies of popular education and the systematization methods used by the Participatory Research Network in order to create spaces for collective reflection on the topics addressed in the research and to elaborate the participatory evaluations (*diagnósticos participativos*) requested by the organizations with which we worked.

We approach systematization from a dialogic and critical perspective, understanding it as a way to reclaim specific experiences and reflect on them as sources of knowledge of the social for the purpose of achieving transformations. The term "systematization" was popularized in the 1950s and 1960s in the field of social work as a way to "reclaim, order, specify, and classify knowledge on social service in order to give the profession a scientific/technical character and raise its status vis-a-vis other specialities" (Ayllón 2002: 21). In contrast to this rather clinical definition, the concept of systematization was resignified in dialogues and praxes with the indigenous and human rights organizations we worked with, as they requested our accompaniment in processes that also responded to their own logics and objectives. This accompaniment took place through three types of workshops: participatory evaluations (*diagnósticos participativos*), collective reflection on specific topics, and healing (*talleres de sanación*).

Although in most cases these workshops responded to the specific concerns of the organizations, they were an invaluable source of information for our research regarding women's experiences in the various spaces of justice and their appropriations and resignifications of discourses on rights. Simultaneously, the cultural and power dynamics that developed in the workshops were a source of ethnographic information for all of us. The great challenge has been to reflect on our own positionality in those organizational rituals of which we were a part.

- I. Participatory Evaluations (*diagnósticos participativos*). In the cases of the justice promoters of the CRAC in Guerrero, the women from Totora Marka in Bolivia, the diploma on "The Indigenous Family, Participation, and Gender Equity" in Colombia, the Municipal Women's Council in Chichicastenango, and the Provincial Network of Rural Kichwa Women's Organizations of Chimborazo (REDMUJCH), the purpose of the *diagnósticos* was to identify the main problems experienced by the women in the various regions, and the strategies they developed to confront them. The researchers' participation facilitating or systematizing these inquiries was requested or allowed by the organizations' members, often as an explicit requirement prior to carrying out any other research activity, as a means to propose topics for research or educational development (in the case of the diploma in Colombia).

Although the methodology of participatory evaluations has been appropriated by many international cooperation organizations and by state bureaucracy as a quick form of "community consultation" before implementing development projects, the *diagnósticos* undertaken in the context of this project were based on the need to jointly seek alternative solutions to the organizations' most urgent problems. The objective was therefore not only to "systematize information," but rather to contribute to critical reflection through intercultural dialogue.

This does not mean that the researchers did not occupy a place in the social hierarchies of class, gender, and generation that was reproduced in those spaces. In the case of those of us who are university professors, the expectation that we had useful knowledge to share with the organization often placed us in a privileged position in the exchange of experiences. But gender and generation had an influence on the way the relations with the authorities were established. Ana Cecilia Arteaga observes,

> My relations were more with the male authorities, both traditional authorities and *estatuyentes*, who were continuously present during the

year and a half of my fieldwork. I believe that this had an influence on the place I occupied during the process of consultation on the statute and on my relationship with the organization, which was more influenced by gender than by generation. One example was how the authorities distributed the collaborators' functions; during most of the process I was assigned to systematizing the deliberative forums, while male collaborators were assigned to facilitating the meetings. When I asked the reason for this distribution, the *jacha mallku* (the territory's highest authority) told me that I was chosen for the task of systematization because women are the men's assistants (Electronic communication, April 5, 2013)

Although our intention was to make systematization a more dialogic process, conditions did not always allow for this, and the dynamics and time frames established by the organizations often determined the degree of participation in the systematization.

The level of organizational strength had a significant influence on the role of the researchers in elaborating the *diagnósticos*, since in the Colombian and Bolivian cases discussed in this volume, the organizations had already advanced in developing the methodologies they wanted to use, which meant that the researchers' participation was mainly limited to systematizing processes that were already under way. These processes involved joint analyses of collective experiences, cotheorizations that in several studies formed a central part of our academic work.

In other cases, like those of María Teresa Sierra in Guerrero and Rachel Sieder in Chichicastenango, the researchers sought support from professionals with a long experience in participatory evaluations, while they, together with the specialists, coordinated the workshops and proposed different work methods. In the former case, members of the Jop'tik association from San Cristóbal de Las Casas supported the CRAC's justice promoters and María Teresa Sierra in elaborating their *diagnóstico* on women's problematics related to customs, rights, and access to justice.

Although the specialists' participation was essential to structure the workshops, the justice promoters actively participated in their development and appropriated many of the popular education methodologies used to develop future workshops. At the political level, the *diagnóstico* played a vital role in making the CRAC's authorities aware of problems affecting women, and of the importance of their participation in the organization's structure. These results were also presented in workshops to the communal authorities and in a final workshop to the authorities of the CRAC, regional coordinators, counselors, and men and women from the communities. The document they produced together is now an integral part of the historical memory of the women in the *Comunitaria* and is one of the many informational products that resulted from the research work.

In the case of Rachel Sieder, the *diagnóstico* centered on the issue of domestic violence, an issue of explicit concern for the women from the Municipal Women's Council. K'iche' social worker Lidia Osorio and the women leaders together defined the structure and methodology to follow. The process allowed for the identification of women within their villages who shared their testimony about their experiences of aggression, prompting the leaders of the Municipal Women's Council to suggest a second phase of collaborative work centered on the organization of workshops to help the victims heal the psychological and spiritual wounds left by the violence they had suffered.

- 2. Workshops for Collective Reflection on Specific Topics. In many instances the purpose of the participatory evaluations was to identify specific issues identified by the participants as central problems that affected their lives so that these could be addressed in subsequent workshops. Some of the workshops, such as those organized by Rachel Sieder, Ana Cecilia Arteaga, Emma Cervone, Cristina Cucurí, and Aída Hernández, addressed legal and legislative issues, with the purpose of contributing to processes of legal or legislative struggle or to provide elements for processes of denunciation in state or international justice systems.

In the case of the workshops organized in Chichicastenango, the initial *diagnóstico* allowed the women to identify the challenge that presenting a complaint represents for women in their communities. The leaders from the Municipal Women's Council determined that an appropriate response was to organize a workshop on the steps involved in filing a complaint (*la ruta de denuncia*) for cases of domestic violence and civil claims for child support and so forth. This was organized together with the Office of the Human Rights Ombudsman in Quiché, whose representative was an important ally of the women's council. In such contexts, the researcher's role was to support and facilitate dialogue between the different bodies and actors that accompany women victims of violence who want to present a formal complaint.

The purpose of the workshops on autonomy statutes and indigenous rights held in Bolivia and Ecuador was for women to learn about the new constitutional order and laws, and to reflect on the possibilities and limitations these posed for indigenous women's access to justice. In the Bolivian case, the Women's Encounter in Totora Marka, coordinated and systematized by Ana Cecilia Arteaga, aimed to facilitate the inclusion of the women's voices and needs in the autonomy statute (since in the first consultation women's participation had been very limited). The call included all women from Totora Marka, ensuring that women in positions of traditional authority in each *ayllu* participated,[5] something that gave a greater weight to the accords signed at the end of the workshop. All nine *ayllus* were represented. The facilitators for this event were Lucila Choque, responsible for gender issues in the Vice Ministry of Indigenous Autonomies, and Ana Cecilia Arteaga. Because of her mastery of the Aymara language, Lucila Choque was in charge of formulating the questions for the event, and Ana Cecilia Arteaga was in charge of presenting the proposals generated by the preceding interviews and also of systematizing all the suggestions made. In response to an explicit request from the participants in the Women's Encounter, the resolutions of the workshops were reworked by the facilitators as proposed articles to be included in the autonomy statute.

The workshops organized by Aída Hernández and the ethnologist Héctor Ortiz with the women from OPIM and Inés Fernández Ortega took place months before Inés's case was presented to the Inter-American Court of Human Rights (IACtHR), and were part of the preliminary research that gave rise to the cultural expert report. After the trial, additional workshops were held to analyze the court's verdict against the Mexican state and the implementation of communal reparations. These initiatives were supported by OPIM's president, Obtilia Eugenio, and one of the members of the organization's Women's Commission, Andrea Eugenio; Obtilia and Andrea not only participated as translators (from Spanish to Me'phaa), but were also facilitators and coordinators of the collective reflection that took place in that language. The IACtHR's verdict included an explicit recognition of "military institutional violence" exercised by the Mexican army, which led to reflection in the workshops about the historic processes of militarization in indigenous regions of Guerrero.

The workshops carried out in the course of Morna Macleod and Mariana Mora's research addressed the issues affecting the participating organizations and communities: in Guatemala, a single workshop was held on the impact of mining on Mam communities; in Guerrero ten focus groups were held to examine the impact of militarization and police impunity in the communities of the Mountain region of Guerrero and consider the community's proposal. The workshop organized by Morna Macleod with the Women's Pastoral of the San Miguel Ixtahuacán parish, in San Marcos, was facilitated by a member of the Tz'ununija' Indigenous Women's Movement. Thirty-three Mam female peasants participated to consider the impact of the Marlin Mine on women's lives. This workshop was held in Spanish and Mam (later translated by a Mam leader). Morna Macleod reflected on the linguistic barriers faced by those of us who do not speak the indigenous languages of the women we work with and on what is lost by limiting ourselves to their discourses in Spanish. She observed, "I was somewhat disappointed with the workshop and with what the women said in Spanish, because it sounded somewhat like a 'learned discourse.' I was therefore very surprised when I read the translated transcriptions: marvelous! This gives us much to reflect on . . ." (Written communication, April 5, 2013). Evidently, our ethnographies are limited by the fact that most of the researchers do not speak the indigenous languages spoken in the regions where we work (with the exception of Cristina Cucurí, who is a Kichwa speaker). This is perhaps one of the main barriers to developing truly intercultural dialogues that allow us to recognize and learn from other epistemologies and other ways of understanding life with dignity and justice.

Finally, Natalia De Marinis first collected a series of testimonies on the violence experienced by displaced Triqui women in the city of Oaxaca, which were key for the lawyers who made up the Truth and Justice Committee for San Juan Copala to present the case of forced displacement before the Inter-American Commission on Human Rights. The process of testimonial collection also allowed for the subsequent production of a video in conjunction with the displaced women themselves. Further audiovisual workshops on historical memory were held in the pro-autonomy communities in the region. These reflected on the histories of male communal leadership and the emergence of a type of leadership that fostered greater participation by women during the project of autonomy. "Everything began with the idea of memory and history, translated in the Triqui language as '*cuento'a*.' After the project was presented in the community, male and female elders came forward to tell of the region's history. Everything from Triqui myths and legends to reflections on historical processes of militarization and different types of leadership was collected in audiovisual materials, which we worked on in meetings with the women" (Written communication with Natalia De Marinis, April 6, 2013). The first product of these workshops was a video that focused on power imbalances between male leaders, which is part of a Triqui myth that was narrated by a woman from the community and illustrated by children in workshops organized by the women. These possibilities for the recovery of historical memory allowed Natalia De Marinis to contribute to the struggle of displaced Triqui by facilitating a reflection on leadership and the origins of the community.

In all of these workshops, our role as researchers and/or systematizers was not to "raise awareness" among the indigenous men and women with whom we worked, but rather to attempt to establish intercultural dialogues that were as horizontal as possible, without ignoring the structural context of race and class hierarchies. As part of these dialogues, our role was to share our knowledge about legal frameworks on indigenous and gender rights, information on the political and economic contexts of the regions where we worked, or concrete knowledge about specific processes of dispossession and militarization. In some cases, these intercultural dialogues facilitated the coproduction of knowledge, as was the case in Cauca, where the participants elaborated their own concepts and epistemologies to analyze gender problematics, situating them within the family, the community, the organization, and nature.

In many cases, these dialogues were fundamental to destabilizing our own preconceptions. They questioned certain constructions of progress and well-being that have been universalized together with conceptions of liberal rights that give sustenance to many of today's democratic struggles. The certainty that as "committed intellectuals" or "feminist activists" we can somehow identify and share strategies to confront domination crumbled before the voices that questioned dominant modernist utopias. Behind these voices are other epistemologies based on alternative conceptions of the person, where the individual cannot be separated from the collective, and where nature is not a resource at the service of humans, but rather a part of the totality of which we are only one small part. They are voices full of contradictions that also reproduce discourses of power reflecting gender ideologies or that naturalize racial hierarchies. Our intention is not to idealize these voices, but to signal their different ways of imagining and perceiving the world, and of theorizing its transformation.

- 3. Healing Workshops (*talleres de sanación*). The third type of workshop organized in the context of our collective research was healing workshops aimed at helping to alleviate the effects of experiences of violence on the bodies and minds of the indigenous women. These workshops aimed not to systematize information or facilitate collective reflection, but to provide tools for psychic and spiritual healing for the women who lived through violence and for ourselves as women activists who work in regions affected by militarization and violence, continuously witnessing and listening to testimonies of repression and impunity.

In the first case, Rachel Sieder, upon request of the women from the Municipal Women's Council of Chichicastenango, organized healing workshops for the women who offered their testimonies during the *diagnóstico* on domestic violence. Although the grievances systematized in that process had occurred years earlier, the "fright and sadness" that invaded their bodies continued to affect their everyday lives, something the women leaders from the Council had perceived during the interviews and conversations. The women explained their afflictions and conditions according to local epistemologies concerning health and illness, so it was decided to invite Sebastiana Pol, a K'iche' healer from Chichicastenango and the daughter of a renowned spiritual guide in the region. She worked in the K'iche' language on topics such as self-esteem, healing, and the body-mind connection. The techniques used included dance, bio-energetic manipulation, medicinal plants, and narration through words, drawings, or play-acting. These workshops were held in private homes in the various villages to ensure their privacy, and the researcher participated only in those dynamics to which she was invited.

These workshops signaled the corporal memory of violence within women's bodies. Although one of our central ethical concerns was to avoid revictimization through the process of collecting testimonies, we were also aware that sometimes verbalization, naming the facts, is part of the process of arranging and resignifying the pain and trauma of the past; as long, of course, as it occurs at the right time and under adequate conditions. However, the healing workshops showed us that verbalization is not sufficient, since the body also stores memories of pain and manifests knowledge. This sui generis experience of feedback or *mano vuelta*, as Morna Macleod calls it, made us think about how the stories of violence we listened to were affecting each of us and about the lack of therapeutic resources available to confront crisis situations that could arise during the interviews or the workshops. With this concern in mind, we invited Clemencia Correa, a specialist in psychological support in contexts of political violence, to give a workshop to the research team. Clemencia had also participated in the elaboration of a psychological expert report in the case of Inés Fernández Ortega, and was familiar with the context of violence and militarization of several of the regions studied in Mexico, Colombia, and Guatemala.

This workshop had the double purpose of identifying tools to help us confront crisis situations and be more sensitive when listening to denunciations and testimonies of violence and human rights violations; but we were also interested in reflecting on the potential effects of fear in contexts of violence, militarization, and impunity on our own physical and mental health. Conceiving ourselves as social actors in the processes we were analyzing implied recognizing not only our privileges as scholars and urban middle-class women, but also our vulnerabilities as activists and women in a context of extreme patriarchal violence. This "healing" workshop allowed us to reflect on our fears, seek resources to confront them, and think collectively about security strategies we could adopt in order to develop the fieldwork and accompaniment in the best conditions possible.

Recognizing our fears and our empathy with the women victims of violence also led us to reflect on the importance of incorporating pain, fear, and sadness in our analyses as fundamental emotions to understand how the women we worked with experienced injustice and impunity. The anthropology of pain of which Veena Das speaks necessarily requires new methodological and textual strategies that allow us to approach the emotions that mediate the experiences of the social actors with whom we collaborate, and also mediate our own representations. These workshops made us reflect on the need to break with "the conceptual structures of our disciplines that lead to a transformation of suffering elaborated by professionals, which takes away the voice of the victim and distances us from the immediacy of her experience" (Das 2008: 15).

Healing processes were also an important part of the workshop to share experiences with the members of the research team and representatives of the organizations we worked with that was held in Cuetzalan, Puebla. The hosts and facilitators of the workshops were the Nahua women from Maseualsiuamej Mosenyolchicauanij ("Indigenous Women Working Together and Supporting Each Other") and rural feminists from the Center for Advising and Development among Women (CADEM). These workshops allowed us to share the participants' challenges and achievements with regard to indigenous women's access to justice. In parallel, accompanied by spiritual guides and traditional healers from Maseual, we worked on the corporal and emotional impacts of contexts of insecurity and violence. The healing techniques, which included corporal dynamics and a *temazcal* (traditional steam bath), allowed the construction of knowledge to be not only an academic exercise, but also a healing and affective experience.

Life Histories: An Approximation to Indigenous Female Subjectivities

Feminist anthropologists and historians have stressed for decades the importance of life histories and oral testimonies as a way to approach women's experiences and their impact on the history of peoples (see Reinharz 1992). These perspectives argue that gender hierarchies translate into unequal access to writing, which means that women's perspectives are generally not recorded in written sources and their voices end up being silenced by traditional historiography. Regarding contemporary societies without access to writing or with high levels of illiteracy, anthropologists have reproduced historians' androcentric perspectives, prioritizing the views of men, who end up representing the voice of "their culture" (see Moore 1996). Reproducing functionalist perspectives of "harmonious communities" without taking gender, class, and generation differences into account, many classical ethnographies reflected hegemonic representations of cultures, failing to recognize dissident voices within those collectivities, which often included women's voices critical of "exclusionary traditions" (see Hernández Castillo 2009).

Women's life histories aim not only at countering the silencing effected by official histories, but at allowing us to approach other dimensions of social life, such as everyday dynamics that are often ignored by androcentric representations of the public and the political. Feminist anthropology has demonstrated that these exclusions prevent us from deeply understanding political, economic, or cultural processes that emerge from domestic or family spaces. Concern over these "incomplete representations of social life," to put it mildly, has led many female anthropologists to vindicate life histories as a feminist methodology par excellence (see Bataille and Mullen Sands 1984).

These critical voices have been present since the origins of anthropology, as is the case with Ruth Underhill, who as early as the 1930s broke with the androcentric tradition of US anthropology by writing the life history of María Chona, a Papago woman from Arizona (Underhill 1936). Since then, life histories of indigenous women have provided new perspectives on the different impacts of colonialism on women's lives. For example, Nancy Lurie's work on a Winnebago woman from the state of Wisconsin denounces the role of Christian internships in the destruction of native cultures (Oestreich Lurie 1961); the work by indigenous intellectuals Anna Moore Shaw (1974) (Pima), Helen Sekaquaptewa (1969) (Hopi), and Maria Campbell (1973) (Métis from Canada) narrates their experiences as women under the neocolonial governments of the United States and Canada. In Latin America, testimonies by Domitila Barrios de Chungara, a Bolivian labor leader, and Rigoberta Menchú, a Maya-K'iche' leader from Guatemala, compiled by the anthropologists Moema Viezzer (Barrios de Chungara and Viezzer 1978) and Elizabeth Burgos-Debray (1985) became key references on the leadership of indigenous women and the racist violence of nation-states.

Although several of these life histories were the product of intercultural dialogues with anthropologists or other social scientists, rarely are the terms of these dialogues made explicit, and there are few critical reflections on the social hierarchies that mark the relations between researchers and the social actors with whom we work. Marie France Labrecque observes,

> In the introductory chapters of life histories, the authors insist on the personal nature of their relations with the informants. Very few face the delicate issue of what each represents for the other at a structural level, failing to acknowledge that these relations are as important as personal relations. Furthermore, I would suggest that, structurally speaking, anthropologists are a part of the life histories of their informants. A life history is a part of a larger conversation, not only between two individuals, but also between two categories of individuals. It is therefore as important to focus on analyzing the hierarchical relations that the life history immediately reveals as the power relations that connect researchers and informants. (1998: 35)

Taking these questions into account, we acknowledge that, despite our position as political allies of the women we worked with, our dialogues with them were always marked by our ethnic and class differences. It was more than evident that the researchers had the time and privilege to analyze and write about political processes on which the women often bet their lives. However, maintaining a permanent dialogue on the "what for" of the life histories and testimonies allowed us to at least minimally compensate these structural inequalities between "two categories of individuals," by transforming these textual strategies into collective forms of knowledge construction, inscribed in broader contexts of struggle for self-representation.

In the context of the collective project, two types of life histories were elaborated: those that were part of the systematization of women's memories of their struggles and resistances in certain organizations—as was the case with the women in the CRAC in Guerrero, the young Triqui women displaced in Oaxaca, and the women threatened by armed groups in Cauca—and those that took the form of testimonies of human rights violations presented before local, national, international, or ethical tribunals—such as the testimony by Inés Fernández Ortega before the IACtHR, the Mam women organized against the Canadian mining company Goldcorp before the Peoples International Health Tribunal, the relatives of Bonfilio Rubio preparing the case that was presented to Mexico's Supreme Court, and the testimonies of domestic violence systematized by the Municipal Women's Council of Chichicastenango.

In the case of indigenous women's memories of resistance, we prioritized accompaniment in the processes of writing and self-representation, as was the case with the books *Mujeres contracorriente* (Women against the Grain) (1998); *La doble mirada: Voces e historias de mujeres indígenas latinoamericanas* (The Double Gaze: Voices and Histories of Latin American Indigenous Women) (2005); *Historias a dos voces: testimonios de luchas y resistencias de mujeres indígenas* (Histories in Duet: Testimonies of Struggles and Resistances by Indigenous Women) (2006); *Bajo la sombra del guamúchil: historias de vida de mujeres indígenas y campesinas en prisión* (Under the Shadow of the Guamúchil: Life Histories of Indigenous and Peasant Women in Prison) (2010); *Género, complementariedades y exclusiones en Mesoamérica y los Andes* (Gender, Complementarities, and Exclusions in Mesoamerica and the Andes) (2012); and *Transgredir para transformar: La disputa como agente de cambio social y cultural* (Transgressing to Transform: Dispute as an Agent for Social and Cultural Change) (2012). All of these books are of collective authorship, in which the indigenous women wrote parts of their lives and decided how to represent themselves and which parts of their collective reflections to share. Giving continuity to these processes of accompaniment, in parallel to this academic book, the justice promoters of the CRAC are working in collaboration with María Teresa Sierra to elaborate a book on women's participation in the Community Police; Morna Macleod wrote the prologue of a book elaborated by the Tz'ununija' Indigenous Women's Movement that systematized the life histories of eight women facing arrest warrants in San Miguel Ixtahuacán (and their accompaniment); and, together with Doña Crisanta (2013), she wrote about the latter's struggle against Goldcorp. Transforming the old role of anthropologists as "narrators of other women's life histories" into one of accompanying processes of systematization of their own histories, and even the creation of own publishing projects such as the Colectiva Editorial de Mujeres en Prisión Hermanas en la Sombra (Sisters in the Shadow Publishing Collective of Women in Prison), in Atlacholoaya, Morelos, whose establishment has been accompanied by Aída Hernández, was part of our efforts to transform the "extractivist" nature of our discipline.

In the case of the testimonies of violence presented before various judicial bodies, the great challenge we faced was to avoid revictimization in the name of denunciation. This has been a permanent concern for those who work in processes of psychosocial accompaniment of victims of sexual violence (see Aranguren Romero 2010). Although the decision to denounce was consciously made by the women victims of violence, in our role collecting and systematizing these testimonies we are concerned about the effects that renarrating the horror of violence experienced can have on the minds and bodies of the victims, as well as the lack of therapeutic resources to accompany those processes in the case of testimonies collected by anthropologists or human rights activists with no training to face situations of emotional crisis. It was in part in response to this concern that the research team requested the support of the psychologist Clemencia Correa during the healing workshop described above, and of the psychologist Alejandra González Marín, then a member of the Tlachinollan team, in the case of Inés Fernández Ortega, to work directly with her in the process of psychosocial accompaniment. In the case of the women from Chichicastenango, the healing workshop was in part a response to the emotions unsettled by the testimonies gathered in the initial *diagnóstico*.

Another part of the problem is the academic use that can be made of these testimonies presented as denunciations in legal spheres; in other words, what to use or leave out of the experiences of women victims of violence. How do we present experiences of pain without trivializing them by theorizing about them? What do we include and exclude from these testimonies? The Colombian psychologist and social researcher Juan Pablo Aranguren Romero describes the contradictory aspects of social research with testimonies of violence, observing that

> underpinning the compilation of memories of pain and making them known is the idea that this represents . . . solidarity and respect for the other: giving voice to the voiceless. [But] who authorizes the other to give voice to the victim? Is there not something of epistemic violence and subalternization in this process? . . . What is lost in the process of translating the victims' testimonies into the language of human rights? . . . What is lost in this process is in principle the same as occurs when translating an experience to a written text, and therefore the same road traveled from an interview to a book or from oral history to a research paper. In all cases we can allude to the fact that what is lost in this transit from the encounter with the 'other' to the written text is the body and the presence of that 'other' in the written text. (2010: 25)

Following the methodological proposals of Joselyn Géliga Vargas and Inés Canabal we consider that the use of testimony and its public collective discussion can contribute to "make visible and legitimize the authors of those testimonies, and to their (self-)recognition as knowledge producers and shapers of history" (2013: 158); it is also a way to generate political alliances among those communities and other collective projects in different social contexts.

Returning to the so-called anthropology of pain, Veena Das (2008) has delved deeply into these dilemmas, arguing that the conceptual structures of our disciplines translate suffering into a different language that deprives the victims of a voice and distances us from the immediacy of their experience. For this author, the testimony is an invitation to share the pain and a form of healing. In the case of the Triqui women, their request to have their testimonies recorded in audiovisual format allowed the women to locate their personal trauma in a collective trauma and their bodies before structural violence, thus mitigating the effects of the individuality of pain, such as shame and silence. It is our intention not to solve all of these conceptual challenges in the book, but rather to recognize the need to seek textual strategies capable of accounting for the experiences of pain and violence without trivializing them through our theoretical interpretations.

Ethnography and Spaces of Justice

Another methodology fundamental to our project was ethnography of the spaces of justice. Ethnography has been one of anthropology's main research methods, and it has contributed to deep understandings of cultural differences. However, our epistemological position demands a reflection on the relationship between ethnography's methodological possibilities and its ethical/political nature. From its inception among those who devoted themselves to the study of so-called primitive societies to the present, ethnography has been a historically situated means of understanding different historic contexts, each with its own, and perhaps radically different, subjects and subjectivities, objects and objectivities (Comaroff and Comaroff 1992: 9–10). In other words, ethnography has described social worlds from a particular viewpoint, the Western, thus standardizing its readings of cultural difference.

This has been a source of criticism both for anthropology itself and for the social groups that have been the subjects of ethnographic representations. Its founding fathers have thus been accused of serving the causes of imperialism, justifying the colonial enterprise, and today it has also been used to deny the legitimacy of indigenous rights. "All ethnographic work has therefore a contained potential and an eventual political use" (Bartolomé 2003: 203). We are interested in considering ethnography beyond its academic dimension, that of exploration and wonder. We are aware of its potential political use as an instrument to regulate difference through authority, but also wish to champion it as a method and window onto different worlds and epistemologies.

While it is true that the authority of the ethnographic method is due in part to its ability to provide broad and detailed depictions of social groups, based on direct and prolonged contact and observation and founded on centralized theoretical precepts, it is important to recognize that this authority is also due to its political nature, and is enacted primarily through power structures. It is precisely because of this that the project made a theoretical/methodological and political turnabout in its ethnographic work.

In our efforts to combine the analysis of power relations in the legal realm with the need to construct research problems in dialogue with the social actors we worked with, we found the theoretical and practical mechanisms to discuss and reformulate our ethnographic work in the contributions of critical legal anthropology, research action, and collaborative research. The focus was hence no longer on impartial observation and description of social groups, but on a dialogue about multiple ways of understanding and confronting political and justice dynamics, in which we recognized structural realities and shared political commitments. An emphasis on the political nature of the ethnographies varied according to the different justice spaces examined: community justice, international justice, ethical tribunals, and state justice. These were understood not as neutral or empty realms but as historic and culturally constructed spaces that needed to be interrogated, and that directly affect the dynamics of research and action. What does it mean to perform an ethnography of juridical spaces in conjunction with an analysis of defense strategies, the role of authorities, and the tensions between the various legal systems? These questions have been central to legal anthropology, whose ethnographies have attempted to examine the social relations involved in disputes, conceiving juridical spaces as spaces for social interaction (Nader 2002). They have also attempted to understand how power and change influence legal processes, where law is conceived in its historic and social context as a product of human agency (Comaroff and Roberts 1981; Starr and Collier 1989; Sierra and Chenaut 2002).

In this project, we approach ethnographically the spaces of community justice in the Indigenous Court of Cuetzalan and in the Mountain region of Guerrero, in the area of influence of the CRAC; of state justice and its appropriation by indigenous organizations in the processes unleashed by the Constituent Assemblies of Bolivia and Ecuador; and the "cultural rituals" that develop in the spaces of international justice.

For Aída Hernández, doing ethnography in IACtHR implied learning to "culturally distance herself" from legal practices that were more or less familiar to her and breaking with the premise that so-called indigenous law and community justice are full of "culture," while international law and its spaces of justice are merely "transparent" expressions of the use of law. In her ethnographic description of the IACtHR, she describes the trial of Inés Fernández against the Mexican state as a space of dispute where cultural referents and power relations between all of the actors who participated in that legal performance came into play. The physical space of the Supreme Court of Lima, Peru, is described as the stage of a performance in which not only the judges and the legal representatives of the parties involved participated, but also a broader audience that included law students, members of human rights organizations, Peruvian indigenous women organized against military violence, and feminist groups struggling against violence. Litigation thus becomes, for ethnographic analysis, a cultural ritual where different conceptions of justice and rights interact.

Final Reflections

One objective in this chapter was to demonstrate the complex connections between forms of thought and practices in the various locations of research, based on specific social relations that not only provide concrete meanings in terms of gender, ethnic group, and class, but also facilitate or hinder access to political spaces and processes of knowledge construction. While this review of the research processes reveals the complexity behind socially committed work, we concluded that writing from a collaborative and critical perspective depends on both encounters and disagreements. In this respect, we identified two key aspects for the development of this type of studies: that knowledge is inter-knowledge and that it always combines the cognitive with the ethical/political (Santos 2009; Hale 2008).

The methodological routes we chose—workshops, life histories, ethnographies of legal spaces—were conceived as means for intercultural dialogue and interknowledge. Our greatest challenge was to transform these dialogues into written texts that accounted for the various epistemologies, social hierarchies, and representations of the world that came into play during these four years. How do we incorporate the pain, the marks left by violence on bodies and minds, the fear in contexts of militarization and paramilitarization, the sadness before death and displacement? These have been some of the challenges we have faced in our search for textual strategies that go beyond this academic book and that include other narrative and visual forms.

Recognizing the plurality of thought and practices allowed us to address the various case studies from the perspective of their complementarities or contradictions. If we accept that different epistemologies historically interact and intertwine (under unequal power relations), we find ourselves before the possibility of resorting to different epistemic referents. In our case, the points of encounter were the concepts of violence, security, and access to justice, which were in turn closely related to the realm of political action, bringing theory and practice together in the research processes.

We hope that the situated knowledges shared here can contribute to critical reflection on the use of law in emancipatory struggles of indigenous peoples in our continent, and that throughout the research process we were able to contribute, albeit minimally, to the construction of an ecology of knowledge that includes, but is not limited to, cosmopolitan subaltern legalities.

NOTES

1. In addition to the academic essays presented here, the outcomes of our research effort include many other informational products elaborated in collaboration with members of the indigenous organizations we worked with, in addition to the generation of mid- and long-term organizational processes.

2. The "action research" concept was developed by the German-US psychologist Kurt Lewin in 1944 to define a research methodology based on democratic and

participatory processes with the local population. The concept was revisited in the 1960s by Latin American social scientists from different perspectives committed to social justice. In this development, the contributions by Brazilian pedagogue Paulo Freire were essential. For an analysis of the development of action research and collaborative research, see Mora 2008.

3. For an analysis of action research from feminist academia, see Lykes and Couquillon 2007.

4. Toledo proposes a series of premises to go from a dialogue of phantoms to a dialogue of knowledges between the "modern" and the "traditional" in the field of communal sustainability.

5. *Ayllu* is an organizational unit composed of several communities and families, with territorial rights through the *sayañas* (family units).

REFERENCES

Aranguren Romero, Juan Pablo. 2010. "De un dolor a un saber: cuerpo, sufrimiento y memoria en los límites de la escritura." *CEIC Papers* 2 (63): 1–27.

Arteaga, Ana Cecilia. 2013. "'Todas somos la semilla.' Ser mujer en la Policía Comunitaria de Guerrero: Ideologías de género, participación política y seguridad." Master's thesis, Centro de Investigaciones y Estudios Superiores en Antropología Social (CIESAS), Mexico City.

Ayllón, Maria Rosario. 2002. *Aprendiendo desde la práctica, una propuesta operativa para sistematizar.* Lima: Asociación Kallpa.

Barrios de Chungara, Domitila, and Moema Viezzer. 1978. *"Si me permiten hablar . . .": Testimonio de Domitila, una mujer de las minas de Bolivia.* Mexico City: Editorial Siglo XXI.

Bartolomé, Miguel. 2003. "En defensa de la etnografía. El papel contemporáneo de la investigación intercultural." *Revista de Antropología Social* 12:199–222.

Bataille, Gretchen M., and Kathleen Mullen Sands. 1984. *American Indian Women: Telling Their Lives.* Lincoln: University of Nebraska Press.

Brown, Wendy, and Janet Halley. 2002. *Left Legalism/Left Critique.* Durham, NC: Duke University Press.

Burgos-Debray, Elizabeth. 1985. *Me llamo Rigoberta Menchú y así me nació la conciencia.* Mexico City: Siglo XXI.

Campbell, Maria. 1973. *Half-breed.* Lincoln: University of Nebraska Press.

Castro-Gómez, Santiago. 1998. "Latinoamericanismo, modernidad, globalización. Prolegómenos a una crítica poscolonial de la razón." In Castro-Gómez and Mendieta, *Teorías sin disciplina,* 169–203.

———. 2000. "Ciencias sociales, violencia epistémica y el problema de la 'invención del otro.'" In *La colonialidad del saber: eurocentrismo y ciencias sociales. Perspectivas latinoamericanas,* edited by Edgardo Lander, 285–303. Buenos Aires: CLACSO-UNESCO.

Castro-Gómez, Santiago, and Eduardo Mendieta, eds. 1998. *Teorías sin disciplina. Latinoamericanismo, poscolonialidad y globalización en debate.* Mexico City: Miguel Angel Porrúa.

CEPLAES. 1998. *Mujeres contracorriente: Voces de líderes indígenas.* Quito: CEPLAES.

Comaroff, John, and Jean Comaroff. 1992. *Ethnography and the Historical Imagination.* Boulder, CO: Westview Press.

Comaroff, John, and Simon Roberts. 1981. *Rule and Processes. The Cultural Logic of Dispute in an African Context.* Chicago: University of Chicago Press.

Das, Veena. 2008. *Sujetos del dolor, agentes de dignidad*. Bogotá: Pontificia Universidad Javeriana.

De Marinis, Natalia. 2011. "Breaking the Silence: State Construction and Violence towards Triqui Women of San Juan Copala, Oaxaca, Mexico." *Development* 54: 480–484.

———. 2012. "Indigenous Rights and Violent State Construction: The Struggle of Triqui Women of Oaxaca, Mexico." In Sieder and McNeish, *Gender Justice and Legal Pluralities*, 156–179.

———. 2013. "En los márgenes de la (in) seguridad. Desplazamiento forzado y relaciones de género y poder en San Juan Copala, Oaxaca." PhD diss., CIESAS, Mexico City.

Foucault, Michel. 1980. *Power/knowledge. Selected Interviews and Other Writings 1972–1977*. Edited by Colin Gordon. New York: Pantheon Books.

Géliga Vargas, Jocelyn, and Inés Canabal. 2013. "Las rupturas de la investigación colaborativa: Historias de testimonios afropuertorriqueños." In *Otros Saberes. Collaborative Research on Indigenous and Afro-Descendant Cultural Politics*, edited by Charles Hale And Lynn Stephen, 154–179. Santa Fe: School for Advance Research Press, Latin American Studies Association.

Hale, Charles. 2006. "Activist Research v. Cultural Critique: Indigenous Land Rights and the Contradictions of Politically Engaged Anthropology." *Cultural Anthropology* 21: 96–120.

———, ed. 2008. *Engaging Contradictions: Theory, Politics, and Methods of Activist Scholarship*. Berkeley: University of California Press.

Haraway, Donna. 1988. "Situated Knowledge: The Science Question in Feminism and the Privilege of Partial Perspective." In *Simians, Cyborgs, and Women: The Reinvention of Nature*, edited by Donna Haraway, 183–203. New York: Routledge.

Harcourt, Wendy. 2001. "Rethinking Difference and Equality: Women and Politics of Place." In *Places and Politics in an Age of Globalization*, edited by Roxann Prazniak and Arif Dirlik, 299–343. Lanham, MD: Rowman & Littlefield.

Hernández Castillo, Rosalva Aída. 2002. "The Struggle for Justice of Indigenous Women in Chiapas Mexico." In *Gender Justice, Democracy and Rights*, edited by Maxine Molyneux and Shahra Razavi, 384–413. Oxford: Oxford University Press.

———. 2003. "Repensar el Multiculturalismo desde el Género. Las luchas por el reconocimiento cultural y los feminismos de la diversidad." *La Ventana Revista de Estudios de Género* 18: 30–68.

———. 2009. "Movilidades transfronterizas, identidades transnacionales: nuevos cruces de fronteras entre los indígenas mames contemporaneous." In *Identidades y movilidades en México y Colombia*, edited by Margarita Chávez, 205–232. Bogota: Universidad Nacional de Colombia.

———. 2015. "Hacia una antropología socialmente comprometida desde una perspectiva dialógica y feminista." In *Conocimiento, Poder y Prácticas Políticas de autoría colectiva*, edited by Xochitl Leyva, 365–398. Mexico City: CIESAS-FLACSO-UNICAH.

———. 2016. *Multiple Injustices: Indigenous Women, Law, and Political Struggle*. Tucson: University of Arizona Press.

Hernández Castillo, Rosalva Aída, and María Teresa Sierra. 2005. "Repensar los derechos indígenas desde el género: Aportes de las mujeres indígenas al debate de las autonomías." In *La Doble Mirada: Voces e historias de mujeres indígenas latinoamericanas*, edited by Martha Sánchez Néstor, 105–121. Mexico City: UNIFEM/ILSB.

Labrecque, Marie France. 1998. "Metodología Feminista e Historias de Vida: Mujeres, Investigación y Estado." In *Los usos de la historia de vida en las ciencias sociales*, edited by

Thierry Lulle, Pilar Vargas, and Lucero Zamudio, 27–52. Colombia: Universidad Externado de Colombia, Centro de Investigaciones sobre Dinámica Social (CIDS)—Institut Français d'Études Andines (IFEA)—Anthropos.

Lykes, M., and M. Couquillon. 2007. "Participatory and Action Research and Feminisms: Towards Transformative Praxis." In *Handbook of Feminist Research: Theory and Praxis*, edited by Hesse-Biber, 297–326. Thousand Oaks, CA: Sage.

Macleod, Morna. 2011. *Nietas del fuego, creadoras del alba: Luchas político-culturales de mujeres mayas*. Guatemala: FLACSO.

Macleod, Morna, and Crisanta Pérez-Bámaca. 2013. *Tu'n Tklet Qnan Tx'otx,' Q'ixkojalel, b'ix Tb'anil Qanq'ib'il, En defensa de la Madre Tierra, sentir lo que siente el otro y el buen vivir. La lucha de Doña Crisanta contra Goldcorp*. Mexico City: Ce-Acatl.

Moore, Henrietta. 1996. *Antropología y Feminismo*. Valencia: Editorial Cátedra.

Mora, Mariana. 2008. "Decolonizing Politics: Zapatista Indigenous Autonomy in an Era of Neoliberal Governance and Low Intensity Warfare." PhD diss., University of Texas at Austin.

Nader, Laura. 2002. *The Life of the Law: Anthropological Projects*. Berkeley: University of California Press.

Naples, Nancy. 2003. *Feminisms and Method: Ethnography, Discourse Analysis and Activist Research*. New York: Routledge.

Oestreich Lurie, Nancy, ed. 1961. *Mountain Wolf Woman, Sister of Crashing Thunder: The Autobiography of a Winnebago Indian*. Ann Arbor: University of Michigan Press.

Reinharz, Shulamit. 1992. *Feminist Methods in Social Research*. New York: Oxford University Press.

Rodríguez Garavito, Cesar, and Boaventura de Sousa Santos, eds. 2007. *El derecho y la globalización desde abajo hacia una legalidad cosmopolita*. Madrid: Anthropos.

Santos, Boaventura de Sousa. 2009. *Una epistemología del sur: la reinvención del conocimiento y la emancipación social*. Mexico City: CLACSO, Siglo XXI Editores.

———. 2010. *Descolonizar el saber, reinventar el poder*. Uruguay: Trilce.

Sekaquaptewa, Helen. 1969. *Me and Mine: The Life Story of Helen Sekaquaptewa*. Tucson: University of Arizona Press.

Shaw, Anna Moore. 1974. *A Pima Past*. Tucson: University of Arizona Press.

Sieder, Rachel. 2012. "Sexual Violence and Gendered Subjectivities: Indigenous Women's Search for Justice in Guatemala." In Sieder and McNeish, *Gender Justice and Legal Pluralities*, 109–132.

Sieder, Rachel, and Morna Macleod. 2012. "Género, derecho y cosmovisión maya en Guatemala." In *Género, complementariedades y exclusiones en Mesoamérica y los Andes*, edited by Rosalva Aída Hernández and Andrew Canessa, 170–200. Copenhagen: IGWIA and Abya-Yala.

Sieder, Rachel, and John-Andrew McNeish, eds. 2012a. *Gender Justice and Legal Pluralities: Latin American and African Perspectives*. New York: Routledge-Cavendish.

———. 2012b. "Introduction: Gender Justice and Legal Pluralities—Latin American and African Perspectives." In Sieder and McNeish, *Gender Justice and Legal Pluralities*, 1–30.

Sierra, Maria Teresa, and Victoria Chenaut. 2002. "Los debates recientes y actuales en la antropología juridical: las corrientes anglosajonas." In *Antropología jurídica: perspectivas socioculturales en el estudio del derecho*, edited by Esteban Krotz, 113–170. Mexico City: Universidad Autónoma Metropolitana.

Speed, Shannon. 2008. "Forged in Dialogue: Toward a Critically Engaged Activist Research." In Hale, *Engaging Contradictions*, 213–236.

Starr, June, and Jane Collier. 1989. *History and Power in the Study of Law: New Directions in Legal Anthropology*. Ithaca, NY: Cornell University Press.

Toledo, Víctor. 2011. "Del 'diálogo de fantasmas' al 'diálogo de saberes': conocimiento y sustentabilidad comunitaria." In *Saberes colectivos y diálogo de saberes en México*, edited by Arturo Argueta, Eduardo Corona, and Paul Hersh, 469–484. Mexico City: UNAM/CRIM and Universidad Iberoamericana.

Underhill, Ruth. 1936. "The Autobiography of a Papago Woman." *Memoirs of the American Anthropological Association* 46: n.p.

NOTES ON CONTRIBUTORS

ANA CECILIA ARTEAGA BÖHRT is a Bolivian anthropologist and a PhD candidate at the Centro de Investigaciones y Estudios Superiores en Antropología Social (CIESAS) in Mexico City.

EMMA CERVONE is an anthropologist scholar with many years of research experience in Ecuador on topics of indigenous policies, gender, and racism. She is the author of *Long Live Atahualpa: Indigenous Politics, Justice, and Democracy in the Northern Andes*.

CRISTINA CUCURÍ is a member of the Provincial Network of Rural and Kichwa Women's Organizations of Chimborazo (REDMUJCH), and has been general coordinator of that network since 2007. She also heads the program of rights and citizenship at the Centro de Desarrollo, Difusión e Investigación Social CEDIS.

NATALIA DE MARINIS is an Argentine anthropologist who holds a PhD from CIESAS in Mexico City. She is a researcher and teacher at CIESAS Golfo in Veracruz.

ROSALVA AÍDA HERNÁNDEZ CASTILLO teaches at the Centro de Investigaciones y Estudios Superiores en Antropología Social (CIESAS) in Mexico City. She is the author of *Multiple Injustices: Indigenous Women, Law, and Political Struggle*.

LEONOR LOZANO SUÁREZ is an anthropologist and independent researcher based in Bogotá. She has worked with indigenous peoples organizations in the Cauca for over two decades.

MORNA MACLEOD teaches at the Universidad Autónoma del Estado de Morelos in Mexico. She is the author of *Nietas del fuego, creadores del alba. Luchas político-culturales de mujeres mayas*.

MARIANA MORA teaches at the Centro de Investigaciones y Estudios Superiores en Antropología Social (CIESAS) in Mexico City. She is the author of *Kuxlejal Politics: Indigenous Autonomy, Race, and Decolonizing Research in Zapatista Communities*.

ADRIANA TERVEN SALINAS teaches at the Universidad Autónoma de Querétaro in Mexico. She holds a doctoral degree from CIESAS in Mexico City.

RACHEL SIEDER teaches at the Centro de Investigaciones y Estudios Superiores en Antropología Social (CIESAS) in Mexico City and is an affiliated senior researcher at the Chr. Michelsen Institute in Bergen, Norway. Her books include *Gender Justice and Legal Pluralities: Latin American and African Perspectives* (coedited with John-Andrew McNeish).

MARÍA TERESA SIERRA teaches at the Centro de Investigaciones y Estudios Superiores en Antropología Social (CIESAS) in Mexico City. She is editor of *"Haciendo justicia": Interlegalidad, género y derecho en regiones indígenas.*

INDEX

accumulation: dispossession, 15, 210, 223; injustices, 214; insecurities, 19, 198, 207–210

ACIN (*Asociación de Cabildos Indígenas del Norte de Cauca,* Association of Indigenous *Cabildos* of Northern Cauca, Colombia), 191n9, 191n13, 191n116, 192n17, 193n29; Justice and Harmony program (tejido de justicia y armonía), 186; Women's Program, 178, 183, 185–186

action research, 266, 269, 283n2, 284n2, 284n3. *See also* collaborative research, methodology

activist: anthropology, 266; environmental, 233; feminist, 275; human rights, 2, 40, 280; research, 2, 4, 269; scholars, 16, 51, 126, 146n5; women, 3, 13, 67, 90, 120, 124, 275n3, 276

Ágel (Guatemala), 222–237, 239n15. *See also* San Marcos

agency, 56, 92n19, 167, 227; feminist conceptions, 97, 118n32; indigenous women's, 4, 11, 98–99, 115

agenda: development, 80; feminist, 45; gender, 4, 31, 74, 89–90, 99–100, 115, 120, 145, 188; government, 72; indigenous organizations, 16, 52, 60, 68, 72, 139; indigenous women, 120, 137–140, 145, 146n5, 167, 174–179; multicultural, 14; neoliberal, 4; women's rights, 124

Agreement on the Identity and Rights of Indigenous Peoples (Guatemala), 90n2

Agreement on Socio–Economic Matters and the Agrarian Situation (Guatemala), 90n2, 91n5

Alausí (Ecuador), 125–128, 136, 147n12. *See also* Chimborazo

alliances, 138, 148, 183, 256, 266, 269, 280

Amazonian indigenous peoples, 7

American Convention on Human Rights, 36, 46n10

anthropological affidavits. *See* expert witness report

APPO (*Asamblea Popular de los Pueblos de Oaxaca,* Popular Assembly of the Peoples of Oaxaca, Mexico), 18, 242–258, 259n4

armed conflict: Colombia, 4, 173–190; Guatemala, 73–85, 237; Mexico, 39, 243–244, 251–258, 268; Peru, 37

Asamblea Popular de los Pueblos de Oaxaca. See APPO

ASDECO (*Asociación de Desarrollo Comunitario,* Association for Community Development, Guatemala), 75–89, 91n12, 91n15, 92n20

ASDI (*Asociación Sueca para el Desarrollo Internacional,* Swedish International Development Cooperation Agency), 76

Asociación de Cabildos Indígenas del Norte de Cauca. See ACIN

Asociación de Desarrollo Comunitario. See ASDECO

Asociación Sueca para el Desarrollo Internacional. See ASDI

Association for Community Development. *See* ASDECO

Association of Indigenous *Cabildos* of Northern Cauca. *See* ACIN

Atlixcala (Mexico), 197–205, 212. *See also* Puebla

AUC (*Autodefensas Unidas de Colombia,* United Self-Defense Forces of Colombia), 192n25

authorities: *cabildo,* 181–187; civilian, 75; communal, 78, 85–86, 98, 104, 144, 165, 169n13, 253–254, 271; community, 3, 32, 45, 57, 77, 85, 100, 144, 154, 228, 252; female, 157–158, 179; indigenous, 77–80, 125, 144, 151–158, 165, 176, 182, 193n29; indigenous authorities, 77–80, 125, 144, 151, 152, 156–158, 165, 176, 182, 193n29; judicial, 33; legal, 82; male, 91n12, 157–160, 167, 198, 212, 267, 270; Mayan, 77; mestizo, 253; military, 30; moral and ethical, 75; municipal, 78, 91n6, 256; state, 68, 82, 87, 132, 144, 186, 217n3; system of, 155–156, 173; traditional, 75–79, 150, 155–156, 175, 188, 190n3, 208, 255–256, 260n24, 270, 272

Autodefensas Unidas de Colombia. See AUC

Autonomous Intercultural Indigenous University. *See* UAIIN

autonomy, 1–5, 12 173–174; indigenous, 2–5, 19, 90n2, 97–99, 144, 151–157, 160–168, 168n6, 169n13, 176–177, 183, 192n22, 202; organizational, 4; regional, 5; right, 2–5; 39; San Juan Copala, 3, 242–258, 274;